The School Counselor as Consultant

An Integrated Model

for School-Based Consultation

RICHARD D. PARSONS
West Chester University

WALLACE J. KAHN
West Chester University

D1569715

THOMSON
BROOKS/COLE

Australia • Canada • Mexico • Singapore • Spain
United Kingdom • United States

For . . .
Two very special women
. . . women of courage
. . . of gentle hearts
. . . inviting smiles
. . . and boundless, unconditional love.

Two very special women, our moms . . . Marie and Edie

THOMSON
BROOKS/COLE

Executive Editor: *Lisa Gebo*
Editor: *Marquita Flemming*
Assistant Editor: *Shelley Gesicki*
Editorial Assistant: *Amy Lam*
Technology Project Manager: *Barry Connolly*
Marketing Manager: *Caroline Concilla*
Marketing Assistant: *Mary Ho*
Advertising Project Manager: *Tami Strang*
Project Manager, Editorial Production:
    Candace Chen
Art Director: *Vernon Boes*

Print Buyer: *Lisa Claudeanos*
Permissions Editor: *Sara Harkrader*
Production Service: *Peggy Francomb,*
    Shepherd Inc.
Copy Editor: *Karen Slaght*
Cover Designer: *Bill Stanton*
Illustrator: *Anne-Marie Gephart*
Cover Image: *Artville*
Cover/Text Printer: *Malloy Incorporated*
Compositor: *Shepherd Inc.*

For more information about our products,
contact us at:
Thomson Learning Academic Resource Center
1-800-423-0563
For permission to use material from this text
or product, submit a request online at
http://www.thomsonrights.com.
Any additional questions about permissions
can be submitted by email to
thomsonrights@thomson.com.

Library of Congress Control Number:
2004109180

ISBN 0-534-62865-6

Thomson Brooks/Cole
10 Davis Drive
Belmont, CA 94002
USA

Asia
Thomson Learning
5 Shenton Way #01-01
UIC Building
Singapore 068808

Australia/New Zealand
Thomson Learning
102 Dodds Street
Southbank, Victoria 3006
Australia

Canada
Nelson
1120 Birchmount Road
Toronto, Ontario M1K 5G4
Canada

Europe/Middle East/Africa
Thomson Learning
High Holborn House
50/51 Bedford Row
London WC1R 4LR
United Kingdom

Latin America
Thomson Learning
Seneca, 53
Colonia Polanco
11560 Mexico D.F.
Mexico

Contents

LIST OF CASES   XIV

LIST OF EXERCISES   XV

PREFACE   XVII

I   The School Counselor as Consultant   1

1   THE SCHOOL COUNSELOR: ADDRESSING THE NEED FOR SERVICE   3

Chapter Objectives   4

Increased Complexity and Quantity of Needs   4

The Inadequacy of a Direct-Service Model of Counseling   7

    School Counselor Role   7

Consultation as Paradigm: More Than Just a Technique   9

Consultation: An Operational Definition   10

    Triadic Relationship   12

    Problem-Solving Focus   14

    Mutual and Voluntary   15

    Dual Focus   16

Special Orientation, Special Skills 16

Summary 17

    Increased Complexity and Quantity of Needs 17

    Inadequacy of Direct-Service Models 17

    Consultation as Paradigm: More Than Just a Technique 17

2 CONSULTING: PROVIDING AN INTEGRATED MODEL OF SERVICE DELIVERY 20

Chapter Objectives 21

The Many Faces of Consulting: Modes and Models 21

    Dimension I: The Nature of the Consult—Crisis or Developmental 21

    Dimension II: Problem and Goal Definition Varying in Depth and Breadth 22

    Dimension III: Theory and Assumptions—Mental Health, Behavioral, Organizational Development 22

    Dimension IV: Consultant Skills Content or Process Expertise 24

    Dimension V: Modes of Consultation—Provisional–Prescriptive– Collaborative–Mediational 25

Integrating Perspectives—Serving the One and the Many 28

    A Continuum of Felt Need 29

    A Continuum of Content–Process Expertise 30

    A Continuum of Collaboration 32

    A Continuum of Breadth of Impact 33

    Integrating Nature, Focus, and Modes 37

Guiding Consultant Decision Making 37

    Guiding the Consultant's Decisions Regarding Form and Focus of Consultation 37

    The Contract as a Defining Element 38

    The Nature of the Problem and Goal 38

    Consultant Orientation 39

    Consultee Experience, Expectations, and Style 39

Summary 40

    The Many Faces of Consulting: Modes and Models 40

Integrating Perspectives—Serving the One and the Many   41

Guiding the Consultant's Decisions Regarding Form and Focus of Consultation   41

II The Needs of One within the Context of Many   45

3 THE SCHOOL AS A SYSTEM: BASIC ELEMENTS   47

Chapter Objectives   48

Systems Introduction   49

System Defined   49

The School as System   50

System Populations: Consumers and Providers   51

Consumers   51

Providers   52

Systems—in Service of Population Needs   53

The Elements of Need Assessment   53

From Individual to Community Needs   54

Knowing Our Ever-Changing Population   54

From Needs to System Goals and Objectives   57

From Goals to Objectives   58

Processes: The Means to Our Desired Outcomes   60

A System Perspective: Implications for Mr. Thomas   63

Summary   65

Systems   65

System Populations: Consumers and Providers   66

Systems—in Service of Population Needs   66

From Needs to System Goals and Objectives   66

Accountability: Creating Processes to Achieve Outcomes   66

4 SYSTEM DYNAMICS: RESPONDING TO CHANGE   68

Chapter Objectives   69

The Evolution and Nature of Systems   69

Open Systems   69

Moving from Open to Closed   70

Toward a State of Entropy   71

Systems: Formal and Informal   72

Formal Systems   72

Informal Systems   72

Formal and Informal: Parallel or Integrated Systems?   75

Organizational Structure   76

Specialization and Structure   77

System Dynamics and Orientation to Change   78

Responding to Change   78

System Change as Inevitable   79

System Dynamics and Counselor Consultation   79

Systemic Dynamics: Implications for Mr. Thomas   81

Summary   82

The Evolution and Nature of Systems   82

Systems: Formal and Informal   83

Organizational Structure   83

System Dynamics and Orientation to Change   83

5   THE CONSULTANT AS AGENT FOR CHANGE   85

Chapter Objectives   86

Consultation—Inevitably Impacting the System   86

Counselor-as-Consultant: Advocating for Client and System   87

Advocate and Adversary   88

Advocate for the Mission   88

When Goals Conflict   88

Reaction and Resistance   89

Resistance as Self-Preservation   90

Specific Conditions Stimulating Resistance   90

Promoting Innovation   93

Principle 1: Keep Innovations Culturally Compatible   94

Principle 2: Shaping—Introducing Change in Small Steps   97

Principle 3: Align Innovation with Opinion Leaders   99

Principle 4: Increasing Value and Power as Consultant   100

Principle 5: Move in a Crisis   105

Summary   108

Consultation—Inevitably Impacting the System   108

Counselor-as-Consultant: Advocating for Client and *System*   108

Reaction and Resistance   108

Promoting Innovation   109

III Facilitating the Consultative Process   113

6 THE STAGES OF THE CONSULTATION PROCESS   115

Chapter Objectives   116

Preentry: Creating Conditions for Successful Consultation   116

Establishing Norms and Expectations   116

Provisions for Preentry   117

Entry: Establishing the Contract for Consultation   118

Exploration: Defining the Problem and Its History   121

Gathering and Organizing the Data   122

Outcome Goals and Objectives: Moving toward Solutions   125

The Creation of Desired Outcome Goals   126

Translating Goals into Objectives   127

Subobjectives: Building on Small Increments of Change   128

Reaching Consensus on Goals and Objectives   129

Strategy Development and Implementation   129

Don't Reinvent the Wheel   130

Link Diagnostic Model to Goal Formulation and Strategy Development   131

Sometimes More Is Better; Or, There's More Than One Way to Skin a Cat   132

Maintenance: Sustaining the Trajectory of Change   132

Termination: Linking Past, Present, and Future   134

Summary   135

Preentry: Creating Conditions for Successful Consultation   135

Entry: Establishing the Contract   135

Exploration   135

Outcome Goals and Objectives: Moving toward Solutions   135

Strategy Development and Implementation   135

Maintenance: Sustaining the Trajectory of Change   136

Termination: Linking Past, Present, and Future   136

7   COMMUNICATION FOR EFFECTIVE CONSULTING   138

Chapter Objectives   139

Communication Skills in Consultation: Purpose and Outcomes   139

Demonstrate Empathy and Build Rapport   139

Inform or Provide Information   140

Obtain Information to Identify and Define Problems   140

Obtain Information to Formulate Goals and Objectives   140

Support and Reassure   140

Affirm and Reinforce   141

Persuade and Influence   141

Creative Data Gathering through Brainstorming   141

Providing Instruction and Directives   141

Skills of Active Listening (Preconditions to Understanding)   142

Attending as a Physical Response   143

Attending—a Psychological Response   144

Minimal Encouraging   145

Paraphrasing Content   145

Skills of Exploration   149

Exploring through the Art of Questioning   149

Guidelines for Effective Questioning   150

Skills of Focusing   153

Clarification   154

Tacting Response Leads   155

Summarizations   157

Written Communication: Special Considerations   160

Integrating: Stages, Purpose, and Communication Skills   160
Summary   161
   Communication Skills in Consultation: Intended Outcomes   161
   Skills of Active Listening   162
   Skills of Exploration   162
   Skills of Focusing   162

8   WORKING WITH RESISTANCE   165

Chapter Objectives   166
Understanding the Sources of Resistance   166
   Resistance: Often a Reasonable Response   167
   Resistance—a Response to Consultant Insensitivity   167
   *Resistance—a Reaction to Consultee Issues
and Concerns*   169
   Resistance—a Reaction to Consultant Style   175
   *Resistance—a Reaction to a Dysfunctional
Consulting Relationship*   176
Recognizing the Manifestations of Resistance   179
   The Push Away   180
   Yes, But . . .   181
   Passive Aggression   182
   Requesting Counseling   182
   Quick Sell/Quick Buy   183
Working with, Not Defeating, Consultee Resistance   185
   The Invitation   185
   Reframe the Resistance   186
   Ameliorating the Source of Resistance   188
Reducing the Risk of Resistance   188
Summary   189
   Understanding the Sources of Resistance   189
   Recognizing the Manifestations of Resistance   190
   Working with, Not Defeating, Resistance   190
   Reducing the Risk of Resistance   190

IV Consultation Foci 193

9 CLIENT-FOCUSED CONSULTATION: THE STUDENT AS CLIENT 195

Chapter Objectives 196

Approach Student Service from a Consultation
Perspective 196

Focusing on the One While Impacting the Many 197

Problem Identification 198

Assessing the Specifics of the Task Demands 199

Assessing the Environment 202

Assessing the Client 204

Goal Setting and Solution-Focused Consultation 209

Basic Tenets of a Solution-Focused Model 210

Considerations for School-Based Consultation 211

Goals for Client, Task, and Environment 211

Setting Priorities and Finding a Place to Start 212

Developing and Employing Solutions 214

Summary 214

Approach Student Service from a Consultation Perspective 214

Focusing on the One While Impacting the Many 215

Problem Identification 215

Goal Setting and Solution-Focused Consultation 215

10 CONSULTEE-FOCUSED CONSULTATION 218

Chapter Objectives 219

The Consultee: A Significant Extrapersonal Variable 219

Collaborating on Knowledge Development 221

Identifying the Problem 223

Interventions 225

Collaborating on Consultee Skill Development 226

Facilitating Skill Development 226

Program Development 227

Training Considerations 227

Regaining Objectivity and Professionalism   228

   Categorizing Loss of Objectivity   229

Confrontation: Aan Essential Intervention   237

   Methods of Direct Confrontation   237

   Guidelines for Effective Confrontation   238

   Methods of Indirect Confrontation   241

Putting It All Together   242

Summary   243

   The Consultee: A Significant Extrapersonal Variable   243

   Collaborating on Knowledge Development   244

   Collaborating on Consultee Skill Development   244

   Regaining Objectivity and Professionalism   244

11 THE GROUP AS CLIENT: FROM TEAM BUILDING TO MEDIATION   247

Chapter Objectives   248

The Three-Legged Stool   249

Systemic Conflict: Unfulfilled Needs and Interests   251

Intrasystem Conflict: Conceptualizing the Triad   255

Facilitating Win–Win Solutions: Getting to Yes   257

   Separate People from the Problem   258

   Focus on Interests   259

   Generate Options   260

   Use Objective Criteria   261

The Forces That Influence Change   265

Planning and Organizing Solution Implementation   268

Summary   272

   Conceptualizing the Triad and Their Goals   272

   Facilitating Win–Win Solutions and Getting to Yes   272

   The Forces That Influence Change   272

   Planning and Organizing Solution Implementation   273

12 THE SYSTEM AS CLIENT: SYSTEM-FOCUSED CONSULTATION 275

Chapter Objectives 276

System-Focused Consultation: When the System Is the Problem 276

When Client Symptoms Reflect System Problems 277

System Diagnosis 277

System Analysis: A Demanding Process 277

Steps in the Diagnostic Process 279

Focusing the Diagnosis 280

Analyzing the Systems—Elements, Forces, and Culture 282

The System's Elements 282

Assessing Forces Impacting the System 284

Assessing the System Character and Culture 285

The Linkage of Artifacts, Values, and Assumptions 288

Diagnostic Tools and Techniques for System-Focused Consultation 289

System-Focused Consultation: Intervention and Prevention 290

General Guidelines 290

Feedback: The First Level of Intervention 291

Fine-Tuning: A Second Level of Intervention 294

Changing the Character and Culture of a System: The Third Level of Intervention 298

Summary 304

System-Focused Consultation: When the System Is the Problem 304

System Diagnosis 305

System-Focused Consultation: Intervention and Prevention 305

13 ETHICAL CONCERNS AND CONSIDERATIONS 309

Chapter Objectives 310

Ethics and Standards of Practice: Guides, Not Fixed Directives 311

Basic Ethical Issues Targeting the Counselor as Consultant 311

Consultant Competence 311

Consultant Values 312

Consultant Cultural Sensitivity 314

Basic Ethical Issues Targeting Relationships   318
  Informed Consent   318
  Confidentiality   319
  Establishing and Maintaining Professional Boundaries   322
  Power   323
Process Issues   323
  Identification of the Client   323
  Efficacy of Treatment   324
  *Evaluation—a Stage of Consultation and an Ethical
  Consideration*   325
  Forms of Evaluation   325
Summary   326
  Ethics and Standards of Practice: Guides, Not Fixed Directives   326
  Basic Ethical Issues Targeting the Counselor as Consultant   327
  Basic Ethical Issues Targeting Relationships   327
  Process Issues   327

14 APPLYING WHAT WE KNOW   330

Chapter Objectives   332
A Review of the Consultation Process   332
A Concluding Thought: Not an End, but a Beginning!   352

INDEX   353

List of Cases

1.1   Tina—Problems with Homework?   5

2.1   The Case of Tommie S.   28

2.2   Case Application—Tommie: Crisis and/or Developmental   30

2.3   Expert-Process Consultation Case Application—Tommie—A Technical or Process Approach   32

2.4   Case Application—Four Modes for Tommie   34

2.5   Case Application—Tommie: Many Targets, Many Goals   36

4.1   Formal and Informal Systems of Operations   73

5.1   Tommy, the Attention Seeker   94

8.1   The Overly "Competent" Consultant   168

8.2   Consultee Vulnerability   174

8.3   Identifying the Source of Consultee Resistance   189

11.1 Specials Who Don't Feel Special   254

12.1 Fine-Tuning the Systems   294

14.1 A View from a Counselor's Window: The Case of Ellen   336

14.2 A Solution-Focused Approach: Benny—A Picture of "Energy"   346

List of Exercises

1.1   Student Concerns—Then and Now   5

1.2   One Week in the Life of . . .   8

1.3   The Counselor's View of Consultation   9

1.4   Consultation: A Triadic Relationship   12

2.1   Multimodes of Consultation   27

2.2   Viewing Problems and Goals along a Continuum of Expansiveness   40

3.1   Goals to Outcome Objectives   59

3.2   Identifying System Process   60

3.3   System Analysis: Components   63

3.4   Systems Consultation   65

4.1   System Analysis: Dynamics   71

4.2   Formal and Informal Systems   74

4.3   Job Performance Analysis   81

5.1   Innovation as Culturally Compatible   96

5.2   Change in Small Steps   98

5.3   Opinion Leaders   100

5.4   Increasing Power and Value   104

5.5   Highlighting and Moving in a Crisis   107

6.1   The Consultation Referral   117

6.2   Setting the Contract   121

6.3   Exploring and Defining the Problem   125

6.4   Translating Goals into Objectives   128

6.5   Outcome Goals and Objectives   129

6.6   Strategy Development and Implementation   132

6.7   Maintenance and Termination   134

7.1   Paraphrasing   146

7.2   Reflection of Feelings   148

7.3   Styles of Questioning   152

7.4   Employing Clarification Skills   155

7.5   Developing Summarization   158

8.1   Recognizing and Working through Negative and Conflicting Expectations   170

8.2   Reducing the Aversive Nature of Consultation   177

8.3   Working with Resistance   186

9.1   The Case of Keith-Focusing on the Task   200

9.2   Keith-An Environmental Analysis   203

9.3   Keith-Assessing the Client   208

10.1   Full Inclusion   222

10.2   Theme Interference   232

10.3   Effective Confrontations   240

10.4   When Consultee-Focused Consultation is Needed   243

11.1   Assessing Needs and Interests   255

11.2   Conducting a Principled Negotiation   264

11.3   Conducting a Force-Field Analysis   268

11.4   PERT Charting a Solution   271

11.5   Groups in Conflict: From Problem Identification to Solution Planning   271

12.1   The Tale of Two Schools   281

12.2   The Impact of Mission on Structure and Process   283

12.3   A Look at One System's Culture   288

12.4   Fine-Tuning Communication Processes   296

12.5   A High School in Need of Change   301

13.1   Identifying Operative Values   313

13.2   Events in Multicultural Context   317

13.3   Maintaining Confidentiality?   321

Preface

To suggest that school counselors face incredible demands is perhaps stating the obvious. This situation of asking too much of too few is not new to school counselors. However, what is different about this situation is that now, not only are counselors asked to deal with the multitude of issues presented by students (and their parents), but also school counselors are asked to be teacher and classroom support personnel, curriculum modifiers, team builders, group mediators, and even system analysts. The requests for counselors to occupy these ever-expanding roles, come not as direct requests, but rather as a natural response to the nature of the problems presented and the need for prevention as well as intervention services.

The school counselor is eager and willing to address these needs. However, tools of individual and/or small-group counseling, although valuable, are no longer sufficient to adequately address the needs of our schools. As such, school counselors are seeking alternative models of service delivery. Models that will assist them to not just intervene and remediate but also to prevent. Models that will not only target the student but also the system. There is now a need for models of service delivery that will help counselors coordinate and integrate all their varied roles and functions. What is needed is a model that directs counselors to a perspective focusing on goals, solutions, and resources. What they are seeking is an integrated model of consultation. It is this model of consultation that is presented in this text.

PERHAPS A WARNING IS IN ORDER?

Perhaps, we should warn the reader, *The School Counselor as Consultant* is not just another skills or "how-to" text. While providing knowledge and skills necessary to function effectively as a school counselor/consultant, *The School Counselor as Consultant* is also a challenge to the very way the school counselor perceives his role and conceives her[1] services. The reader may find that the text calls to question many of her professional assumptions and challenges him to embrace a new paradigm of professional service. Such a shift of paradigm is neither easy nor painless.

Consultation as presented within this text is *not* simply an add-on task or an additional tool for school counselors to perform, in addition to that which they already do. As presented here, consultation is not merely one of the three components to a comprehensive counseling program—counseling, consultation, and coordination. No, consultation will be presented as an integrated model for all school-based services—one to supplant current approaches and result in expanded efficiency and impact. Consultation will be presented as the umbrella under which all school counselor services can be conceptualized and delivered.

As with any new model or paradigm, consultation will require a shift in the counselor's perspective of role and function. The model will call counselors to redefine the who with whom they work, the focus of their diagnostic and intervention efforts, and even their definition of successful outcomes. This redefinition is necessary if school counselors are to be effective.

AN INTEGRATED MODEL
IN AN INTERACTIVE TEXT

The School Counselor as Consultant is really neither a "how-to" book nor an esoteric attempt at model building or theory explication. Because consultation is a complex mode of service delivery that must be founded on a sound base of knowledge and the application of specific attitudes and skills, it calls for a text that *blends theory and practice*.

The School Counselor as Consultant articulates a solution-focused, collaborative model of consultation that operates within a systems view of a school. In addition to presenting an integrative model of consultation, the text distinguishes itself in its pedagogical approach. In line with its emphasis on skill development as well as knowledge acquisition, the text includes learning objectives, practice exercises, case simulations and illustrations, chapter summaries, and Internet links.

---

[1]The authors have chosen to alternatively use feminine and masculine pronouns.

TEXT FORMAT
AND CHAPTER STRUCTURE

Each chapter will provide a blending of theory, practice, and personalized application. Each chapter will engage the reader in the application of specific concepts and principles presented within the chapter. Each chapter provides guided personal reflections, directed learning activities, and case illustrations as tools for helping the reader apply what was learned. Specifically, each chapter will include

- An opening vignette that will serve as an ongoing, unitary case, developed across chapters
- Chapter objectives
- Personal reflection guides
- Cooperative learning exercises: Ethical dilemmas
- Case illustrations
- Summary
- Important terms

AN OVERVIEW

Section I, "The School Counselor as Consultant," provides the reader with an operational definition, the rationale and the specific model of consultation that serves as the core to this text. In chapter 1, the reader is provided an overview of the many demands confronting today's school counselor. The chapter highlights the reality of "too much being asked of too few" and the need for a new, more efficient approach to service delivery. In chapter 2, the traditional methods of defining consultation services are discussed, including the various roles (provisional, prescriptive, mediational, collaborative), major theories (behavioral, organizational development, mental health), different skills (expert, process), and foci (crises, developmental). Chapter 2 also provides a *multidimensional model* for conceptualizing and employing all these varied approaches in an *integrated,* theoretically sound, and empirically supported model.

The chapters found in Section II redefine the nature of the school counselor from that of direct-service provider, assisting the individual student, to counselor as agent of change, serving students as part of the larger school system. Whereas chapters 3 and 4 provide the basic outline of the school as a system, chapter 5 provides insight into what is required for a counselor to function as an agent of change, be it for a single student or for an entire school.

The three chapters presented in Section III, "Facilitating the Consultative Process," highlight the unique nature and process of consultation (chapter 6). Chapter 7 presents the communication skills required to foster and develop a collaborative relationship, and chapter 8 addresses the resistance often encountered by those employing a consultation form of service delivery.

Section IV, "Consultation Foci," walks the reader through the application of this integrated consultation model where the target is the student as client (chapter 9), the consultee as client (chapter 10), the group as client (chapter 11), and the system as client (chapter 12). These chapters highlight the specific skills and approaches to be employed in both the problem identification and intervention stages. Chapter 13 highlights the ethical concerns and considerations that are faced by the school counselor as consultant, and the final chapter, "Applying What We Know" (chapter 14), provides the reader with a flowchart that can be used to navigate the consultant through the process of consultation starting with her point of entry and moving through to the final evaluation. This chapter also provides extended case illustrations and case exercise that will help to bring the previous information and skills together in one final capping experience.

Although the text is intended to meet the needs (both conceptual and skill based) of those employing consultation, it is only a start. Ongoing training and supervision are essential if one wishes to be an effective, ethical consultant. It is our hope that the current text will serve as a foundation for such ongoing professional development.

ACKNOWLEDGMENTS

Throughout the text, numerous researchers and theorists have been identified and cited for their contribution to our knowledge and practice of consultation. However, the real substance of this text and our work comes from the many individuals—students, parents, teachers, and administrators—with whom we have worked. It is their shared experiences that have given form to the many case illustrations and examples provided within this text. It is their shared experience that provides us with the courage to put forth this model of school counselor. It is to these many "forward"-looking consultees who have invited us to share in their growth that we say "Thank you."

Also, with much appreciation we recognize all those sometimes anxious, always challenging, and ever-giving graduate students who have endured our rambling for more years than we care to remember. It has been their probing questions, requests for concrete examples, and challenging commentary that have served as a source of much insight and growth. To all those, too many to mention, we say "Thank you."

Finally, we want to acknowledge the encouragement and support we received from Marquita Flemming, Julie Martinez, and Shelley Gesicki at Wadsworth, and the excellent work done by Peggy Francomb and Karen Slaght at Shepherd Incorporated.

The School Counselor as Consultant

1

⌒

The School Counselor

Addressing the Need for Service

Don't you just love it? It's 7:30 a.m., and I haven't
even removed my coat and here's a Post-it note!
"Please see Ellen M. IMMEDIATELY! This
kid has real problems! Signed: Dr. Jamison!"
Okay, so I need to see Ellen "immediately" . . . somewhere
between the IEP meeting I have to attend, the SAP
conference, the two parent conferences, and. . . .

The feeling expressed by this counselor is certainly not new to anyone who works within a school system. School counselors know all too well the feeling of having too much asked of too few. There is an incredible demand for counselor services within our schools. It would be rare to find a school counselor whose day *is not* filled with a multitude of tasks, including individual, academic, vocational, and personal counseling; group interventions and mediation; teacher support; parent conferences; and IEP meetings—just to name a few.

The need and request for school counselor involvement has not only increased but also the nature of the issues for which their help is requested has changed dramatically. This added demand for service, along with the changing forms of services required, has forced counselors to review and reconsider their role and models of service delivery. This need for a new form of service delivery serves as the focus of this chapter.

CHAPTER OBJECTIVES

After completing this chapter, the reader should be able to

1. Describe the nature of the increased demands being experienced by the school counselor in the twenty-first century
2. Identify the specific limitations to a direct service approach to these demands
3. Describe consultation as paradigm

INCREASED COMPLEXITY
AND QUANTITY OF NEEDS

Walking into your office on any one day and finding a long list of notes, requests for service, e-mail and telephone messages, and so on would be unnerving even for the best of us. But walking into an office and experiencing this barrage daily is, in fact, the experience of many school counselors.

Abundant evidence, both anecdotal and empirical, suggests that our society is in crisis (e.g., Brown, 1996; Lockhart & Keys, 1998; Luongo, 2000). Statistics on divorce rates, poverty, sexism, racism, violence within and outside our families and institutions, drug and alcohol abuse, sexual abuse, joblessness, and homelessness all give evidence of a people under stress and a society in crisis—a stress that is pervasive across all strata of our society and one from which our students are far from immune. For example, according to the Substance Abuse and Mental Health Services Administration (SAMHSA) report (1998), 15% to 22% of all children and adolescents have significant emotional impairment requiring treatment. Further, as of 1996 suicide remained the third leading cause of death among adolescents, with estimates of attempts ranging from 10,000 to 20,000 a year (Brown, 1996). And, as of 1999 there were more than 5 million children with special educational needs receiving services within our schools (Kupper, 1999), a number that is expected to climb. To say that our society is facing myriad mental health issues is stating the obvious. What may also be just as obvious is that these crises do *not* stop at the school door nor cease with the ringing of the first-period bell. In fact, given the shortages in community-based services (Luongo, 2000), these crises are now being laid at our schools' doorsteps with increasing frequency.

In addition to the increased number of individuals needing the services of our school counselors, the nature and complexity of the problems brought to the counselor's office have changed dramatically. The problems confronted by today's school counselor would stretch the competency and professional adequacy of any one service provider. A student upset about peer teasing, who once only needed a caring, supportive ear or perhaps assistance with the development of social skills, now shares realistic fears for his or her well-being, given the prospects of bullying and violence in our schools. The student who has become lax in homework may need more than a pep talk or a behavior modifi-

---

CASE 1.1   Tina—Problems with Homework?

Consider the situation wherein a school counselor is presented with a student failing fifth grade. Not many counselors today would be shocked to find that this student, who is struggling to pass, is at the same time attempting to adapt to a home life in which she serves as the primary caretaker of her four siblings. But even beyond this social condition, which serves as a primary deterrent to that child's academic functioning, it would not be totally out of the question or the experience of today's counselor to find that this household is one in which the mother is a drug addict and her transient boyfriend physically and sexually abuses the children in the house.

---

cation program. Discovering that there is quite a bit more to a student's concern than what first appears is becoming the rule rather than the exception. Consider Case 1.1. This case provides one illustration of a simple presenting concern that unfolds rapidly and tests the limits of this counselor's professional resources.

The case is certainly dramatic and may not be one experienced by all school counselors. The truth, however, is that most school counselors can identify with the experience of approaching what appeared to be a manageable issue only to have it rapidly unfold and reveal a more serious concern. It is not unusual to find that the failure to complete homework is compounded and/or exacerbated by many other crises in the child's life (e.g., learning disability, negligent or absent parents, family alcoholism). Exercise 1.1 is designed to provide you firsthand knowledge of the realities of school-based counseling in your area.

EXERCISE 1.1

Student Concerns—Then and Now

There was a time when the biggest concerns facing a school counselor were how to assist a new anxious student adjust to a new school environment, or how to assist a student to develop some time management and organizational study skills. Although these needs continue to exist and are successfully addressed by the school counselor, the nature of student concerns and issues have extended well beyond adjustment anxiety and study skills acquisition. The current exercise invites you to become familiar with the changing needs of today's students and the impact that has on the role and function of today's school counselor.

Directions: Visit three school counselors—an elementary-, middle-, and high school-level counselor. Find a counselor who has been working as a school counselor for at least 5 years. Ask them each of the following questions.

Continued

EXERCISE 1.1 CONTINUED

1. How long have you been working as a school counselor?

   _____

2. In the early years of your career, what were the problems or student's concerns you most typically experienced?

   _____

   _____

   _____

   _____

   _____

3. In the last few years (or year) have you noticed a change in the nature of the concerns and problems students now present? If so, in what way have these changed?

   _____

   _____

   _____

   _____

4. Please identify the degree or extent to which you encountered each of the following, first during the early years of your career and next, most currently. (Code response as: none, very few, some, quite a few, a lot).

Student Problem or Concern	Early Part of Career	Most Recent Part of Career
Eating disorders (anorexia, bulimia)		
Special learning needs (e.g., learning disorders, attention deficit, medical conditions)		
Mood disorders, including major depression and bipolar disorders		
Anxiety disorders, including specific phobias, obsessive-compulsive disorders, generalized anxiety		
Drug and alcohol dependency or addictions		
Sexual orientation problems		
Explosive or hostile behavior		
Bullying and victims of bullying		
Homeless		

EXERCISE 1.1 CONTINUED

Student Problem or Concern	Early Part of Career	Most Recent Part of Career
Family related concerns—separation, divorce, domestic violence, etc.		
Social or peer group problems		
Other: (indicate)		

THE INADEQUACY OF A DIRECT-SERVICE MODEL OF COUNSELING

The provision of one-on-one counseling service to students exhibiting mental health problems continues to be a mainstay of school counselors' role and function. Further, given the anticipated increase in the number of students presenting with significant psychosocial problems (e.g., Kupper, 1999; SAMHSA, 1998) the provision of direct counseling services is likely to increase. It is this very possibility of the significant increase in need for service that calls to question the adequacy of the method of service delivery typically employed. It would appear that the school counselor's roles and functions are expanding, and with it comes a need for alternative methods of service delivery.

School Counselor Role

The role of the school counselor will certainly vary according to context and population. But even with that as a caveat, it is safe to say that most school counselors find themselves called on to serve in a variety of capacities. The provision of individual and group counseling services will certainly remain a mainstay of the counselor's role and function. However, as noted by Bailey, Deery, Gehrke, Perry, and Whiteledge (1989), the role of interventionist is simply inadequate. "It's like the story about a school. It was commended for rescuing so many students from the river of problems. A wise person visited the school and was impressed with the programs and strategies for helping drowning students. 'However,' he asked, 'has anyone gone up the river to see who is throwing them in?" (p. 7).

The American Counselor Association has for years called on counselors to employ developmental, preventive models of services within the school (Campbell & Dahir, 1997). In addition to providing individual and group counseling services, most school counselors will find themselves called on to provide developmental educational and guidance instruction (American School Counselor Association, 1999).

School counselors are also being asked to serve as career development and educational planning specialists (Herr & Cramer, 1996; Niles, 1998), crisis interventionists (Sink, 2000), and given the recent experience of violence within our schools, counselors now are called on to serve as violence prevention programmers (Campbell & Dahir, 1997). Add to this list of growing job demands the additional roles of advocate for students with special needs, agents of multicultural sensitivity, and even advocates for school reform, and it quickly becomes obvious that attempting to do one's job by sitting behind an office door, seeing each child one-on-one, is simply inadequate (see Exercise 1.2).

EXERCISE 1.2

One Week in the Life of . . .

Not only have student concerns and problems increased in depth and complexity, but also the school counselor is now asked to serve in a variety of support roles, such as those listed (planning specialist, crisis interventionist, violence prevention programmer, etc.). These multiple demands and job requirements take the counselor out of the office and away from one-on-one student contact. It will be the extent to which the counselor not only balances these multiple demands but also finds a way to integrate each demand as part of a comprehensive counseling program that will determine his/her level of effectiveness.

Directions: While you can, and most likely have, read accounts of the various roles and functions school counselors perform, the lived experience can prove much more insightful. Your task is to

1. Ask a counselor to keep a diary or a professional calendar marking their various activities throughout a one-week period. Review the diary with the counselor assessing the degree to which this reflects a typical week.

2. Ask that counselor if you could "shadow" him or her for a single day. Keep a journal of all of the planned and unplanned services and activities in which that counselor was asked to engage. Keep your own reflections as you go through the day.

3. Based on these two tasks, write a summary of what you learned about the role and function of the school counselor.

4. What have you identified as the knowledge, skills, and attitude you will need to be effective in this professional role?

School counselors recognize that it is too much (both in number and complexity) for any one counselor to adequately handle all of the tasks that confront them. As such, they have become increasingly aware of the essentiality of working together. School counselors are not only being called on to share their expertise, but are also recognizing the value of working with others (teachers, learning specialists, parents) in a collaborative relationship of shared expertise and resources. With this increased awareness of the need and utility of such collaboration comes the increased use and valuing of consultation as an essential model for school counseling services delivery.

CONSULTATION AS PARADIGM: MORE THAN JUST A TECHNIQUE

The idea of coordinating services, sharing expertise, and consulting is far from a new or novel idea. In the early 1960s, consultation was highlighted as an essential element of the school's counselor role and function (Wrenn, 1962).

Consultation is an activity embraced by the profession and practiced by many school counselors (Schmidt, 2003). For some, however, consultation continues to be viewed as a service, a technique that is provided in addition to the many direct services already offered. Thus, although praising the value of consultation, these school counselors simply fail to have the time or the energy to do one more thing or to use one more technique (see Exercise 1.3).

EXERCISE 1.3

The Counselor's View of Consultation

Consultation, as presented in this chapter, is a mode of service delivery—a new paradigm or perspective from which to implement all the tasks counselors are called to perform. However, many counselors have embraced consultation, not as an umbrella for all service delivery but as an added technique, a technique for which they have neither time nor energy to employ.

Directions: Using the same three schools that you used in Exercise 1.1, or other schools, interview three school counselors, again across grade levels (i.e., elementary, middle, and high school). Ask each of them the following.

1. Do you ever approach your work as a consultant? (An alternative way of asking, is: Do you employ consultation in your role as a school counselor?)

2. If not, why not? (List all the reasons.)

3. If yes,

   A. Would you tell me what consultation is for you?

   B. When and where do you employ a consultative approach?

   C. What, if any, are the benefits of using consultation as a method of service delivery?

   D. What, if any, are the drawbacks or costs to using consultation as a method of service delivery?

Finally, review your data, looking for reasons that may explain the limited or lack of use of consultation as a mode of service delivery. Keep this listing handy, and as you read through this text, begin to identify the knowledge, the skill, and the attitude you will need to develop to employ consultation in a way maximizes the impact of your services, while reducing your costs (in terms of time and energy).

As will be emphasized throughout this text, consultation is *not* just an additional technique. Therefore, to reap the full benefits of a consultation as a mode of service delivery, school counselors will need to make a paradigm shift. They will need to embrace consultation not simply as an added tool in their counselor toolbox . . . but as a whole new way of viewing their role and function within the school.

Consultation, as presented here, is a perspective from which to view the role and function of all that the school counselor does. The invitation throughout the text is for readers to reconfigure their frame of reference, professional orientation, and approach to school-based service delivery. This does not require readers to abandon their models of counseling or the techniques they may have found so useful. Rather, it is an invitation to employ consultation as the umbrella beneath which to modify and deliver numerous forms of intervention, prevention, and postvention services. In so doing they expand the effectiveness and efficiency of their efforts.

CONSULTATION: AN OPERATIONAL DEFINITION

The forms of service and interaction that have been grouped under the rubric of consultation are many and quite varied. The term *consultation* has been applied to activities as varied as the informal discussion between friends regarding an issue of importance, or a husband and wife consulting their calendars to plan a dinner party, to the process of sharing of advice and service by an expert or one with specialized training. In each of these illustrations, the use of the word *consultation* implies the provision of advice and/or services. Although this soft definition of consultation as one providing advice or service may apply in many arenas, such a colloquial definition fails to engender the value, the uniqueness, and the complexity of consultation (Gallessich, 1982).

Numerous professions (e.g., medicine, mental health, business, education) have employed the term *consultation* to refer to myriad professional roles, activities, and relationships (see Brown, Pryzwansky, & Schulte, 2001). Further, a multitude of definitions of consultation have been offered in the professional literature (e.g., Brown et al., 2001; Friend & Cook, 1992; Gallessich, 1982; Parsons, 1996). However, attempts to identify a single operational definition of consultation that would be applicable across the spectrum of human services has been less than successful. Much of the difficulty stems from the fact that various practitioners and theorists tend to emphasize different elements of consultation in their definitions and approaches. For example, one author (Parsons, 1996) reviewing the literature identified five dimensions that appeared to differentiate the unique forms of consultant function and focus. These dimensions are

1. *The point of focus*—whether it is on a specific, technical content or a unique process.

2. *The nature of the interaction*—be it in response to a crisis or as a form of prevention and developmental programming.

3. *The modality of service*—the role to be played by the consultant. At times the consultant will provide the service or prescribe to another how to perform the service. Others, see the consultant as employing a collaborative role in which work and reward are mutually shared.

4. *The theory employed*—for example, Adlerian consultation, behavioral consultation, systems or organizational development.

5. *The systemic level of entry*—the definition of goals and problems; that is, whether the consultation focused on a single client or an entire organization.

Even with the variations of focus and the subtleties of differences in definitions, a number of core characteristics can be articulated and at a minimum serve as the components to the operational definition employed within this text. Consultation can be characterized as a helping, problem-solving process involving a help giver (the consultant), a help seeker (the consultee), and another (the client). This voluntary, triadic relationship involves mutual involvement on the part of both the consultant and consultee in an attempt to solve the current work-related problem in a way that it not only stays solved but also that future problems may be avoided and or more efficiently handled (prevention).

Thus, consultation can be defined as a form of counselor service delivery in which the counselor (as consultant) works with a second person or persons (as consultee) for the purpose of benefiting a third person or persons (as client). Consequently, consultation is always a **triadic** relationship, although the nature of the relationship will vary depending on (1) the party initiating the consult, (2) the severity of the problem presented, (3) the capability of the consultee in resolving the problem, (4) the parameters of client and consultee definition, and (5) the extent of accountability existing between consultee and client. With variability in each of these five conditions, the form and function of school-based consultation are both complex and idiosyncratic. In spite of this variability, certain features of the triadic relationship will emerge. The five considerations offered will help define the nature of this triadic relationship.

The party initiating the consult is usually the consultee, but can also be the consultant. Counselor consultants can be reactive or proactive in their role and function. The severity of the problem presented will determine the form of response (i.e., counseling modality) indicated for the counselor consultant. The capability of the consultee in diagnosing and resolving the problem will also determine the modality of consultation employed. The client will frequently be an individual such as a student, a parent, or even a teacher (typically when the administrator is the consultee), but it is not uncommon for the client to represent a group (e.g., the fourth grade) or even a larger system, such as an entire school. Likewise, the consultee can also serve as a group or a larger system.

The relationship between the consultee and client is one of accountability and responsibility. The consultee is responsible for the actions (i.e., behavior, academic performance) of the client and engages the consultant in a process that will benefit the client. Implied by this accountability relationship is the requirement that the goals and objectives of the consultation process must reflect the desires of the consultant or at least the agreement of the consultee when the consult is initiated by the consultant.

Regardless of the modality employed, two constants will always characterize school-based consultation. First, whenever a consult is initiated the counselor consultant must first meet with the referring consultee to define the problem and determine the consultation modality. Second, collaboration between consultant and consultee (i.e., collaborative modality) is always the preferred mode of consultation. As you will see in our discussion of consultation modalities, the advantages of consultant–consultee collaboration outweigh all other forms of school-based consultation. This is true even when a more provisional modality is requested and initially employed. Even in this situation the consultant will be working toward increasing collaboration.

Triadic Relationship

As noted, previously, consultation is by definition a process involving a help giver (i.e., the consultant), a help seeker (i.e., consultee), and the person for whom the consultee is directly responsible, that is, the client. The triadic nature of this helping relationship immediately distinguishes it from direct-service counseling, which involves only two roles in the helping encounter, that of "helper" (i.e., counselor, therapist) and "helpee" (i.e., client, patient).

In consultation, the consultee could be a parent, a teacher, a supervisor, a manager, or a fellow human service provider. The consultee is the party generally (although not always) initiating services. The consultee has responsibility for the client's work-related behavior and is experiencing some concern or difficulty in relationship to that client or that client's performance. The consultant is a person who is perceived as having special knowledge or skills sought by the consultee in relationship to a current work-related problem. Exercise 1.4 will help further clarify the triadic nature of the consultation.

EXERCISE 1.4

Consultation: A Triadic Relationship

Directions: For each of the following scenarios, label the Consultant (C), the Consultee (c), and the Client (cl). Remember, the client is the person exhibiting a problem for which the Consultee, the party responsible or accountable for the client's performance, is seeking help. Finally, the consultant is the individual who, although not directly responsible for the client's performance, is serving as a help giver to the consultee.

Example: Sheila, a third-grade teacher expresses great concern about her difficulty getting Joel to refrain from calling out in class. She has gone to speak with Mr. Thomas, the school counselor, knowing that he previously worked with Joel.

Consultant: Mr. Thomas

Consultee: Sheila

Client: Joel

Scenario 1: Reginal, the reading specialist at Elmwood Elementary, is approached by Al, the fourth-grade language arts teacher, who expresses a concern about one of his students, Louis, who appears to have difficulty following along in class.

Consultant:

Consultee:

Client:

Scenario 2: Dr. Peterson, the school psychologist, asks to talk with Mrs. Zaborowski, who serves as Fatina's school counselor. Dr. Peterson has attempted on numerous occasions to engage Fatina, but with no success. He has heard of the long-standing counseling relationship that Mrs. Zaborowski has with this student and is hoping she can provide some insight into what may be interfering with his own attempts to create a helping relationship with her.

Consultant:

Consultee:

Client:

Scenario 3: Dr. Morton, the principal of Hatfield High, approaches Len Spikel, the director of guidance, expressing his apprehension about needing to confront a teacher about a possible drinking problem. Although Dr. Morton does not reveal the name of the teacher, he is very concerned about learning the most effective approach to such a confrontation and is hoping that Mr. Spikel can help.

Consultant:

Consultee:

Client:

Scenario 4: Louise, the principal of P.S. #142, contacts the local community mental health center to request assistance with providing some AIDS awareness programming for her senior high students.

Consultant:

Consultee:

Client:

Unlike direct-service models, such as counseling, which have relationships that are linear with the service provider working directly with the client (see Figure 1.1), consultation as a triadic form of service means that the work to

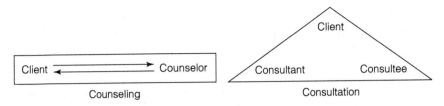

FIGURE 1.1 Direct and Indirect Service

be accomplished will at some level involve the consultee in both the problem-defining and problem-solving processes (see Figure 1.1).

Thus rather than having a one-on-one, linear relationship with the client, the consultant is now involved in a nonlinear way with both the consultee and the client. For example, the consultant may work with the consultee gathering information about the client and in turn provide recommendations to the consultee for implementation or may implement the interventions herself. Chapter 2 provides a more detailed explanation of these various ways a consultant can act.

The types and number of focal points for the helping relationship are clearly multiplied once the service moves from dyadic, as in counseling, to triadic, as in consultation. The inclusion of this third party as coparticipant in the problem-solving venture provides additional resources and perspective. In addition, the inclusion of this third party also requires the counselor-now-consultant to develop a new shift in focus and employ a new set of skills previously unused in a direct-service model. Understanding and coordinating multiple perspectives, varied terminology, turf concerns, and power issues are but a few of the additional variables included in the dynamics when one moves to a consultative model of service delivery.

Problem-Solving Focus

Consultation is most often characterized as a problem-solving process in which the target of such problem solving is the work-related role and function of the client. In most definitions the work referred to is broadly conceived to include any and all mission-driven needs for the institution, agency, and/or consultee. The intent of focusing consultation on work-related issues is to highlight the fact that the consultant is *not* providing the consultee with mental health counseling or psychotherapy, but rather the focus of service to the consultee is always performed with an eye to impacting the performance of the client. This is not to suggest that the consultee may not also grow in personal insight or emotional well-being, or that the focus of the interaction cannot be centered on the skills, knowledge, or objectivity of the consultee. What is being highlighted is that consultation, even when taking such a consultee-centered focus (see chapter 10) emphasizes problem solving around issues of the client's performance, as opposed to therapeutic personal insight and growth for the consultee.

This definitional element requires that the consultant employ helping interaction while at the same time avoiding developing a personal, therapeutic contract with the consultee. Although this may appear clear cut and relatively simple, the truth is that it is not always easy to walk the fine line between consultative help and personal therapy. Consider the following case of Allen T.

Allen was a high school history teacher with 42 years of teaching experience. He requested the consultative services of the school psychologist because he was very worried about a young boy in his class. Allen described Dennis as "a good boy, who last year was quite prompt in completing assignments. This year however, Dennis has been frequently late with assignments and (I) must always give him extra time." Continuing, Allen stated: "I think he's going through some very painful times. His dad died only 6 months ago!"

As the consultant worked with Allen, two things became quite clear. First, the student, Dennis, was grieving the death of his father. However, his grief reaction appeared appropriate in both intensity and duration. Also, Dennis was involved in supportive counseling with his family, which seemed to be very effective. The second, and perhaps more essential, issue identified by the consultant was that Allen's objectivity and professional approach to Dennis had been comprised. Allen, by his own admission, was overly solicitous of Dennis and provided him more freedom in meeting deadlines than he normally would allow. It became apparent that Dennis was responding to the extra time given him by making the most of it. It was also apparent that Allen's personal issues surrounding the delayed grieving of his own parents' deaths and the anticipatory grief connected to his upcoming retirement were interfering with his professional objectivity and ability to hold Dennis responsible for deadlines.

Although the consultant needed to help Allen see the connection between his overreaction to Dennis and Dennis's lack of performance in class, it was imperative that he avoid focusing his energies and interventions on Allen and Allen's own delayed grief. This is not to suggest that recommendations to Allen to consider some individual work would be inappropriate. What is being presented is that the contracted nature of the consultation should remain on resolving the work-related problem of the client and not the therapeutic needs of the consultee. Knowing how to walk the fine line between work-related problem solving and personal therapy is essential for the counselor working from a consultative frame of reference.

Mutual and Voluntary

Although consultation has most often been presented as an expert relationship (Friend & Cook, 1992), most definitions acknowledge the need for the participants to share, if not completely, collaborate in the process (Gutkin, 1999). The value of a mutually contributing model in which both the consultant and consultee approach the consultation as coequals, sharing in the ownership and responsibility for the consultation interaction and outcome, has been emphasized by many (e.g., Block, 1981; Caplan, 1970; Parsons, 1996). But even when less than collaborative approaches have been discussed or employed, the value of consultee involvement and ownership and the value of teamwork has been highlighted (see Gutkin, 1999).

Moving the relationship to one in which mutual responsibility and shared ownership for the process and ultimate content, while valuing the individual differences in perspective and expertise, requires that the counselor–consultant develop additional interpersonal skills aimed at reducing consultee resistance and equalizing psychosocial power differentials. These skills will be discussed in Section III.

Dual Focus

One of the primary values of a consultation model of service delivery is that it does more than target the work problem for intervention. More than simply intervening to resolve a current work problem (remedial–intervention focus), consultation, as presented here, attempts to resolve the current dilemma in such a way that it not only "stays fixed" (Block, 1981) but also in a way that the consultee is left better prepared to avoid similar problems in the future or handle future problems with increased skillfulness and efficiency (prevention focus).

Including a prevention goal into our consults forces us to expand our perception of the problem as well as the work that needs to be accomplished. It is important to approach each problem situation with a desire to resolve along with the hope of promoting growth and development (Kurpius & Fuqua, 1993). The preventive focus of consultation requires that strategies be conceptualized and enacted that will facilitate the spread of effect or generalization of impact to other, nonreferred clients. The prevention focus moves us to employ strategies that promote the emotional well-being of all members of a particular situation and not just the identified client.

For many counselors, trained to work with pathology or dysfunctionality, the invitation to work in a preventive mode can be both challenging and somewhat unsettling. Shifting focus from one of remediation to one of prevention requires counselors to expand their perspective to include not only the client but also the ecology, the environment, and the extrapersonal factors affecting the client. Further, as a preventionist, the counselor–consultant must now accept that they are agents of change, proactive in conditions that may prove detrimental to the well-being or continued functioning of those involved. Thus with this preventive focus, the counselor–consultant moves from being reactive and responsive in time of need, to proactive and preventive (educative) prior to needs emerging.

SPECIAL ORIENTATION, SPECIAL SKILLS

Consulting is much more than advice giving or conversing with another. Because of its uniqueness as a paradigm of service conceptualization and delivery, it will require a modification of professional attitudes and orientation, along with the development of additional professional skills. It is the development of this knowledge and skill that serves as the focus for the remainder of this text.

SUMMARY

Increased Complexity and Quantity of Needs

The nature of the issues now confronting those working within our schools has changed dramatically. These changes have created significant challenges for our students, our teachers, and as such the very role of our counselors. These changes necessitate new ways to approach the role and function of school counselors.

Inadequacy of Direct-Service Models

School counselors are called on to provide

- Individual and group counseling services
- Developmental educational and guidance instruction to classes and large groups
- Career development programs, as well as serves as
  - Educational planning specialists
  - Crisis interventionists (Sink, 2000)
  - Violence prevention programmers

Given these various roles and functions, it quickly becomes obvious that operating strictly from a one-on-one direct-service model is inadequate.

Consultation as Paradigm:
More Than Just a Technique

The idea of coordinating services, sharing expertise, and consulting has been an essential element of the school counselor's role and function from at least the early 1960s. However, rather than simply employ consultation as an additional strategy or technique in the counselor's toolbox, the need calls for a shift in school counselor paradigm, to one in which consultation is embraced as a perspective and through which all counselor functions are viewed.

IMPORTANT TERMS

Collaborative relationship	Counselor role and function	Intervention
Consultation	Crisis interventionist	Paradigm
Consulting	Direct service	Prevention
Coordinating services	Indirect service	Postvention

SUGGESTED READINGS

Baker, S. B. (2000). *School counseling for the twenty-first century* (3rd ed.). Upper Saddle River, NJ: Prentice Hall.

Campbell, C. A., & Dahir, C. A. (1997). *Sharing the vision: The national standards for school counseling programs.* Alexandria, VA: American School Counselor Association.

Parsons, R. D. (1996). *The skilled consultant.* Boston: Allyn & Bacon.

WEB SITES

American Counseling Association—home page for the professional organization. http://www.counseling.org

American School Counselor Association—home page for school counselors' professional organization. http://www.schoolcounselor.org

School Counseling Resources—excellent listing of links for counseling and psychology resources for children, youth, and adolescents. http://www.libraries.wright.edu/libnet/subj/cou/cpmeta/sc.html

REFERENCES

American School Counselor Association. (1999). *Position statements* [Online]. Retrieved from http://www.schoolcounselor.org

Bailey, W. R., Deery, N. K., Gehrke, M., Perry, N., & Whiteledge, J. (1989). Issues in elementary school counseling: Discussion with American School Counselor Association leaders. *Elementary School Guidance and Counseling, 24,* 4–13.

Block, P. (1981). *Flawless consulting.* San Diego, CA: Pfeiffer & Comp.

Brown, D. (1996). Training consultants: A call to action. *Journal of Counseling and Development, 72,* 139–143.

Brown, D., Pryzwansky, W. B., & Schulte, A. C. (2001). *Psychological consultation.* Needham Heights, MA: Allyn & Bacon.

Campbell, C., & Dahir, C. (1997). *The national standards for school counseling programs.* Alexandria, VA: American School Counselor Association.

Caplan, G. (1970). *The theory and practice of mental health consultation.* New York: Basic Books.

Erford, B. T. (2003). *Transforming the school counseling profession.* Upper Saddle River, NJ: Merrill/Prentice Hall.

Friend, M., & Cook, L. (1992). *Interactions: Collaboration skills for school professionals.* New York: Longman.

Gallessich, J. (1982). *The profession and practice of consultation.* San Francisco: Jossey-Bass.

Gutkin, T. B. (1999). Collaborative versus directive/prescriptive/expert school-based consultation: Reviewing and resolving a false dichotomy. *Journal of School Psychology, 27*(2), 161–190.

Herr, E. L., & Cramer, S. H. (1996). *Career guidance and counseling through the lifespan* (5th ed.). New York: HarperCollins.

Kupper, L. (1999). *Questions often asked by parents about special education services* (4th ed. Briefing paper). Washington, DC: National Information Center for Children and Youth with Disabilities.

Kurpius, D. J., & Fuqua, D. R. (1993). Introduction to the speed issues. *Journal of Counseling and Development, 71,* 596–697.

Lockhart, E. J., & Keys, S. G. (1998). The mental health counseling role of school counselors. *Professional School Counseling, 1,* 3–6.

Luongo, P. F. (2000). Partnering child welfare, juvenile justice and behavioral health with schools. *Professional School Counseling, 3,* 308–314.

Niles, S. G. (1998). Developing life-role readiness in a multicultural society: Topics to consider. *International Journal for the Advancement of Counseling, 20,* 71–77.

Parsons, R. D. (1996). *The skilled consultant.* Needham Heights, MA: Allyn & Bacon.

Schmidt, J. J. (2003). *Counseling in schools: Essential services and comprehensive services* (3rd ed.). Needham Heights, MA: Allyn & Bacon.

Sink, C. A. (2000). The school counselor as a psychoeducational resource specialist: Reframing our role for the next century. *Professional School Counseling, 3,* ii–iii.

Substance Abuse and Mental Health Services Administration (SAMHSA). (1998). *National expenditures for mental health, alcohol and other drug abuse treatment.* Washington, DC: SAMHSA, Department of Health and Human Services.

Wrenn, C. G. (1962). *The counselor in a changing world.* Washington, DC: American Personnel and Guidance Association.

2

Consulting

Providing an Integrated Model of Service Delivery

It certainly looks like Dr. Jameson is really concerned about Ellen.
But then again, he sometimes reacts as if everything were a crisis.
I know he wants me to see Ellen IMMEDIATELY but
I think I will try to see him first.
I need to see him as soon as he returns to his office to get
a little more information on what it is that is concerning him.
Hopefully, by seeing him first, I may be able to
understand what he expects me to do as well as
share with him my hopes of working together.

It is clear that Dr. Jameson is concerned. What may also be clear in the brief "referral" is that Dr. Jameson, at least at this juncture, expects our counselor to work directly with Ellen to address his concern.

In reading this brief description of the counselor's reflections, we begin to see the counselor's valuing of responding to the referral, but doing so in a way that conveys to Dr. Jameson that his input is sought and valued. Meeting with Dr. Jameson, as you will soon discover, is more than merely the politically correct thing to do. It is more than a nice and caring response to a colleague in distress. It is the first step necessary to developing a collaborative consultation approach to the issue at hand. It is the first step to a process, which if successful, will not only result in the intervention of this specific concern but will also lay a foundation for the prevention of this and similar issues in the future.

CHAPTER OBJECTIVES

The current chapter presents consultation as model of service delivery that allows counselors to integrate all roles and functions in a way that maximizes the impact of their services. After completing this chapter, the reader should be able to

1. Differentiate characteristics or dimensions of the various activities and services deemed to be consultation
2. Describe how each specific form or type of consulting would approach a single problem
3. Discuss a multidimensional model to consultation that allows the integration of the variety of approaches, goals, and services
4. Identify guidelines or decision criteria to guide the practicing consultant in the selection of the form of consultation most appropriate to a given situation

THE MANY FACES OF CONSULTING:
MODES AND MODELS

A review of the consultation literature will highlight both the many arenas in which consultation is practiced (e.g., schools, mental health services, hospitals, industry) and also depict the diversity in role and functions defined as consultation. One model that has been employed to differentiate the various forms of consultation function and consultant role is that presented by Parsons (1996). This model, which is presented here in abbreviated form, categorizes consultation along five dimensions: nature, problem–goal, theory, skills, and modes. Although such a depiction may assist in identifying the various subtleties of consultation, the true value of consultation is maximized, when these components are integrated into a flexible, multidimensional approach to consultation (Parsons, 1996, p. 21).

Dimension I: The Nature of the Consult—
Crisis or Developmental

Consults that are of a crisis nature are those in which the individual consultee or consultee system experiences pain or dysfunction and requests the consultant's assistance. The consultant's form of response and the degree to which he/she can take time to fully develop the nature of the problem and the various options for intervention depend to some extent on the intensity and duration of the crisis along with the consultee's and consultee's system resources. Consultation services that focus on human potential by promoting self-enhancement, self-awareness, and actualization are developmental in nature. Similarly, consultation activities that focus on increasing human adjustment by improving interpersonal skills, problem-solving abilities, and stress management skills are also considered developmental and preventive in nature. Finally, consultative activities that alter potentially inhibiting or detrimental elements in one's physical–social–psychological environment also reflect a developmental or preventive focus to the consultation.

Unlike the crisis-orientated consultation, developmental consultation is quite often initiated by the consultant (as opposed to the consultee). Further, developmental consultation may be introduced at a time when the consultee and/or consultee's system appears to be operating and functioning appropriately. As a developmental activity, the focus for this form of consulting is on growth and prevention rather than pain reduction and remediation.

The absence of crisis allows the consultant and the consultee the luxury of time to plan and implement the most growth-filled form of service. However, the same absence of pain and crisis often reduces the felt need for such service. Thus developmental consultation may be met with resistance. Overcoming this "if it ain't broke, don't fix it" mentality requires additional interpersonal marketing skills on the part of the consultant to enlist the consultee's cooperation and ownership of this developmental process.

Dimension II: Problem and Goal Definition
Varying in Depth and Breadth

A second way consultation can be differentiated is based on the way the problem and thus the specific goal is defined. Problems can be conceptualized as varying in breadth and depth. The breadth of a problem can be restricted to a single student or more broadly identified as involving a group or department or even the entire system. A problem can be defined as varying in depth, from a single issue to involving multiple issues, from a surface problem to a more hidden, implied, or convoluted issue. Further, the problem can be defined as either one of a technical nature to one involving a human systems or process glitch.

Just as the problem definition can vary along breadth and depth dimensions, so can the goal statement and focus. Goals can be operationalized to involve changes in a person (client, consultee, etc.), a policy, or a system structure or process. The size of the goal can vary from micro to macro and to anywhere in between (Gallessich, 1982).

Dimension III: Theory and Assumptions—Mental
Health, Behavioral, Organizational Development

Like other forms of helping, the consulting process and focus will be guided and shaped by the consultant's operating set of assumptions or theory of helping. The role the consultant employs, the outcomes expected, and the strategies chosen are usually derived from the consultant's assumptions about how change can best be effected. Three major models of consultation—mental health consultation, behavioral consultation, and organizational consultation—are briefly described next.

Mental Health Consultation   Popularized by Gerald Caplan (1970) and presented in its updated version (Caplan & Caplan, 1993, 1999), the mental health model of consultation is practiced in community agencies (Rogawski, 1979); school settings (e.g., Curtis & Zins, 1981; Meyers, Parsons, & Martin, 1979), and even business or industrial settings (Gallessich, 1985). The triadic relationship, which has been identified as a core characteristic of consultation, is evident in the mental health model of consultation. For example, Caplan worked as consultant to a small staff of psychologists and social workers responsible for the mental health needs of immigrant children in Israel. His efforts were initially aimed at simply providing the staff (i.e., the consultees) with new techniques for coping with the problems they had identified with the children (i.e., the clients). Unlike a number of the earlier expert models, in which the consultant would diagnose the problem and provide authoritative, expert prescription, the keystone to Caplan's approach was the nonhierarchical or coordinate relationship that existed between the consultant and the consultee. Caplan conceptualized this relationship as one of equals, wherein the consultant had no direct-line authority over the consultee. The mental health consultation model, although focusing on the client's (i.e., an individual, group, or organization) functioning, did so with emphasis given to the role of the consultee's knowledge, skill, and objectivity in relationship to both the remediation and prevention of the problem at hand. The basic premise was that increasing the knowledge, skills, or professional objectivity of the clinical staff would not only result in the amelioration of presenting concern but also serve a preventive function, reducing the need for future consultation on similar type of issues.

The mental health model of consultation views consultation as a pyramid in which the mental health professional, at the apex, consults with and educates the consultees, in the middle of the pyramid, who in turn work in the agencies that provide the direct service to the client. By affecting the consultee, the consultant gains an extended impact in that the consultee is now better prepared to cope with other clients in that environment. Gallessich (1982) noted that this "spread of effect" concept is central to the mental health approach to consultation. From this orientation, the consultant is not only a service delivery expert but also an educator and facilitator.

Behavioral Consultation   A contrasting set of assumptions about the targets for both problem identification and resolution can be found within the behavioral model of consultation (Bergan & Kratochwill, 1990; Bergan & Tombari, 1976; Kuehnel & Kuehnel, 1983; Martens, 1993). Unlike the mental health model, behavioral consultation was founded on social learning theory and as such focused on the overt behaviors of the consultee and the client.

Behavioral consultation emphasizes learning principles and the effect of one's environment on current functioning. Further, most consultants operating from a behavioral model employ intervention strategies drawn from behavioral and social learning theory (e.g., contingency management, shaping, social modeling). Behavioral consultants often assume a directive role of monitoring the consultees' implementation of a prescription. They may be directly active in observing client behavior or client–consultee interaction and gathering descriptive data about the conditions and frequency of the particular problematic behavior. If not directly collecting the needed information, they will be actively involved in directing the consultee to collect similar observational information as methods for diagnosis, intervention planning, and intervention monitoring.

Organizational Consultations   Organizational consulting (Argyris, 1970; Beckhard, 1969; Bennis, 1969; Rockwood, 1993; Ross, 1993; Schein, 1969, 1989, 1990) has, in fact, two significant paths of service. One path is the expert, who is able to provide technical specialization and support to an agency. In this situation, the consultee or the consultee's system calls on the consultant to work in a variety of roles, including technical adviser, applicator, trainer, or mentor. In this form, the organizational consultant may be involved in designing and defining work tasks, overseeing employee selection and training, and implementing skill development training. In either case, the consultant tends to be expert in focus and directive (i.e., provisional, prescriptive) in mode of delivery.

As more attention was given to the human side of the business enterprise, consultants shifted focus from tools, technical skills, or structures to the social dynamics and processes involved in the work setting. The second path organizational consulting has taken is one involving combined knowledge of social–psychological, cognitive–behavioral, and ecological–systems theories and principles. The target for this approach is to improve the socioemotional dynamics of the workplace. Research on the importance of quality of work life, leadership style, group dynamics, and morale to productivity encouraged organizations to review and monitor their systems and processes.

One consultant, Edgar Schein (1969), championed the value of process consultation. In this form of consultation, the members of an organization become more aware of the events and processes in their work environments and the impact of these processes on their performance. The process consultant is an organizational consultant interested in improving the interpersonal skills, interpersonal climate, and social dynamic existing within the work setting.

From this orientation, the organizational consultant was not only the prescriber or provider of expert knowledge, but also a facilitator of effective interpersonal behavior. The roles played by such a process consultant include systems analyst, administrative coach, action researcher, and educator/trainer.

Dimension IV: Consultant Skills Content
or Process Expertise

In the previous discussion on organizational models of consulting, it was noted that some organizational consultants employ a technical focus, providing content or technical expertise, whereas others focus more on the organizational structures and process. Although it is obvious that consultation always involves some level of expertise, the focus or emphasis of the expertise may vary from content/technical expertise to process expertise.

The consultant who is operating as a content expert will most often directly provide intervention or problem solving (Kurpius, 1978). From the role of content–technological expert, the consultant's goal is to provide the needed information, material, principles, or programs aimed at resolving the problem. The operative assumption underlying the role of content expert is that the current concern can be resolved by the direct application of specific knowledge or techniques. It is assumed that the consultant possesses knowledge and techniques that are needed and that the consultee lacks.

Process consultation, on the other hand, involves working with a consultee to actively implement a planned change process. The process consultant operates from the assumption that those within the system are unaware of the recurrent processes that have been or could be significantly affecting their performance and may be the source of their current difficulties. The process consultant will attempt to increase the consultee's awareness and understanding of the nature and impact of their system's patterns or processes. The process consultant may attend staff meetings to point out significant patterns of interaction, communication, or decision making; with the consultee review formal communication processes or lines of authority and decision making; or even employ actual critical incident situations to have the consultee review the dynamics of an event to better understand the processes operating and the impact of those processes. The focus of the process consultation would be on those individual roles and functions, intergroup and intragroup dynamics, communication patterns, leadership styles, or decision-making mechanisms that appear problematic. The operational assumption is that through such increased awareness the consultee will be able to adjust or in some way change the problematic process and thus increase the effectiveness or productivity of the system. Because the shift of emphasis is on the increased awareness and effectiveness of the consultee, the process consultant will typically employ a less-directive role in which there is more shared responsibility (ownership) and focus on education/prevention. The process consultant operates more as a facilitator than director, more as a coordinator, and less as the expert problem solver.

Dimension V: Modes of Consultation— Provisional–Prescriptive–Collaborative–Mediational

A fifth way to differentiate the various examples of consultation is to contrast consultation as a function of the particular role played by the consultant. Kurpius (1978) describes four modes of consultant behavior that could be used to differentiate consultation. Kurpius (1978) named these modes the provisional mode, the prescriptive mode, the collaborative mode, and the mediational mode.

In the provisional mode, or what has been termed a "pair-of-hands" role (Block, 1981), the consultee retains full control of the focus of the consultation, and the consultant is expected to apply specialized knowledge (content and process expertise) to implement action plans toward the achievement of goals defined by the consultee. It is as if the consultant, while possessing specialized knowledge or skill, functions as an extension of the consultee, employing his/her specialization in the manner that achieves the consultee's outcome objectives. Even though the consultant is providing specialized service, he or she does so at the specific request of the consultee. As such, the consultant defers to the consultee for determination of the problem and formulation of a desired outcome. The consultee judges and evaluates the process and outcomes, whereas the consultant attempts to make the system more effective by the application of specialized knowledge, providing a direct, yet reactive (i.e., crises oriented) service. In this role, two-way communication is limited (consultee initiates, consultant responds) and control rests with the consultee. Clearly the effectiveness of the consultant's intervention is strongly affected by the accuracy of the consultee's diagnosis of the problem and selection of desired outcome.

The prescriptive mode is also somewhat reactive and crisis focused in nature. In this form of consultation the consult is typically initiated by the consultee and typically out of a sense of need.

Although the service provided may tap the consultant's content or process expertise, the focus of the role is for the consultant to serve as a diagnostician and a provider of prescriptions for intervention by the consultee. The application of the intervention is the responsibility of the consultee, who may be directed and guided in this application by the consultant.

In the collaborative role, the consultant assumes that joining his or her specialized knowledge and skill with that of the consultee will increase accuracy of problem identification and maximize intervention resources and approaches. It is assumed that through such an expansion of resources and perspective the probability of effectiveness will be increased. In the collaborative mode, both the consultee and consultant play an active role. Responsibility for data gathering, analysis, goal setting, and intervention planning are shared. The responsibility for success and failure of the consult is also shared, and communication is two way.

As with the preceding modes, the collaborative mode is viewed as reactive, with the consultant being invited into the referral, typically because of the consultee's concern. Because of the interactive, mutual nature of the collaborative consultation, it allows for targeting the dual goals of intervention and prevention. It is hoped that by working together—sharing expertise and perspective—not only will the current problem be resolved, but the consultee will also be better able to resolve or prevent similar problems in the future.

Finally, the consultant who is operating from a mediational role or mode will take a much more proactive stance than would be the case from any of the previously discussed modes. The consultant in the mediational mode will initiate the consultation contact with the consultee. The consultant will initiate the contact, having recognized a recurrent problem, prior to the consultee's recognition or experience of need. In this mode the consultant will gather, analyze, and synthesize existing information as a way of defining the problem and develop an intervention plan for implementation.

When operating from a mediational mode, the consultant not only has to address the problem at hand, but "sells" the need for intervention to the consultee. The consultant will have to demonstrate to the consultee the wisdom and value of the need for consultation because up to this point the consultee has been operating without crisis or need. It is as if the consultant is trying to demonstrate the value of fixing something when the consultee feels that same something works and has worked well. Exercise 2.1 will help further clarify these varied modes of consultation.

EXERCISE 2.1

Multimodes of Consultation

Directions: With a colleague, classmate, or supervisor, discuss how a consultant operating from each of the previously described modalities might approach the following case. Discuss which mode you feel would be most effective.

Scenario: As a director of guidance you are asked for assistance by one of your counselors, Ron. It appears Ron is having a very difficult time working with one of his students, Nicole. Ron is brand new to the school, and this is the first time he has ever worked in an all-girls high school. Ron explains that no matter what he does, it simply seems that Nicole won't follow through on the suggestions. Further, he notes: "She's always coming down to see me, but when I ask what is up . . . she just goes silent, on me!" Ron, continues: "I have no idea what to do. Would you see her for me?" As you listen to Ron's concerns, you are clearly aware of his call for help, but are somewhat overwhelmed yourself trying to cover 1,200 girls, with only three full-time counselors. You just are not sure how much time you can give.

Provisional mode: _____

_____

Prescriptive mode: _____

_____

Collaborative mode: _____

_____

Mediational mode: _____

_____

Your choice? (Why?): _____

_____

CASE 2.1　The Case of Tommie S.

Referral

Tommie S. was referred to your office, by his teacher, Ms. Casey. Tommie is in fifth grade. He lives at home with his mother (a corporate lawyer) and his father (a psychiatrist). Tommie has an older sister (Julie) who is a senior in high school and an older brother (Alex) who is attending Columbia University Law School.

Ms. Casey sent Tommie with a note that read: "Tommie needs your help! He is a disturbed child. I found Tommie dropping his pencil in class in order to look up the dress of the girl who sits behind him. I also found some drawings that I would be embarrassed to show you. Tommie is inattentive. He is always fidgeting in his seat, looking around in class, and doing things (like dropping his pencil) to get peoples' attention.

I have tried talking to Tommie, I have kept him after school, I have talked to his parents and NOTHING works. It seems I spend more time calling out Tommie's name than teaching, please help him to get it together!"

Observations

In meeting Tommie you note that he is a very neat, mannerly, and articulate youth. Tommie admits that he was looking up the girl's dress, but stated, "It's just a game, other guys do it, too!" Tommie complained that Ms. Casey is always on "his case" and that she is really "boring."

In describing his home life, Tommie noted that he really misses his older brother (who had been at home up until this past month). He explained that he has a small job (taking care of his neighbor's dogs) after school and it keeps him busy from the time he gets home (3:00) until the time his mom comes home from work (4:15). Tommie discussed the many hobbies and sports activities he enjoys and noted that his dad has been the coach for both his soccer and baseball teams.

INTEGRATING PERSPECTIVES—
SERVING THE ONE AND THE MANY

Although each of the previous descriptive classifications has value in highlighting a particular aspect or characteristic of a consult, such classification can be misleading if it is interpreted as reflective of real distinctions. In practice, consultations rarely fit into one or another of the previous classifications. More often a consultation involves a mix of a number of these dimensions. Further, it is not unusual for the nature, focus, and target of the consultation to change as it develops over time. Therefore, rather than attempting to develop unique camps of consultation, it is much more functional and supportable to view the nature and form of consultation as a multidimensional, integrated activity that takes shape and distinctiveness by moving along a continuum reflecting consultee felt need, consultant expertise, degrees of collaborative involvement, and expansiveness of impact. The Case 2.1 will be used throughout this section to demonstrate each of the continua discussed next.

CASE 2.1   Continued

Tommie has been described by other teachers as a "good kid" who is somewhat of an "itch."

About the Consultee

Ms. Casey has been a teacher for the past 27 years. Ms. Casey has taught grades K through 2 for most of her career. This is the first year she has ever taught fifth grade. Ms. Casey stated that "she loves teaching and wouldn't know what to do if (she) couldn't have her classroom."

She expressed concerns over the real possibility of being forced to retire, and as such she wants to "demonstrate to the administration that (I) can be in complete control of (my) classroom." She noted that other children in her class have "discipline problems" and appear a bit "itchy." She noted, however, that she is concerned about referring these children for counseling because "a good teacher should be able to handle her own problems within the classroom!"

About the School

The school contains grades K through 5, with a student population of 520 students. The school has 18 classroom teachers, 3 supplementary teachers, a school psychologist, a learning specialist, and 2 school counselors. Within the last five years the community has grown significantly in size, educational background, and financial status. Most of the children come from homes in which both parents work in professional capacities, and the family expectations are that education will be valued and achieved.

The goals of the school are to: "foster academic development, inspire pride in self and country and to promote the development of self-control and responsible decision making." Informally, the school seems to value calmness, order, and neatness.

The school employs a self-contained mode of classroom education and as such teachers are responsible for all subject curriculum (with the exception of physical education).

FIGURE 2.1 Continuum of Felt Need

A Continuum of Felt Need

Rather than seeing consultation as either crisis or developmental in nature, it is much more effective to view each consultation as existing on a continuum of crisis or felt need (see Figure 2.1).

From this perspective, each consult is viewed as involving both a degree of felt need, either immediate or remote, and the potential to address possible future difficulties (i.e., developmental/preventive opportunity). This will become clear as we return to our sample case of Tommie (see Case 2.2).

CASE 2.2   Case Application—Tommie: Crisis and/or Developmental

We can begin to more clearly see how consultants operating from either a crisis or developmental focal point would differentially approach a consult by reviewing the case of Tommie S.

A consultant operating from a crises frame of reference would have a number of points of contact in the case of Tommie. Clearly, Ms. Casey is in need of assistance (in crisis). Providing remediation for Ms. Casey's limited understanding of typical fifth-grade behavior or ineffectual classroom management skills would seem appropriate. Similarly, intervening with Tommie, who is also in crisis, being bored and in trouble with Ms. Casey, would appear appropriate. Working with Tommie and Ms. Casey perhaps in developing a behavioral contract aimed at increasing his time on task and

positive classroom behavior would appear to be a potential useful plan for crises consultation.

Even though the referral was made in a crisis, a consultant with a developmental orientation may see other potential problems that need addressing. A consultant approaching this situation from a more developmental perspective may target each of the following as points for preventive programming.

- Teacher in-service and preparation, especially in light of new grade level assignments
- Retirement planning and transitional support
- After-school programming for latchkey children
- Sex education curriculum development

Clearly, the consultee in this case, Ms. Casey, was experiencing an immediate need for intervention. However, conceptualizing the consult from only a crisis orientation would have blinded the consultant from the preventive potential of the consultation. The consultant who viewed this interaction as one starting at the extreme left side of the felt need continuum would perceive the value of moving up the continuum toward the prevention end as the immediacy and severity of the need subsides. Thus, in addition to assuring Ms. Casey that something can be done to reduce Tommie's disruptive behaviors in her classroom, this consultant will also have an eye to prevention, looking forward to ways to assist this consultee to better cope with the demands of a new type of student population (i.e., fifth graders) in the future.

A Continuum of Content–Process Expertise

The position taken here and elsewhere (see Parsons, 1996) is that it is more effective to conceptualize consultation as moving along a content–process expert continuum as opposed to being either a content/technical focus or a process focus (see Figure 2.2).

In each consultation, the consultant is expected to possess specialized knowledge and skill. In the case of the school counselor, this expert knowledge centers around the processes of human behavior. But in addition to

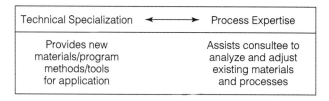

Technical Specialization ◄─────► Process Expertise	
Provides new materials/program methods/tools for application	Assists consultee to analyze and adjust existing materials and processes

FIGURE 2.2 Content-Process Expertise—Need for both

possessing expert knowledge and technical materials and resources, the counselor–consultant will have the skills to facilitate the identification and utilization of the consultee's own knowledge and skills as applied to the current situation. A number of elements (e.g., consultee need, original consultation contract, consultee expectations) can be used to determine which end of the expertise continuum the consultant will initially emphasize. However, the point for consideration is that regardless of the level of emphasis, both technical and process expertise is important.

Without fostering the consultee's understanding and awareness of the process by which the problem emerged or the processes that are available to the consultee for reducing the likelihood of this problem reoccurring, hopes of prevention may be blocked. Again considering the case of Tommie (see Case 2.3), it is apparent that a consultant skilled in behavioral techniques (content expertise) could certainly provide a specific remedial program for the client to be applied by either the consultee as part of classroom management or by the consultant or by both. Similarly, from a process orientation, the consultant could support and facilitate the consultee's own analysis of the situation, along with her or his own identification of the specific factors characterizing classroom process that may contribute to the current problem.

Through the support of the process consultant, the consultee may begin to identify those elements that can be employed to remediate the current difficulty and prevent future similar problems from emerging.

Given the high level of experienced stress, the history of her own unsuccessful interventions, and the expectation that the consultant will "help him get it together," the consultant, working with Ms. Casey, may elect to start by providing a number of specific technical steps to be taken. For example, the consultant could remove Tommie from the classroom and begin a behavioral contract system with him, which focuses on his attending behavior. In addition to such technical intervention, the consultant will want to help Ms. Casey identify elements in her own style and classroom process and the impact these may have on the behavior of her students, including Tommie. Further, the consultant, acting as a process expert, may facilitate her understanding of this impact and the possible modification to her style that would augment the work the consultant is doing with Tommie. In this way a consultant is employing both content/technical expertise and process expertise in the delivery of the service.

**CASE 2.3   Expert–Process Consultation
Case Application—Tommie—
A Technical or Process Approach**

A consultant approaching the case of Tommie clearly has a number of targets that he could address (Tommie, Ms. Casey, the classroom, etc.) and from a number of theoretical perspectives. But regardless of the target or the theoretical model, the consultant could emphasize either content/technical expertise or process expertise.

The content expert may

1. Provide Ms. Casey with a specific set of behavior modification recommendations; or
2. Offer a packaged in-service program for teachers regarding classroom management, preadolescent sexuality, or even retirement planning; or even
3. Suggest to the school board or building principal the inclusion of a sex education component to the curriculum or the development of an after-school latchkey program.

Regardless of the target or the model, the content expert consultant brings to the situation a formulated set of principles, techniques, strategies, or programs that he believes have value to the current difficulty.

The process consultant, although certainly attempting to bring expertise to the resolution of the problem at hand, will approach it with a different focus. As such, she may

1. Assist Ms. Casey to review her current classroom management decisions and procedures in attempting to increase her awareness of how these processes may be impacting the current difficulty; or
2. Identify a faculty ad hoc group who will begin to discuss common professional concerns and generate possible actions to be taken (which may include the development of inservice training); or finally
3. Review with the relevant administrators operating procedures for teacher grade-level placement, teacher evaluation processes, or retirement programming, as they may come to bear on this one specific work-related difficulty.

A Continuum of Collaboration

Unlike others (e.g., Kurpius and Fuqua, 1993), who conceptualize collaboration as a separate mode of consultation, the position taken here is that collaboration can be a *style* of consulting that can employed, regardless of the specific mode. Rather than artificially distinguishing the various modes of consultation as if they were exclusive and distinctive, it is suggested that it is more effective to view the role of consultant along a continuum of collaboration (see Figure 2.3).

The least collaborative mode of consulting would be that in which the consultant provides specialized services (i.e., provisional mode). The most collaborative form of consultation would be one in which the consultant and consultee engage in a coordinate relationship, mutually sharing diagnostic observation and coequally owning and developing intervention strategies.

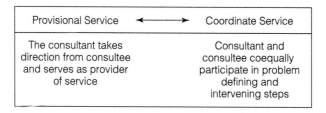

Provisional Service	←——→	Coordinate Service
The consultant takes direction from consultee and serves as provider of service		Consultant and consultee coequally participate in problem defining and intervening steps

FIGURE 2.3 Continuum of Collaborative Style

These two positions are identified as idealized poles at the extreme of the collaborative continuum, with the reality falling somewhere in between.

Regardless of the position on the continuum, collaboration as a process is valued. Thus even while serving in a provisional role, the consultant values the need for the consultee's input into the specifics of what is to be provided, as well as the values needed to provide educative and preventive feedback to the consultee. Similarly, the consultant operating from a prescriptive stance, values and employs collaborative skills to ensure not only consultee understanding of the prescription but also consultee ownership of the intervention plan.

It is our position that the effective consultant attempts to maximize the mutuality of input and ownership and therefore includes elements of collaboration into each consult. This would appear to be true in the case of Tommie (see Case 2.4).

The consultant in this case may want to enter the relationship with Ms. Casey at the level of provisional service, because that is what she is requesting, but would attempt to maximize the active involvement of Ms. Casey along the entire process. Including Ms. Casey's input into this process not only increases the probability of developing a successful intervention plan but also would provide the avenue through which preventive programming could be initiated.

A Continuum of Breadth of Impact

Historically consultation has been presented as a mode of service delivery that indirectly serviced the client, as opposed to counseling, which would be considered a direct form of service. The position taken here and elsewhere (Myers, Parsons, & Martin, 1979; Parsons, 1996; Caplan & Caplan, 1993, 1999) is that direct service, including counseling, can be placed under the rubric of consultation if there is evidence of a triadic element showing the consultant interacting with the consultee.

Viewed from such a perspective, one could envision consultation as focusing on a more or less expansive target in efforts to effect client change. At one end of this continuum, one may employ a crises intervention with a client focus, in which there is direct contact with the client by the counselor-consultant. At the other end of this continuum, we may see a counselor-consultant attempting to effect change in a client by changing policies, procedures, or specific elements within the school system itself (Figure 2.4).

CASE 2.4   Case Application—Four Modes for Tommie

In order to more fully appreciate the role differentiation suggested by the aforementioned discussion around modes of consultation, consider how a consultant from a provisional, prescriptive, collaborative, or mediational mode would service Ms. Casey.

Provisional: As an added pair of hands, the consultant might take Ms. Casey's request to ". . . please help him to get it together" literally. As such, the provisional consultant may meet with Ms. Casey to more concretely identify what she sees as the problem and what she wants the consultant to do with Tommie. Perhaps Ms. Casey wants Tommie removed from her class because he is such a disruption. She may also want the consultant to see that his parents get Tommie professional help. Should the consultant modify Tommie's schedule to place him in another class and speak to the parents about professional counseling for Tommie, s/he would be operating from a provisional mode.

Prescriptive: Because Ms. Casey is in crisis, the consultant may respond to her need by providing suggestions on what to do with Tommie and/or for herself. Perhaps after getting a better understanding of the nature of the problem, the prescriptive consultant might suggest the following.

1. Ms. Casey should talk to the principal about moving Tommie to the other fifth grade;
2. Ms. Casey should use the filmstrip and programmed unit on respecting each other (provided by the consultant) as a way of helping the class modify such behavior (looking up skirts); or even
3. Instruct Ms. Casey to review material (provided by the consultant) on the behavior

modification principles of extinction, shaping, and reinforcement so that she would be more competent to apply these principles to shape Tommie's behavior.

Collaborative: Although each of the recommendations either enacted by the consultant in the provisional mode or provided to Ms. Casey in the prescriptive mode may have value, they were generated from only one source (either the consultee or the consultant). As a result of this unidirectional action, understanding and complete ownership for the interventions may not be shared, and a second potential resource went untapped. The collaborative consultant will attempt to work with Ms. Casey to come to common agreement regarding the nature of the problem. As a result of their discussions Ms. Casey and the consultant may agree that although Tommie is most likely neither an evil child nor a child with a sexual problem, his behavior in class is somewhat disruptive and should be modified. Further, from a sharing of principles of what could be done (from the consultant) and the identification of the natural conditions of the classroom environment and the procedures that have already been applied (from the consultee), a new, situationally specific application of the behavioral principles may emerge to which both the consultant and consultee had input and ownership.

Mediational: Even though the consultant has been asked to intervene in the case of Tommie and thus is reacting to a crisis, the conditions of the referral also provide a number of targets from mediational consultation. Although the immediate concern of Ms. Casey is Tommie, it is

Continued

CASE 2.4   Continued

clear that the process of teacher evaluation and the eventuality of her retirement also loom as future stressors that may negatively impact her professional performance and the performance of her students. The mediational consultant will attempt to elevate Ms. Casey's awareness of the potentially detrimental effects of these possible stressors and help her begin to plan methods for reducing the negative stress of these events and/or increasing her ability to cope and adjust to such stress.

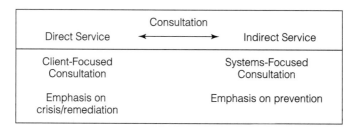

FIGURE 2.4 Expanded Focus

As suggested in Figure 2.4, client-focused consultation (chapter 9) allows for direct assessment of the client by the consultant and thus is the most direct form of consultation. Consultation focusing on the system (chapter 12) uses techniques that may completely remove the consultant from direct contact, thus proving to be the least direct form of service delivery. Each of these levels requires specific diagnostic and intervention skills and as such will be discussed in greater detail in later chapters (see chapters 9–12). However, a brief overview of each is provided following.

Level I: Client-Focused Consultation   The consultant seeking to modify the behavior, attitudes, and feelings of a particular client or clients may gather diagnostic data either directly (e.g., interviewing, individual testing, observation) or more indirectly through the consultee. In either case, the focus of both the diagnoses and intervention is on the client.

Level II: Consultee-Focused Consultation   Consultee-focused consultation still attempts to impact the client, but does so somewhat more indirectly, by focusing intervention on changing the behavior, attitudes, or feelings of the consultee.

It is reasoned that by increasing the consultee's knowledge, skill level, confidence, or professional objectivity, benefits will be accrued by the client.

Level III: Group-Focused Consultation   Quite often a consultant is asked to assist in a situation in which the functioning of dyads or small groups within the organization is faltering. For example, with the realities of limited resources within our schools, it would not be unusual to find departments competing for space or materials, a competition that may result in increased tension and reduction of cooperation of these departments. Under these conditions, the counselor–consultant may attempt to assist the groups in their goal setting, communication, and conflict-resolution processes (Cadence Group, 1995; Hale, 1998).

Level IV: System-Focused Consultation   Because a system consists of a number interdependent elements, it could be argued that a consultant's efforts to influence the client or the consultee is, in fact, employing a system intervention. There are times, however, when the specific client's need is best met by a modification of the processes or structures of the system within which the client operates. It is under these conditions that system-focused consultation is performed.

The goal of a system-focused consultation is to improve organizational functioning of the system. It is assumed that optimizing the processes, structures, and functioning of the system will indirectly increase the mental health and general functioning of the client and consultee within that system. Although system-focused consultation is the least direct of all the forms of consultation, it provides the greatest opportunity for affecting the largest number of potential clients and consultees with the highest degree of primary prevention (Parsons, 1996; Parsons & Meyers, 1984).

These various targets and extent of breadth and depth of impact can be more fully illustrated by once again returning to our case of Tommie (Case 2.5).

CASE 2.5   Case Application—Tommie: Many Targets, Many Goals

Again, a review of the case of Tommie (Case 2.1) might clarify this issue of how a consult could be differentially defined and approached along this dimension of problem and goal conceptualization.

In reviewing the case of Tommie, it may appear obvious that the breadth of the focus of the referral could be narrowed and restricted to working directly with Tommie or defined more broadly to include working with the Ms. Casey's entire fifth grade. Further, goals may be established and intervention procedures employed that attempt to produce changes in various targets. The breadth of the intervention and goal may be limited to an individual, for example, modifying Tommie's inattentive behavior or increasing Ms. Casey's classroom management skills. Goals and interventions could also be expanded to include changes within a group, for example, educating the student's in Ms. Casey's class around the issues of preadolescent development. Or even more broadly defined goals could include the development of institutional policies and procedures that would protect against inappropriate teacher–grade assignments or provide a system of supports for preretirement planning.

Integrating Nature, Focus, and Modes

As with any categorization and compartmentalization of consultation, the model presented here is artificial and if employed as a lockstep view of consulting can interfere with the flexibility needed for effective consulting. It is hoped that this conceptualization of consultation along a continuum of direct–indirect foci will provide readers with a cognitive map to employ as they proceed in the process of diagnosing and intervening in any one consultation contract. For example, in a client-focused consultation that may have originated with a client problem (crises) and a consultee who is seeking direct services (provisional) or recommendations (prescriptive), the consultant employing a multidimensional, integrated model of consulting can identify opportunities for preventive programming by targeting the consultee and/or the system at large. (See Exercise 2.2)

GUIDING CONSULTANT
DECISION MAKING

Guiding the Consultant's Decisions Regarding
Form and Focus of Consultation

A consultant truly needs to be a jack of all trades and master of some. In assuming an integrated, multidimensional approach to consultation, the consultant enters a consultation relationship without a predetermined, fixed plan of operation. The consultant will be flexible and responsive to both the demands and opportunities of the situation, shifting the consult in terms of its nature, focus, content, and mode.

With so many modes of operation and points of focus possible, one may soon become overwhelmed with role of consultant. To be effective, the consultant needs to be able to select the level of service (e.g., client focused, consultee focused, system focused) and the form of consulting (i.e., degree of collaboration) that will provide the greatest degree of immediate remediation and provide the highest level of prevention potential. Although there are no hard and fast rules to direct a consultant in her decisions, there are a number of considerations that could be used as guidelines when selecting the form and level of a consultation. The process of selecting a form and focus for a particular consult will be influenced by the nature of the consultation contract, the definition of the problem and goal, the consultant's orientation, and the consultee style. Each of these inputs (i.e., the consultation contract, the nature of problem and goal, consultant orientation, and consultee style) must be brought into the decision process as guidelines for the consultant's choice of mode, style, and focus. As such, each of these inputs will be briefly described and expanded on in later chapters.

The Contract as a Defining Element

It may seem obvious, but the consultant's form of operation will be at least initially defined by the nature and limits of the consulting contract. A counselor working within the school must be sensitive to requirements of the contract that defines their role and function. Regardless of whether this is a formal written contract or merely an implicit agreement between the counselor and the principal or representative of the school system, the contract establishes a number of conditions that must guide the counselor-as-consultant's choices.

The contract marks the entry stage of any consult and involves achieving a level of acceptance and empowerment to perform the role of consultant. It is during this stage of the consultation process that the consultant needs to discern between what is expected by the consultee and what is required. Further, the consultant needs to begin to identify system and consultee openness to consultation as a way of discerning what is optimal from what is possible. How the consultant is accepted and empowered to work (i.e., entry) will influence the way a problem can be conceptualized and the level (i.e., client focused, consultee focused, group focused, or system focused) on which it can be approached. However, as will become evident throughout the remaining chapters, the process of consulting is fluid, and the effective consultant will continue to look for opportunities to reenter and even renegotiate the consultative contract at levels that allow for more preventive and systemic impacts.

In the process of gaining entry and developing the working contract, the consultant should identify the nature and limits to the consultant's role, the objectives of the consult, and the expectations and role of others (e.g., consultee, client) in the consult, as well as other specific details of time schedule and manner of feedback or evaluation. It is important that the consultant be clear about the expectations of the contract, both in terms of what the consultant can and will do, as well as what the consultant will not do.

With this in mind, it is suggested that consultants approach contract formulation as an opportunity for intervention and education. It is important to establish, where possible, a broad-based contract that includes direct client and consultee contact along with indirect (systems) services. Further, it is important to contract to provide services of both a crises and preventive nature. Finally, it is extremely important to emphasize the value of a collaborative mode of consulting along with specifying the specific expectation of collaborative relationships. Clearly, establishing such a broad-based contract will allow more flexibility in decision making on the part of the consultant.

The Nature of the Problem and Goal

In the ideal world, the mode of consultation, the form of intervention, and the style of consultation employed should all be responsive to the specific nature of the problem presented, along with the nature and conditions of the goal(s) desired. However, there are many ways to conceptualize a presenting complaint. Any one presenting concern can be defined or conceptualized as one calling for client-focused, consultee-focused, group-focused, or even system-focused consultation.

Thus, although the consultant could possibly define both the problem and the goal at a number of levels, with each level helping determine the nature and direction of the consultation, the consultant needs to adjust this conceptualization to make it coordinate with the conceptualization of the consultee. Although there may be an optimal way of defining this or that problem and the subsequent goals, it is more important to present the problems and goals in ways that the consultee can embrace.

Consultant Orientation

Gallessich (1982) argued that the factor most influencing a consultant's choice of approach is the mind-set produced by her professional training and experiences. Because our own personal and professional paradigm can be so influencing, it is important for us to be on guard that our diagnosis and intervention planning reflect the problem at hand, as opposed to our biased approach. The consultant needs to be aware of his orientation and sensitive to the possibility that his professional orientation or set can shape the way he defines a problem. The consultant also needs to be cautious that the strategies employed reflect the needs as presented and not simply the comfort level of the consultant with some strategies as opposed to others.

While being clear to operate in ways consistent with one's level of training, experience, and supervision, it is also incumbent that the consultant operating from a flexible, integrated, multidimensional perspective continue professional development through ongoing training and supervision. It is important that as a consultant one become increasingly aware of the variety of approaches available and begin to discern those methods, those choices that are most functional and applicable to each situation. Such breadth of understanding and flexibility will require constant updating of professional skills and knowledge, as well as ongoing supervision and self-monitoring.

Consultee Experience, Expectations, and Style

When considering the manner in which one may consult, a consultant needs to understand the previous experience (both positive and negative) of the consultee and others within the system with consultation. It is important to identify how this previous experience and knowledge of consultation may impact the current expectations.

In selecting an approach or focus for one's consultation, the power of expectations needs to be taken seriously. Approaching the consultee with a style or focus that is so completely dissonant with expectation may result in consultee resistance or defensive posturing.

Although it is possible to continually shape (or reshape) the consultee's expectations, this may have to occur in small steps. It is important for the effective consultant to keep in mind that congruence between consultee expectations and experience with a consultant is a requisite to success.

EXERCISE 2.2

Viewing Problems and Goals
along a Continuum of Expansiveness

Directions: Following you will find three consultation scenarios. For each scenario identify a specific or restricted problem and corresponding goal. Next, review the same scenarios redefining the problem more broadly and making the goal more encompassing. Share your perspective with a colleague, classmate, or supervisor to see additional perspectives.

Scenario I: The high school basketball coach approaches you for possible assistance in helping his team relax at the foul line. He wants you to teach team members stress-reduction techniques. As you discuss the proposed program with the athletic director, you are informed that this is to give the team that little edge over the competition. You are also told that this is a highly competitive school, and winning isn't everything, it "is the only thing." The coaches need every advantage to keep the principal off their backs.

Scenario II: You are asked by your principal to meet with the sixth-grade team of teachers. It appears that the members of this team have been a bit on edge. The principal stated that these "four teachers have been pretty argumentative and I won't have that among my faculty." He continued: "These four are going to be working as the sixth-grade team for the remainder of the year, and they better start pulling together!" Your task is to get these four faculty to work out their problems with each other.

Scenario III: You are working in a small school district that is about to merge with its sister district. According to the principal of your school, some faculty appear to be more interested in chatting about the rumors than doing their job. He wants you to help him get them "back in line—doing their job more and gabbing less!" His feeling is that what goes on at district level is not their business, and they should be focusing on their classrooms. As he notes: "Even the kids are getting off task!"

SUMMARY

The Many Faces of Consulting: Modes and Models

A review of the consultation literature will highlight both the many arenas in which consultation is practiced (e.g., schools, mental health services, hospitals, industry) and also depict the diversity in role and functions defined as consultation. The model employed here, as elsewhere (see Parsons, 1996), differentiates the various forms of consultation function and consultant role categorizes consultation along five dimensions: nature (crisis–developmental), problem–goal focus (client, consultee, group, or system), theory (mental health, behavioral, organizational), skills (content or process), and modes (provisional, prescriptive, collaborative, and mediational).

Integrating Perspectives—
Serving the One and the Many

In practice, consultations rarely fit into one or another of the classifications just listed. More often a consultation involves a mix of a number of these dimensions. Further, it is not unusual for the nature, focus, and target of the consultation to change as it develops over time. Therefore, the approach taken within this text is to view the nature and form of consultation as a multidimensional, integrated activity that takes shape and distinctiveness by moving along a continuum reflecting consultee felt need, consultant expertise, degree of collaborative involvement, and expansiveness of impact.

Guiding the Consultant's Decisions Regarding
Form and Focus of Consultation

To be effective the consultant needs to be able to select the level of service (e.g., client focused, consultee focused, group or system focused) and the form of consulting (i.e., degree of collaboration) that will provide the greatest degree of immediate remediation and provide the highest level of prevention potential. The process of selecting a form and focus for a particular consult will be influenced by the nature of the consultation contract, the nature of the problem and goal, the consultant orientation, and the consultee style.

IMPORTANT TERMS

Behavioral consultation

Client

Client-focused consultation

Collaboration

Collaborative mode

Content expertise

Consultant

Consultation

Consultee

Consultee-focused consultation

Crisis-orientated consultation

Developmental consultation

Dual focus

Group-focused consultation

Mediational mode

Mental health consultation

Mutual

Prescriptive

Prevention

Problem solving

Process expert

System-focused consultation

SUGGESTED READINGS

Barcus, S. W., III, & Wilkinson, J. W. (Eds.). (1995). *Handbook of management consulting service* (2nd ed.). New York: McGraw-Hill.

Caplan, G., & Caplan, R. (1999). *Mental health consultation and collaboration*. Prospect Heights, IL: Waveland.

Erchul, W. P., & Martens, K. (1997). *School consultation: Conceptual and empirical bases of practice*. New York: Plenum Press.

Zins, J. E., Kratochwill, T. R., & Elliot, S. E. (Eds.). (1993). *Handbook of consultation services for children*. San Francisco: Jossey-Bass.

WEB SITES

Conjoint Behavioral Consultation (CBC)—resources for school psychologists and counselors. http://tc.unl.edu/schoolpsych/cbc.html

Process Consultation—support and information for Edgar Schein's process consultation model. http://www.cape.org/2002/schein.html

Behavioral Consultation—resource for operationally defining behaviors of real concern and organizing consultation approaches. http://www.cecp.air.org/fba/problembehavior/text.htm

Technical Aid Packet on School-Based Client Consultation, Referral, and Management of Care—this document is a hard copy version of a resource that can be downloaded at no cost. http://www.smhp.psych.ucla.edu/qf/student_tt/topic3-reading.pdf

REFERENCES

Argyris, C. (1970). *Intervention theory and method: A behavioral science view*. Reading, MA: Addison-Wesley.

Beckhard, R. (1969). *Organization development: Strategies and models*. Reading, MA: Addison-Wesley.

Bennis, W. G. (1969). *Organizational development: Its nature, origins and prospects*. Reading, MA: Addison-Wesley.

Bergan, J. R., & Kratochwill, T. R. (1990). *Behavioral consultation and therapy*. New York: Plenum Press.

Bergan, J. R., & Tombari, J. L. (1976). Consultant skill and efficiency and the implementation and outcomes of consultation. *Journal of School Psychology, 14,* 3–14.

Block, P. (1981). *Flawless consulting*. San Diego, CA: Pfeiffer & Comp.

Cadence Group, The (1995). Team building. In S. W. Barcus III & J. W. Wilkinson (Eds.), *Handbook of management consulting services* (2nd ed., pp. 26.1–27.0). New York: McGraw-Hill.

Caplan, G. (1970). *The theory and practice of mental health consultation*. New York: Basic Books.

Caplan, G., & Caplan, R. (1993). *Mental health consultation and collaboration*. San Francisco: Jossey-Bass.

Caplan, G., & Caplan, R. (1999). *Mental health consultation and collaboration*. Prospect Heights, IL: Waveland. (Original work published in 1993)

Curtis, N. J., & Zins, J. E. (Eds.) (1981). *The theory and practice of school consultation*. Springfield, IL: Charles C Thomas.

Gallessich, J. (1982). *The profession and practice of consultation*. San Francisco: Jossey-Bass.

Gallessich, J. (1985). Toward a meta-theory of consultation. *The Counseling Psychologist, 13,* 336–354.

Hale, J. (1998). *The performance consultant's fieldbook*. San Francisco: Jossey-Bass.

Kuehnel, T. G., & Kuehnel, J. M. (1983). Consultation training from a behavioral perspective. In J. Alpert & J. Meyers (Eds.), *Training in consultation*. Springfield, IL: Charles C Thomas.

Kurpius, D. J. (1978). Consultation theory and process: An integrated model. *The Personnel and Guidance Journal, 56,* 335–338.

Kurpius, D. J., & Fuqua, D. R. (1993). Introduction to the speed issues. *Journal of Counseling and Development, 71,* 596–697.

Martens, B. K. (1993). A behavioral approach to consultation. In J. E. Zins, T. R. Kratochwill, & S. E. Elliot (Eds.), *Handbook of consultation services for children* (pp. 65–86). San Francisco: Jossey-Bass.

Meyers, J., Parsons, R. D., & Martin, R. (1979). *Mental health consultation in schools*. San Francisco: Jossey-Bass.

Parsons, R. (1996). *The skilled consultant*. Needham Heights, MA: Allyn & Bacon.

Parsons, R., & Meyers, J. (1984). *Developing consultation skills*. San Francisco: Jossey-Bass.

Rockwood, G. F. (1993). Edgar Schein's process versus content consultation model. *Journal of Counseling and Development, 71,* 636–638.

Rogawski, A. S. (Ed.). (1979). *New directions for mental health services: Mental health consultation in community settings* (No. 3). San Francisco: Jossey-Bass.

Ross, G. J. (1993). Peter Block's flawless consulting and the homunculus theory: Within each person is a perfect consultant. *Journal of Counseling and Development, 71,* 639–641.

Schein, E. H. (1969). *Process consultation: Its role in organization development*. Reading, MA: Addison-Wesley.

Schein, E. H. (1989). Process consultation as a general model of helping. *Consulting Psychology Bulletin, 41,* 3–15.

Schein, E. H. (1990). Organizational culture. *American Psychologist, 45,* 109–119.

The Needs of One within the Context of Many

3

The School as a System

Basic Elements

Well, I really expect Dr. Jameson is going to be a bit surprised and maybe confused by the fact that I want to see him—even before I see Ellen. The counselors have always been used in crises, to put out fires, and to react to teacher, administrator, and even parent requests to work directly with students. I know that this has been the expectation of the counselor, to be a direct-service, hands-on provider.

For such a small high school, especially one that is so very conservative in values and entrenched as an agricultural, rural community, trying something new is neither easy nor always welcomed. I better go slowly. But I do think Dr. Jameson needs to understand my rationale for not seeing Ellen first. It's the only way I'm going to be able to begin to develop the expectation of collaborative consultation.

Attempting to perform one's job the way we see fit is not always an easy task. Every job that receives monetary compensation is formed, influenced, and maintained by the social and physical environment in which it exists. School counseling is no exception. Thus, the role and function that Mr. Thomas is expected to perform in helping Ellen, and in responding to Dr. Jameson's request, is influenced, not just by Mr. Thomas's perspective of the problem, but also by an array of social and environmental forces.

Most of these forces, such as the needs, values, and beliefs of his teaching colleagues, his students, and their parents existed long before he joined the school staff. These forces manifest and reflect the unique needs, beliefs, and values of the local community, the school board, the administration, the district's teachers and support staff, and every individual involved with this school (and district) since its inception.

What appears to have been a simple request for service is truly an invitation for Mr. Thomas to step into the history, trajectory, and current dynamics of his school community. Without an understanding and appreciation of the nature and influence of this evolving, dynamic *system*, his efforts to respond to this one request for service may prove less than effective.

Mr. Thomas does not operate in a vacuum. His work is to some degree guided by the culture of his school, the rules and regulations established, the nature of the internal workings, and the expectations of all involved. And although he may assume his job is that of guidance, the truth is that his counseling program at Kirkwood High School is just one of many subsystems of this school community that was designed to meet the various needs of the numerous groups comprising this system. As such, Mr. Thomas's job description with its roles and functions is directly and indirectly influenced by the dynamic needs, values, and beliefs that characterize these school community groups. Each component of his counseling program—his counseling, consulting, and coordination (Gyspers & Henderson, 2000)—must be responsive and accountable to these systemic forces. Whether considering the broad scope and sequence of his comprehensive program or just one component, such as his consulting role, his effectiveness as a school counselor (as consultant) will be influenced by these systemic forces. Moreover, his effectiveness will be measured by his ability to successfully address the needs and goals of his professional colleagues, students and their parents, community members, and stakeholders who have a vested interest in the learning and development of his students.

From this systems perspective, Mr. Thomas must not only be a skilled counselor to successfully carry out his duties, but he must also be knowledgeable and skilled in understanding and working with systems and system influence. The same is true for you!

CHAPTER OBJECTIVES

School counselors must be knowledgeable about and sensitive to these systemic forces if they are to be effective. To this end, chapter 3 will describe the basic elements of a school as a system and explain their relationship to the many functions of school counselor consultation.

After completing this chapter the reader will be able to

1. Describe the basic elements of a school as a social system
2. Explain the interrelationship of these basic components in building, maintaining, and revising the program of services offered by the school counselor
3. Explain the nature of school counselor consultation from a systemic perspective

SYSTEMS INTRODUCTION

What does Mr. Thomas need to know about the system (and its various sub-systems) in which he works? Before we address this question for Mr. Thomas at Kirkwood High School, we need to define and describe the basic components of systems in general. As you read through the following section, think of the systems in which you currently operate. The elements to be described can be applied to your workplace or school, the class you may be taking, and even your own family. Attempting to identify these specifics elements in your life will help them come alive.

System Defined

According to one author (Kurpius, 1985), a *system* is "an entity made up of interconnected parts, with recognizable relationships that are systematically arranged to serve a perceived purpose" (p. 368). So what are these interconnected parts?

Systems receive resources (input) from their environment (population) and use those resources to execute operations (processes) in order to produce purposeful effects (output) that meet environmental (needs) (Jerrell & Jerrell, 1981). These five basic elements—**population, need, output, process,** and **input**—are the parts that are interrelated and interdependent and need to operate in synchronicity to keep the system functioning efficiently and effectively.

The definition of *system* is applicable across the spectrum of systems with which you engage daily. Physical systems such as computers, cell phones, and automobiles employ these same systemic properties, using energy (input) to perform operations (processes) designed to create conditions (output) that help individuals to meet their (needs). At a more personalized level, organ systems such as our respiration, circulation, and musculature use chemical nutrients to maintain their respective bodily functions to keep us alive, alert, and able to read this book. Further, any changes in any single component will alter the entire system and its capacity to do the job for which it was designed. For example, consider the effect of extensive exercise on your ability to do further exercise. As lactic acid builds in the striated muscles during rigorous exercise, these chemical changes (input) restrict muscle relaxation and contraction (processes), causing you to slow down and take a rest (output). With rest, the proper chemical balance in the cell tissue is restored, and the system can renew its work, or exercise.

Just like our bodily systems, our social systems, those created by people to achieve desired outcomes and resolve critical needs, are composed of these same components and operate from the same dynamic principles. Some of these man-made systems are designed to produce products (outcomes) that we purchase and use to meet physical, social, entertainment, and emotional needs. Burlington Coat Factory produces products to keep us warm, McDonald's Restaurants produce products that satisfy our appetite, and

Disney Corporation produces outcomes that titillate our senses and mobilize our fantasies. Each of these social systems produces a product that meets our needs. Likewise, many social systems are created and maintained by people to provide services (output) that address other critical needs. Hospitals are systems designed to provide the requisite medical care to keep us healthy and alive, whereas law enforcement systems exist to keep us safe and secure within the parameters of acceptable and unacceptable behavior.

Each of these social systems provides an array of services that use resources (input) to create and deliver services (processes) in order to achieve (output or outcomes) critical to the health and safety of society (population).

The School as System

In addition to being consumers of our health and law enforcement systems, each of us has utilized another one of our social systems—the school.

In the early part of the nineteenth century, with the industrial revolution in full gear, American society recognized the critical importance of a literate, informed, and educated workforce. It was acknowledged throughout the nation that this need for literacy and numeracy existed for all segments of American society with the exception of targeted minority populations. Anglo-European youth were expected to enter adulthood, and the workforce, being able to read, write, and perform mathematical calculations. They were also expected to exercise values and beliefs of citizenship and good character. No mechanism or institution then existed to achieve these goals, therefore institutions had to be created with the resources and commitment emanating from the prevailing need. Those locally established institutions became our public schools.

Each community constructed educational systems composed of schools organized as administrative systems within explicit geographical boundaries. Community leaders further entrusted specifically qualified individuals to organize these schools and deliver a program of studies leading to desired levels of literacy and numeracy. During these formative years, public schools were expected to educate students to basic levels of performance required by local business, religious, and industrial institutions (also social systems). These specialized individuals entrusted with this task or mission were called educators, teachers, and administrators, and they constructed basic curricula and teaching methodology around achieving the charge given to them by their community leaders. Schools were new, resourceful, innovative, for that time, and operated within the full view and blessing of their local community. At their point of origination, these schools are flexible and able to adapt to changing circumstances. At this point, the school can be considered to be an **open system** with processes linked to desired outcomes that in turn were derived from population needs. This system dynamic (i.e., open or closed systems) will be discussed in the next chapter. For now, we narrow our focus to the specific components of the school as a system.

SYSTEM POPULATIONS:
CONSUMERS AND PROVIDERS

Before we begin to isolate and discuss each component of the school system, it is important to note that the actual boundaries of our school system could be defined as narrowly as the individual classroom or as broadly as the State Department of Education and beyond. This continuum of smaller to larger highlights the reality that systems exist within systems, which in turn exist within larger systems, and so on ad infinitum. In actuality, the single classroom can be viewed as a subsystem of a grade, which is a subsystem of a school, which is a subsystem within a curriculum level (elementary, middle school, high school), which operates as a subsystem of a larger system called a district, and so forth (see Figure 3.1). With this continuum as the backdrop, it becomes obvious that any one specialized process such as a comprehensive guidance program, although serving the needs of the system (i.e., school) in which it is embedded, is also, in and of itself, its own system. Thus each of the subsystems within a school contains the same basic components and dynamics of systems in general. What distinguishes these systems within a system is the specific population–need–outcome–process–input parameters that it employs.

Consumers

All social systems exist because people experience needs and are willing to put their resources into processes designed to meet those needs. Consider the illustration of a single school, Kirkwood High School, our case illustration. Kirkwood High School exists to serve the unique needs of the specific population attending its programs. Further, Kirkwood High School is maintained by the population of taxpayers and governmental agencies that provide its input. As such, Kirkwood High needs to be responsive to two populations— those who receive the services (i.e., educational program) offered by the school and those who provide the resources necessary to keep the services

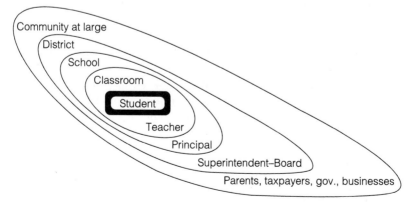

FIGURE 3.1 Systems within Systems

operating. Typically, those receiving services are referred to as consumers. But who are these consumers?

In looking at Kirkwood High, we see that those receiving services include students, parents, and even community stakeholders (e.g., employers, institutions of higher education). This group of consumers who exist outside the school and who come to partake of or in some way share its services can be designated as external consumers.

In addition to this external population, schools employ teachers, administrators, staff, and support personnel, who may also serve as a consumer population. For the school counselor, this group of teachers, administrators, staff, and support personnel are all potential partakers of their services and thus constitute internal consumers. Even though these internal populations are employed by the same system, they receive critical services from their counselor colleagues. Consequently, their demographics and needs (relative to performing their job) deserve important consideration when formulated and implementing programs and services.

Providers

A second population to whom a system needs to be responsive are those who provide the resources necessary to keep the school operating. This group will be referred to as *providers*. The overlap that occurs in these two groups is most evident in the population of parents whose children attend the school and whose property taxes support the school's operation. Serving as both consumers and providers, these parents are strong stakeholders in the cost effectiveness of the school's enterprise. Consequently, their needs, values, and beliefs must be given significant consideration in the development of the mission and outcomes of their school.

It is somewhat ironic that for most school systems, the population that frequently has the strongest and most direct influence over the school's policies, procedures, and operations are local taxpayers, even those without children within the system. And yet the largest population of consumers—those for whom programs are targeted (i.e., the students attending the school)—although having a strong vested interest in the school's successful operation, may have the least influence over the school's operation.

Similarly, local, state, and federal governmental agencies that filter tax dollars to particular school programs provide resources without direct receipt of school services. Because they provide input without direct benefit of outcome, this provider population frequently has different investment and agendas as stakeholders in the school. Their financial needs often manifest in fiscal conservatism that takes precedence over school reform and expansion. In some communities the parents of school-attending children represent only a small minority of citizens supporting the school through its property taxes. It should not be surprising that these communities will elect conservative school boards with the charge to monitor and curtail educational expenditures, even when those consumers express needs for services of a different sort.

Whether serving as consumers, providers, or both, it is the needs, values, and beliefs of this external population that drive the mission and desired outcomes for the schools. Consequently, it is incumbent on all school personnel to know the demographic features of their consumers and providers and use this knowledge to identify the extant needs, values, and beliefs of each diverse group comprising its population. It is only through ongoing, accurate assessment of these needs that a school can maintain realistic outcomes reflecting the actual needs, values, and beliefs of their population. As such, the issue of needs and need assessment becomes the second of our school system components to consider.

SYSTEMS—IN SERVICE OF POPULATION NEEDS

We all experience needs and seek to meet their satisfaction. Dehydration creates the need for fluids, and thus, we seek something to drink. The fuel measure in our car approaches "empty," signaling the need for more gas. A student who resolves interpersonal conflicts through verbal and physical aggression is in need of anger management and conflict resolution skills. In each instance, a need has been recognized, and some step to fill that need, or remediate the situation, is employed.

The Elements of Need Assessment

Each of the preceding illustrations demonstrates the essential characteristics of a need and the elements of a needs assessment. First, in each of the three instances a *current state* (i.e., what is now) was identified. The athlete, following her workout, experiences bodily cues that signal her current experience of dehydration and need for fluids. Similarly, the blinking light on the fuel gage announces to our driver the low volume of fuel within his tank. And the many disruptions within the classroom or the frequent acts of aggression exhibited by our student clearly announce the need for alternative conflict resolution skills.

A second element that typically follows on recognition of a current state is the formulation of what is sought, that is, the *desired state*. Thus our athlete seeks fluid balance, our driver fuel availability, and our student effective conflict resolution skills. The **gap** that exists between the current and desired states represents a need, and the extent of that gap often reflects the intensity of need and the importance or priority given to its resolution.

The term *need satisfaction* simply means that the gap between "what is" and "what is desired" has been narrowed sufficiently so that the need has diminished in strength and motivation. Thus the driver no longer is motivated to seek fuel after topping off his gas tank, nor is our athlete in search of fluid, following ingestion of water. The gap between what is and what is desired has been narrowed. The same would be true for our student who now finds the new skills of conflict resolution and anger management provide him with the experience of his state as "desired state." Each of the actions taken to narrow these gaps, obtaining a cool drink, stopping at the next gas station, or participating in a conflict resolution counseling group was taken or developed as a process directly linked to the respective needs.

From Individual to Community Needs

Just as individuals have needs, so too can whole communities. School community populations have needs for which they seek satisfaction from their local schools. In addition to those academic skills most often sought, consumer and provider populations experience an array of social, emotional, career, citizenship, and character needs for which they look to the school for satisfaction. The schools attempt to create processes that are directly linked to these respective needs and are intended to close the gap between "what is" and "what is desired." Thus, counselors and counseling programs may be charged to develop and deliver processes that will satisfy some of these identified needs. Career guidance, individual and small-group counseling, academic placement, and parent education are just a few of the processes undertaken by school counselors to meet this charge.

But for our system, be it the entire school or a counseling program, to be effective, it must have an accurate understanding of the population's needs and develop programs specifically linked to those needs. Maintenance of this link is the critical factor in keeping any school system, or guidance program, current and effective. Keeping the link accurate and viable requires constant vigilance.

Knowing Our Ever-Changing Population

Program development and evaluation, critical functions for the counselor as consultant, are based on identifying and maintaining this dynamic and empirical link between population need and system process. We know that the demographic characteristics of communities change over time. Rural becomes suburban; people age; new and diverse populations migrate in and out of the community; business, industrial, and economic opportunities reflect the constantly changing marketplace, all creating a constant of change. With the inexorably changing demographic come new needs, new priorities, and new processes targeted to satisfying those needs. Thus, for our programs and processes to remain relevant and effective, we must engage in needs assessments.

These assessments would certainly be called for any and each time there is evidence of a significant shift in population demographics. A community that is experiencing the opening or closing of major community resource or the influx of a new group of residents or the shifting of the economic theater, as may occur when a previously rural, agrarian community becomes more suburban and light industry driven, is signaling the need for a needs assessment. But it is not just under conditions of dramatic shift that needs should be assessed. The specific needs of the population being served are constantly changing. Under the most typical life cycle of a community, we find members moving, families growing, individuals aging, and a host of subtle cultural changes that are operative and impact the needs of our populations. Thus, even when dramatic change has not been evidenced, needs assessment of our population should certainly be considered within 5 year cycles.

Formal Needs Assessment   Formal needs assessments may often take the form of a survey directed to the targeted population or a series of open-ended questions directed to a small, representative sample (i.e., focus group) of the population being assessed. The needs assessment survey may be constructed as a series of statements that describe the developmentally appropriate state, condition, or behavior of the respondent and ask the respondents to identify the degree to which that state exists. For example, if we were conducting a needs assessment of high school students, we may want to know if they can effectively use conflict resolution skills. Consequently, we build our needs assessment survey to include the following statement: "I can effectively resolve conflicts with others in peaceful ways." The student would be asked to respond to this statement as it reflects the degree to which this need is important **and** to the degree which they feel that need is satisfied. As you can see by the following example, the statement is worded as the *desired* state. The importance of this wording will become clear when we discuss prioritizing needs and converting them into outcome goal statements. Our need statement and response categories would be stated as follows: Need Statement: "I can effectively resolve conflicts with others in peaceful ways."

		No	Low	Medium	High	Very High
a.	Need Importance:	1	2	3	4	5
b.	Need Satisfaction:	5	4	3	2	1

In this example, **Need Importance** reflects the value that the respondent places on the behavior (knowledge or skill) stated, in this case, the ability to resolve conflicts with others in peaceful ways. The response levels are offered in a Likert-type scale ranging from "No" importance to "Very High" importance. Even if the need does not currently exist, the student could still mark "Very High" if the value of that behavior was very strong to them. The second response category, **Need Satisfaction** reflects the extent to which that particular behavior is currently in the repertoire of the student. In other words, the extent to which that particular need is being met, and thus presents no, some, or a significant gap. To assess Need Satisfaction, the student is offered response levels ranging from "No" satisfaction to "Very High" satisfaction. For the student who feels devoid of any conflict resolution skill, the "No" level would be marked, whereas the student who is confident in their conflict resolution skill would indicate a "Very High" level of satisfaction.

The inclusion of these two response categories for each need statement serves a few important purposes. For each need (behavior) that we assess, it is crucial that we know the importance or value of the behavior to the respondent and the degree to which that respondent already employs that behavior. A respondent might report that a behavior has "Very High" importance, but we cannot know if that behavior reflects a high priority need until we assess their current level of satisfaction with that behavior. Even if they deem it very important, and if they already experience "Very High" satisfaction in performing the behavior, it may not warrant such high priority attention as an outcome goal. With such a response, you might inquire how the student acquired the conflict resolution skill. If it was learned from a school-based intervention, that information may be your best justification for maintaining that process intervention.

A low priority would also be given to a need in which the student revealed no importance. Regardless of the student's level of satisfaction of that particular behavior, a no or low importance response would relegate that need as unimportant. The greatest gap between the current and desired state is revealed when the respondent reports that a particular behavior has very high importance but currently receives no satisfaction in the performance of that behavior.

Student responses can be quantified in terms of a *Need Score* using the following procedure. These need scores depict the degree to which a gap exists.

Need Scores In order to quantify student responses, we first place values on each level of our two response categories. Notice in our example need statement that each response level has a numerical weight. In the category of Need Importance, the weighted levels range from "1" for "No" to "5" for "Very High." Conversely, the weighting of Need Satisfaction ranges from "5" for "No" to "1" for "Very High."

When we add the scores of both categories, we derive a Need Score. The higher the score revealed, the stronger is our confidence that a gap really exists between the current and desired states. Thus, the greatest gap is revealed when the Need Importance is "Very High" (receiving a score of 5) and the level of Need Satisfaction is "No" (receiving a score of 5). Consequently, the Need Score would be a 10, the highest possible indication of existing need. Little or no gap is revealed when the behavior has "No" importance (score of 1), and the level of satisfaction is "Very High" (score of 1). A moderate need, for example, would be identified when the Need Importance and Satisfaction are expressed at the "Medium" level, equating to a Need Score of 6.

Through this calculation we can derive a Need Score for each statement that can range from 1 to 10. In this way we can quantify and prioritize each need and have confidence that our highest priority needs reflect the reported state of this one specific consumer population.

Because we are only speaking of students at this juncture, it is important to recognize that a similar needs assessment should be performed on each of our consumer populations (e.g., parents, teachers, taxpayers) to get a complete picture of current need states.

Informal Assessment   In addition to employing such a structured, formal method of assessment, needs can be assessed in more informal ways. An unplanned observation of a student's behavior in the classroom or playground or crises that are brought to the attention of the counselor can serve as forms of immediate needs assessment. Students at severe risk present significant gaps between current and desired states.

In many situations, it is these crisis needs assessments that serve as the primary, if not sole, form of needs assessment. Although crises will certainly occur and call for timely response, a truly comprehensive guidance program that addresses the needs of all consumer populations requires a deliberate, systematic, proactive stance by the counselor. An integral part of the counselor's daily schedule should be devoted to the development, delivery, and evaluation of needs-based services (processes) that are developmental and preventive in nature. Such a needs-based program of services easily becomes accountable to its consumer and provider populations because identified needs form the bases for establishing desired program outcomes. The establishment of viable, desired outcomes represents the third component of our school as a system.

FROM NEEDS TO SYSTEM
GOALS AND OBJECTIVES

As previously mentioned, a need represents a gap between an existing state and a desired state. When needs assessments are conducted, priority attention is usually directed to the needs revealing the largest gap. This information is essential in program development, revision, and evaluation. Once needs have been empirically assessed and prioritized, the information can be directly translated into outcome goals and objectives. This process is relatively simple if the need statements clearly describe the desired condition (behavior) and assess its importance and level of satisfaction to the respondent. In most instances, the description of the desired state can be directly converted, often verbatim, into a desired outcome goal, often verbatim. For example, let's assume that on the Need Statement, "I can effectively resolve conflicts with others in peaceful ways," the average Need Score was 8.0 for the 9th grade, 6.1 for the 10th grade, 4.8 for the 11th grade and 3.9 for the 12th grade student population. These data suggest that the 9th-grade population experiences a relatively strong gap between their current and desired ability to employ peaceful conflict resolution strategies. A further analysis of the 9th-grade data might reveal a mean of 4.2 on Need Importance and a mean of 3.8 on Need Satisfaction. These data elevate this particular need to a high priority status for the 9th-grade students. The 10th-, 11th-, and 12th-grade means for this need are moderate and do not warrant prioritization. Based on these data results, the counselor employing such a needs assessment process might decide that the acquisition and use of peaceful conflict resolution skills by the 9th-grade students should be addressed and as such sets that as an important outcome goal for department programming.

The formulation of this outcome goal is simply a reiteration of the Need Statement. The only change that occurs is to replace the words "I can" with the words "All 9th-grade students will . . ." Consequently, our outcome goal for this particular need is "All 9th-grade students will effectively resolve conflicts with others in peaceful ways."

Outcome goals for social systems such as schools typically describe the demonstration of knowledge, skill, or attitude (to be manifest in action). However, these outcome goals are often presented as broad, general, and non-operational descriptions of a desired state or condition. As such, although they offer some direction for desired change and its related accountability, they lack the quantitative or qualitative specificity required to know that the desired state has been achieved. Presenting outcomes in vague, generalized language fails to describe the actual criteria that confirms the attainment of the desired state and thus reduction of the need. Further, just outcome goals provide little information needed to inform the processes that might be employed to further facilitate outcome goal attainment.

From Goals to Objectives

In order to achieve operational specificity, accountability, and informed process construction, outcome goals must be translated into *outcome objectives*. Whereas outcome goals are vague and undefined, outcome objectives are descriptive, concrete, and measurable. They describe the actual behaviors (actions) that will be performed when the desired outcome goal is achieved. In effect, outcome objectives are the evidence that shows the successful performance of the outcome goal. In revealing the evidence of goal attainment, outcome objectives also provide the standard level of acceptable performance implied in the goal statement. Because outcome goals are so broad, general, and undefined, they usually have multiple pieces of evidence determining their attainment. A single goal, such as "effectively resolving conflicts with others in peaceful ways," might require numerous pieces of evidence to conclude that it has been achieved by our 9th-grade students. Each piece of evidence constitutes an objective, and the aggregate of objectives confirms that the desired goal has been achieved.

In translating an outcome goal into its constituent objectives, it is helpful to ask, "How will I know when that goal is achieved? What will the students be doing that will show that they are resolving their conflicts peacefully? What have I seen in others (and even in myself) that I will characterize as effective, peaceful conflict resolution?" These and similar questions that get to the actual doing of the outcome goal will generate observable, measurable evidence that forms the basis of outcome accountability and process (program, service, intervention) construction. Exercise 3.1 provides examples of outcomes objectives along with an opportunity for you to practice translating goals to concrete outcomes objectives.

EXERCISE 3.1

Goals to Outcome Objectives

Directions: Review each of the following illustrations of outcome objectives as they reflect the goal: "All 9th-grade students will effectively resolve conflicts with others in peaceful ways." Notice the specificity with which the outcome objectives are written, along with the way the goal has been operationalized. After reviewing the examples, develop two additional outcome objectives of your own. Ask a colleague to review the objectives listed and to assess the degree to which these objectives could be quantified and observed.

Samples:

1. When angry and frustrated in an interpersonal situation the students will identify their feeling (subobjective) and express it to others as an "I" statement (subobjective).

2. Students will employ deep breathing relaxation regimen (subobjective) or remove themselves from the conflict situation (subobjective) when becoming angry in an interpersonal situation.

3. When presented with a conflict situation, the students will describe a problem-solving strategy that enables each participant to get something positive from resolving the conflict. This is often referred to as a win–win solution.

Practice:

1. When angry and frustrated in an interpersonal situation, students will

2. When presented with a conflict situation, the students will

---

The three sample outcome objectives presented in Exercise 3.1 represent some of the actual behaviors as evidence that "effective conflict resolution in peaceful ways" has been achieved. Certainly, more objectives could be formulated, and our sample objectives could be even more defined, specifying who, when, where, and the exact level of performance desired. However, even at this level of specificity, we can have confidence in knowing when our 9th-graders have attained their desired goal of resolving their conflicts peacefully. Further, as you review the sample outcome objectives, it may become apparent that they also provide very helpful direction in *how* we might expedite goal attainment for our consumer population.

PROCESSES: THE MEANS
TO OUR DESIRED OUTCOMES

A discussion of how we facilitate outcome goal attainment brings into focus the fourth component of our system: process. System processes are all those programs, services, activities, and interventions that exist in a system that serves as the means to the desired end. The system processes are the vehicles by which the system attains outcome goals and satisfaction of consumer needs. Whether we refer to these processes as operations, programs, services, curriculum, or interventions, the process component of a system represents what employees of the system actually *do*. More precisely, process elements describe the array of services offered to its consumers (e.g., counseling, consulting, and coordinating), the way that the services are structured (e.g., organization) and managed (e.g., administration), the procedures for delivering the services to their intended consumers, and the role and function performed by each employee of the system. Exercise 3.2 will further assist you in understanding the nature and extent of system process.

EXERCISE 3.2

Identifying System Process

Directions: As noted, process elements describe the way services are structured (e.g., organization) and managed (e.g., administration), as well as the procedures for delivering the services to the intended consumers and the role and function performed by each employee of the system. The following exercise will help you to begin to understand the nature and extent of a system's process.

Contact a local school guidance department and gather the following information.

1. What type of services does the guidance department offer (e.g., counseling, consulting, and coordinating)?
2. How is the guidance department structured or organized (e.g., administration)?
3. How are the various services delivered (e.g., request students to come to the office, teacher referral, go into classrooms, group presentations)?
4. How would they define the primary role and function of the counselors in this school?
5. Finally, ask them what might be unique about the services offered or the manner in which they are organized, administered, and delivered that reflects the unique of their student and student need.

If you look at the data you collected in Exercise 3.2, you may begin to understand the scope and complexity of the processes offered by just one department, within one school, in one district. But beyond identifying these processes, the question one could ask could be, "But why *these* processes? Why not others?" The question of how a system determines the processes it will employ is an essential question to be answered in developing and maintaining effective systems.

The sequence in which we have presented the components of a system, that is, population demographic, needs, outcomes, process, and input, is the same sequence to be followed when building, altering, or just evaluating the system's processes. Therefore, from a system perspective, population should determine needs, needs should determine outcome goals and objectives, **outcomes should determine processes,** and as you will see shortly, processes should determine input. Consequently, when deciding on the composition of our program of services, activities, and interventions, the critical question to ask should be, "What experiences can we create for our consumers that will enable them to achieve our desired outcome objectives?" In answering this question we want to look to empirically validated services that have successfully demonstrated the desired cause–effect relationship with similar consumer groups. Table 3.1 lists a menu of process elements that may comprise a comprehensive school guidance program. It is essential, however, that one not take a cookbook approach to developing a systems guidance program (process). It is important to remember that it is first and foremost the *needs* of our consumers, translated into outcomes, that give shape to an effective system process, or in this case a guidance program. As such, the cogency of any one service or activity can only be ascertained by its link to desired outcomes and to the other system components of that school.

Now let's return to Exercise 3.2. If this exercise were repeated with another school, which serviced a different and unique consumer population, would we expect to see the same types of processes? If a system has developed its processes in response to the identified needs of its consumers, it would be fair to assume that schools servicing different populations may employ or prioritize different processes.

The attainment of outcome objectives should be the major criteria in considering processes. The activity, service, program, or intervention that a system creates is simply the means to desired ends and thus its appropriateness is primarily determined the degree to which it is effective in achieving outcome objectives. Although effectiveness of processes in achieving outcome objectives is the essential element in selecting and implementing processes, it is not the only consideration. Once the most effective means to the desired ends have been identified, attention needs to be given to the issue of needed inputs (resources). It is important, however, to allow the element of inputs to be addressed *after* the desired processes are identified. If inputs are considered prior to identifying potentially effective processes, a system may restrict its ability to creatively link effective processes with desired outcomes. It is not unusual for systems to eliminate potentially very effective processes because it

Table 3.1 Process Elements: Content Examples

Programs/Services/Interventions
Individual Counseling
Referral
Intervention
Communication: Contacts and record keeping
Evaluation
Group Counseling
Referral
Intervention
Communication: Contacts and record keeping
Developmental Guidance (Prevention)
Development
Provision
Administration
Evaluation
Career Education (Curricular)
Career Guidance (Individual)
Individual vocational assessment
Career and postsecondary guidance
Referral and recommendation
Consultation
Teacher (individual and group), IST, staff development
Parent (school and home visits), parent conferences
Administration: Crises intervention
Due process facilitation and record keeping
Coordination
IST, child study, SAP, adapt
Transition articulation: Student orientation
Assessment (academic, affect) screening for gifted
Communications (public relations, information
   dissemination), guidance newsletter, Web page
Student support services: mental health, wraparound
Drug and alcohol
Academic scheduling
Community service activities
Peer tutoring
Peer mediation
Administration
Program development: Planning
Program evaluation
Data/records storage and retrieval
Budget
Participation in meetings
Other
Instructional (academic): Teaching
Special duties: Bus, lunch, study hall, etc.
Professional development

does not currently have the input to support them. This shackle of existing or perceived input will diminish creativity in both developing effective processes and then obtaining the input necessary to bring them to reality. Often, the identification of effective processes greatly enhances your ability to creatively find input solutions and persuade providers to support your process efforts.

Because of this population–need–outcome–process–input link, the ideal school guidance program is one that maintains this link empirically and consistently. Every school guidance program (process) needs to reflect its unique link to its population providers and consumers. As a result, it can be expected that the content elements of the school guidance program will naturally vary from school to school and consumer to consumer. What may not be as apparent is that any one school guidance program (process) should vary across time, as its own specific consumer population changes or the specific needs of these consumers change.

A SYSTEM PERSPECTIVE: IMPLICATIONS FOR MR. THOMAS

If we return to our ongoing case of Mr. Thomas, we may begin to understand his dilemma a bit more once we realize that he is only in his second year at Kirkwood High. Because he is new to the area and the school, he is just beginning to really learn about the system and its five systemic components. Mr. Thomas, just as you may expect of any new employee, has focused his attention on the **process** elements under his charge. His first concern has been to understand his own role and function within the school. Thus he may not have a complete grasp of all the other components of this system and how they operate.

With time and experience, he will acquire a much better understanding of the other four components of his system. Whether it is through formal or informal channels he will begin learn about the unique demographics of his school and the specific needs of each of its consumer groups. Further, he will begin to see how these needs give birth to goals and how these goals will both provide him direction and basis for being accountable for his efforts. Exercise 3.3 is provided to assist you in seeing how these connections may evolve.

EXERCISE 3.3

System Analysis: Components

Directions: Select an educational system such as an elementary, middle, high school, or even a postsecondary school. Your selection may be a system in which you have worked or have had some experience. Schedule a meeting with an administrator or counselor in that system and discuss the following questions.

1. What are the demographic characteristics of the consumers of guidance services in your school?
2. Have needs assessments ever been done on the consumers of guidance services?
3. Does the guidance program have outcome goals and objectives?
4. What are the various guidance programs, services and activities (i.e., processes) offered at this school?
5. How was it decided to incorporate these processes into your guidance program?
6. How does this guidance program obtain the resources necessary to operate the program?

Data Analysis: Perhaps with a colleague, review the data you collected from your interview. Consider the following.

1. Can you see the linkage between consumer need, outcome goals, and specific forms of programs, services, or activities?
2. Looking at the specific consumer group, identify three needs you know or could anticipate exist. Translate these needs into outcome statements. Finally, identify one process (program, activity, service) that would prove effective in satisfying this need. List your finding in the following table.

Consumer Needs	Outcomes	Process

As Mr. Thomas's knowledge about these system components increases, he will become more confident, resourceful, and assertive in securing and using the critical input necessary to perform his job effectively. And just as is true for Mr. Thomas, your own increased understanding of and sensitivity to the unique components of systems will enable you to influence and be influenced by every segment of this school community in purposeful, proactive, and predictive ways. Further, with this expanded system perspective, you (and Mr. Thomas) will be able to move beyond the boundaries of a one-on-one, direct-service provider to that of system consultant, and in so doing extend your impact over the entire school system, providing student, teacher, and parent consumers the most effective processes possible. Our final exercise (Exercise 3.4) will help you apply the information provided within this chapter.

EXERCISE 3.4

Systems Consultation

Assume that you are Mr. Thomas, the 9th- and 10th-grade counselor at Kirkwood High School. Use a systems approach to build a process (program, service, activity, intervention) that would respond to each of the following concerns.

Concern #1

Dr. Jameson, Assistant Principal, just sent you an e-mail stating that "a large number of 10th-grade students have been performing very poorly on their standardized tests. These students have also reported academic difficulties in their AP math classes and severe apprehension about taking the PSAT." He closed his e-mail by asking for your help with this problem.

Concern #2

The school nurse stops by your office to report that a number of 9th- and 10th-grade girls appear to be engaged in cutting and self-mutilation. These reports came from teacher observations as well as students seeking medical attention at the school infirmary. The nurse estimates that between 12 and 15 girls have been identified.

Concern #3

Ms. Holden, the permanent teacher of the 9th-grade emotional support class, left on a medical leave six weeks ago. Her long-term substitute, Ms. Novice, recently graduated from college and has never had full-time responsibility over these special needs students. Over the past few weeks she has reported to Dr. Jameson that "many of these students are out of control, unruly, and disrespectful. Their parents are accusing me of being incompetent and responsible for their misbehavior." Twice, Ms. Novice appeared at Dr. Jameson's office in tears, threatening to quit. A replacement for Ms. Novice is not possible now, so Dr. Jameson has appealed to you for help.

SUMMARY

Systems

A system is "an entity made up of interconnected parts, with recognizable relationships that are systematically arranged to serve a perceived purpose."

Systems receive resources (input) from their environment (population) and use those resources to execute operations (processes) in order to produce purposeful effects (output) that meet environmental (needs).

System Populations:
Consumers and Providers

All social systems exist because people experience needs and are willing to put their resources into processes designed to meet those needs. This group of consumers, who exist outside the school and who come to partake or in some way share its services, can be designated as external consumers.

In addition to this external population, schools employ teachers, administrators, staff, and support personnel, who may also serve as a consumer population. This group represents the internal consumers.

A second population with whom a system needs to be responsive are those who provide the resources necessary to keep the school operating. This group will be referred to as providers. Overlap of these groups can occur, as in the case of parents, whose children attend (consumers) the school and whose property taxes support the school's operation (providers).

Systems—in Service of Population Needs

Systems, as noted, exist to meet identified needs. A need is represented by the gap that exists between the current (i.e., what is now) and the desired state (i.e., what is sought).

Program development and evaluation are critical functions based on identifying and maintaining the dynamic and empirical link between population need and system process.

From Needs to System
Goals and Objectives

Once needs have been empirically assessed and prioritized, the information can be directly translated into outcome goals and objectives. In order to achieve operational specificity, accountability, and informed process construction, outcome goals must be translated into outcome objectives.

Where outcome goals are vague and undefined, outcome objectives are descriptive, concrete, and measurable. They describe the actual behaviors (actions) that will be performed when the desired outcome goal is achieved. In effect, outcome objectives are the evidence that shows the successful performance of the outcome goal.

Accountability: Creating Processes
to Achieve Outcomes

System processes are all those programs, services, activities, and interventions that exist in a system that serve as the means to the desired end.

From a system's perspective, population should determine needs, needs should determine outcome goals and objectives, outcomes should determine processes, and processes should determine input.

IMPORTANT TERMS

Consumer	Internal population	Process
Cost effective	Objective	Provider
Demographic	Outcome	Stakeholder
External population	Need	System
Goal	Need importance	
Input	Need satisfaction	

SUGGESTED READINGS

Hanson, G. B. (1995). *General systems theory beginning with the whales.* Washington, DC: Taylor & Francis.

Vanzant, C. E., & Hayslip, J. B. (1994). *Your comprehensive school guidance and counseling program.* New York: Longman.

Wittmer, J. (Ed.). (2000). *Managing your school guidance program: K–12 developmental strategies* (2nd ed.). Minneapolis, MN: Educational Media Corp.

WEB SITES

Comprehensive Counseling and Guidance Program: A resource for reviewing the elements of comprehensive school guidance programming. http://www.cnw.com/~deets/guidance.htm

Brint: A listing of more than 200 articles on information systems research, theory, and practice. www.brint.com/papers/misbibl.htm

Swenson Links: This page contains links and articles on systems theory. www.css.edu/users/dswenson/web/System.htm

Systems Theory and Systems Thinking: Links to articles and information on systems theory. www.ed.psu.edu/insys/ESD/Systems/menu.html

REFERENCES

Gysbers, N. C., & Henderson, P. (2000). *Developing and managing your school guidance program* (3rd ed.). Alexandria, VA: American Association for Counseling and Development.

Jerrell, J. M., & Jerrell, S. L. (1981). Organizational consultation in school systems. In J. C. Conoley (Ed.), *Consultation in schools* (pp. 133–156). New York: Academic Press.

Kurpius, D. J. (1985). Consultation interventions: Successes, failures, and proposals. *The Journal of Counseling Psychology, 13*(3), 368–389.

4

~

System Dynamics

Responding to Change

So much of my time is taken up by reacting to crises. Everybody—
administrators, teachers, parents, and even students—expect that
I will be on call for their immediate concerns.

I know that I am here to help all these people, but by continually working
from a reaction mode, it almost seems like everyone else is writing my job
description. It does feel good to help in a crisis, but I wonder if I am really
serving the needs of all my students, parents, and fellow teachers?

I don't know. Why bother thinking about all this? Trying to change
the way things run around here would be monumental. After all, I'm
new here, and all of my predecessors have seemed to embrace this
reactive role. It is simply the way things are done around here!

Trying to change the expectations of others, or trying to modify the way a system operates is anything but easy. If there is going to be any hope for our counselor–consultant, Mr. Thomas, in his quest to make change, he is going to have to understand not only the components of his school as a system but also the way that they interact. These components, which we discussed in chapter 3, are not static. As such, Mr. Thomas will need to understand their dynamics if he is to achieve the changes he desires.

CHAPTER OBJECTIVES

In chapter 3 we looked at the five components of the school. We addressed each component as static entities and as linearly related to each other. Our decision to present each component sequentially was born of convenience more than the reality of social systems. Now that you understand the nature of each component and their synergistic interdependence, we can look at the dynamic qualities of influence and change that are inherent in every social system. It is these fluid, dynamic forces extant in all systems that give a system its life. It is this dynamic that will be the focus of the current chapter.

After completing this chapter, the reader will we able to

1. Describe different perspectives on the nature of change within systems
2. Describe the characteristics of an open system
3. Describe the characteristics of a closed system
4. Explain how systems evolve from open to closed states
5. Describe consultative procedures that school counselors can take to ensure that their programs remain open and cost effective

THE EVOLUTION AND NATURE OF SYSTEMS

You may recall from chapter 3 that all social systems are created by individuals (external populations) in order to meet certain needs. At their inception, the systemic processes (with their respective inputs) were directly and explicitly informed by these needs. With these needs acknowledged and clearly defined, the processes (programs, services, activities, and interventions) were created with the sole intention of satisfying those needs and eliminating the gap between what is and what is desired. Consequently, at their birth, all social systems are responsive to the needs of their consumers and are flexible in this responsiveness.

Open Systems

At their point of origin, all systems are considered to be open. That is, they tend to be flexible and adaptive. In new systems in which processes (structures and functions) are piloted and monitored for effectiveness, change can occur rapidly. Creativity and innovation are encouraged and reinforced as the system, often employing trial and error planning, strives to build processes that work. The norms created in this culture of flexibility and innovation nurture pragmatism and openness to information from all sources. In schools that are open, boundaries between subsystems such as instructional, administrative, and pupil services are transparent and permeable, facilitating a free flow of communication and information exchange, with communication open and multidirectional. In this culture the way that things are actually done is accepted as the way that they are supposed to be done. But this doesn't always stay that way.

Moving from Open to Closed

Systems do not always remain open. Some move from what was once flexible and responsive to that which is no longer adaptive, adjusting, or servicing the needs of its consumer. Over time established processes become institutionalized as "our way" of operating. During this steady state phase of system evolution, those providing and administering "our" processes become invested in perpetuating their existence, or maintaining the status quo.

Change, of course, must be resisted to maintain the status quo. Consequently, all the feedback mechanisms (e.g., demographic analyses, needs assessment, outcome evaluation) that were instrumental in creating the system and keeping it open become ignored and dismantled. In the absence of such corrective data, the system becomes closed. The many manifestations and responses to system resistance will be our topic for chapter 5.

The prevailing thinking of a closed system becomes, "What is the incentive for collecting, analyzing and using information that may challenge what we already know? And besides, we all know how we do things around here!" At this point in the system's maturation (or more accurately decline), programs, services, and interventions are more than routine; they become codified and acknowledged as formal policies and procedures. Any deviation from the status quo is punished with formal and informal sanctions. Although everyone recognizes that alternative processes might work, "Our way is considered the best." Table 4.1 offers criteria that can be used to differentiate open from closed systems.

Table 4.1 Criteria for Open and Closed Systems

Open Systems
Are flexible and adaptive
Processes are piloted and monitored for effectiveness
Change can occur rapidly
Creativity and innovation are encouraged
Norms of flexibility and innovation flourish
Boundaries between subsystems are transparent and permeable
Communication is open and multidirectional
Measure the outcomes of what they *do*
Are accountable to their various consumers
Closed Systems
Are rigid and resistant to change
Processes are not targeted to consumer needs or outcomes
Outcomes are not measured
Formal and informal systems are in conflict
Governance and communication are centralized and top down (hierarchical)
Rigid boundaries exist between groups and subsystems
Job descriptions are narrow and specialized

Exercise 4.1 provides an opportunity to identify systems that are open and closed.

EXERCISE 4.1

System Analysis: Dynamics

Use the same system that you selected for Exercise 3.1. Investigate the system by reading documents; interviewing employees, consumers, and providers; and simply observing the system by just walking around and watching what goes on. From your investigation try to answer the following questions using the criteria for open and closed systems appearing in Table 4.1.

1. Where would you place this system on an open (1)–closed (10) continuum?
2. Describe the characteristics of this system that are open.
3. Describe the characteristics of this system that are closed.
4. If you were a consultant to this system, what recommendations would you make to make this system more open?

Share your responses with a colleague and seek their perspective on your recommendations.

Toward a State of Entropy

If systems continue to move toward increasing complexity, inflexibility, and nonresponsiveness the emphasis on sustaining the status quo takes center stage and what was once "our way of doing things" becomes "The Way." You can imagine the resistance to change that must be maintained to sustain a status quo that ignores the reality of and need for change. Myopic belief in and perpetuation of the status quo leads the system to a state of entropy, the final stage of its existence.

Entropy represents the natural state of a closed system. It is the state in which the system devotes much of its energy to boundary maintenance to preserve its processes (structure and function) vis-à-vis its external environment. But in entropy the system no longer has the energy to even maintain the status quo. The input required of the system to keep going is reduced or eliminated by external populations of providers and consumers whose needs have been ignored and who experience the system as unresponsive, unaccountable, and irrelevant. And so these populations look elsewhere for need satisfaction, and the system in entropy eventually stops. No input, no process!

Some systems, such as businesses and industries that are continually accountable to a population that is both provider of input and consumer of goods and services, will reach a state of entropy rapidly unless they make concerted efforts to remain open. Marketing research (needs assessment) and quality control measures are mechanisms used to keep systems open. Other systems, however, such as governmental agencies and schools, whose providers and consumers represent different populations, may experience a very long tenure in a steady state before they eventually reach entropy. We all know of sick (in system terms) schools that have perpetuated the same processes (curriculum, teaching methodology, services, policies, and procedures) for what seems like forever, despite significant change in their external populations. Sometimes these schools are literally taken over by their disgruntled populations in a desperate attempt to create change within the system. Privatization of urban schools is one of these desperate measures.

SYSTEMS: FORMAL AND INFORMAL

The more systems close, the more rigid and codified their processes become. As the system moves from processes, which are seen as "A Way," to those that now are viewed as "The Way" of operating, creativity and innovation are discouraged and even punished. In these systems, "The Way" becomes codified in manuals, policies and procedures documents, contracts, and charts. This codification conveys the very clear message that: "This is the way that this system *is* to operate!" This appearance of this strict codification of rules, regulations, procedures, and processes defines a system's transition from what was once informal to what is now formal.

Formal Systems

In the formal system, everyone should know his or her role and function because these are clearly spelled out. The formal system prescribes the what, when, where, and how of virtually every process element. Moreover, job descriptions are explicitly drawn from these prescriptions as well as the hierarchical and bureaucratic structures that explicate the chain of command, decision making, and accountability. Although the formal system appears to offer stability, safety, and unambiguous expectations for performance, it is that very formality and standardization that propels it even further toward entropy.

Informal Systems

In most systems, however, the internal populations that come into direct contact with their consumers and providers are confronted with the reality of those populations. This reality may often be in stark contrast to what the systems formally depict to be the way things are—or should be! Every day teachers are faced with learning disabled and behaviorally disordered students. Counselors encounter emotionally distraught students and teachers who feel bewildered and defeated in their classrooms. This is the front line of education, and these professional educators will do whatever it takes to meet the needs of their respective consumers. Unfortunately, the prescriptions offered by the formal system do not always work, leaving these frontline educators to find alternative means of achieving success. These alternative processes for achieving success (or simply surviving in a closed system) represent the informal system.

Whereas the formal system explicates how things are supposed to be done, the informal system reveals how things really get done in this system (see Case 4.1).

CASE 4.1 Formal and Informal Systems of Operations

Case 1: Instructional Support

In our first example, the formal policy employed by a school principal requires a teacher with a child who is not learning to file a formal (official) referral form with the school's Instructional Support Team. This team must conduct an extensive curriculum-based assessment of the student's academic functioning and submit a formal report before the teacher can expect any guidance or relief, a process that could take months. In the meantime, the teacher experiences the reality of this student's learning problems daily. The formal system is inadequate in addressing the exigencies of this situation. Consequently, the teacher chooses to ignore the referral process and **informally** seeks out an experienced colleague who has had extensive experience with these kinds of learning problems. Together, the two educators formulate an instructional strategy that capitalizes on the student's strengths and unique learning style. Thus, an informal system has been created that obviates a formal system that does not work.

Case 2: Questions of STDs

A second example will further elucidate these parallel phenomena. When an 11th-grade female student approaches her counselor with questions about sexually transmissible diseases the counselor faces a dilemma. The official school policy (as determined by the school board) explicitly restricts all district counselors from discussing birth control, pregnancy, abortion or any other sexual matter with students. The official, formal message to the counselors is clear, but the reality of this student's predicament requires immediate action. The student is "madly in love" with a senior at the same school. She has been sexually active with this boyfriend for six months, and has used birth control measures up to the present. Neither her parents nor her family doctor are aware of her sexual activity, and she is convinced that her parents will "throw me out of the house" if they find out. Consequently, she refuses to tell them. Within the past week her boyfriend has pressured her to engage in intercourse without the use of prophylactics. He has been telling her that prophylactics are unnecessary and has reassured her that nothing bad will happen from their love making. She confesses to the counselor that she is ignorant and confused about birth control and sexually transmittable diseases and doesn't know how to reply to her boyfriend as he increases the pressure to engage in unprotected sex.

CASE 4.1   Continued

Believing that an informed response to her boyfriend might lessen the pressure, she appeals to the counselor for guidance. Since she refused to discuss this dilemma with anyone else, she states that she will succumb to his pressure if the counselor cannot help her.

In violation of district policy, and at the risk of losing her job, the counselor agrees to meet with the student. At the **"informal"** meeting the counselor shares information about birth control and STDs, framing the information within a problem solving and decision-making context. The counselor also instructs the student in assertiveness skills that could be applied with the boyfriend.

It is clear in these case examples that the formal system does not operate in the best interest of the students. The counselor in Case 2 is very knowledgeable about the information needed by the student to assert her needs and rights. Additionally, the counselor is confident that it would require only a few counseling sessions to help her to establish the control that she desires in this relationship. But to conduct these sessions would violate established, formal policy and possibly jeopardize the counselor's job. In weighing the cost and benefit of risking informal measures in helping this student, the counselor reluctantly agrees to provide the information (and support) she requested. In so doing, the informal system takes precedence over the formal. Recognition of the formal and informal dynamics of a school's operation will help the school counselor differentiate what is supposed to occur from what actually occurs and which offers the greatest efficacy. Exercise 4.2 will give you practice in recognizing this important distinction.

EXERCISE 4.2

Formal and Informal Systems

Select a system with which you are very familiar. Your choice could be your past or present employment, a school that you have attended, or a system with which you have been a frequent consumer. Identify those elements (explicit, formal norms, policies, procedures, directives, etc.) that reflect the formal system. Then identify those elements that reflect the informal system. For example, you might identify a school that has a formal zero tolerance policy that requires a 10-day suspension for any student engaging in physical conflict. In your investigation, however, you might find that most physical infractions result in a verbal reprimand by the principal. As you identify formal and informal characteristics of this system, answer the following questions.

1. To what extent are the formal and informal systems in conflict?

2. How did the informal system evolve?

3. How aware and accepting is the formal system of the informal system?

4. How might the formal and informal systems merge or become more compatible?

Share your responses with a colleague or mentor to gain their perspective on your responses.

Formal and Informal: Parallel or Integrated Systems?

As systems close, these formal and informal systems may operate in parallel fashion. For example, when problems occur in their systems, such as when a school experiences increases in student failure or student pregnancies, the administrators are responsible to act, mobilizing the resources available to solve the problem. These system managers (or administrators in schools) are formally at the top of the chain of command. This chain is referred to as a line, with the top administrator having line authority. As such, they are responsible and accountable to those employees (teachers, counselors) further down the chain. However, if they are not aware of the problem (or the informal remediation attempts), they cannot respond in a timely fashion. In each of our sample cases, the school administration was employing official policies and procedures that it thought were effective. The administrators in both cases thought that they knew how their system was operating. However, in both cases, informal procedures were employed unbeknownst to those administrators. Often, it is only when the problem has become a crisis that the informal system sounds the bugle for the formal system to rescue.

The brief case illustrations (Case 4.1) also demonstrate the conflict and stress created by formal, rigid, and relatively closed systems. Employees who adopt informal processes will usually do everything that they can to conceal their actions from the formal system, for fear of official sanction. The consequences of these parallel phenomena in systems are highly stressful to the employees, confusing to both providers and consumers, and destructive to the system as a whole.

An additional problem that emerges when formal and informal systems operate in parallel form is that of access to resources (input). The formal system controls the input (resource) distribution. Informal processes need resources to operate, and when those resources are not easily accessible, both the processes and the consumers can suffer. Moreover, when the informal system needs resources to do its work, it must either reveal its deception to the formal system or employ surreptitious means of getting its resources. In either case, increased tension and system disruption typically result.

Merging the disparate formal and informal systems into one can minimize the deleterious effects of these parallel phenomena. This consolidation or integration can only be achieved by maintaining a formal system that invites innovation, creativity, and experimentation by all its internal populations. In many instances it is the informal processes that work best, and it is truly a prudent administrator who invites these processes into the formal system.

Richard Friday (2002), in researching the nature of work in America today, has found that employees place the opportunity for creativity as their most desirable feature in a job. Creativity can no longer be left to our informal systems. Creativity—innovation and flexibly responding to change—needs to be built into our schools' formal systems of operation.

The school counselor, often privy to both formal and informal processes, can actively facilitate linkages between the two systems and serve as an agent of change (see chapter 5). Through the collaborative efforts of the counselor-consultant, system effectiveness and employee morale will be increased and homeostasis established throughout the system.

ORGANIZATIONAL STRUCTURE

As systems evolve and slowly close, they build increasingly more complex organizational structures with many layers of bureaucracy between the frontline employees and top administrators. Relative to closed systems, open systems operate from simple organizational structures. Often open systems will employ a chain of command that is clear, efficient, and short, permitting easy access to all individuals within the chain. If a classroom teacher, for example, has a concern or helpful suggestion, an open system would afford her easy and timely access to the school administrator. But as systems evolve toward closing, they develop and employ complex hierarchies that comprise multiple layers and levels.

These hierarchies contain within them the inherent mechanisms for system closure. The flow of information is severely restricted and when it does occur, it follows a top-down direction. The central control and command from the top results in critical decisions for the system without counsel from those lower on the chain. Those at the bottom of the chain, usually the frontline employees, receive these decisions as edicts from above. Without any sense of involvement or ownership of these administrative edicts, it is not surprising that execution of these directives is unmotivated, lackadaisical, and even sabotaged.

Perhaps even more destructive to the system is the absence of critical information flowing from bottom to top. Through frequent contact with their consumers, frontline employees are often much better informed of changing consumer needs and the new and revised processes that could more effectively address these needs. With communication channels discouraged or even closed, we have all the ingredients for the creation of the informal system we discussed previously. Moreover, as the system closes, it invests more of its resources in maintaining boundaries between the layers of its hierarchy that are both impermeable to outside influence and impervious to internal change.

Mechanisms that inhibit the increasing complexity and closure of systems attempt to spread the locus of control over the entire system. This can only be done by keeping the system structure and function as simple as possible. Some innovative systems that have remained open have purposely flattened their hierarchy to form vertical or lateral subsystems that are permeable and accessible to each other. Not only do these subsystems talk to each other, but they collaborate in making critical decisions that affect the entire system. This decentralized decision making by those in the know conserve many of the characteristics of open systems.

Specialization and Structure

When subsystems are communicating and open to change and innovation, they experience an interdependence that brings unity and cohesion to the system. This interdependence nurtures mutual respect and a collaborative spirit, both valuable characteristics of open systems. In contrast to closed systems that nurture independence, with well-defended boundaries, open systems maintain structures that support the free flow in information within and between all components and elements of the system.

In this culture of interdependence and collaboration individuals can be involved in all aspects of system processes. Consequently, the open system values its internal population as generalists, knowledgeable and skilled in many of the system's processes. Conversely, closed systems prefer that their employees be specialists who can only perform their function within the narrow boundaries of their subsystem. This *specialization of function,* with its matching job description, enables the closed system to restrict communication, buttress its subsystem boundaries, and sustain the status quo. Specialization of role and function also expands the gulf between those responsible for processes (i.e., the experts) and their consumers and providers. As increasing numbers of specialists operate system processes, external populations of consumers and providers feel intimidated by the system and experience less involvement (i.e., oversight and accountability) with the system. Of course, intimidation and alienation also pervades the system's internal populations as specialized experts proclaim exclusive knowledge and skill to perform their job. Not surprisingly, this is a very effective way to bring closure and entropy to a system. However, even with that knowledge it is very difficult to resist the dynamic of specialization.

In most systems specialization enhances job security and decreases ambiguity about individual role and function. Territorial boundaries are clearly drawn. In a school, specialization reflects academic discipline, educational credentials, and professional experience. We want our teachers to have expertise in their discipline (as well as how to teach that discipline) and administrators who can manage a school budget. But the more that each of these internal populations can know and understand what each other is doing, the greater they can respond to each other with appreciation, respect, and empathy. Moreover, they may be surprised and pleased about the help and support that they could provide each other if given a chance to cross boundaries of specialization.

Keeping lines of communication open and empowering others (students, teachers, parents) to engage in proactive decision making are crucial functions that the counselor–consultant can undertake. A counselor as consultant can help school communities to make school-based management and strategic planning viable mechanisms for systemic change.

SYSTEM DYNAMICS
AND ORIENTATION TO CHANGE

The natural evolution of systems from open to closed can be expedited or reversed by specific system dynamics. For example, according to general system theory (Hanson, 1995; Malinowski, 1948; Parsons, 1971) goal-seeking systems such as schools should have and employ a feedback mechanism. This feedback mechanism provides information about each system component to the system's internal population (i.e., teachers, administrators, counselors) so that adjustments can be made. Such a continuous feedback loop is essential if effective goal attainment can be maintained (Weiner, 1948).

As previously noted, when the flow of information about each system component is current, accurate, and used in problem solving and decision making, the system is said to be open. Open systems are by definition need–outcome focused. However, closed systems are process–input focused, with the processes impervious to change. These closed systems restrict this flow of information to preserve their processes (structure and function).

This difference in focus usually stems from the degree of outcome data desired, available, and obtained. These conditions of outcome data typically lead to different approaches to demonstrating accountability. The open system is able to obtain and use data from all five components of the system to show accountability, whereas the closed system, bereft of population, need, and outcome information, is left with only process and input data when called on to demonstrate accountability.

When open, the system uses empirically valid information to continually adjust to the naturally occurring changes within and between the system components. Paradoxically, although appearing unstable and inconsistent, this purposeful adjustment actually maintains a healthy balance within the system, keeping all components working in synergy to achieve desired goals. Therefore systems that can maintain this balance, this homeostasis, are able to sustain themselves even in light of changes in its environment (i.e., consumer and provider populations).

Responding to Change

Just as with biological and mechanical systems, social systems manifest the paradox of being pulled toward continuous change while at the same time holding to the desire for the status quo. A number of models or theories have been developed to explain this dynamic. One model of systems, the structural–functional view (Malinowski, 1948; Parsons, 1971) sees systems as striving for equilibrium and balance. With equilibrium as a goal, any change, which by definition causes disruption of equilibrium, tends to be resisted unless it occurs slowly enough to allow the system time to adjust. An alternative view of systems is that of the conflict theory (Collins, 1974; Simmel, 1950). This model views change in social systems as being both divisive and consensual. According to this model, change has both associative (binding) and dissociative (disintegrative) forces and pressures for a system. One type of associative force found within a system is systemic norms. These systemic norms represent the implicit and explicit structures and functions that are adopted and perpetuated by a specific system. The establishment of systemic norms, such as an adopted curriculum, a standing committee such as an instructional support team, or a school calendar, act as associative or binding pressures. In contrast to such binding forces, pressures that result from an economic downturn in the school community, the retirement of key system employees, or new governmental mandates for specialized services for targeted populations represent dissociative pressures. Although the relative influence of these pressures will vary over time, the resulting change will always invigorate and mobilize the system.

As you might surmise, unlike the structural–functional theorists who decry change as destructive to the system, the conflict theorists welcome change.

System Change as Inevitable

As might be obvious, change is inevitable. Social systems that attempt to fight change through entrenchment in fixed ways of performing, although perhaps maintaining the "security" of the status quo, will soon experience system atrophy and even system death.

Although system change is inevitable, it need not be inevitably destructive! Responding, adjusting to change is certainly a challenge. It confronts our innate desire for stability, control, and the security of the status quo. But change also announces an opportunity. Change announces the system's opportunity to grow, to evolve, to respond more effectively to the changing needs of it's consumers, and/or the changing nature of it's resources (inputs). Even in the face of change, system homeostasis can be preserved if those individuals functioning within systems accept the inevitability of change and devote their energies to the accommodations required in response to that change. The school counselor is in an ideal position to fulfill that role of systems change agent. As a consultant to all consumers and providers within the school community, the school counselor can inform, mobilize, and collaborate in initiatives that will keep the system responsive, flexible—open.

SYSTEM DYNAMICS
AND COUNSELOR CONSULTATION

The realities of system evolution, impact of system structures—formal and informal—along with the system's response to change are realities that the counselor–consultant must understand to be effective. Through an understanding of the nature of systems, system dynamics, and the characteristics of open systems, the school counselor-as-consultant can be proactive in building, maintaining, and revising their comprehensive guidance program. Many of these initiatives will involve actions that school counselors can take to maintain their school (and guidance program) as an open system. Most of those actions involve the counselor as a consultant to both internal and external populations. The school counselor–consultant will occasionally be asked to help other professional colleagues in the performance of their job. A teacher experiencing classroom management problems, a special teacher who can't seem to connect with her students, a cafeteria worker who fails to stop bullying at lunch, and a new teacher who fails to submit lesson plans for administrative review are all examples of jobs that are not getting done. When called on to help rectify such problems, the counselor–consultant must first assess what is inhibiting effective job performance. Are there certain criteria for effective job performance that are not being met?

Five criteria must be met for any individual to be able to perform their job optimally. First, they must possess the competence (knowledge and skill) required to perform the tasks of the job. If they cannot do it, they will not do it. Second, the individual must have the authority (permission) to carry out the functions prescribed by the job. Without authority, fear can preempt the performance of tasks. Often accompanying authority is the third criteria, the resources necessary to perform the work. Without critical materials, space, time, and technology, most jobs could not be performed adequately. Fourth, the individual must be accountable (responsible) for the commission and results of the job. Without accountability, individuals can easily lose the motivation to perform the job effectively. And finally, individuals need the motivation (extrinsic and intrinsic) to do quality work and achieve quality outcomes. The research literature (Cherrington, 1989; Jex, 1998; McClellend, 1985) offers an array of motivation techniques that will inspire workers to want to perform their jobs effectively.

A deficiency in any one of these five criteria will interfere with a person's job performance; multiple deficiencies can severely obstruct one's job performance. By applying the five criteria to someone's job performance, the counselor–consultant can help the individual and his system to target remediation to the deficiencies identified. Competence deficiencies can be remediated through formal and informal instruction and training. System managers can clearly and formally grant the authority to individuals to perform the various aspects of their job. At the same time, those system managers can also ensure that their workers have the requisite resources to perform their job. Accountability can only be regained through the establishment of clear, accurate, and reasonable objectives and the consistent assessment of those outcomes. The results of those assessments must be used for both formative and summative evaluations. And finally, motivational strategies for job performance can be introduced that cogently tailor incentives and consequences to the unique needs, desires, and values of workers.

Exercise 4.3 provides an opportunity for you to identify job criteria in a selected job and develop an intervention for each criteria not met.

EXERCISE 4.3

Job Performance Analysis

Select a current or recent position of employment that you have held. As you reflect on that job, consider the extent to which each of the five job performance criteria were (or are being) met. For any criteria that are not being met, describe what changes are needed for that criteria to be met. As with previous exercises share your response with a colleague or mentor as a way of gaining from their perspective and insights.

Performance Criteria

1. Competence (knowledge and skill)
2. Authority (permission)
3. Resources
4. Accountability (responsibility)
5. Motivation

SYSTEMIC DYNAMICS:
IMPLICATIONS FOR MR. THOMAS

Mr. Thomas's comments at the beginning of this chapter suggest that Kirkwood High School is experiencing some of the characteristics of a closed system. The reactive role of counselors is a well-established norm in this school. Counselors are expected to respond to concerns brought to them and perform their remediation directly with the referred client (e.g., Ellen) without active involvement by the referring consulted (e.g., Dr. Jameson). This pervasive norm, maintained by both internal and external populations, defines the counselor's role and function (and de facto job description). Moreover, within such a restrictive and reactive function, the school counselors are impeded in serving all their consumers, prompting Mr. Thomas to question whether he is serving the needs of all of his students, parents, and fellow teachers.

Some other characteristics of closed systems can also be gleaned from Mr. Thomas's comments. It appears that the guidance program at Kirkwood High School is strongly invested in the status quo and resistant to change. From Mr. Thomas's questioning whether he is serving the needs of his consumers, we can draw a few conclusions. First, the needs of his consumers have not recently (or ever) been assessed. Without current and empirically valid measures of his consumers' needs, he is unable to establish accurate outcome goals and objectives and thus have the empirically based standard by which to answer his question. Second, in the absence of valid outcome goals and objectives, Mr. Thomas has no basis for building, maintaining, or changing his program (processes), other than perpetuating "Our Way" or "The Way" of doing things. The empirical support that he will need to formulate a direction and rationale for change in his program, and thus his job description, requires a current assessment of his consumers' needs. As a prudent, systemic agent of change, Mr. Thomas realizes that measures to open his system will take time. He knows that he will have to maintain his reactive role while he begins to shape norms that are congruent with an open system. Perhaps his first step in this systemic sea of change should be to have an informal conversation with Dr. Jameson about Kirkwood High School as a system. Although Dr. Jameson can be a valuable source of information about Kirkwood High School, it is just as critical that Dr. Jameson also begin to think about Kirkwood High School as a system.

Finally, when Mr. Thomas questions his effectiveness, he might consider the five job performance criteria. He knows what he is expected to do and appears to have the competence to perform his job. In fact, he has the competence to do much more if given the opportunity. He also has the authority to do the job as defined for him, but questions whether he has the authority to initiate empirically supported changes in his program. The line authority will be critical to his success. So far, he has been responsible for reactive and remedial interventions. The extent of his accountability to his line authority, as well as his consumers, is still unclear. It appears that responding to crises and putting out fires is his primary responsibility. The most problematic criteria in performing his job are clearly the accuracy of his efforts. Only by collaborating with his colleagues (starting with Dr. Jameson) in opening his system will he be able to attain the level of accuracy that he desires.

SUMMARY

The Evolution and Nature of Systems

At their point of origin all social systems are responsive to the needs of their consumers and are flexible in this responsiveness and therefore considered to be open.

Systems do not always remain open. Some move from what was once flexible and responsive to that which is no longer adaptive, adjusting, or servicing the needs of its consumer. Under these conditions the system is considered a closed system.

With energy given to maintaining the status quo, systems often find themselves in a state of entropy, the final stage of its existence. Entropy represents the natural state of a closed system in which the system devotes much of its energy to boundary maintenance to preserve its processes (structure and function) vis-à-vis its external environment.

Systems: Formal and Informal

The more systems close the more rigid and codified their processes become. This appearance of this strict codification of rules, regulations, procedures, and processes defines a system's transition from what was once informal to now that which is formal.

Although the formal system appears to offer stability, safety, and unambiguous expectations of performance, it is that very formality and standardization that propels it even further toward entropy.

Whereas the formal system explicates how things are supposed to be done, the informal system reveals how things really get done in this system.

As systems close, these formal and informal systems may operate in parallel fashion.

Organizational Structure

As systems evolve and slowly close, they build increasingly more complex organizational structures with many layers. The flow of information is severely restricted, but when it does occur, it follows a top–down direction.

Mechanisms that inhibit the increasing complexity and closure of systems attempt to spread the locus of control over the entire system.

System Dynamics and Orientation to Change

When open, the system uses empirically valid information to continually adjust to the naturally occurring changes within and between the system components. Systems that emphasize equilibrium as a goal will view any change as disruption of equilibrium, and thus something that needs to be resisted.

IMPORTANT TERMS

Accountability	Formal system	Open system
Associative pressures	Homeostasis	Staff authority
Closed system	Informal system	Status quo
Cybernetics	Job performance criteria	Steady state systemic
Dissociative pressures	Line authority	
Entropy	Norms	

SUGGESTED READINGS

Banathy, B. (1991). *Systems design of education.* Englewood Cliffs, NJ: Educational Technology Publications.

Frick, T. (1993). A systems view of restructuring education. In C. Reigeluth, B. Banathy, & J. Olson (Eds.), *Comprehensive systems design: A new educational technology* (pp. 260–271). Berlin: Springer-Verlag.

Gleick, J. (1987). *Chaos: Making a new science*. New York: Penguin Books.

Kuhn, T. (1970). *The structure of scientific revolutions*. Chicago: University of Chicago Press.

Maccia, E. S., & Maccia, G. S. (1966). *Development of educational theory derived from three theory models*. Washington, DC: U.S. Office of Education, Project No. 5-0638.

WEB SITES

Optimize Magazine: part of the TechWeb business connection. Offers resources and references on organizational operations, change, and dynamics. http://www.optimizemag.com/issue/007/culture.htm

Center for School Change: This is a program of the Humphrey Institute of Public Affairs at the University of Minnesota. It offers resources for educators, parents, and businesspeople concerned about student achievement and quality education. http://www.hhh.umn.edu/centers/school-change/

Systemic Change in Education: The New England Complex Systems Institute (NECSI) is an independent educational and research institution dedicated to advancing the study of complex systems. http://www.necsi.org

REFERENCES

Cherrington, D. J. (1989). *Organizational behavior: The management of individual and organizational performance*. Needham Heights, MA: Allyn & Bacon.

Collins, R. (1974). *Conflict sociology: Toward an explanatory science*. New York: Academic Press.

Friday, R. (2002). *The rise of the creative class*. New York: Basic Books.

Hanson, G. B. (1995). *General systems theory beginning with the whales*. Washington, DC: Taylor & Francis.

Jex, S. M. (1998). *Stress and job performance: Theory, research and implications for managerial practice*. Thousand Oakes, CA: Sage.

Malinowski, B. (1948). *Magic, science and religion*. Glencoe, IL: Free Press.

McClelland, D. C. (1985). *Human motivation*. Glenview, IL: Scott Foresman.

Parsons, T. (1971). *The system of modern societies*. Englewood Cliffs, NJ: Prentice Hall.

Simmel, G. (1950). *The sociology of George Simmel* (Kurt H. Wolf, Trans.). New York: Free Press.

Weiner, N. (1948). *Cybernetics*. New York: Wiley.

5

⚬⚬

The Consultant as
Agent for Change

I can't believe the reactions I'm getting. It seems like almost anything I
try to initiate or anytime I ask Dr. Jameson or any of the teachers to do
something that in their mind is out of the ordinary, they look at me like
I'm an anarchist or something. I am just trying to do my job and help
Ellen and all the students. Why the resistance? I'm only trying to help!

Only trying to help? Although that is certainly true, it is also true that
Mr. Thomas, our counselor–consultant is also trying to introduce
change and innovation. This really should not come as a surprise.
Counselors are in the business of change. The client who is in pain and seeks
assistance from a counselor clearly expects that things will be different (better)
as a result of the client–counselor interaction. The client anticipates that some
change will be experienced as a result of counseling.

The same is true for the counselor-as-consultant. The consultee enters a
consultative relationship expecting that the consultant will provide, promote,
or facilitate some form of change (improvement) in the conditions that led to
his/her invitation into the consult. As such, the counselor-as-consultant will
function as an agent for change.

There is some potentially significant difference, however, between the
counselor as agent of change for the client and the counselor–consultant as
agent of change. These differences may at first be uncomfortable for the counselor new to consulting and will often be unsettling to the system in which
he or she is consulting.

CHAPTER OBJECTIVES

This chapter will provide a look at the dynamics involved in the process of instituting innovation and change within an organization or system and highlight the role of the consultant as one of change agent and innovator. Further, the chapter will discuss the basis of resistance often encountered by agents of change and provide a model for initiating change in the face of such potential resistance.

After completing this chapter, the reader should be able to

1. Explain how the role of consultant is inevitably one of change and innovation
2. Describe how consultation is advocacy for system and client
3. Explain the basis for system resistance to change
4. Describe the principles of diffusion of innovation, which may help reduce resistance and facilitate change

CONSULTATION—INEVITABLY
IMPACTING THE SYSTEM

Perhaps when we think of organizational change or system innovation, we envision massive reallocation of resources or realignment of structures and processes. With this as our focus, it may seem that the school counselor is an unlikely candidate for initiating such innovation. But system change comes in many forms—some less dramatic, less encompassing then others—and many fall clearly within the competency and job domain of our counselor–consultant.

Because the members of a system, along with the processes, structures, procedures, and products found within a system, are by definition interdependent, efforts taken to effect change in the client, the consultee, or any one of these process or structure elements effect change within the system. For example, consider the situation in which our counselor–consultant helps a student develop assertive skills. By providing this client with the skills and belief structures needed to assert her needs, the counselor is impacting the system. Just consider how her change in attitude and behavior will cause disruption in her relationships with friends, family, and teachers significant in her life. Or consider the situation in which a counselor runs a group on nonviolent conflict resolution. What happens when these students attempt to use their problem-solving skills when encountering a disagreement with a teacher or administrator? Providing these skills to one element of the system, the students, sets in motion the wheels of change within the entire system.

Thus even without intending to impact the system, the counselor–consultant will inevitably function as an agent of system change. This element of the counselor–consultant role, that of agent of change, becomes even more pronounced when placed within context of the model of consultation offered here.

As previously noted, consultation is considered to be a process that is not only triadic, but is also one that emphasizes extrapersonal factors as contributors to a client's current problem. This approach to consultation assumes clients do not function within a vacuum or exist immune from the influences of those around them. It is assumed that the client's behavior occurs within the context of his/her psychosocial–physical environment. As such, to be effective, the counselor–consultant needs to focus not only on the client's intrapersonal dynamics but also on the extrapersonal factors (e.g., role of the consultee, the tasks assigned, and the environment) contributing to the existence and maintenance of the current problem.

Further, if the intent of the counselor–consultant is to have long-lasting impact, then her efforts must be targeted to impact not only the client but also the extrapersonal variables in the client's environment (Kurpius, 1985). This is especially true when the target of consultation goes beyond remediating the current situation to establishing means and mechanism for prevention of this difficulty in the future. These foci or goals of consultation necessitate that the counselor–consultant consider the way extrapersonal variables may be changed to both maintain client change and to ensure prevention.

This emphasis on extrapersonal factors and prevention necessitates that in addition to effecting change within the client, the counselor-as-consultant will also—by design and intent—effect change within the system (Friend & Bauwens, 1988; Parsons & Meyers, 1984). To that end, it is essential that the counselor–consultant help consultees recognize the level of interdependence that exists between the problem diagnosis, the intervention, and the contextual influence of the system in which they work (Fuqua & Gibson, 1980; Kurpius, 1985).

COUNSELOR-AS-CONSULTANT:
ADVOCATING FOR CLIENT *AND* SYSTEM

In some settings, counselors are assigned, formally or informally, the role of advocates for the system and the status quo. In these settings counselors are asked to fix the problem student in such a way that the student fits in to the existing school environment. However, there are other times and other settings in which counselors are perceived as the advocate for the student. In these settings, the counselor is perceived as one in an adversarial position with teachers and administrators. In these situations counselors are often resisted or dismissed as the school's equivalent of a bleeding heart always fighting the status quo and pushing for change, in service of their client—the student. But the counselor-as-consultant need not be in an adversarial role pitted against the system. It is possible to be an advocate for both the student–client and the school system.

Advocate and Adversary?

The consultant's role, especially when involving innovation of systemic change, is often confused with the role of advocate, even though their goals and boundaries are different. The traditional view of advocacy is one of conflict. That is, there are a number of partisan groups within a system and organizational procedures (e.g., tracking, curriculum development, promotion procedures, supervisory models) that are to the advantage of some and the disadvantage of others. The advocate in this orientation attempts to gain advantage for her constituency at the expense of some others. It is not unusual for a counselor to be perceived as an advocate, an advocate whose recommended innovations come at the expense of the teacher and the teacher's way of teaching. This view places the counselor in conflict with the teacher and proves detrimental to the student, the counselor–consultant, the teacher, and the system as a whole.

Advocate for the Mission

In consultation the adversarial role is eliminated or at least minimized. Does that mean the counselor–consultant won't at times seek changes that are beneficial for the student? Certainly, this is not what is being suggested. No, contrasted to the traditional role of advocate who, while not only seeking to support his client most often does so by implementing adversarial actions on the client's behalf, the counselor–consultant seeks to support the client as a way of facilitating the system's achievement of its mission and publicly stated goals.

The model of consultation presented here does not oppose the client with others in the system. It is not a matter of student versus teacher or teacher versus administration. The client is an interdependent part of the system, just as the consultee is a part of the system. Change in the client, change in the consultee, or change in the process and structure of the system are all innovations in the system (Parsons, 1996). Each is intended to better service the system as well as all those involved as they attempt to fulfill the mission of that system. Consultation as presented here is advocacy for both client and system.

When Goals Conflict

The idea of the counselor as advocate for system and client is based on the assumption that the goals of the system and those of the individual are not antagonistic. In this situation, the consultant who is facilitating the development and healthy functioning of the individual within the system is also increasing the health of the system. Further, by improving the organizational structure and processes so that they are more mission driven, it is assumed that the goals of the individual will find a context that is more supportive and facilitative.

Although it is desirable for a consultant to work with systems in which she feels congruent with both mission and goals, sometimes this is either not possible or not readily apparent. When the consultee or systems members are actively engaged in unethical or illegal behaviors, then clearly the consultant must confront these behaviors, and terminate contracts when they are not ceased.

Although very few counselors will experience situations in which there is gross violation of ethical or legal principles, many may encounter systems in which the goals and processes, although not so radically incongruent with their own, do create conflict between the organization and the individuals within. Such conflict interferes with the system's goal attainment. Change in the individual, the system, or both is needed, and change that results in reduced conflict and increased harmony is the type of goal-directed change suggested here.

At times counselor–consultants will advocate system change. When the organization's functioning, decision making, and communication processes are incongruent with its own mission and goals, the consultant as change agent will address these incongruencies. The realignment of the system functioning with stated goals and mission will have a positive impact on all of those within the system (i.e., consultees and clients). Similarly, when the operation and procedures of the system are detrimental to the members, the counselor–consultant's task may be to assist the system to redefine the responsibilities or reenvision its modus operandi in light of the original mission and purpose.

REACTION AND RESISTANCE

As noted in our previous chapter, systems are notorious for resisting any significant change in their current condition or manner of functioning (e.g., Argyris, 1970; Blake & Mouton, 1976; de Jager, 2001; Wickstrom & Witt, 1993). This resistance is often difficult to penetrate and may require a major sociopolitical or economic force to open a system to change and innovation. For example, the 1958 National Defense Education Act following the launching of the Russian *Sputnik* satellite forced the American educational system to reconsider its current curriculum. Change was quick to follow. Similar systemic change occurred as a result of the passage of the Education for All Handicapped Children Act (Public Law 94-142) in 1975 and the extension of that law's requirement of free and appropriate education to all handicapped children (P.L. 99-457). These forces caused significant adjustments in the teacher preparation, school curriculum, and even plant physical organization. Although radical and rapid system change typically requires such major sociopolitical and economic forces, change is possible even when the counselor–consultant lacks the power of major sociopolitical force.

To initiate and maintain system innovation and change under less-dramatic conditions, the counselor–consultant needs to understand the base of system resistance and be skilled in the employment of the principles underlying successful diffusion of innovation.

Resistance as Self-Preservation

As noted previously, systems may start out as open, flexible, and responsive to the changing needs of the people they serve, but quite often they begin to stabilize and concretize their structures and processes. These systems evolve into a state of stability, homeostasis, and potentially one of stagnation and death.

With this transition to a more stable, formal structure comes a diversion of energy and resources. Now the system employs its resources for two ends. Some energy and resources are deployed to continue its mission-driven activities of the system. Other resources, however, are redirected to maintain the system's own structure and function. With the goals of self-maintenance or system preservation in mind, systems create organizational structures, role definitions, formal lines of communication, and a variety of procedures and policies aimed at keeping the style of operation and current character in its present form and configuration. Thus where once change and adaptation were the rule of the day, now innovation, experimentation, and change are not only ignored but also actively resisted. Change is viewed as a threat not just to the organization's stability but to its very identity—its very existence. Any force, person, or idea that would indicate that the existing system be changed—be it as minute as expanding or modifying a job definition or as complicated as decentralizing the form of management or changing curriculum—will run contrary to this self-maintenance goal and evoke system self-preservation resistance (Napierkowski & Parsons, 1995).

Specific Conditions Stimulating Resistance

Although any change may evoke a self-preservation response and thus system resistance, four specific conditions appear to actively evoke system resistance. These conditions, which are discussed in detail later, involve changes that: threaten the balance of power, suggest the risk of sunken costs, create miscommunications, and/or challenge group norms (Kast & Rosenzweig, 1974). Understanding and ameliorating these conditions is essential if the counselor–consultant is to reduce system resistance to change.

Threats to Balance of Power   A primary source of resistance is the fear that innovation will upset the balance of power between the various subgroups existing within the system. Consider the situation in which the counselor-as-consultant attempts to promote a change in the way children with special needs are included within the school's curriculum and activities. If the innovation is perceived as giving those in special education added resources or power to direct curriculum, it may arouse resistance from those regular education departments and faculty. This resistance may be further supported by parents, who view a shift in the utilization of school resources and therefore tax dollars to the detriment of their own children. Similarly, the counselor–consultant who attempts to use nonprofessional staff in an educational setting, to expand counseling services (e.g., peer counselors, paraprofessionals, or regular classroom teachers as members on the child study team) may evoke some resistance from the professional counselors, who feel they are losing some professional distinction and power.

Clearly, innovations that appear to be to the benefit of all members of the system or innovations that require the least amount of loss of power to any one group will be those that meet the least resistance. Counselors working from a consultation perspective need to be sensitive to the different constituencies within the system and the perceived impact their recommendations and innovation may have on each constituent's role, function, and power.

Sunk Costs   In systems such as schools in which resources are limited, there is always concern over the way these limited resources—be they time, energy, or capital—are to be utilized. Thus, a consultant seeking to introduce change and innovation may be perceived as expending school resources on a yet to be proven program or process. From this perspective, it is viewed as a cost without return. Without a clear sign of the payoff this innovation will accrue, these costs, which are real and immediate, are viewed as sunken, without return. Naturally such a perception of cost without return will stimulate resistance.

The counselor–consultant seeking to diffuse innovation needs to be sensitive to this type of cost perception. Further, it is important to note that costs anticipated extend beyond those of resource and energy. The psychological costs (e.g., stress, frustration, anxiety) that accompany change also serve as a base for resistance.

With this in mind, the counselor–consultant needs to plan introduction of change in a way that keeps costs (both tangible and psychological) to a minimal, while at the same time demonstrating real, concrete, and immediate payoffs or returns on the investment in change.

Miscommunications   Quite often the individuals who are aware of the need (and potential benefit of change) fail to communicate the need and nature of the change in ways that can be understood and accepted by others within the system. Rumors, miscommunication, and conflicting data elevate system anxiety and confusion and with it increased resistance (Lewis, 2000).

It is not usual to hear that a counselor's request to visit a classroom to observe a student is really a ruse for evaluating the teacher. Or that a counselor who is attempting to facilitate the inclusion of a student with special needs into a particular class is really attempting to open the floodgates and eventually move all the children with unique needs to that classroom.

These misperceptions need to be corrected, and steps need to be taken early in consultation to reduce the possibility of their occurrence. It is important for the consultant to clearly communicate to all involved the purpose and process of the consultation (Lewis, 1999). Further, it is of great value to provide objective, clear, and consistent data as a base from which to derive consensual agreement on the nature of the problem and the possible strategies and avenues to pursue. The clarity and consistency of these data will highly affect the degree of resistance or acceptance experienced.

Protecting Tradition A fourth source of resistance stems from a desire to maintain and protect tradition. In many schools the culture is rich with history. The way things are done have long historical roots, and often those within the system value they way things are done, simply because it is the way they always have done it. Tradition is a powerful form of resistance. Change is not only a risk, especially if the traditional way of doing things has worked pretty well, but when change is viewed as a challenge to a procedure that has become normative, almost sacred, resistance will be maximized.

Quite often the original reason for a particular process or procedure may have long passed, and in fact those involved with the original decision to employ such a process or procedure may no longer be around, yet tradition can dictate that it be continued. It is not so much that the process is viewed as having much value; it is simply that the process is a part of the system's identity—"they way we do things." Tampering with this process may be mistakenly interpreted as tampering with the system's identity and thus elicit system resistance.

For example, consider the experience of Mr. Alvertson, the ninth-grade counselor at Haberson High. Mr. Alverston is in his first year at Haberson, having worked in a nearby district for the past 7 years.

Over the course of his first semester, Mr. Alvertson became aware of the large number of students who were being suspended. It appears that Haberson is known for its no-nonsense approach to discipline. Further, the previous dean of students (who retired last year) had developed a strict disciplinary code, which included the use of internal and external suspensions for a variety of offenses.

In working with some of the students, Mr. Alverston began to realize that this strict approach, although perhaps having some value for some students, was impacting many of the students in a very negative way. Students who had previously not demonstrated a history of school offenses were developing a negative, hostile attitude to what they perceived to be an overly oppressive system.

In an attempt to reduce this negative perception among students as well as reduce this high rate of suspension, Mr. Alvertson attempted to incorporate a peer court system, which he had found extremely effective at his previous school. The proposal included a process in which students who were facing suspension could have the option to go to student court rather than directly to the dean of students. For those choosing the student court, their case would be reviewed by a select body of their peers, and if found in violation, the court of peers would assign some form of consequence. These consequences could include those previously dictated under the code of conduct, a referral to the dean of students, or the assignment of the student to do some form of school-based service.

Mr. Alvertson suggested that rather than simply removing the students from classes, as was the procedure with in-house and external suspension, that it would be more productive to assign these violators to pro-social activities, such as tutoring, helping with the recycling of school refuse, or participating in one of the school's afterschool programs. Mr. Alvertson suggested that this student court approach would help the students understand the value of the school code and give them opportunities to engage in pro-social activity rather than simply being removed from the school, which for some, was actually a positive experience.

Although the proposal was well thought out, Mr. Alverston immediately began to experience resistance, not just from the dean of students, but from the principal and most of the faculty as well. When asked what the point of objection was, most were hard-pressed to provide an answer other than to simply state that the dean of students *always* enforced the code.

For the counselor–consultant confronted with resistance based in tradition, the goal is not to compete with tradition or in any way attempt to demean the status quo, but rather attempt to offer change as an alternative or suggest a minor adjustment that can be used to affirm the value of the traditional way (Brown, Blackburn, & Powell, 1979). In this situation where the dean of students had traditionally been the court of no appeal, returning power to the dean would be essential. Thus, Mr. Alverston revised the original proposal suggesting that rather than the counselor or the students deciding on who would have the opportunity to have their case heard by the student court, it would be up to the dean of students. Further, Mr. Alverston proposed that this option could be employed for those students having minor offenses and that such a process may reduce the amount of time that the dean had to spend with these cases, allowing him more time and energy for the more serious student problems. Although this was but a small step in modifying the discipline system at Haberson High, it was an introduction of innovation, which no longer threatened the tradition of empowering the dean of students as the school's disciplinarian, and as such was accepted as a pilot program.

Even though school counselors have the creativity and insight to develop wonderful programs for remediating and even preventing potentially problematic situations, it must be remembered that these programs are only as good as they are implemented. Further, for a program to be successfully applied, it must be embraced by those responsible for its implementation. Therefore, to be successful, a counselor–consultant will not only need to recognize sources of resistance but will also need to employ those techniques and strategies that reduce these forms of resistance and facilitate the diffusion of innovation within the school.

PROMOTING INNOVATION

As an agent of change, the counselor–consultant operates within two different systems. The first system is that which currently exists. It is the way things currently operate, and it is the one that the counselor is seeking to change. The second system is the one which the counselor is attempting to create. It may only be a system with a minor adjustment or change from that which is, but it is a change, and it is different than the status quo.

This second system is envisioned to have a way of operating that will make it more effective than that which is or will in some way reduce the problem currently encountered by the counselor operating within the old system. But for this change to be effectively implemented, the counselor–consultant needs to act as the bridge between these two systems of "what is" and "what is hoped." The consultant will need to employ strategies and techniques that reduce the system's resistance to innovation and bring these systems in line so that the new information, program, or process can be disseminated and accepted.

There are variety of models of planned change (Argyris, 1970; Bartunek & Louis, 1988; Ellsworth, 2000; French & Bell, 1990; Mohrman et al., 1989; Schmuck & Runkel, 1985). However, five principles culled from the classic work of Rogers and Shoemaker (1971) appear to be particularly useful for the school counselor attempting to introduce innovation and change. The principles are: (a) keep innovations culturally compatible, (b) introduce change in small steps, (c) align change with opinion leaders, (d) increase consultant power and value, and (e) move in a crisis.

Principle 1: Keep Innovations Culturally Compatible

Acting as a bridge between the old system of status quo and that of innovation, the counselor–consultant needs to understand the original system's norms and values. Further, the consultant seeking to diffuse innovation needs to shape and form the innovation in ways that make it compatible with these existing norms and values (Eldridge, 2001). To introduce change that is compatible to the existing system culture, the counselor–consultant needs to shape that innovation in a way that

1. Is in line with the mission and purpose of the system
2. At a minimum approximates the operating values and norms
3. Is sensitive to the unique internal and/or external forces or pressures impacting the system, as well as the unique history and tradition that may be affected by the change

The Case 5.1 (Tommy, the Attention Seeker) will help to more fully demonstrate the importance of this principle.

CASE 5.1   Tommy, the Attention Seeker

The fifth-grade teacher at J. R. Turnball elementary school requested to meet with the counselor. It appeared that over the course of the last five weeks, Tommy, a fifth-grade student, had been calling out in class and making inappropriate "animal noises." The teacher, Ms. Zaborowski, reported employing a number of techniques to stop Tommy, but all have proven unsuccessful. The teacher noted that she has (a) verbally chastised Tommy when he called out, (b) kept him in at recess, (c) made him take his seat out in the hallway, and (d) even threatened to send him to the principal.

CASE 5.1   CONTINUED

In observing the class, the counselor–consultant noted that Tommy was isolated from the rest of the class. Whereas, the other class members worked in groups on learning projects, Tommy sat at his desk working on individual worksheets. When asked as to the reason for this classroom arrangement, the teacher reported that this was a result of Tommy's disruptive behavior in the learning groups.

The counselor–consultant also observed that the teacher, who was in her first year of teaching, exhibited a lot of energy and enthusiasm going from table to table to work with the different groups of students. However, it was only when Tommy called out or made an "animal noise" that she would attend to him.

Following these observations, the consultant suggested to the teacher that Tommy was simply seeking attention and that her chastising and negative attending were actually reinforcing Tommy's inappropriate behavior. The consultant suggested that the teacher begin to ignore Tommy's inappropriate behavior (as a process of extinction) and begin to praise Tommy when he was working on his worksheets (as an attempt to shape appropriate behavior). The teacher understood the concepts of shaping, extinction, and reinforcement and said she would try.

The recommendation failed. Tommy's behavior grew more disruptive, and the teacher lost confidence in the consultant. When the consultant followed up on the recommendation, she found that the teacher failed to stick with the agreed upon plan.

To understand what happened, one needs to understand the basic profile of the system in which the innovation was introduced.

Ms. Z.'s fifth-grade class was in a private elementary school. Among the many things the school valued and attempted to promote were respect, self-control, obedience to authority, order, and compliance. Further, a norm operating within the system was that every teacher was responsible for his/her own classroom and its management and that a good classroom (and thus a good teacher) was one in which the children **were quietly working** on tasks and **the teacher was actively in control**. The innovation recommended by the counselor–consultant, although theoretically sound, has a number of unique dimensions that seem incompatible with the culture of this school and therefore made the recommendation unacceptable to the consultee (i.e., Ms. Zaborowski).

Behavior that was intermittently reinforced and that is now undergoing an extinction process at first tends to increase in frequency and/or intensity. As such, the recommendation made by the consultant to ignore Tommy's inappropriate behavior led to an increase in the disruptive behavior. This increase in Tommy's calling out was in direct violation of the norm of working quietly. Further, the fact that compliance, obedience, and authority are valued and the teacher is expected to be in control appeared to run contrary to the consultant's request for the teacher to ignore (or as she explained, "do nothing") when Tommy acted out. Because of the felt incompatibility of the innovation with the norms, values of her own system's culture, the teacher simply failed to follow through.

Exercise 5.1 provides you with practice in creating interventions that are culturally compatible with the target system.

EXERCISE 5.1

Innovation as Culturally Compatible

Directions: Following you will find a brief case presentation. After analyzing the presenting concerns, along with the description of a number of specific system characteristics, review each of the intervention plans suggested. With a colleague, classmate, or supervisor discuss the degree to which each intervention is compatible or incompatible with the current system profile. Which of the interventions provided would be most compatible? Could you create a fourth intervention that would be even more compatible and thus more likely to be accepted?

Problem
In general there is increasing tension and conflict between faculty serving regular education and those in special education. The school's faculty were feeling unsupported by the administration and were now contemplating union action.

Situation
School A is a high school located in an upper-middle-class, suburban district. School A has a long-standing history of both academic and athletic excellence. The school is proud of its large number of AP students, state athletic championships, and a three-year track record of placing in top 1% on state standardized testing.

The district has a strong teacher's union, and the teachers have enjoyed support from parents in each incident of their contract negotiations. Parents have been very supportive, given the academic and athletic achievements that have been made. All previous contract negotiations have been quite amicable, with all involved working for the betterment of the students and the maintaining of the highest quality. Up to this year the relationship among various departments, as well as between faculty and staff, has been highly supportive.

At the beginning of the school year the faculty were informed by the principal that the district was implementing "full inclusion" policies, and as a result many if not most of the regular education faculty would now have classrooms in which students with special needs would be included. Faculty were further informed that the inclusion policy being adopted provided for full participation in academics and all extracurricular activities. The principal stated that this was policy and as such it was up to the faculty "to make this happen." Faculty were also informed that a number of specialists had been hired by the district to serve as curricular advisers and consultants to the regular education teachers. The principal directed the faculty to work with these advisors.

Throughout the first two months of school a number of conflicts arose. Parents confronted teachers with concerns about anticipated drops in academic and athletic excellence. Parents with children with special needs were upset that some teachers failed to meet the children's needs. As a result the faculty felt in the middle, being damned if they did and damned if they didn't. Further the faculty felt unsupported—abandoned by the administration—who kept reiterating that it was their (the faculty) job to make it work!

Faculty began to take out their frustrations on the consultants. They refused to meet with consultants and began to blame the consultants for anything that went wrong. Rumors suggesting that this was just the beginning and that their school would eventually become a special education center started to be circulated. With this increasing tension, the faculty meetings became gripe sessions with the focus on the intrusion of these "specialists in our school." Faculty expressed resentment about having to change their curriculum and in general their way of doing things, which previously had proven successful. Many faculty threatened to make this an issue for union action.

Recommendations

1. Have a town meeting in which the faculty and parents can voice their concerns to the superintendent.

2. Have the school principal meet with those faculty refusing or resisting the process and confront them with the reality of the district's decision and the choices and consequences they have.

3. Develop strategic work groups composed of faculty, consultants, parents, and administration to develop strategies for effectively maintaining levels of excellence and meeting the needs of all children.

4. Develop a representative body of school administration, teachers, and parents to pressure the central office to reconsider their decision and reduce the breadth of their inclusion plan.

5. Use the union as a agent for negotiation with the administration, and make this a matter of contract renegotiation.

6. (Write your recommendation):

_____

Principle 2: Shaping—Introducing Change in Small Steps

Although attempting to present innovation as culturally compatible, the reality is that any innovation, by definition, alters the way an organization will function and thus can never be completely compatible to the existing culture. Thus, in addition to introducing change that is most compatible, innovation must be presented in ways that are perceived as tolerable and only minimally disruptive to the status quo.

Radical adjustments or changes are more likely to be met with resistance than those requiring small steps. Systems, like individuals, can be shaped toward change. Introducing the elements of innovations as small approximations of the desired goal may help to reduce the resistance to the innovation. Weick (1984), for example, found that a sequence of small wins (i.e., a measurable outcome of moderate importance) set up a pattern that can "attract allies, deter opponents and lower resistance . . ." (p. 43).

Research suggests, that innovations proving most acceptable will be those that: (a) require the least amount of change, (b) require the least amount of resource expenditure, (c) require the least amount of adaptation of roles or development of skills and knowledge, and (d) prove least disruptive to the organization's schema or frame of reference (Bartunek & Moch, 1987; Torbert, 1985).

Change that is least perceptible and, in fact, least disruptive to day-to-day functioning will be change that elicits the least resistance. Thus, changing the way morning messages are delivered will be less disruptive and therefore less resisted by faculty than changing the scope and sequence of a curriculum. As one proceeds to the higher levels of perceptual change, one will experience an increase in the general anxiety level of the system. Further, with higher levels of change, there will be an increase in amount of resources required. As such, a counselor–consultant attempting to promote change may experience more resistance when that change requires a complete shift or reframing of the organization's schema. Again, embracing such a significant change is facilitated by the process of shaping. Exercise 5.2 will help assist you in using the concepts of shaping in the development of an intervention plan.

EXERCISE 5.2

Change in Small Steps

Directions: For each of the following scenarios, use the principle of shaping to move the system in small steps toward the ultimate goal. Your task is to generate a subgoal that may help you begin the process of innovation while at the same time attempting to be least disruptive to the existing system. Discuss this intervention with a colleague, classmate, or supervisor attempting to identify points that may stimulate system resistance to its adaptation.

Scenario A: Over the course of the summer PS27 has been wired for high-speed Internet and in-house computer networking. The principal wants to have faculty place all lesson plans, roll books, and grading on the computer central network. He feels this will provide him easy access to information should a parent request data about a child or a specific teacher. The faculty has had neither prewarning nor preparation for this computerization of the school.

Goal: Place all curricula, lessons plan, roll book records, and grading on central database.

Subgoal: _____

Scenario B: The St. Edmunds High School Counseling Department is attempting to move from a 3 Cs model of counseling (i.e., counseling, coordination, and consultation), in which each task is often viewed and performed in isolation of the others, to a model that coordinates all services under the rubric of a triadic consultation approach. The faculty and administration have historically referred students (only) to counseling and expected these students to receive direct, one-on-one counseling services.

Goal: To use counselors as consultants, operating from a triadic, indirect model of service delivery. Counselors will expand the target for their services to include students, faculty, administrators, and the system.

Subgoal: _____

Principle 3: Align Innovation with Opinion Leaders

Another principle to follow when attempting to diffuse innovation and enhance the possibility that suggested changes will be embraced is to focus energy on personally aligning with the system's opinion leader(s) (Beer & Spector, 1993; Gray, 1984; Lippitt, 1982). The benefit of aligning innovation with opinion leaders is that those within a system who are respected and valued are given more leeway in violating group norms. The introduction of innovation is by definition a variance from the existing norm. Thus once aligned to these opinion leaders, the variation appears more acceptable.

Opinion leaders are not always those individuals who occupy the formal positions of power, such as a department chair or principal. The counselor–consultant needs to be alert to identify those who appear most influential within the system, regardless of their formal role or title. Further, the counselor–consultant would do well to forge alliances with these formal or informal leaders.

Identification and alignment with such opinion leaders often happens by engaging in the informal mechanisms and rituals in a system. Quite often taking a coffee break at the same time as those who appear to be the opinion leaders or by engaging in committee work, formal social activities, and informal gatherings (after-work volleyball or end-of-the-week "happy hour," etc.) can provide the mechanism by which the counselor can come to know and be known by the opinion leader(s). Although there are no hard and fast criteria from which to identify an opinion leader, any evidence that a person exerts influence over the functioning of the group's attitudes and behavior would be indicative of an opinion leader. Sometimes simply paying attention at faculty meetings may give the counselor the clues needed to identify the opinion leaders in the school.

Exercise 5.3 may help you in identifying the opinion leaders in your current situation.

EXERCISE 5.3

Opinion Leaders

Directions: The following can be employed either at a faculty meeting, work group meeting, or any gathering of members of your system in which opinions are being shared and decisions made. Identify by name, and where appropriate formal title or role, four individuals who are active in that group. Place a check mark under the name of the individual who most exemplifies the indicators listed. Next share your observation with another member of that same group. Covalidation may be indicative of the identification of the group's opinion leader.

Name of Group: _____

                                                                    Names/ Roles

Indicators: 1 _____ 2 _____ 3 _____ 4 _____
1. Keeps the group on task.
2. Sets direction for group.
3. Most directly influences
   mood or tone of group.
4. Tends to be most
   listened to.
5. Most often sought out
   for advice.
6. Individual with whom
   others wish most to relate.
7. Perceived as most important
   to the group.
8. Most often sought out at
   breaks in the group's meetings.
9. Individual whose absence
   would be most missed.
10. Seen as the prime resource
    for the group.

Principle 4: Increasing Value and Power as Consultant

Just as innovation and change may be more acceptable when presented by an opinion leader, a counselor–consultant who is perceived has having special value to the system will be more effective in introducing change. When consultants have demonstrated a value to those of the client system, they are more likely to have the power to effect system change and to have innovation embraced. This perception of value to those within the system can be enhanced by: (a) doing something, and (b) increasing expert and referent power.

Do Something Quite often the counselor, especially one new to a system, may face an uphill battle when attempting to gain respect and value. Without a history of demonstrated effectiveness to draw on, the counselor–consultant may feel like he has to constantly sell his services. Under these conditions, the counselor–consultant would do well to identify any role or function that may serve as of value to the members of the system and attempt to implement that role or function (Willing, 2002). The concept of doing something is not restricted to the realm of the esoteric or strictly professional. Quite often a counselor–consultant can begin to be perceived as valuable after serving a very practical function. Consider the following case illustration.

Mr. R. was a counselor assigned to work in a particular inner-city elementary school. The school had a history of bad experiences with previous counselors, and as a result members of the school were nonresponsive to Mr. R.'s attempts to work with the teachers and staff. Mr. R. attempted a number of different approaches such as sharing interesting articles that he had read, going to faculty meetings, and contributing to discussions, but nothing seemed to break through the resistance. Despite all his professional competence and sophistication, the event that resulted in his breaking through the resistance involved his driving ability.

The school had scheduled a day at the zoo for the lower grades (1–3) as a reward for children's participation in a read-a-thon. As might be anticipated the children were extremely excited about the day, and teachers although somewhat apprehensive about monitoring the children, all felt that it would be a wonderful experience. Because of a mix-up with insurance paperwork, the bus company contracted to transport the children the half mile to the zoo canceled on the morning of the planned trip. As fate might have it, Mr. R. was licensed to drive a school bus, and he volunteered to transport the children (a total of 5 trips both ways). Further, he suggested calling the central office to see if a small bus could be made available to the school. Not only was his suggestion successful, but his willingness to role up his sleeves to help with this problem, along with the rapport he demonstrated with the children as he transported them to the zoo, impressed the teachers and parents involved and resulted in a lowering of their resistance to working with him.

As a consultant, one would naturally seek to be valued for professional competence. With time the effective counselor–consultant will in fact gain power and acceptance as his or her interventions prove effective. However, as illustrated in the previous example, although a counselor–consultant, may want to gain value as a result of his or her demonstrated professional competence, quite often he or she may find that an increase in perceived value comes as a result of meeting any of the system's felt needs—even when those needs require practical rather than professional knowledge and skill.

Increase Value by Increasing Expert and Referent Power At first blush, counselors may feel some resistance to the idea of employing power to influence another. Yet, as mental health providers and as educators, we do exert power in service to others. We must exert power if we are to be effective. The power that we are speaking of provides the ability to influence another person's attitudes and or behavior. For example, encouraging a student to expand her perspective on an issue or adjust his way of responding to certain situations are times that as a counselor we may exert our power—our power to influence.

There are many forms of social power. In a now-classic look at power, French and Raven (1959) identified the following forms of social power.

1. Coercive power or the ability to reward and or punish another.

2. Legitimate or traditional power, that is, the power that stems from society's sanctioning of a person's role and authority to control the attitudes and behavior of another, as may be the case with a parent or public official.

3. Informational power is that power accrued because the information provided by one person is viewed as highly relevant and useful by the second.

4. Expert power, or the power that we associate to a person who is perceived as having special knowledge and skill that is valued or necessary by another. This is similar to informational power except that the focus is on the person (in expert power), whereas in informational power it is on what the person says.

5. Referent or identification power is the power to influence that accrues to a person because she is attractive, a person whom another wants to like and be liked by—in short a role model. Most often in referent power a party is viewed as having characteristics similar to the second person or desired by the second person, and as such the second party identifies with the first. It is this process of identification that serves as the source of influence.

When considering increasing the ability of a counselor–consultant to influence another's attitude and or behavior, it would appear that two of the preceding forms of power, expert and referent, are appropriate avenues for a consultant to demonstrate value within the system. As such, they are discussed in more depth following.

Expert Power The very nature of asking the consultant for assistance would suggest that the consultant is perceived as having some form of expertise and thus expert power. When the counselor–consultant's particular knowledge or skill proves useful to those within the client system (e.g., the consultee), then the consultant's value and resultant power are increased. And as might be assumed, as the consultant's value and power increase, resistance to the consultant and her innovations should decrease.

Research demonstrates that the perception of expertise and the resulting assignment of expert power to another can be enhanced by indications of advanced education, relevant experience, and higher social status, for example: awards, citations, or affiliation with prestigious institutions (Martin, 1978). Therefore consultants attempting to increase their expert power should find ways to communicate their experience and education and highlight factors that could increase their perceived social status (e.g., articles written, testimonials from other consultees, special awards or recognitions received). In addition to these general indicators of expertise, a consultant seeking to effect change, should develop a small number of content areas of real expertise over and above his/her general knowledge and competency.

Expert power is clearly a useful tool for effecting change. However, as presented here, consultation is a relational process. It is a process in which the consultee needs to feel as if she can approach the consultant and work openly with him. Thus in addition to having specialized knowledge and skill, which makes the consultant "different" from the consultee, the consultant must also exhibit conditions that facilitate rapport and connectedness with the consultee (Caplan, 1970; Dinkmeyer & Carlson, 1973; Parsons & Meyers, 1984). In fact, relying solely on expert power may be detrimental to the effectiveness of the consultant in that it places the consultant in a one-up position inviting the consultee to anticipate prescription or provision from the "expert" consultant. Bennis, Benne, and Chin (1969) noted: "the extent to which a change agent is successful (that is, influential) is dependent on the degree to which he is perceived as susceptible to influence by the client" (p. 148). Thus one could argue that the more a consultant is perceived as the "expert" the less he or she may be perceived as open to influence by the consultee. Therefore, although exhibiting some expert power, it is important to develop a collegial relationship, one in which the consultant is perceived as coequal, approachable, and susceptible to consultee influence. Under these conditions, a second form of power, referent power, seems to hold special value.

Referent Power When the consultee perceives the consultant as manifesting feelings, attitudes, interests, and behaviors similar to his/her own or to those that he/she would like to possess, the consultant has referent power. Thus the consultant's effectiveness will be enhanced when he shares certain values, personal characteristics, behaviors, background experiences, knowledge, and interest with the consultee. Being able to relate to the local sports teams or political scene; sharing a common cultural background; or simply enjoying the same type of food, music, or entertainment increase one's referent power. Clearly the directive is for the consultant to empathically and nonjudgmentally get to know the consultee while at the same time providing appropriate and parallel self-disclosures. This is often best achieved in informal settings such as the lunchroom, after-work social settings, break rooms, or even at the water cooler.

Blending and Balancing Power The use of expert and referent power might at first appear somewhat incompatible because it is difficult to highlight one's unique expertise while at the same time emphasizing one's similarity. Yet a proper blending of expert and referent power is what is called for. Research suggests that too much expertise reduces one's attraction value, and logic dictates that too much referent power, where the consultee sees the consultant as having the same expertise and knowledge as they do, will result in the consultee not seeking the consultant's advice. Thus the consultant who has accrued a good deal of referent power will benefit from emphasizing her expertise. This is often the case in which a counselor who previously had spent years as a faculty member may, when stepping into the new position of counselor–consultant, have to emphasize his or her new knowledge and skills. Under these conditions it may be important for the consultant to publicize recent professional involvement or scholarship, communicate (even using professional jargon) knowledge of relevant information, and demonstrate (perhaps by providing in-service training) competency in specific areas of expertise.

On the other hand, the consultant who is perceived as expert will do well to balance this perception by highlighting points of commonality between himself and his consultee. This may especially be true for the counselor–consultant new to the system or called in to assist another system. Their presence in the school may have been preceded by information regarding previous training and experience and perhaps even testimonials of success, but the *person* of the consultant is still an unknown. Under these conditions, the counselor–consultant would do well to spend time in the informal settings getting known and getting to know the consultee.

Demonstrating practical and immediate usefulness (i.e., doing something) along with developing expert and referent power are useful tools for the consultant seeking to decrease resistance and diffuse innovation. Exercise 5.4 will help the reader more fully understand the concepts described and begin to concretely apply these concepts.

EXERCISE 5.4

Increasing Power and Value

Part I directions: Following is a description of a presenting complaint, along with the characteristics of the consultee and the system involved in this consult. After reading the descriptions, answer the questions that follow. It would also be beneficial for you to share your response with a colleague, classmate, or supervisor because each consultant differs in both areas of expertise and referent abilities and thus will most likely respond differently to the opportunities presented.

Presenting Complaint
The consultee (Dr. Seronita Torres) is principal of Elwood Good Alternative High School. She comes to you with a problem she is having with one of her students. The student, Regina, is 14 years old and a 10th grader at Elwood Good High. Regina is an IV drug user (heroin) who was court assigned to the alternative high school. In addition to her drug involvement, Regina has been living on the streets for the past three months and recently has met a man (age 31) whom she feels she loves. Regina told Dr. Torres that she was considering secretly trapping her boyfriend into marriage by becoming pregnant. Dr. Torres has attempted to get Regina to see the potential danger involved with her decisions, but nothing she has said appears effective. Dr. Torres admitted that she does not know what to do with Regina and would really like your assistance.

Consultee and Consultee Setting

Dr. Torres is a 57-year-old principal with a doctorate in education from the University of Mexico and a master's in counseling (having been a counselor for 8 years prior to becoming a principal). Dr. Torres has been in this country 18 months and has been working at her current position for only 9 weeks. She states that she feels somewhat "out of her element" working in her current setting.

The school services an inner-city, poor population of identified SED students. Most of the students are either Hispanic Americans or African Americans. Dr. Torres revealed that she has limited knowledge and experience working with this population and that she took this position as a temporary post while she gained experience as a principal. Dr. Torres noted that she was able to get the job because of her political connections.

Dr. Torres comes from a very affluent and influential family in Mexico City. She expressed her difficulty with truly understanding the experience of the people with whom she works, given her background, which included private schooling, extensive family affiliations, and "strict Catholic values." Dr. Torres also expressed her interest in and concern about the role and future of females within the Hispanic culture, and she is very politically active on women's rights.

You are the first counselor to be used by the staff at the school. Previously, all mental health services were out serviced. It is clear that although Dr. Torres wants some assistance, she is also very concerned about how her peers and supervisors may perceive her if they know she sought consultation.

Consider each of the following and discuss in as concrete terms as possible.

#1. Expert Power: What specific area of expertise do you bring to this situation? How might you convey this expertise to Dr. Torres and to the other staff, as a way of diffusing the potential resistance to your presence?

#2. Referent Power: Identify at least two areas of dissimilarity and two areas of similarity between yourself and Dr. Torres. What elements could you highlight as a way of eliciting referent power? How would you reduce the perception of difference?

#3. Do Something: Given the concerns expressed by Dr. Torres, what one, immediate thing would you do to demonstrate your value?

Principle 5: Move in a Crisis

The old adage "If it ain't broke, don't fix it" bodes poorly for those of us with prevention focus. When systems are at points of equilibrium and stability and are not experiencing pain, resistance to change will be at its maximum. Thus, a final principal of diffusion of innovation is to be alert to signs of instability and disequilibrium as opportunities for diffusing innovation. Thus the directive for the counselor–consultant is to move in a crisis.

When experiencing a crisis, individuals and systems are placed into a disequilibrium and what results are feelings of imbalance and urgency. For example, consider the impact that recent incidents of school violence and sensational news stories have had on creating a multitude of "safe schools" and "at-risk" initiatives. One local school district, for example, installed expensive security systems within its school, even though the district was facing fiscal crises. Similarly, numerous schools have implemented zero tolerance policies in regard to school violence and the use of "terroristic" language. Other schools have trained teachers and staff in lock-down procedures. All these innovations, disruptive as they were to the normal way of operating, were rapidly implemented with little resistance. The ability to diffuse this type of change was facilitated by the crisis nature of the times.

When a system is in pain, it is more receptive to possible solutions that will help lead it back to a point of stabilization. Thus the counselor–consultant, seeking to act as an agent of change, needs to be sensitive to points of disequilibrium and to be able to respond at moments of these crises. Consider the case of Ms. L. Jackson, a counselor at a rural elementary school. After attending a professional conference on "Postvention: Responding to School Suicide," Ms. Jackson returned and developed a proposal for a postvention response plan for her school. The plan outlined the steps to be taken and the community resources that could be brought in for support. Although her program was well developed and in line with the sample programs she acquired at the conference, the principal and the school board were resistant to even considering such a program. The general feeling was that these programs are needed in urban schools where, as the principal explained, "these type of things (suicide) happen . . . not here!"

Over the course of the next two years, Ms. Jackson attempted to reshape her proposal so that it would be more palatable to administration, but to no avail. Sadly, it was the joint suicides of two 5th-grade students that moved the system to adopt her program.

On a Monday in October, the school returned to the news that two 5th-grade students had committed suicide the previous Sunday. The school was thrown into absolute chaos. Students and teachers flooded Ms. Jackson's office showing signs of shock. Parents hysterically called the school and attempted to remove their children. And the principal was completely frustrated by his inability to gain any direction from the central office as to what steps he should take.

Ms. Jackson stepped into this crises and gained permission to contact her community resources and to begin the procedures that she had attempted to implement two years prior. Although no hard data was collected, it may be fair to assume that the existence of a well-thought-out program and this counselor's ability to make contact with community mental health providers, who were able to come to school to provide immediate crises counseling for all, helped this school community avoid even further disaster.

However, waiting for the disruption to the stability of the organization before having innovations embraced may not be desirable. Consultants may need to use data feedback pointing to problems and possible implications as a way of highlighting the sense of urgency and crisis. If successful, this will produce the disequilibrium that can allow innovation. For example, the consultant who provides a principal with demographic data and projections on the declining tax base for the school district may find that the data serve as the stimulus for consideration of innovation to the way counseling services are delivered within the school. Or the counselor–consultant, attempting to introduce a peer mediation program may find it helpful to present data showing (a) the increase in number of incidents of student conflicts, (b) the increase amount of time spent by teachers and the vice-principal in resolving student conflict (time taken away from other more professional duties), and (c) the predicted increase in student conflict, which may result as a function of next year's merger with a previous rival school. These data may help to elevate the principal's "felt" pain to the point where the discomfort of change appears to be less than the potential costs (in terms of student conflict) of nonchange. Although we may like to believe that good ideas can simply stand on their own merit, when it comes to change, we agree with Kurpius, Brack, Brack and Dunn (1993) that it is "the frame that one's pain is reducible that is critical to implementing the motivation to change" (p. 424). Exercise 5.5 will help clarify this point of moving in a crisis.

EXERCISE 5.5

Highlighting and Moving in a Crisis

Part I directions: For each of the following scenarios identify
a. The felt or perceived area of crisis
b. How you as consultant could use that as a point of diffusing innovation and as an aid to reaching the listed goal

Scenario 1
Conditions: The consultee is a high school principal. Her school has recently experienced an increase in student population and faculty as a result of absorbing the students and faculty from a neighboring school that was forced to close. Recent student conflict (gang fights) has stimulated the principal to call you in to provide assertive discipline training for the teachers so that they can learn to intervene before problems emerge.

Problem: Besides the student problem with assimilating, the faculties from both schools were exhibiting symptoms of burnout. Faculty from the school that had closed had not adequately grieved the loss of their school and its tradition. The host faculty felt resentment toward the new faculty and anger at the crowding caused by their presence. The host faculty were also somewhat jealous of the attention the new faculty were receiving. Both faculties reported feeling disempowered, having not been consulted or really even advised about the move until the very last moment.

Goal: To reduce the faculties' feelings of disenfranchisement and facilitate faculty ownership and decision making around the steps to be taken to develop a blended identify of the two schools.

Consultant strategy:_____

Scenario 2: Middle School Guidance Department. Although there are no immediate problems that the chair or the other counselors have reported, you observe that the amount of work as well as the complexity and severity of the cases managed has clearly increased over the course of the last year.

Problem (identify potential problem area):

_____

_____

Goal (identify change in the current operation that may prevent the problem from developing):

_____

_____

Strategy (identify how you, as counselor–consultant, could reframe the lack of pain to encourage change):

_____

_____

SUMMARY

Consultation—Inevitably Impacting the System

The role of the consultant is clearly one of change. A consultant not only intervenes with the client, but also does so in ways that impact the extrapersonal variables affecting the client. It is important to remember that even when the specific focus of the consultation *is not* on organizational change, the preventive–extrapersonal focus of consultation will result in system change.

Counselor-as-Consultant:
Advocating for Client *and* System

The counselor–consultant is truly an agent of change, working to bring the system goals and individual goals into harmony in order to reflect the mission for which they have come together. Attempting to serve as advocate for the client and advocate for the system is possible, but not without points of tension and conflict.

Reaction and Resistance

Systems have developed a number of mechanisms through which they attempt to maintain the status quo and thus by definition resist any form of change that may be perceived as threatening to the balance of power, the utilization of resources, or simply the existing state of functioning. Consultants need to be able to recognize these points of system resistance and navigate through them using a model of planned change.

Promoting Innovation

Innovation, or change, is most readily embraced when a number of principles are taken into consideration. The principals discussed were (a) keep innovation culturally compatible; (b) introduce innovation in small steps, shaping; (c) align innovation with system opinion leaders; (d) increase consultant's value and power within the system; and (e) introduce change at times of system crises.

IMPORTANT TERMS

Adversarial role

Advocacy

Agent for change

Balance of power

Culturally compatible

Diffusion of innovation

Doing something

Expert power

Extrapersonal factors

Group norms

Miscommunications

Mission

Move in a crisis

Opinion leaders

Power

Referent power

Resistance

Self-preservation

Stability

Sunken costs

SUGGESTED READINGS

Bartunek, J. M. (2003). *Organizational and educational change: The life and role of a change agent group.* Mahwah, NJ: Lawrence Erlbaum Associates.

Ellsworth, J. (2001). Eric Digest: A survey of educational change models. *Teacher Librarian, 29*(2), 22–25.

Kezar, A. (2001). Organizational models and facilitators of change: Providing a framework for student and academic affairs collaboration. *New Directions for Higher Education,* 116.

Marcus, E. C. (2000). Change processes and conflict. In M. Deutsch, & P. T. Coleman, (Eds.), *The handbook of conflict resolution: Theory and practice* (pp. 366–381). San Francisco: Jossey-Bass.

WEB SITES

National Education Policy Network: Checklist of components of a Crisis Prevention Program. http://www.renew.net/prevstat.htm

Visionomics: The comprehensive process for understanding, measuring and enhancing any organizational workplace culture. http://www.visionomics.com

Applied Learning Labs: Learning and knowledge map tools to make organizational change happen. http://www.appliedlearninglab.com

Journal of Educational Change: Comprehensive review and updates on educational change. www/wkap.nl/jmltoc.htm/1389-2843

REFERENCES

Argyris, C. (1970). *Intervention theory and method: A behavioral science view.* Reading, MA: Addison-Wesley.

Bartunek, J., & Moch, M. (1987). First-order, second-order and third-order change and organizational development interventions: A cognitive approach. *The Journal of Applied Behavioral Science, 23*(4), 483–500.

Bartunek, J. M., Louis, M. R. (1988). The interplay of organization development and organization transformation. In W. A. Pasmore & R. W. Woodman (Eds.), *Research in organizational change and development* (vol. 2, pp. 97–134). Greenwich, CT: JAI.

Beer, M., & Spector, B. (1993). Organizational diagnosis: Its role in organizational consultation. *Journal of Counseling and Development, 71*, 642–650.

Bennis, W. G., Benne, K. D., & Chin, R. (Eds.). (1969). *The planning of change.* New York: Holt, Rinehart & Winston.

Blake, R. R., & Mouton, J. S. (1976). *Consultation.* Reading, MA: Addison-Wesley.

Brown, D., Blackurn, J. E., & Powell, W. C. (1979). *Consultation.* Boston: Allyn & Bacon.

Caplan, G. (1970). *The theory and practice of mental health consultation* New York: Basic Books.

de Jager, P. (2001). Resistance to change: A new view of an old problem. *Futurist, 35*(3), p 24.

Dinkmeyer, D., & Carlson, J. (1973). *Consulting: Facilitating human potential and change processes.* Columbus, OH: Merrill.

Eldridge, C. R. (2001). Organizational congruent values: Effects on attitudes for planned change and innovation in a production environment. *Dissertation Abstracts,* No. AAI3028847. Ann Arbor, MI: UMI.

Ellsworth, J. B. (2000). Surviving change: A survey of educational change models. Washington DC: Office of Educational Research and Improvement. (ERIC Document Reproduction Service No. ED443417)

French, J. R. P., Jr., & Raven, B. (1959). The bases of social power. In D. Cartwright (Ed.), *Studies in social power.* Ann Arbor: University of Michigan Institute of Social Research.

French, W. L., & Bell, C. H., Jr. (1990). *Organization development* (4th ed.). Englewood Cliffs, NJ: Prentice Hall.

Friend, M., & Bauwens, J. (1988). Managing resistance: An essential consulting skill for learning disabilities teachers. *Journal of Learning Disabilities, 21*(9), 556–561.

Fuqua, D. R., & Gibson, G. (1980). *An investigation of factors related to the durability of organizational innovations in human service systems.* Paper presented at the annual convention of the American Psychological Association, Montreal, Canada.

Gray, J. L. (1984). *Supervision: An applied behavioral science approach to managing people.* Boston: Kent Publishers.

Kast, F. Z., & Rosenzweig, J. E. (1974). *Organization and management: A systems approach* (2nd ed.). New York: McGraw-Hill.

Kurpius, D. J. (1985). Consultation interventions. *The Counseling Psychologist, 13*, 368–389.

Kurpius, D. J., Brack, G., Brack, C. J., & Dunn, L. B. (1993). Maturation of systems consultation: Subtle issues inherent in the model. *Journal of Mental Health Counseling, 15*(4), 414–429.

Lewis, L. K. (1999). Disseminating information and soliciting input during planned organizational change: Implementers' targets, sources, and channels for communicating. *Management Communication Quarterly, 13*(1), 43–75.

Lewis, L. K. (2000). "Blindsided by that one" and "I saw that one coming": The relative anticipation and occurrence of communication problems and other problems in implementers' insight. *Journal of Applied Communication Research, 28*(1), 44–67.

Lippitt, G. (1982, August). Developing HRD an DOD, the profession and the professional. *Training and Development, 36,* 67–74.

Martin, R. (1978). Expert and referent power: A framework for understanding and maximizing consultation effectiveness. *Journal of School Psychology, 16*(1), 49–55.

Mohrman, A. M., Jr., Mohrman, S. A., Ledford, G. E., Jr., Cummings, T., Lawler, E. E., III, & Associates. (1989). *Large-scale organizational change.* San Francisco: Jossey-Bass.

Napierkowski, C., & Parsons, R. (1995). Diffusion of innovation: A model for implementing a change in role and function of counselors within the schools. *The School Counselor, 42,* 364–369.

Parsons, R. (1996). *The skilled consultant.* Needham Heights, MA: Allyn & Bacon.

Parsons, R., & Meyers, J. (1984). *Developing consultation skills.* San Francisco: Jossey-Bass.

Rogers, E. M., & Shoemaker, F. F. (1971). *Communication of innovations.* New York: Free Press.

Schmuck, R. A., & Runkel, P. J. (1985). *The handbook of organizational development in schools* (3rd ed.). Palo Alto, CA: Mayfield.

Torbert, W. (1985). On-line reframing. *Organizational Dynamics, 14*(1), 60–79.

Weick, K. E. (1984). Small wins. *American Psychologist, 39*(1), 40–49.

Wickstrom, K. F., & Witt, J. C. (1993). Resistance within school-based consultation. In J. E. Zins, T. R. Kratochwill, & S. N. Elliot (Eds.), *Handbook of consultation services for children* (pp. 159–178). San Francisco: Jossey-Bass.

Willing, L. F. (2002). Making difficult change. *Fire Engineering, 155*(8), 81–84.

Facilitating the Consultative Process

6

⟨∾⟩

The Stages of the Consultation Process

Well . . . miracle upon miracle. I finally got
Dr. J. to meet with me. I know he's got a lot going on but
I really want him to work with me in trying to decide
what if anything needs to be done for Ellen.

I really need to think about this first meeting. This first
meeting is key if I am going to be able to establish a collaborative
relationship, one that will continue through the entire process.
So I need to really do a little planning for that meeting.

Our consultant, Mr. Thomas, is certainly aware of the need for his own premeeting preparation. This first meeting will set the stage for all that is to follow. He is also aware that regardless of the mode of consultation to be employed, the process of consultation involves a series of specific and recognizable stages of action, and each of the stages requires planning if the entire process is to be successful. It is these specific and recognizable stages of consultation along with the unique task demands of each stage that serve as the focus for this chapter. Additionally, we will introduce aspects of brief or solution focused interventions that can enhance the formulation of goals and the creation of solutions. A much more comprehensive discussion of solution focused consultation will be offered in chapter 9.

It should be noted that although this chapter offers a thorough exposition of each of the stages of consultation, a caveat is in order. The stages are presented and described as if they are separate, discrete, experiences, but such is not the case in the world of application. In the practice of consultation the consultant will experience the stages sometimes occurring in neat, linear order, whereas at other times, the experience will suggest that the consultation process is cycling in and out of various stages almost simultaneously. Thus, although the discrete, linear presentation makes it easier for this book presentation, it is not to be assumed that these stages will occur in neat, discrete, or invariant order within the real world of practice.

CHAPTER OBJECTIVES

After completing this chapter, the reader should be able to

1. Describe the overall scope and sequence of the consultation process
2. Describe each of the six stages of the consultation process with respect to rationale, relationship factors, and consultant and consultee roles and functions
3. Describe some of the unique features of a solution focused approach to school-based consultation

PREENTRY: CREATING CONDITIONS FOR SUCCESSFUL CONSULTATION

As with any service provided by a school counselor, careful, deliberate planning is required if consultation—as a mode of service delivery—will be successful. This planning and preparation starts well before the reception of the first request for service.

Establishing Norms and Expectations

How teachers, parents, administrators, and even students approach the school counselor for help, or even if they choose to do so, cannot be a matter left to chance. The systemic norms that exist in any school prescribe the expectations for the counselor's role and function in resolving school problems and achieving certain outcomes. The counselor seeking to employ a consultation mode of service delivery needs to establish the expectation among those employing her service that as a resource for change, she approaches her duties as a collaborative process, a partnership if you will. This is a critical systemic norm that must be established and maintained by the counselor.

Implied in this norm is the schoolwide belief that everyone who experiences a concern about another person or group can easily refer themselves to the school counselor for help in resolving this concern. Furthermore, in referring themselves for help they are agreeing to be active participants in the resolution or change process. Whether this agreement is implicit or explicit in the form of contracts and codified protocols, its existence is essential for consultant–consultee collaboration to occur.

Our case example of Dr. Jameson's referral of Ellen to the school counselor is indicative of a school norm that mitigates against consultant–consultee collaboration. In Dr. Jameson's referral, he asked Mr. Thomas to see Ellen as quickly as possible to begin the diagnostic–remediation process. Implied in Dr. Jameson's referral is the expectation that Mr. Thomas will take over the change process, and that Dr. Jameson's role in the process ends with the referral. This traditional clinical model of the school counselor's role and function places all responsibility for diagnosis and remediation of the problem in the hands of the counselor and diminishes the role of the referring person to that of passive observer. Unfortunately, it is the school counselor's desire to be helpful and competent that easily prompts the counselor to succumb to the trap, thus perpetuating the norm that individuals refer others to the counselor for help, and that the counselor will fix them up and send them back to the referring person.

Upon receiving the referral from Dr. Jameson, Mr. Thomas was acutely aware of the challenge and opportunity to shape a school norm of collaborative consultation. Instead of seeing Ellen for counseling or observing/diagnosing her functioning directly, Mr. Thomas wisely choose to schedule a meeting with Dr. Jameson to discuss the referral and build a collaborative, working relationship. By meeting with Dr. Jameson first, Mr. Thomas established the critical norms that are the foundation of collaborative consultation.

Provisions for Preentry

Creating conditions for collaboration is the goal of preentry. This goal can be accomplished in a number of ways. First, all the counselor's prospective consultees must be informed that the counselor is a resource for consultation. Second, the counselor must establish and maintain an efficient and timely referral procedure that is accessible to and understood by every consumer of counseling services. Third, in every occasion that an individual refers himself to the counselor for help with a third party (client), he needs to understand and expect that the counselor will meet with him first. Further, the consultee needs to accept that he is committing himself to a consultation relationship that will last until the identified concerns are resolved. These are the critical norms that need to be established and maintained as part of the preentry stage of consultation. In Exercise 6.1 you will write a referral that will initiate our consultation process.

EXERCISE 6.1

The Consultation Referral

Directions: Select an educational setting (K–12) in which you are a teacher, parent, student, or administrative consultee. Formulate a real or fabricated situation in which you, as the consultee, write a referral to the counselor–consultant about a concern that you have about a client. This referral will form the basis for your work in subsequent exercises in this chapter. Address the following areas in your referral.

1. Identify the setting.
2. Identify the names and roles of the consultant, consultee, and client.
3. Briefly describe the concern that prompts your referral.
4. Briefly describe what you hope will result from your referral.

Outcome: Share your referral with a colleague, classmate, or instructor. This referral will be used in later exercises.

ENTRY: ESTABLISHING THE CONTRACT FOR CONSULTATION

The first meeting between counselor–consultant and consultee implicitly and explicitly shapes the formation of the working relationship. Each party in the consult brings a host of expectations about how the process will proceed, the criteria that will determine success and failure, and the role and function performed by the consultant, consultee, and client. How do we want to work together? What expertise and expectations does each of us bring to our cooperative problem solving and decision making? These are the questions to be addressed as the parties enter the consultation process.

If the consultee has no previous experience with consultation or with this particular counselor, it is incumbent on the consultant to provide sufficient structure to the first meeting so that the aforementioned questions are addressed and the consultee leaves the session feeling optimistic and that the first meeting was productive. The focus of the initial discussion will, to a very large extent, depend on the severity of the concern brought by the consultee. On occasion, a teacher, parent, or administrator has struggled with a problem unsuccessfully to the point that they feel highly frustrated, angry, defeated, and helpless. Their referral of themselves to the counselor for help may be the culmination of many failed efforts. Consequently, they begin the consultation with trepidation and discouragement. A heightened level of helplessness may cause them to defer all diagnostic and remedial responsibility to the consultant. In these more extreme crisis situations, the consultant must quickly and astutely decide if the consultee currently possesses the resources and motivation to collaborate in the diagnostic or remediation process. If the consultant believes that the consultee is not ready for collaboration, and thus fails to display a positive perspective that encourages the goal and potential for readiness, the consultant will initiate a provisional or prescriptive modality for consultation. Even under these conditions of less than full engagement, the consultant will invite the consultee to participate and collaborate as much as possible. In this case the consultant encourages the consultee to "tell their story" and express their feelings that emanate from that story. The structuring issues to be described will still need to be addressed, even within these consultant-directed modalities.

In some cases the consultee will be capable of fully entering into a collaborative consultation but will need to express their story and feel heard and understood by the consultant. The credibility and expert power of the consultant will increase significantly as the consultant is able to demonstrate accurate empathy with the consultee. The use of active listening skills (the subject of chapter 7) to hear and reinforce consultee self-disclosure is an essential ingredient in the consultant's repertoire of skills throughout the consultation process, but especially in the stages of entry and exploration.

When the consultee is in crisis over a client, structuring issues should be deferred until the consultee has satisfactorily expressed the concern. Fortunately, most school-based consultations will not be under crisis conditions. Consequently, the consultant can address structuring issues before plunging into exploration of the consultee's concerns. The purpose of structuring the consult is to establish clear, practical, and acceptable guidelines for when, where, how, and why the consult is to occur. The key points to be addressed when structuring the consult are

- Emphasize that the outcome objective of the consult is resolution of the consultee's concern.

- When possible, the process leading to that outcome will involve a working partnership (collaboration) between the consultant and consultee.

- Decide on convenient times and locations for meeting. Frequently, the best location for meeting is in the work environment of the consultee. This increases the comfort of the consultee and sensitizes the consultant to the working conditions of the consultee.

- Each meeting will be structured with a specific purpose and agenda and can be initiated by either the consultant or consultee.

- The consultee brings critical (expert) knowledge about the client and the environment in which the consultee and client are working. The consultant's expertise may be technical or in the facilitation of change processes. Optimal success of the consult will require the expertise of both parties.

- Any decision for the consultant to work directly with the client (for diagnostic or remedial purposes) will be made collaboratively by the consultee and consultant.

- The professional ethics of confidentiality (and privileged communication where appropriate) apply to the consultant–consultee relationship just as it would in individual counseling. The exceptions to confidentiality under Duty to Warn considerations equally apply in consultation. The consultee should be informed that whenever a threat to the consultee or anyone else is perceived by the consultant, this information must be reported to the appropriate authorities (probably the school principal) for action.

■ These structuring points can be codified into a written contract
that can be discussed and signed by the consultant and consultee.
A sample of such a contract can be found in Figure 6.1.
Exercise 6.2 is provided to further assist you in this stage of
consultation.

POINTS OF AGREEMENT
IN THIS CONSULT

The outcome objective of the consult is resolution of the consultee's
concern.

■ Pursuing this outcome will involve a working partnership
(collaboration) between the consultant and consultee.

■ Our consults will occur at times and locations that are acceptable
to both parties.

■ Each meeting will be structured with specific purpose
and agenda and can be initiated by either the consultant or
consultee.

■ The consultee brings critical (expert) knowledge about the client
and the environment in which the consultee and client are
working. The consultant's expertise may be technical or in the
facilitation of change processes. Optimal success of the consult will
require the expertise of both parties.

■ Any decision for the consultant to work directly with the client
(for diagnostic or remedial purposes) will be made collaboratively
by the consultee and consultant.

■ The professional ethics of confidentiality (and privilege
communication where appropriate) will be maintained throughout
this consult. The exceptions to confidentiality under Duty to
Warn considerations will also be maintained. Whenever a threat
to the consultee or anyone else is perceived by the consultant this
information must be reported to the appropriate authorities after
discussion with the consultee.

_____   _____   _____

CONSULTANT   CONSULTEE   DATE

FIGURE 6.1 Sample Consultation Contract

EXERCISE 6.2

Setting the Contract

Directions: Using the structure provided by the consultation contract (Figure 6.1), you are to role-play a consult at the entry level that revolves around the contract issues. You will perform this role play with colleague or classmate, rotating the roles of consultant and consultee. For each role play the consultee will use the referral written in Exercise 6.1 as the basis for the meeting. The consultee will share their referral with the consultant, and the consultant will then conduct the first session of entry using the contract.

Outcome: Share your signed contract with a colleague or instructor as a means of monitoring the completeness of the contract.

Once structuring issues have been addressed, the consultation moves into an exploration of the problem or concern experienced by the consultee.

EXPLORATION: DEFINING THE PROBLEM AND ITS HISTORY

By the time that a consultee has made a referral to the school counselor, the consultee has already invested time and effort into resolving the problem. The consultee's experience (albeit subjective perception) of the problem as it exists in the present as well as its history are best understood by the consultee. Moreover, the consultee and consultant may feel strongly that a productive consult can only occur if the consultant has a clear, thorough understanding of the consultee's perspective. Consequently, the consultant will use active listening and communication skills to elicit problem-related information from the consultee. The consultee will be encouraged to describe the problem or concern as it currently exists, the relevant background and history of the problem, and all successful and unsuccessful previous efforts at problem resolution. This thorough exploration of the presenting problem culminates only when the consultant and consultee have achieved consensual validation of the consultee's perspective. The attainment of this consensus can be ascertained when the consultant is able to accurately summarize the perspective offered by the consultee. When the consultee replies, "Yes, you've got the entire picture correctly" in response to this summary, the consultant can be confident that exploration is accurate and complete.

The emphasis placed on a thorough exploration of the problem has recently been questioned by those individuals embracing a brief or solution focused approach to consultation (e.g., Davis & Osborn, 2000; De Jong & Berg, 1998). The position taken here is that such a solution-focused approach to purposeful change need not be in conflict with the model of consultation offered here. This point will be elaborated on later within this chapter and again in chapter 9. For now, we will look at those strategies that will produce an accurate understanding (i.e., diagnosis) of the concern or problem brought by the consultee.

Gathering and Organizing the Data

Consultees will disclose a great deal of information as they "tell their story." Sometimes their exposition will be clear and well organized. The description of *what* is occurring and the diagnosis for *why* will be cogently understood and articulated by the consultee. This level of clarity is not always present, however, and the problem that is described and explained by the consultee may be confusing, incomplete, incongruent, or even inaccurate. Such deficiencies in consultee disclosure can result from consultee bias, stress created by the crisis itself, or the consultee's inability to reflect on and organize problem-related information. This latter cognitive deficiency results when the consultee lacks an organizing schema with which to recognize and differentiate relevant problem information and organize that information so that patterns can be recognized and understood.

The teacher who can only describe random and disconnected anecdotes about the problem (and client) may be unable to see the problem holistically and thus lacks the schema or paradigm that would enable them to approach the problem diagnostically and prescriptively. For example, consider the case of a teacher who is exasperated by what appears to be a student's frequent and random acts of violence and aggression. The teacher perceives each act of bullying or fighting by the student as disobedience and brutality and responds with punitive disciplinary action. The punishments employed include lecturing, removal of privileges, and internal and external suspension. These prove ineffective. However, even though these fail to produce change in the behavior, the teacher continues to employ these strategies anyway.

Had this teacher used a cognitive schema or paradigm for understanding aggression in children, she or he might have seen the broader dynamics of this student's world. The absence of empathy skills, the presence of aggressive role models (i.e., parents or siblings), the absence of successful pro-social and academic experiences at school, and the possibility of emotional and cognitive disabilities such as depression and Attention Deficit Hyperactive Disorder all come into focus when a problem is viewed through a comprehensive and integrative schema.

Regardless of which model or empirically valid organizing framework is used, it is imperative that the consultant and consultee conduct their exploration through a congruent organizing filter. In addition to helping us understand the human experience, these organizing frameworks offer clear, congruent strategies for purposeful change. When consultees enter a consult without an organizing schema, often the most salutary benefit that they derive from the consult is the organizing schema that is modeled by the consultant.

One such organizing schemata is the cognitive–behavioral paradigm (Kahn, 1999), which is discussed in the next section. "Another, the multimodal approach of Arnold Lazarus (Lazarus, 1989), will be presented in chapter 9. Readers interested in a more developed presentation of either of these models are referred to Kahn (1999) and Lazarus (1989), respectively. These two models offered by the authors for organizing information provided by the consultee have been empirically validated (Cormier & Nurius, 2003; Spiegler & Guevremont, 1998) and are easily expandable to each of the six stages of the consultation process.

The A-B-C Model   The components of the A-B-C (cognitive–behavioral) model follow a linear or chronological sequence. Thus we will start with the "A" component, the external environment or context in which our behavior occurs.

A   This is the *a*ntecedent stimulus or external environmental event that starts the behavioral episode. The "A" is something (time, place, person, object, or event) in the external environment that signals the start of your thinking and acting behavior.

Some antecedents signal or enable behavior to occur, thus we can think of these as green light "As." These green light "As" tell us that certain thoughts or actions will lead to desirable consequences. Other antecedents prevent behavior from occurring or signal not to perform the behavior because the consequence will be undesirable. We might call these red light "As." Whether these external stimuli inform us to "go" or "stop," they derive their intent from the perceived consequences that will result from our actions.

B/Covert   The covert behavior represents the content and process of how we think. These covert behaviors comprise the subjective world that exists in your head and are comparable to the cognition modality in the multimodal model.

These covert behaviors represent the subjective world that exists in our heads. These thoughts can be labeled *covert behaviors* because although you cannot see or measure them directly, they can be purposely generated or eliminated, much like our actions (acting behavior or operants). Many of our thoughts consist of our interpretation of the messages sent from our external environment (i.e., "A"), the array of responses we could give to these messages (i.e., "B"), and the consequences (i.e., "C") that would result from the behavioral responses we choose to make. We might experience these thoughts as images or self-talk that essentially inform us: "When this **A** occurs . . . I better do this **B** . . . if I want this **C** to result. Each covert response is probably based on some past experience, and each will elicit its own behavior. Also, these thoughts can provoke emotional reactions to experiences and in turn prompt subsequent actions leading to further thoughts and emotions.

Our emotions are a critical dimension of our covert experience and represent the subjective meaning and associated label that we use for the feeling or emotion connected to any particular experience. Emotions are the meaning or interpretation we give to the composite A-B-C of an experience. And the affective labels (typically formed as adjectives) that we use, such as

sad, frightened, angry, excited, worried, or guilty, are the language symbols
that we use to convey the As, Bs, and Cs of our immediate experience.

B/Respondent In the A-B-C Model respondents are our involuntary,
physiological–biochemical responses to either *antecedent* stimuli or the covert
expectation of a particular consequence (i.e., "C"). In the expectation of a
punishing or aversive consequence, our body mobilizes itself physically (i.e.,
increasing muscle tension and arousal) in preparation to cope (fight or flight)
with the perceived threat. We often call this increased mobilization anxiety,
and our coping response the general adaptation syndrome (Selye, 1974).

B/Operant Behavior that is voluntary and operates on the environment to produce desirable consequences is referred to as operant behavior. We choose to
do operant behavior because we expect (covert expectations stored in our
head) that it will either get us something desirable or enable us to avoid or
escape something undesirable. In most instances clients will experience problems that result from inappropriate behavior that they do too much of or at the
wrong time and place or not enough at the appropriate time and place. The
appropriateness of operant behavior is determined by its success in achieving
the desired consequences. This leads us to the last component of the model.

C Consequences represent the immediate or long-term results of the operant
behavior preceding it. Consequences can occur as objects, events, or activities
that we experience as desirable or undesirable. We tend to engage in behaviors
that produce desirable consequences (i.e., positive reinforcement) or prevent
undesirable consequences (i.e., negative reinforcement). In both cases, reinforcement can be experienced as either extrinsic (from the environment) or
intrinsic (from within ourselves). Whereas positive and negative reinforcement
tends to motivate and increase behavior, unpleasant consequences can deter
behavior or prevent it from occurring altogether. Punishment (i.e., receiving
an aversive or painful consequence) can stop behavior or prevent it from
occurring. Likewise, the removal of positively reinforcing consequences will
stifle motivation and extinguish behavior. Consequently, it is crucial to identify the antecedents–behavior–consequences that clients and consultees
experience in understanding their concerns and their desire for change.

The value of an organizing model, such as this A-B-C model, is that it
offers templates or guides for systematically assessing the client's situation.
As such, the model enables the consultant and consultee to more specifically
and more concretely define the nature and scope of the client's concern as the
first step to formulating useful and achievable goals and outcomes.

In consulting with teachers and parents (as well as counselor education students) one author will usually place a large, blank piece of paper on the table
and organize the information provided by the consultee within an A-B-C
framework. This collaborative exploring and organizing reinforces consultee
disclosure and helps to bring order and understanding of events that seemed
chaotic and random. The building of an A-B-C perspective of the problem is

solely collaborative as the consultant and consultee add pieces to the problem puzzle. The final product is a shared perspective that easily leads to consensual validation of the problem and direct implications for our subsequent stages of goal/objective and strategy formulation. Perhaps the most valuable and long-lasting benefit of a collaborative exploration with an organizing schema is the consultee's mastery of the schema and its subsequent use in defining and resolving problems.

You may recall that we said that consultation has both a remedial and a preventive focus. As such, a critical objective of collaborative consultation is to help our consultees to be autonomous problem solvers spurred on by an internal locus of control. Helping them to formulate comprehensive, valid, and practical organizing schemata will move them significantly toward that goal. Exercise 6.3 will help you employ some of what we just discussed.

EXERCISE 6.3

Exploring and Defining the Problem

Directions: For this exercise two colleagues or students will work together using their referrals (written in Exercise 6.1) as the reference for data collection. Each colleague/student is to serve as the consultant using the consultee's referral as the basis for doing an A-B-C analysis of the client in the referral. The consultant and consultee are to identify (or fabricate) data about the client and the situation so that an A-B-C profile of the client emerges. Each analysis is to be conducted collaboratively. After the first analysis is completed, the roles are to be reversed and the second analysis is to be performed with the new consultant.

Outcome: Each written analysis is to be reviewed and discussed.

As consensual validation of the problem is achieved, the focus of collaboration will move from "What is happening now?" to "How do we want things to be?" We are ready to formulate our outcome goals and objectives.

OUTCOME GOALS AND OBJECTIVES:
MOVING TOWARD SOLUTIONS

Every consultee is seeking change. Although the target for this change is most often the client, as we will see in subsequent chapters, quite often a change in the thoughts and actions of the consultee, or even a change in the system, may be required to eventually affect a change in the client. But regardless of the specific target, change will be desired. The nature and direction of that change will usually become clear as the existing concern is defined, clarified, and agreed upon.

Whether a consultant takes a traditional problem exploration and definition approach to establishing goals and outcomes or employs a solution-focused model of goal setting (see chapter 9), the formulation of viable outcome goals and objectives is crucial to purposeful change. Consideration of how the consultee would like it to be (for client, system, or self) when consultation is successfully completed prompts the formulation of broad outcome goals.

How would you like things to be? How will you know if our consultation is successful? How could you tell if the problem no longer existed? These are all questions posed by the consultant to the consultee for the purpose of formulating desired outcome goals. These are also the questions that move us from problem focus to goal orientation. Whereas the importance of goal setting has recently been discussed in the solution-focused literature, application of such a solution-focused approach to consultation has only recently began to appear in the literature (Juhnke, 1996; Kahn, 2000; LaFountain & Gerner, 1996; Mostert, Johnson, & Mostert, 1997; Paull & McGrevin, 1996; Santa Rita, 1996). The assumptions and considerations of this approach for consultation have been incorporated here and will be more fully developed in chapter 9.

The Creation of Desired Outcome Goals

In chapter 3 we differentiated between systemic outcome **goals** and **objectives.** The same distinctions exist when we construct goals and objectives within the consultation process. Outcome **goals** are broad, general, undefined, and quite vague. They reflect the general form of the desired state or outcome but lack the concrete evidence revealing its actual occurrence. It is most common for consultees to frame their desired state as vague goals and then begin the process of operationally defining those goals into viable objectives. The following are typical examples of broad goal statements.

1. I'd like Frank to get along better with others.
2. Kulina needs to take more responsibility for her work.
3. I wish Todd and Jason would stop picking on Lorraine and Cheryl. They should just be kind and respectful to them.
4. Yolanda hates school. I wish she looked forward to going to school each morning.
5. Ms. Franklin's class would do so much better if she used effective classroom management.
6. We need a policy and set of procedures for dealing with bullies.

There are a few characteristics of these six broad goals that need to be noted. First, each goal statement describes a general, vague change exhibited by a client population. Secondly, each goal statement is worded in positive terms, what the consultee *would like to happen or occur more frequently.* Framing a desired goal in positive terms keeps the focus on what the client (and correspondingly the consultee) will be **doing** when the consult is successful. Third, a critical criterion for any outcome goal is that it describes what the client (or consultee) will be **doing** as opposed to what the client will **not be doing.** One helpful approach in applying these criteria is to use the "Dead Person" standard. If a dead person can perform the stated outcome, then the outcome needs to be restated in **doing** terms. For example, if our first goal example were stated as "I wish Frank would stop fighting with others," it would not meet the Dead Person criterion. A dead person could easily "stop fighting with others." In fact, a dead person never fights with others. Words such as **not, never, stop, eliminate,** and **cease** are adverbs or verbs that are typically used in violation of the Dead Person standard. In other words, your outcome goal needs to describe the **presence** of something rather than the **absence** of something.

Our third goal example, "I wish Todd and Jason would stop picking on Lorraine and Cheryl" clearly violates this criterion. If Todd and Jason were dead they would most certainly stop picking on Lorraine and Cheryl. The next sentence, however, rectifies the violation by stating the desired outcome in the positive, "They should just be kind and respectful to them." Being kind and respectful are behaviors that Todd and Jason can **DO,** and these new behaviors can be modeled, taught, and reinforced. The Dead Person standard equally applies to our formulation of outcome objectives, where the standard is much easier to meet if the criterion is used in formulating the goal. Finally, because the desired change is an increase in specified behavior, that behavior can be taught, and shaped using established principles of behavior change (Cormier & Nurius, 2003; Kanfer & Goldstein, 1991; Kazdin, 1993) that emphasize stimulus control, shaping, and positive (reinforcing) contingency management.

Translating Goals into Objectives

Stating broad goals as desired behavior also facilitates the translation of broad goals into specific outcome objectives. As discussed in chapter 3, outcome objectives are the concrete **evidence** that each goal has been attained. For each goal the objective(s) tells us how we will know, what we will see or hear, the proof that the goal is realized. As the quantitative or qualitative measure of goal attainment the objective offers a clear, unambiguous direction for change as well as a valid means for assessing accountability for our efforts.

Because any single goal can have multiple pieces of evidence, most goals will translate into many objectives. The translation of our six outcome goals into their respective objectives will illustrate this point. Our first goal calls for Frank to get along better with others. If we assume that Frank is a seven-year-old second grader (and knowledge of his age and grade will help us to formulate developmentally appropriate objectives) Frank could demonstrate "getting along better with others" by (a) actively participating in a language arts cooperative group activity, (b) sitting and communicating with a peer at lunch, (c) sharing play equipment with his peers at recess, or (d) expressing his needs as requests and accepting compromise when his needs are not met. When displayed by Frank, each of these four actions provides evidence that Frank is truly "getting along with others."

Exercise 6.4 presents five outcome goals and asks you to formulate *at least* two objectives for each goal.

EXERCISE 6.4

Translating Goals into Objectives

Directions: For each of the following outcome *goal* statements formulate two *objectives.*

Goal 1. I (principal is consultee) would really like the new students who transfer into our school during the year to make quick and successful adjustments.

Goal 2. I (teacher is consultee) don't like the way my Latino and African-American students get along in my class. I wish they could get along and support each other.

Goal 3. I (teacher is consultee) really wish that the parents of my students would give them more academic support and discipline at home.

Goal 4. I (parent is consultee) really have a hard time getting through to Mr. Simon (teacher). I wish he had a better understanding and compassion about my son's learning disabilities.

Goal 5. These kids are really unruly on my bus. I (bus driver is consultee) really wish that they would settle down and behave themselves so I can drive the bus.

Objective: Share your written answers with a colleague or instructor for review and feedback.

Subobjectives: Building on Small Increments of Change

Once outcome objectives have been established, it is helpful to match the client's (or consultee's) **current** behavior with those desired outcomes. It is not uncommon to find a large gap between "What is" and "What is desired." Of course, the **current** behavior is the presenting problem and has already been defined in the consult. For example, let's reconsider Frank. In reference to the four outcome objectives formulated for Frank, we might find that Frank's **current** behavior (also referred to as Frank's baseline level of performance) consists of social withdrawal, isolated play, refusal to share or cooperate with peers, and impulsive and aggressive need satisfaction. Relative to our four outcome objectives, Frank has a long way to go. If we scaled Frank's baseline and outcome objectives along a continuum of "1" (Frank at his absolute worst) to "10" (Frank's outcome objectives), we might place Frank's current behavior at the "3" level. Any expectation that Frank will quickly perform at the "10" level is unrealistic, and to pursue such a drastic change only sets up Frank and the consult for failure. However, Frank may be able to demonstrate progress to the "4" level, which might see him simply sitting quietly with his language arts cooperative group, eating lunch at the same table as his peers, shooting baskets with a peer and the recess aide, and asking his teachers for help in meeting his immediate needs. Although they do not demonstrate ultimate success for Frank and the consult, these subobjectives are reasonably attainable and provide evidence of change in the right direction. This process of **goal scaling** (Davis & Osborn, 2000) is an integral part of the solution-focused approach to be discussed at the end of this chapter.

Reaching Consensus on Goals and Objectives

Once outcome objectives have been formulated, it is important that the consultant and consultee demonstrate a clear understanding and consensus of agreement for those outcomes. Mutual understanding and consensus are essential for the commitment to action that will be required in the strategy development and implementation stage of the consultation process. Unresolved differences about desired outcome objectives will impede further collaboration, and the success of the consult, whereas a clearly informed consensus will reinforce the collaboration, empower consultant and consultee alike, and build the foundation for subsequent stages of the consultation. (See Exercise 6.5)

EXERCISE 6.5

Outcome Goals and Objectives

Directions: For this exercise two colleagues or students will work together using the analysis that they completed *as the consultee* in Exercise 6.4. Each colleague/student (as consultee) will share his analysis with his consultant. After the analysis is presented and understood by both parties the consultant is to collaboratively help the consultee to formulate outcome goals *and* objectives using the analysis as the reference.

Outcome: Written goals and objectives for each consultee should be shared and discussed. Review the criteria for objectives listed within the chapter to ensure those written meet the criteria.

STRATEGY DEVELOPMENT
AND IMPLEMENTATION

With consensual agreement about baseline and desired outcome, the consultant and consultee are ready to address the question, "What can be done to facilitate a process of change that will move the client from baseline to the desired outcome objectives?" The wording of this question is quite deliberate and warrants some analysis. The first part of the question asks, "What can be done?" This phrasing is meant to be inclusive of every resource available that can help in the change process. It doesn't ask, "What can I (consultant) do?" Nor does it ask, "What can you (consultee) do?" It doesn't even ask, "What can we (consultant and consultee) do?" By keeping the question inclusive, it presumes a collaborative effort to creatively mobilize resources and strategies that will create (facilitate) conditions for change. The opening question also presumes that change will be a process that will move the client (and consultee) to a desired outcome. Purposeful change strategies are as diverse as the idiosyncratic baseline and objectives formulated in our consultations. Throughout the remainder of this text the authors will discuss purposeful change that is directed toward the client, the consultee, and the broader system in which both parties do their work. In introducing this stage of the consultation process, the authors will offer some general guidelines to the development and implementation of effective change strategies.

As stated previously, in times of crisis the counselor–consultant will quickly develop and implement change strategies (e.g., provisional mode) or formulate strategies that can be implemented by the consultee (e.g., prescriptive mode). The development and implementation of effective change strategies is, at best, a collaborative effort on the part of both the consultant and the consultee. At first glance it might appear that the consultant following this collaborative mode will bring both content and process expertise to the formulation of strategies, and the consultee will perform the bulk of the strategy implementation. On closer inspection, many successful change strategies already exist within the repertoire of the consultee, only to be recognized with the help of the consultant. Moreover, effective client change is often enhanced when, as part of a comprehensive strategy, multiple interventions are employed, requiring action by both parties. Let's look at each of these realities of strategy development and implementation separately.

Don't Reinvent the Wheel

When consultees refer to a consultant for help, they frequently feel that they have exhausted all their ideas and resources for helping a problematic client. Whatever strategies that they have tried in the past have failed to produce the desired change, yet they continue to try the same strategies again and again. This repetition of failed effort can be demoralizing and lead to feelings of hopelessness and helplessness. Often these same consultees have experienced considerable success with others using tailor-made strategies that they only associated with particular individuals. For instance, Mr. Spitoli, Frank's second-grade teacher might have continually tried to lecture Frank about the value of sharing and cooperation, only to see Frank withdraw further from others. Coincidentally, the previous year a new student, Jerome, had enrolled in Mr. Spitoli's class at midyear and experienced social adjustment problems. One winter day Jerome and another popular student were feeling slightly ill and requested to stay in their classroom during lunch and recess. Mr. Spitoli agreed to let the two boys eat their lunch in the classroom with him. As the lunch progressed, the two boys enjoyed a lively conversation, and by the close of recess Jerome had established a friendship that flourished and expanded to other students for the remainder of the year. The opportunity for Jerome to interact with only one student, who possessed considerable friendship and support skills, within the safe confines of his classroom and with the support of Mr. Spitoli enabled him to take social risks and experience the joy of friendship and acceptance. With the help of his new friend, Jerome's school adjustment was smooth and successful.

Unfortunately, a year later, Mr. Spitoli failed to link his success with Jerome with the problems that he was experiencing with Frank. It was only when the consultant asked him when he had successfully worked with socially withdrawn students that he remembered Jerome. As a result of linking a past success with a comparable, current concern, Mr. Spitoli and the consultant were able to formulate a strategy involving a series of classroom lunches attended by Frank, a socially skilled and supportive peer, and Mr. Spitoli. Although this strategy represented only one of a number of interventions employed to help Frank, it illustrates that many consultees are already successful with strategies that could certainly be transferred to problems that they are currently experiencing. They do not have to reinvent the wheel.

Link Diagnostic Model to Goal Formulation and Strategy Development

Just as the organizing schema should provide the framework for an empirically based diagnosis of a problem brought by a consultee, it should also inform the construction of change strategies. Organizing schema can provide the framework for empirically based diagnosis, the formulation of goals and objectives, and the development of strategies for change.

For example, the interdependent components of the A–B–C model comprise the essential diagnostic picture of the problem experienced by the consultee. Excessive thoughts and actions performed by the client occur within specific environmental context and cause undesirable consequences to themselves and/or others. Likewise, deficit thoughts and actions can present the most problematic conditions. In most cases, the consultee's desired objectives reflect a decline or termination of the excess thoughts and actions and/or an increase in those thoughts and actions deemed deficient. As the consult moves into the change strategy phase the profile offered by the A–B–C model will direct attention to those antecedents and consequences that can be altered to support the desired behavior change. Application of this schema to the case of Frank will illustrate this point. In order to help Frank "get along better with others" we can create antecedents that make it safe and easy for Frank to "try out" some of his social skills. This form of stimulus control is exactly what Mr. Spitoli employed with his classroom lunches. Through the consequences of friendly responses from his peer and the verbal praise from Mr. Spitoli, Frank's attempts at social interaction could be carefully shaped from baseline to objective. By introducing a socially adept peer into the classroom lunches, Mr. Spitoli could use peer modeling, vicarious learning, and direct instruction in the treatment intervention.

More attention will be given to the application of this orienting schema in later chapters. Before we leave our discussion of this stage of the consultation process however, one additional consideration is in order.

Sometimes More Is Better: Or, There's More
Than One Way to Skin a Cat

During the creative give and take that occurs during a strategy development consult, as many change strategies as possible should be generated and considered for implementation. Some strategies will involve actions that the consultee will pursue within the educational environment of the client. Changing behavior contingencies, altering communication, revising curriculum or teaching methodology and adoption of specific learning accommodations are some of the more viable interventions that consultees can implement. At times a collaborative decision will be made for the consultant to provide direct service to the client in the form of individual and/or group counseling. Such direct service by the counselor will provide the individual and small-group problem solving, skill building, shaping, and relationship building that will supplement intervention conducted by the teacher, parents, or others. When direct services are included in the treatment plan, it is imperative that the consultee's goals maintain their focus and commitment, even though client goals may emerge from the individual and/or group counseling.

Exercise 6.6 provides you with the opportunity to practice developing strategies tied to goals.

EXERCISE 6.6

Strategy Development and Implementation

Directions: For this exercise two colleagues or students will work together using the goals and objectives that were formulated when they were the consultee in Exercise 6.5. With the one serving as consultant, they are to collaboratively formulate change strategies that will help to achieve their outcome goals and objectives.

Outcome: Change strategies should be reviewed and discussed as they reflect a linkage to the goals and objectives and appear feasible, given the realities of the consultee work situation.

MAINTENANCE: SUSTAINING
THE TRAJECTORY OF CHANGE

How are we doing? Are we on track in meeting our objectives? What changes have occurred? What changes still need to be made? These are the questions that guide our consultation once our change strategies are implemented. As the change process proceeds and strategies are formulated and employed, it is crucial that the changes exhibited by the client (and consultee) be monitored and documented. If outcome goals have been accurately translated into objectives, the nature of the data and its assessment methodology should be clear and straightforward. Moreover, the actual assessment procedures employed, such as observation, testing, interviewing, and surveying, will be shared by both parties in the consult. These data attesting to change, or the absence of change, will be brought to each consultation for analyses and decision making. When the data reveal that the trajectory of change is on track, the consult will adjust focus to be on the maintenance of successful strategies. During the maintenance phase it is important for the consultant to provide recognition of the consultee's efforts and contributions. This recognition is helpful in facilitating the consultee's adoption of an internal locus of control regarding the process and outcome. This internalization of control is essential if the consultee is to feel empowered to act proactively and autonomously in the future.

The systematic monitoring of change is the only objective way of knowing that planned strategies are having the desired effect. At times the data will be disappointing, suggesting that our strategies need to be "tweaked," revamped, or reconstructed entirely. Slower than expected change may indicate minor revisions in existing strategies or an agreement to lower expectations and increase patience. When change occurs in the desired direction at a slower pace, it is often prudent to celebrate even the smallest increments of change while motivating everyone involved to stay on track and expect (look for) even more change.

When the data reveal no change or deleterious effects, the following questions are helpful to answer.

1. Was the real problem identified and defined?
2. Could other factors, which were not identified during the exploration phase, be contributing to the problem?
3. Could sources of resistance be operating that could mitigate change?
4. Were systemic forces supportive of change mobilized?
5. Were antagonistic forces addressed?
6. Were the goals and objectives appropriate for the client, consultee and the system?
7. Were strategies that were created and implemented appropriate and reasonable? And were they truly employed in the manner in which they were designed?

By addressing these questions together, the consultant and consultee can review the consultation process in a chronological and comprehensive manner. The answers will suggest minor or major changes to be considered collaboratively. Problem solving and decision making about any aspect of the consultation must be the purview of both parties in the consult with modifications in the process both expected and welcomed. Through frequent overview of the consultation process and the contributions of each member of the consult the foundation is laid for a successful termination.

TERMINATION: LINKING PAST, PRESENT, AND FUTURE

With or without strategy revision, at some point in the consultation process the review of the data will confirm that the outcome objectives have been achieved. Or the existing data will show sufficient progress prompting the consultant and consultee to consider termination of the consult. In either instance, the decision to terminate should be consensual. Once decided, however, closure should not occur until the consultant conducts a culminating meeting to address the following questions.

1. What did we accomplish?
2. How did we do it?
3. What did each of us contribute?
4. What actions can be taken to sustain the progress made?
5. What did we learn for the future?

By answering these five questions collaboratively, the consultant will have the opportunity to review and reinforce successful elements of the change process as well as the method employed to guide the process. Success is certainly reflected in goal attainment. However, an equally important outcome of a successful consult that concludes with consideration of these questions is the knowledge and skill that the consultee learned from the process. Furthermore, the feelings of helpfulness, efficacy and pride will engender future feelings of hopefulness, autonomy and empowerment.

EXERCISE 6.7

Maintenance and Termination

Directions:

Part A. For this exercise two colleagues/students will work together as consultant and consultee using the data from Exercises 6.5 and 6.6. Each student will share their goals/objectives and change strategies that were formulated when they were in the role of consultee. As they share their data, the students serving as consultant will consider maintenance factors with the consultee. The following questions can be used.

1. How will the change be monitored?
2. What forces (person or system) might interfere with progress? What can be done to offset this?
3. What forces (person or system) might support progress? How can they be mobilized?
4. How can change strategies be sustained and where might they need revision?

Part B. List the five questions that need to be addressed in order for termination to be successful.

Outcome: Review and discuss your notes from Part A and your answers to Part B. Share these with your supervisor and/or instructor.

SUMMARY

Preentry: Creating Conditions for Successful Consultation

Collaborative consultation starts *before* the initial meeting with a consultee. It is important for a consultant to establish efficient and timely referral procedures. Further, the counselor–consultant needs to take steps to promote the norm of collaborative consultation as the mode of operations.

Entry: Establishing the Contract

The working relationship between the consultee and consultant is established during the first meeting. While addressing the consultee's crisis, it is important to structure the relationship and the expectations in line with a collaborative consultation model. As such, emphasis is given to the development of a shared, coequal, and mutual working relationship.

Exploration

From a traditional perspective, once a contract has been established, efforts will be targeted to identify both the depth and breadth of the problem as well as possible resources that can be brought to bear on the solution. As such, this is a stage in which data are collected and with the help of an organizing schema, such as the A–B–C model, are analyzed.

Outcome Goals and Objectives: Moving toward Solutions

In this stage, broad goals of desired outcome will be identified. In addition to these goals, objectives will be established that provide the concrete evidence that each goal has been attained. Because a single goal can have multiple pieces of evidence, most goals will translate into multiple objectives. As with other stages it is important that both the consultant and consultee demonstrate clear understanding and consensus of agreement.

Strategy Development and Implementation

With consensual agreement about desired outcome, the consultant and consultee are ready to address the question: What can be done to facilitate a process of change that will move the client from baseline to desired outcome objective? The development and implementation of effective change strategies is contingent on the understanding and owning of the strategy by both consultant and consultee. It is also helpful to employ the same organizing schema that provided the framework for defining the problem to inform the construction of change strategies.

Maintenance: Sustaining the Trajectory of Change

The systematic monitoring of change is the only objective way of knowing that planned strategies are having the desired effect. This monitoring of speed and direction of change allows the consultant and consultee to identify what is working and modify what is not.

Termination: Linking Past, Present, and Future

Once the outcome objective has been achieved, termination of the consultation can be considered. As with each step in the consult, termination should be a collaborative decision. As part of the termination process, the consultant and consultee should review the experience to identify: (a) What was accomplished? (b) How was it achieved? (c) What actions can be employed to sustain progress? and (d) What was learned for future use?

IMPORTANT TERMS

A-B-C model

Constructivism

Entry

Exploration

Goal

Goal scaling

Internal locus of control

Objective

Organizing schemes

Preentry

Solution-focused approach

Structuring

SUGGESTED READINGS

Brown, D., Pryszwansky, W. B., & Schulte, A. C. (2001). *Psychological consultation: Introduction to theory and practice* (5th ed.). Boston: Allyn & Bacon.

Gingerich, W. J., & Wabeke, T. (2001). A solution-focused approach to mental health intervention in school settings. *Children & Schools, 23,* 33–47.

Kazdin, A. E. (2001). *Behavior modification in applied settings* (6th ed.). Pacific Grove, CA: Brooks/Cole.

McNamee, S., & Gergen, K. J. (1992). *Therapy as social construction.* London: Sage.

White, M., & Epston, D. (1990). *Narrative means to therapeutic ends.* New York: Norton.

WEB SITES

The Solution Focus Links: Listing of sites providing information on the application of solution focus strategies in a variety of settings.
www.thesolutionsfocus.com/linksh.cfm
Bright Futures: Tools for professionals.
www.brightfutures.org/mentalhealth/pdf/professionals/school_cnsltn.pdf

National Center for Family Resource Support: Provides various packets of resource information, including packets on collaborative consultation.

www.casey.org/cnc/support_retention/packet_school_collaboration.htm

REFERENCES

Cormier, S., & Nurius, P. S. (2003). *Interviewing and change strategies for helpers* (5th ed.). Pacific Grove, CA: Brooks/Cole.

Davis, T. E., & Osborn, C. J. (2000). *The solution-focused school counselor: Shaping professional practice*. Philadelphia: Accelerated Development.

De Jong, P., & Berg, I. K. (1998). *Interviewing for solutions*. Pacific Grove, CA: Brooks/Cole.

Guterman, J. T. (1994). A social constructionist position for mental health counseling. *Journal of Mental Health Counseling, 16,* 226–244.

Juhnke, A. (1996). Solution-focused supervision: Promoting supervisee skills and confidence through successful solutions. *Counselor Education and Supervision, 36,* 48–57.

Kahn, B. B. (2000). A model of solution-focused consultation for school counselors. *Professional School Counseling, 3*(4), 248–254.

Kahn, W. J. (1999). *The A-B-C's of human experience*. Pacific Grove, CA: Brooks/Cole.

Kanfer, F. H., & Goldstein, A. P. (1991). *Helping people change* (4th ed.). New York: Pergamon.

Kazdin, A. (1993). Psychotherapy for children and adolescents: Current progress and future research directions. *American Psychologist, 48,* 644–657.

LaFountain, R. M., & Gemer, N. E. (1996). Solution-focused counseling groups: The results are in. *The Journal of Specialists in Group Work, 2* (1:2), 128–143.

Lazarus, A. (1989). *The practice of multimodal therapy* (2nd ed.). Baltimore: Johns Hopkins University Press.

Mostert, D. L., Johnson, E., & Mostert, M. P. (1997). The utility of solution-focused, brief counseling in schools: Potential from an initial study. *Professional School Counseling, 1,* 21–24.

Paull, R. C., & McGrevin, C. Z. (1996). Seven assumptions of a solution-focused conversational leader. *NAASP Bulletin, 80,* 79–85.

Santa Rita, E. (1996). The solution-focused supervision model for counselors teaching in the classroom. (*ERIC Document ED393524*)

Selye, H. (1974). *The stress without distress*. New York: Lippincott.

Spiegler, M. D., & Guevremont, D. C. (1998). Contemporary behavior therapy (3rd ed.). Pacific Grove, CA: Brooks/Cole.

7

❦

Communication
for Effective Consulting

Well that seemed to go well. I was happy that I was able to structure the
relationship and explain confidentiality. Dr. Jameson was quite concerned
about Ellen and really wanted to talk about her problems and what he had
done to help her. I'm glad I was able to use my reflective listening and
summarizing to show him I understood and empathized with his view of
the problem. He certainly seemed appreciative of my encouraging him to
tell his story. Plus my tacting leads helped him to describe specific, recent
occurrences of the problem (and also the absence of the problem). I feel
like we were really on the same page and that he was enthusiastic about
the homework of formulating two outcome goals that we could use to
measure success in our consult. Yes, we made quite a bit of progress in our
first meeting, largely because our communication went so well.

O ur consultant has certainly learned one important lesson; the essence
of any helping relationship is the manner and effect of the communication displayed. Our consultant's complex theories, intricate strategies, and best intentions will surely fail if his verbal, nonverbal, and written
communications are not clear, open, honest, and purposeful. Every verbal and
nonverbal communication by the school counselor–consultant should be purposeful and selective, always in service of the demands of the specific phase of
the consultation process. As such, the current chapter will focus on the skills
necessary to be an effective counselor–consultant.

CHAPTER OBJECTIVES

The current chapter will not only review skills of communication for consultants, but will also begin with an overview of the many purposes to which communication skills are directed. This means–end connection will then be further linked to the specific stages of the consultation process.

After completing this chapter the reader should be able to

1. Describe and demonstrate the array of verbal, nonverbal, and written communication skills
2. Explain the purpose of each communication skill
3. Describe the locus and rationale for using the various communication skills within the stages of the consultation process

COMMUNICATION SKILLS IN CONSULTATION: PURPOSE AND OUTCOMES

If the communication skills of the counselor–consultant are to result in a successful consult, they must be employed selectively and purposefully. But what are the desired effects for which we selectively employ these skills? A review of the communications literature for both counseling (Ivey, 1994) and consulting (Brown, Pryzwansky, & Schulte, 2001) suggests at least nine purposes of our communication. Although overlap exists in terms of the outcomes achieved through any one communication, enough differentiation exists to discuss each purpose separately.

Demonstrate Empathy and Build Rapport

Everyone who seeks the help of a counselor–consultant wants assurance that they are heard and understood. This understanding is fostered by and actively demonstrated through the use of active and accurate listening. Through accurate reflective listening and the resulting demonstrated empathy (Brammer, 1994), the helper nurtures and sustains the relationship enabling the helper to become significant and influential in the helpee's life.

With accurate empathy at its core, rapport is developed as the consultant displays genuine interest in and acceptance of the consultee (Wilcox-Matthew et al., 1997). The critical importance of rapport in building and maintaining helping relationships has been well established (Ivey, 1994). More specifically, the consultee's ability and willingness to disclose information is predicated on the rapport that is established by the consultant.

Inform or Provide Information

Throughout the consultation process, the consultant will want to communicate clear, accurate, and relevant information to the consultee, client, and client system. The consultant's expert and information power is often reflected in the unique knowledge and skill that the consultant shares with others. In every instance, the consultant wants to be sure that the information is **clear, accurate, relevant to the consultation, timely,** and conforms to the **legal and ethical standards** of confidentiality.

Obtain Information to Identify and Define Problems

Consultants employ specific forms of communication as a way of identifying and defining the target for the consultation. Questions such as the following needed to be answered. What is the consultee's concern? What are the client's excesses and deficits? How is the consultee conceptualizing the problem and its history? What does the consultee expect of the consultant and the consulting process? How does the client system view the presenting problem? To be answered, each of these questions requires information from the consultee and others. And as was the case with communication used to inform, the nature of information gathered needs to be clear, accurate, relevant, timely, and conform to legal and ethical standards of confidentiality.

Obtain Information to Formulate Goals and Objectives

A special category of information that is crucial to the success of consultation consists of descriptions of future goals and objectives. Whereas problem-focused inquiries identify and define past and present events, the formulation of goals and objectives calls for speculation and extrapolation from what is to what could be. The ability of consultees to identify and define outcomes goals and objectives frequently requires creativity and the ability to hypothesize change. Consultants can facilitate this process through their use of active listening and focused questioning.

Support and Reassure

When consultees have tried for weeks or even months to ameliorate the problem, they may come to the counselor–consultant frustrated, angry, pessimistic, and feeling helpless. They may hold this inability to resolve the situation on their own as testimony to their incompetence and inadequacy. As they share their story of failed effort, they need considerable support. They need to experience a genuine appreciation of their efforts, as well as reassurance that consultation will lead to successful resolution of the situation and a change in their client.

Affirm and Reinforce

Once the consultation process is under way the consultee will actively be engaged in diagnostic or remedial interventions with the client. At the very least they will be monitoring and reporting client progress to the consultant. The counselor consultant needs to affirm the commitment and effort expended by the consultee and positively reinforce the consultee for even the smallest contribution to the change process.

Persuade and Influence

Effective consultation requires purposeful change in the thinking, feeling, and/or behavior of the consultee, client, and client system. Thus, the counselor–consultant will be called on to use an array of motivational strategies to influence others as they become involved in the consultation process. Although affirmation and reinforcement will follow actions occurring throughout consultation, strategies of persuasion and influence will attempt to motivate others to action, thus preceding their efforts. Encouragement, structuring goal-directed tasks with minimal response cost, and emphasizing the primary and secondary gain to be achieved through manageable action will often persuade and influence a reluctant consultee, client, or client system to action.

Creative Data Gathering through Brainstorming

Numerous communication and assessment skills will be employed in the accumulation of information throughout the consultation process. This gathering and organizing of data into integrated patterns requires linear and convergent thinking. Creative problem solving and decision making, however, require the vast resource of information that can only come from divergent thinking. Although there are various ways to tap this infinite well of ideas, of particular value is the communication skill of brainstorming that facilitate the creative formation of consultation goals, objectives, intervention strategies, and resources.

Brainstorming is a procedure designed to stimulate convergent and divergent thinking by removing barriers of judgment, censoring, stereotyping, and the pull (of) past practice. Under the rules of brainstorming (Jones, S. & Sims, D., 1985), individuals are given free reign to think about problems and solutions in new and innovative ways—to think "out of the box."

Providing Instruction and Directives

Although active and empathic listening are necessary elements of consultant communication, they are not sufficient for successful consultation. At various times throughout the consultation process the consultant will provide directives for consultee action and even didactically instruct the consultee (or others) in knowledge and skills that will enhance consultation success. Through description, explanation, modeling, and guided practice the consultant will teach the consultee whatever is necessary for success.

During an actual consultation session a consultant may wish to direct a consultee in the performance of a new skill such as conducting a functional behavior analysis or creating a goal scale with a client, or any manner of skill that will aid the consultee. These "in-session" directives will place the consultant in a teaching role that will require the same pedagogical skills employed by all effective teachers (Ryan & Cooper, 1988; Schmidt, 2003).

The rationale for a directive should reflect the specific stage within the consultation process. Homework directives should logically occur toward the end of a consultation session and naturally connect to the progress of the session. A directive to observe a client within a specific environment or activity will reasonably occur in conjunction with early stages of the consult whereas directives to alter a client's environment, tasks, or behavior–consequence contingencies will be congruent with later stages of the process. Directives should be given concretely. Consultants should provide examples and tasks that are practical and manageable for the consultee. Directives always ask for voluntary action and allow the consultee discretion in carrying out the directive. In most cases the best directives are those constructed collaboratively.

Regardless of how the directive is constructed, after it is given the consultant should ask the consultee to repeat (paraphrase) the entire directive as a check for understanding. Failed directives are often the result of consultees not understanding the specific tasks involved in the directive. When directives are particularly complex or challenging, the consultant should guide the consultee in a discussion on anticipated glitches, roadblocks, or barriers and strategies for dealing with those contingencies.

As you can see, effective directives require sufficient time, often a large proportion of a consultation session, but the time and effort can greatly enhance efficiency and effectiveness of the consultation.

SKILLS OF ACTIVE LISTENING
(PRECONDITIONS TO UNDERSTANDING)

In our typical day-to-day conversations, be they at the watercooler or at home over morning coffee, we may find ourselves enacting the role of listener, which is best characterized as being quiet, polite, and noninterruptive. Such a passive approach to listening, although certainly socially acceptable, could actually interfere with our understanding of another person's message. Often in our polite quietness, we may find that we are listening with half an ear and understanding with reduced accuracy. The same can be true in consultation. The consultant who engages in listening quietly and passively to the consultee, may find himself drifting off into a daydream (What a great day for golf!) or focusing on a personal concern (Where do I have to be this afternoon?) or even jumping to conclusions about what is being said (. . . oh, I know where this is leading!).

If one is to be helpful in a consultation interaction, one must understand what the consultee is attempting to convey. These tendencies to jump to conclusions or become inattentive or self-absorbed must be avoided. Further, the consultant will need to not only fully attend to the consultee but also demonstrate to the consultee that she is attending.

Attending as a Physical Response

Attending or "being with" another requires both a physical posture and a psychological orientation. Gerard Egan (1977), for example, pointed out the importance of one's body orientation in the accurate reception of information during a face-to-face encounter, such as is found in consultation. The critical dimensions of nonverbal attending include space (proximity), position, posture, and eye contact.

One interviewing technique suggested by Gerald Caplan (Caplan & Caplan, 1993) is to sit beside, as opposed to opposite, the consultee. When the consultee and consultant are collaborating on writing or reading materials, they may want to sit side-by-side at a desk or table. This positioning gives nonverbal support to the psychological tone the consultant is trying to attain. In sitting side-by-side, the message conveyed is that this consultation will be an elbow-to-elbow mutual problem-solving venture. Rather than sitting across from one another in a role of problem teller (i.e., the consultee) and problem solver (i.e., the consultant), the side-by-side posture suggests a mutuality to both the understanding and resolution of the problem.

Physical seating may be at an angle so that the consultant and consultee are not fixedly staring at each other, but can see each other with a slight turn of the head. The distance between consultant and consultee should reflect and respect both the consultee's and the consultant's comfort level. Violating a consultee's physical space will only create anxiety and a detrimental distraction to both parties.

The key to appropriate posture is that the consultee use a natural posture that reflects the tenor of the discussion. If the consultee leans forward in an excited desire to communicate, the consultant will want to "mirror" that posture by also leaning forward. A relaxed, reclining posture by the consultee should be met with similar posture by the consultant. This mirroring of the consultee's nonverbal expression also applies to facial expressions.

Eye contact is a critical reinforcer of consultee communication. Although eyeball-to-eyeball, fixed staring will usually cause the consultee (and client) to feel uncomfortable, the consultant's eye contact must assure the consultee that the consultant is attentive and listening. The appropriate zone for eye contact can extend from the consultee's forehead to chest and from shoulder to shoulder. By maintaining eye contact within this zone, the consultant can observe critical nonverbal expression, and the consultee will feel that they are being heard.

These suggestions for physical attending must be offered with the caveat that each attending skill must be sensitive to the consultee's (or client's) cultural norms of nonverbal behavior. A number of excellent references

(Atkinson & Hackett, 2004; Pederson & Carey, 1994) address the specific cultural dimensions of verbal and nonverbal communication. This consideration will receive further discussion in chapter 13.

Attending—A Psychological Response

In addition to taking an actively receptive physical stance, the consultant must also be **psychologically active** in the communication exchange. Too often in our communications we simply hear the words, but fail to truly understand the message. For example, consider conversations you may have had with a friend or colleague in which you felt and perhaps stated, "(They) don't understand!" This sense of frustration along with the reality that although words may be heard yet the message misunderstood is evidenced in the following exchange between Jack, a high school physics teacher, and Nick, the school counselor–consultant.

> **Jack:** Nick, could you help me with one of my senior students who seems to have given up in my class? He's been doing average work throughout the year but since he got accepted to college, he has really slacked off. He's stopped turning in his assignments and has been absent a lot this term.
>
> **Nick:** Yeah, this "senioritis" seems to infect these kids this time of year. I wouldn't expect much from this term. Just let it go.

It is clear that Jack is truly concerned about this student and takes pride in his teaching. He wants his students to succeed. Nick looked at Jack's student (client) through the eyes of an experienced educator who is well aware of the manifestations of senioritis and the effects of early acceptance to college. Although Jack's words were heard, the message was missed! Jack really needed more affirmation than the simple, "Just let it go."

The recommendations suggested for improving counselors' ability to listen and understand (Carkhuff, 1987) have similar value for consultants. They are

1. Remember our reason for listening. Our attention and our listening will increase, if we remember that we are attempting to gather data, clues—from the consultee's words, tone, and manner—that will help us understand the nature of the problem or the goals presented.

2. Suspend our personal judgment. We need to remember to focus on what the consultee is actually saying and not our personal judgment or evaluation of the comments. Fixing on our own opinion, evaluation, or frame of reference could prevent us from understanding the consultee's (Friend & Cook, 1992). Clearly at some point in the relationship we may want to share our opinions or values, but for now it is important to "hear" the consultee's position, not ours!

3. Focus on the consultee. It may seem obvious, but the effective consultant will resist distractions and keep his/her focus on the consultee's explicit messages as well as the more subtle indications of the consultee's experience. This focusing on the consultee may be the most important

thing the effective, active listener can do. Focusing on the consultee to the degree that we psychologically step in the consultee' frame of reference so that we can experience what she experiences or see and hear as she sees and hears will clearly increase the accuracy of our understanding. With such active, empathic listening, we will hear the consultee's message as she actually intended and experienced it.

Accurate empathy is demonstrated through minimal encouraging and paraphrasing the consultee's communication. We will discuss each skill set separately.

Minimal Encouraging

Throughout much of the consultation process the consultant will want the consultee to have as much "air time" as possible. This is especially true when the content of a session must come from the consultee. Moreover, the consultee may need to be encouraged to take that air time. The use of minimal encouragers can help in this process. Each of the following consultant responses can serve as a minimal encourager.

1. Physical responses such as smiles, head nods, and hand gestures can both encourage and reinforce consultee disclosures.
2. Verbal responses such as "Ah ha," "Yes," "Right," and "Um" can also be encouraging and reinforcing.
3. In addition to encouraging and reinforcing consultee communication, minimal encouragers can serve as **bridges** that connect consultee disclosures and invite the consultee to clarify or elaborate whatever has been disclosed. Effective bridges include single words such as "and," "but," "although," and "so" that are posed in a questioning manner.
4. Repeating the last few words of a consultee's disclosure such as ". . . and you're not really sure," ". . . you'd really like to," ". . . whenever he's absent" will reinforce the consultee's disclosure as well as invite continuation, elaboration, and clarification.

Paraphrasing Content

Paraphrasing is the process by which the consultant takes the basic message provided by the consultee and, in her own words, **reflects** the content of that message to the consultee. This can be very helpful in letting the consultee expand or clarify issues as well as to invite them to correct any misunderstanding. Consider the following brief exchange.

Consultee: I've been a teacher for 34 years. I have never encountered a situation as the one I have with Jeremy. I want your help in developing some techniques, strategies—something to help me manage him in class!

Consultant: Jeremy's behavior appears to be something that you have never encountered in all your 34 years of teaching, and you're hoping that perhaps I could assist you with some approaches to managing Jeremy in class?

Consultee: It is not just his behavior, I have had students who were itches like him, but—it is more his attitude—he really seems almost "mean.'"

The consultant reflected the content of the consultee's message by correctly identifying the length of teaching experience and the purpose for the consultee's engaging with the consultant (i.e., to gain management strategies). However, the assumption that it was Jeremy's behavior that was causing the most problem for the teacher was corrected by the consultee and expanded to include if not emphasize Jeremy's attitude. Thus, the paraphrase demonstrated that the consultant was attending and had accurately received this initial information. Further, the paraphrase provided the consultee an opportunity to expand and clarify the information presented.

In responding to the content of the consultee's message the effective consultant rephrases that content in his own words to demonstrate understanding. It is important that the consultant attempt to reflect the consultee's message but not simply parrot back the words, exactly as initially presented. This is not a test of memory nor is it an exercise in mirroring the consultee. The goal is to share with the consultee our understanding of what it was that the consultee is attempting to explicitly convey to us. Exercise 7.1 will help you become familiar with the process of paraphrasing the content of the consultee's message.

EXERCISE 7.1

Paraphrasing

Directions: For each of the following read the paragraph and

Part 1. Identify the key experiences—who or what is involved along with the consultee's expressed feelings and actions.

Part 2. Write a response summarizing in your own words these explicit experiences, behaviors, and feelings. Start your response with either: "In other words . . ." or "I hear you saying . . ."

Part 3. Share your responses with a colleague or colearner and compare responses. Did you stay with the explicit message and NOT interpret? Did you simply parrot the consultee, or did you place the message in your own words?

Example:

Frustrated teacher: These darn kids. I've had it. I am so frustrated, I could scream. I tried my best—spent hours—worked hard on developing an exciting lesson and today nothing. They don't care, they goofed off rather than pay attention, why bother?

Part 1.
Experiences: Kids, teacher, and lesson

Behaviors: Teacher prepared lesson; kids unresponsive, inattentive.
Feelings: Frustrated, had it, doubt.

Part 2.
Paraphrase: I hear you saying how frustrated you feel and how you are even beginning to doubt the value of working so hard, because you worked hard on the lesson and the students didn't respond.

1. **Consultee** (a drug and alcohol counselor): Susan is coming in for an appointment today. I'm stuck. I have tried to confront her about her drinking, but she continues to deny that this is a problem for her, even though she has been arrested as DUI. I have no idea what else I can do.

Part 1.
Experiences:
Behaviors:
Feelings:

Part 2.
Consultant Paraphrase:

2. **Consultee** (third-grade-teacher): These kids are getting out of hand. They don't listen anymore, they do whatever they darn well please. It's like you got to yell or scream or threaten them before they listen. I don't want to be that kind of teacher. It is really upsetting.

Part 1.
Experiences:
Behaviors:
Feelings

Part 2.
Consultant Paraphrase:

3. **Consultee** (college residence assistant): I am about to call it quits. I don't think I can take it anymore. No matter what I try I can't get the girls on 5-b to adhere to the quiet time rules. Study time comes and I go ask them to turn down the music and return to their rooms and no sooner do I leave the floor than I get a call from somebody on 5-a complaining about the noise. I have no idea what to do.

Part 1.
Experiences:
Behaviors:
Feelings

Part 2.
Consultant paraphrase:

Reflection of Feelings   In addition to hearing the words of the consultee and accurately reflecting those words, the effective consultant must also begin to recognize the feelings, the emotions underlying those words. It is very important to note, however, that in consultation, unlike therapy or counseling, the goal is not to direct the consultee to a discussion of these feelings. Generally, the consultant's interest in the consultee's feelings is simply to register the consultee's feelings as essential information that will color the way the content of the message needs to be interpreted. For example, perceiving the residence assistance cited in Exercise 7.1 as being extremely frustrated, and perhaps anxious about the possibility of losing her much-needed job, will help the consultant to appreciate the crisis nature of this problem and not approach it as simply a minor issue of conflict over power and authority. The one exception to this rule is when the consultee's emotional reaction is the source of the client's problem. In this situation the consultant will focus on the consultee's feelings, not in and of themselves, but as they directly impact the current work-related problem. This point will be elaborated on in chapter 10.

Like paraphrasing, reflection of feelings requires you to provide a brief statement reflecting the essence of the message received. However, where paraphrasing generally reflects the facts of what was said, reflection of feelings reflects the emotions related to those facts. For example,

> **Consultee:** I don't know what's wrong with our student assistant team (voice somewhat shaky, with frown on brow). We used to be so close, real tight, would approach every work issue with a single mind, now nothing, a big void, nobody seems to care or feel connected (voice pitch trails off, looks down).
>
> **Consultant:** You feel confused, saddened, and somewhat anxious about the transformation you perceive is happening with your team.

For a consultant to accurately reflect the consultee's feelings, he must learn to listen with his eyes as well as his ears. How does the consultee look as she shares her story? What might she be expressing by her posture, facial expressions, or gestures?

Exercise 7.2 will help you begin to develop the ability to accurately reflect feelings.

EXERCISE 7.2

Reflection of Feelings

Direction: After reading each of the following statements and attending to the behavioral expressions, ask yourself: "How would I feel saying these things?" and "How do I usually feel when I act or sound that way?" Then write a response using the formula "It seems that you are feeling . . ." or "You're feeling . . ."

It is helpful to share and compare your response with that of a colleague or colearner. Did you agree on the feelings expressed? If not, which cues were you using? Did you agree with the level of intensity? If not, again, what cues were you each picking up and responding to?

Example:

Consultee: (sighing) I just don't know what to do (looks down to the ground, with a frown in her brow and sighs a second time).

Consultant: It seems that you are feeling confused and somewhat hopeless about what to do.

1. **Consultee:** (sitting up on the edge of the seat—turning red in the face, and raising his voice) "If you only knew what I got to put up with attempting to teach these unruly students! (smacks his hands down on the chair).

Consultant: You seem to be feeling . . .

---

2. **Consultee:** But you have got to help . . . (voice is high pitched, facially appears pleading, actually reaches toward you), I am not tenured and if the principal sees my class out of control I could be finished here.

Consultant: You're feeling . . .

---

3. **Consultee:** Oh, you got to hear this. . . (sitting up, gesturing with hands and smiling as she speaks) that technique we talked about, well you are not going to believe what happened.

Consultant: You feel . . .

SKILLS OF EXPLORATION

This process of exploration entails a real reconnaissance or exploration of the consultee's total experience so that all the relevant data can be gathered and processed. As will become more obvious after reading the next chapters, the quantity and diversity of the information a consultee gathers during this exploration stage can become overwhelming. The consultant will attempt to gather data, not just on the client, but also relevant information about the consultee and the consultee's system. The specific types of information to be gathered will be discussed in the upcoming chapters. The focus here is on the "how" of exploration, with specific emphasis given to the art of questioning.

Exploring through the Art of Questioning

The art of questioning is a keystone to the exploration process. The consultant who has mastered the use of questions can elicit very helpful information from the consultee and do so in a way that is nonthreatening and even comforting to the consultee.

One of the primary values of questioning to the consultant in the exploration stage is that it serves as a vehicle from which to **probe** more deeply into the issue. For example,

> **Consultee:** I just don't understand—I invite the others to provide input and take part in decision making—but they still seem reluctant to do so.
>
> **Consultant:** Take part in the decision making? What is it that you are hoping they will do?

Questions can also be used to **highlight** a certain piece of information for further **clarification.** For example,

> **Consultee:** "O.K., so I tend to be a little gruff with the staff. I know I snap at Ellen (my secretary) and tend to get emotional with Frank (the assistant principal) and Barbara (the psychologist), but gads, is it really that bad? So I am a little rough around the edges.
>
> **Consultant:** You say you are **a little rough around the edges,** but it seems that a number of people, in more than one role and at more than one time, have expressed real concerns about your style of interaction. Can you help me understand why so many people may be concerned about what you call **a little rough?**

Guidelines for Effective Questioning

Questioning can be a very useful tool for a consultant to use to begin to gain a real understanding of the issues confronting the consultee. However, questioning, if done inappropriately, can do much to block a helping, facilitative consultation relationship. The effective use of questioning will be guided by the following principles: (a) be purposeful; (b) be clear, concrete and simple; and (c) ask as few questions as possible. Each of these guidelines is discussed in more detail following.

Be Purposeful   It may be said that one of the most basic rules governing the use of questioning is that questioning and data collection should be purposeful. We can ask questions for a variety of reasons. We could use questions as a form of small talk or use questions as a way of backing another into a corner, almost as a prosecuting attorney may use questions.

We must remember that unlike other times in which we are engaged in social interchanges, we are there to assist or to help another. We are not simply asking questions for our own benefit or as a way of peeping into another person's life. We are attending and questioning because we wish to understand the nature of the problem at hand, as well as the possible avenues for intervention that may be available.

Be Clear, Concrete, and Simple   A second guideline for asking questions in the context of consultation is to keep our questions clear and simple.

Questions should be asked in a manner and with a language that the consultee can understand. Asking compound questions or using slang or jargon will not only be confusing to the consultee but may make the consultee increasingly nervous and thus block communications.

For example consider the following scenario.

Consultee: Gads, I'm nervous. I don't know why . . . just kind of seems strange having to talk to a consultant, I'm so use to handling my own problems.

Consultant: Is it strange that you have to talk with someone, or are you saying it is strange for you to be talking with someone—you know, is it a commentary on your social style, or the fact that your ego defenses block you from seeing yourself as a person who would need help—any thoughts?

With a consultee who has already expressed some anxiety and nervousness about talking to a consultant, it is clear that the multiple questions and the introduction of terms such as *social style* and *ego defenses* may be somewhat unnerving and actually block the exploration of the issue. A related problem is the use of multiple-choice questions where the questioner poses a question and then offers one or more answers for the responder to choose from. An example is if the consultant were to ask, "Why do you think he's so afraid to try? Is it his past failures? Could it be his perfectionism? Or do you think he's just lazy?" Multiple-choice questions severely restrict the consultee's perspective and can often lead to answers that are inadequate or completely inaccurate.

Be Conservative—Ask as Few Questions as Possible   The third guideline is that we need to use as few questions as are needed to gather all the relevant data required to help another, as opposed to making the interaction sound and feel like an interrogation.

Consultee: I don't know where to begin.
Consultant: Tell me about your problem.
Consultee: O.K., I'm the new librarian in this school and I am having . . .
Consultant: Where did you work last?
Consultee: Pine Ridge High School.
Consultant: So when did you arrive here?
Consultee: I started here in September, at the start of school.
Consultant: So you already have a problem. What is it? Who's it with? What are you hoping I can do?
Consultee: Well as I started to say, I am having a problem with the reading specialist.
Consultant: Are you supposed to work with her? Who does she report to?

Asking a set of rapid-fire, interrogating questions does little to place the consultee at ease and may, in fact, force the consultee into a shutdown, protective mode. Questions that can be answered with a simple yes or no response or that can be answered with a few-word, multiple-choice style are generally considered **closed questions.** This type of closed questions not only set the stage for the consultee's feeling as if they are on the witness stand, but they also will create a pattern of communication that places all the responsibility for its structure and direction on the consultant as opposed to allowing the consultee to give the direction they need. Thus, if the consultant is attempting to create an atmosphere of mutuality and collaboration, closed questions, presented in such an interrogating style may prove very counterproductive.

In contrast to this style of **closed** questioning, the effective consultant will develop the ability to employ questions that **invite** the client to **expand, elaborate** and **expound** on a point, rather than simply answer yes or no. Questions that invite the consultee to expand on their point and elaborate as they wish are considered **open questions.** Although many authors, especially in the counseling and psychotherapy literature, will emphasize open questions, almost to the exclusion or even prohibition of using closed questions, such restriction is not suggested here. Open questions are valuable as invitations for the consultee to speak but in effective consultation, systematic inquiry will include the use of both open and closed questions. During the early stage of the consultation, when a consultant is attempting to explore the depth and breadth of the consultee's problem, open questions appear to be most useful. But in the later stages of the interaction, when problem identification and specific intervention strategies are being developed, closed-ended, focused questions may prove to be more useful. Exercise 7.3 provides an illustration of the differential effect of closed and open-ended questions.

EXERCISE 7.3

Styles of Questioning

Directions: Review the following two dialogues between a consultant and a consultee. In both situations the consultant is attempting to **explore** the nature of the problem. The first consultant employs a number of closed-ended questions, whereas the second consultant relies on an open questioning style. Answer and discuss the questions following each of the dialogues.

Scenario I: Closed Questioning

Consultee: Boy am I having a problem with Alfred!
Consultant: Is he refusing to do his work?
Consultee: No, not exactly.
Consultant: Oh, is he disrespectful?
Consultee: Well . . . it's a bit more than that!
Consultant: So he's really acting out, causing a disruption in class. Maybe even undermining your authority?
Consultee: Yeah, I guess you could say it like that.

For consideration and discussion:

1. Who is controlling the content of the session?
2. How do you think the consultee feels at this moment?
3. What is the consultee expecting about this relationship?
4. What has the consultant learned about the consultee?
5. What has the consultant learned about the nature of the problem?

Scenario II: Open Questioning

Consultee: Boy am I having a problem with Alfred!

Consultant: When you say problem, what is it you mean?

Consultee: Well, Alfred is one of the brighter boys in my fifth-period World History course. For the first two months of class he was polite, attentive, and very productive. Lately, he has been late with assignments, doing poorly on quizzes, and appears to have some very strong negative feelings toward me.

Consultant: Strong negative feelings toward you? Could you tell me more about that?

Consultee: Well, I tried to talk to him about his poor performance one day after class. He was standing with a group of his friends, and I walked over and simply said that I need to talk to him about his class production. Well, he gave me this look like he wanted me to drop dead. And then when he did walk over to me he said that he doesn't understand why I am picking on him. Picking on him! I really like this kid, I am just trying to help.

For consideration and discussion:

1. Who is controlling the content of the session?
2. How do you think the consultee feels about the interaction up to this point?
3. What is the consultee expecting about this helping relationship?
4. What have you learned about the consultee?
5. What have you learned about the nature of the problem?
6. Contrast the data you received using open questions as opposed to that in Scenario I. What type of information was attained? What amount of return on consultant energy was received for both approaches?

SKILLS OF FOCUSING

Following the initial exploration and facilitation of a consultee's telling of their story, the consultant needs to assist the consultee to begin to identify and define, in clear, specific, concrete terms, the nature of his concern and the nature of the problem. This process of focusing is facilitated through the proper use of **clarifications, tacting leads** and **summarization.**

Clarification

As an individual shares her story and explores its various dimensions, she may employ inclusive terms (e.g., *they* and *them*), ambiguous phrases (e.g., *you know*), and words with a double meaning (e.g., *stoned, trip*). When the consultee presents such vague, generalized, or ambiguous descriptions, the consultant, through the use of clarification, will invite him to elaborate or expand on the topic. A clarification not only assists the consultant in developing a fuller understanding of the issue under discussion, but also serves as a tool to assist in focusing the conversation.

Typically, the consultant's request for clarification is posed as an open question and simply asks the consultee to elaborate on something that is vague or ambiguous to the consultant.

For example, assume that a consultee stated the following:

Consultee: It makes me bonkers when Conrad pulls that nonsense!

Obviously, it will be hard to assist the consultee in this situation unless the consultant clearly understands what is meant by terms such as *bonkers* and *nonsense*. Through the use of a clarifying question, the consultant will attempt to gain a better understanding (i.e., clarification) of what the consultee is intending. For example, the consultant might say,

"What exactly do you mean when you say *that nonsense?*"
or
"Perhaps you could give me an example of what it is that you call *nonsense?*"

A **tacting lead** (to be discussed shortly) would cause the consultee to describe the **last time** that the concern actually occurred and would simply ask, "When was the last time that Conrad pulled that nonsense . . . did he do it today?" When the consultee cites a recent incident, the consultant will ask, "Tell me about what happened."

A request for clarification from the consultant will not only provide a more accurate picture of what it is the consultee is experiencing, but depending on what it is the consultant selects to have clarified, it may also actually act to focus the discussion. In the preceding example, the consultant asked for clarification on the term *nonsense* as opposed to asking for clarification on the term *bonkers*. This selection will focus the consultee away from a discussion of personal feelings and concerns and will invite her to speak more about what is happening in a work-related situation.

Clarification may also prove to be the help that the consultee is actually seeking. Mehrabian (1970), in discussing counseling, suggested that clarification is actually one of the major steps to problem resolution. It is the position here that the same is true in consultation, in that it is often the consultee's initial lack of clarity about the nature of the problem that lends to feelings of helplessness and blocks his/her own appropriate problem solving. As the consultee gains increased clarity about the specific behaviors, attitudes, and factors involved in his/her problem, the feelings of confusion and helplessness diminish, and direction for resolution may become more apparent.

Exercise 7.4 provides an opportunity to identify vague, generalized, and ambiguous terms and to develop a request for clarification.

EXERCISE 7.4

Employing Clarification Skills

Directions: For each of the following consultee messages, develop a sample clarification response. Before responding, ask yourself:

- What has the consultee told me?
- What parts of the message are either unclear, vague, or maybe missing?
- How can I request information focusing the consultee on the part I want clarified?

Discuss your response with a colleague or classmate. If you have selected different points for clarification, why? What might be the effect of such different focusing?

   1. Consultee: Gads, I've really screwed up! I promised the class that our field trip would be this Friday, and the bus was scheduled for next Friday.
   Consultant: _____

   2. Consultee: O.K. so I ran over budget on the project. The boss is ragged out and the staff is about to jump ship. Big deal. I got things under control!
   Consultant: _____

   3. Consultee: Look, I already have five special needs students in my class. It's not fair that I have to take another one. Why do I have to get dumped on all the time?
   Consultant: _____

   4. Consultee: That group is just a bunch of babies. They are always on my back complaining about something. I'm their principal, not their mother.
   Consultant: _____

Tacting Response Leads

One especially effective clarification technique is the use of **tacting response leads** (Delaney & Eisenberg, 1972). Through the use of consultant tacting leads, the consultee will associate important information with behavioral events and environmental circumstances. Tacking leads achieve this empirical specificity by causing the consultee to identify and describe **the most recent** occurrence of whatever they are discussing. For example, a consultee said, "Every time I talk to this student's parent, we get into an argument." The key term that needs to be defined is *argument.* To define *argument* concretely, the consultant would first use a closed question, "When was the **last time** you experienced this argument?" or better yet, "Did you have this argument **today**?" After the consultee identifies the most recent occurrence, the consultant will pose the open question "Tell me about that." Thus, the tacting lead comprises a series of two questions (closed then open) that cause the speaker to provide a concrete and most recent example of vague and undefined disclosures. A few more examples of tacting leads will illustrate how effective they can be in each stage of the consultation process.

Entry:
> **Consultee:** I'm confident that we can solve this problem.
> **Consultant:** When was the last time you worked with a counselor on a problem?
> **Consultee:** It was last year at Glen Falls Middle School.
> **Consultant:** Tell me about how that went.

Exploration:
> **Consultee:** Frank's behavior has really been bizarre lately.
> **Consultant:** When did you last notice him acting bizarrely? Did you notice anything today?
> **Consultee:** Yeah, this morning during social studies he . . .

Goal Formulation:
> **Consultee:** I guess I'd like him to act more kindly toward his peers.
> **Consultant:** When was the last time you noticed him being kind to his peers?
> **Consultee:** I guess it was last week when Herb spilled all his crayons on the floor.
> **Consultant:** Tell me what happened.

Strategy Development:
> **Consultee:** I am not sure what I could use to positively reinforce his staying on task.
> **Consultant:** What activity has he been doing recently when he's given a choice?
> **Consultee:** Every chance he gets lately he likes to draw his cartoons.

Termination:
> **Consultee:** Thanks for all your help. I just hope this class continues to work together.

Consultant: When did they last work together well?
Consultee: Gee, this morning when we passed out the lab equipment.
Consultant: What did you and your class do?

Summarizations

In summarizing, the consultant pulls together several ideas or feelings, provided by the consultee, into a succinct, concrete statement that is then reflected to the consultee. Such a summarizing process has been found useful in bringing a discussion around a particular theme to a close or even to explore a particular theme more thoroughly (Brammer, 1994). This is a point to remember.

Often, with very enthusiastic and verbal consultees, a consultant may feel as if the consultation is out of control. For the consultant who feels as if she has lost control of the interaction, summarization provides a tool to bring a given conversation to closure. The appropriate use of summarizations, followed by the intentional employment of questions, can provide the consultant with the tools needed to regain control and direction for the interaction.

For example, consider the situation in the following example of a consultant attempting to respond to a consultee who has a tendency to ramble on in many directions.

Consultee: Wow, what a week. You gotta hear this and then I'll tell you what happened with my confrontation with Alice. You know the thing we decided on telling her. Well, anyway it's Monday and I'm going in to schedule her feedback session, just like we planned. But you ain't going to believe what happened! First I go to get in my car and the battery is dead. So I call road service and have to wait 45 minutes until they get there. I get a jump and now I'm off (late, of course) for the meeting. Well traffic is bumper to bumper on the expressway. So I'm now a good hour and a half late for the meeting. You can just imagine how Alice must be reacting.

Oh but it doesn't end there. Sitting in traffic the car starts to overheat. Do you believe this? This car is the absolute worst. I've had nothing but bad luck since I got it last year. The damn thing cost me $16,000 . . .

Consultant (interrupting): It appears that you have had a number of problems with the car, sounds frustrating, but despite all of that, you did have your meeting with Alice. Perhaps you could tell me how that meeting went.

The consultant's brief summary of the ongoing discussion of the car invites the consultee to end the discussion of that particular topic and focus on a more thorough presentation of the experience of the meeting with his employee, Alice.

In addition to closing a discussion or focusing on an aspect to develop, summarizations can be used to focus the consultee's scattered thoughts and feelings. As the consultee's story unfolds, the consultant needs to attend to certain consistencies or patterns—of feelings (e.g., anger, sadness), behaviors (e.g., avoidance, procrastination), and experiences (e.g., abandonment, rejection)—shared by the consultee. These consistent patterns, or **themes,** will be repeated or referred to over and over as the consultee shares her/his story. For example, imagine that in talking with a consultee, you become aware that he has provided four separate instances, with four different students in which he (the consultee) has lost his anger. Further, you discover that each time he loses his anger, he blames the students in an almost victim-like tone. You could use a summarization to pull together these various experiences around this single theme of victimization. You may suggest: "As you have been talking, I have become aware that you have spoken consistently about being an innocent victim, feeling as if the students do things to you and only you and that you have no control or role in the interaction. Perhaps this issue of being an innocent and powerless victim, is one that you may want to focus on."

Inviting the consultee to consider the possible existence of a pattern or theme in their experience may begin to move them to a fuller understanding of himself, as opposed to simply attending to a discussion of what at first appears to be a set of separate, unconnected events.

As evident in the examples provided, summarization requires the consultant to

1. Attend to and recall varying verbal and nonverbal messages presented by the consultee
2. Identify specific themes, issues, feelings conveyed by the consultee
3. Extract the key or core ideas and feelings expressed and integrate them into a concrete statement

As with many of the skills of helping employed in consultation, summarization is not an easy skill to develop or employ. It is one, however, that becomes easier and more effective with practice. Exercise 7.5 is provided to assist you in that practice.

EXERCISE 7.5

Developing Summarizations

Directions: For each of the following consultee presentations consider the following questions and develop a simple, concrete summarizing statement. Share your summaries with a colleague or classmate and discuss points of similarity and difference. In your discussion identify the possible impact each summarization may have on the direction of the consultation interaction. Questions to consider in preparing your summaries are:

1. What is the message the consultee is sending?

   What are the key elements (feelings? content?)

2. Is there a recurrent message (i.e. patterns, themes)?

3. Which of the consultee's words can I incorporate into a summary statement?

> **Consultee 1:** I've tried to speak with him but he just won't listen. It is so frustrating. I describe what I expect him to do, but he ignores me. It's like he has his mind made up and what I say just isn't important. Hell, I am his father. Should I just lay down the law?

Summarization: _____

_____

_____

> **Consultee 2:** (this is the third time you have met, and each time you come up with a plan of action the consultee comes up with an excuse as to why she can't do it) Boy I bet you are going to be really angry! I know we decided last week that I would contact Mr. and Mrs. Spellman about Colleen, and begin to problem solve around her difficulty with completing assignments on time but I had so many projects to do this week that I just couldn't get around to calling them. I know that I had some problem doing it the last two weeks as well, but this is really a busy time. You know we had the Christmas Play, mid-term exams, and parent meeting all over the past few weeks. It can really get overwhelming.

Summarization: _____

_____

_____

> **Consultee 3:** I really feel like such a wimp, I can't seem to assert myself. I should never have taken on this responsibility. I've been made the department chair and I am supposed to keep everybody on task. Al and Harry are deliberately bucking me. They refuse to hand in their schedules and grades on time. They come late to our department meetings. It is going to make me look pretty bad if these grades don't get sent out on time. I just wish they would cooperate.

Summarization: _____

_____

_____

WRITTEN COMMUNICATION:
SPECIAL CONSIDERATIONS

Beginning with the consultee's referral to the counselor consultant, the parties in a consultation will sometimes rely on written communication. Although the same considerations of purpose, clarity, timeliness, and confidentiality that apply to verbal communication will bear on written communication, a few specific caveats to writing warrant attention.

1. Referrals, codified observations, anecdotal and progress reports, written goal scales, and contracts are all appropriate forms of written communication within the consultation process. Over the course of a consultation these documents provide a paper trail of the content and process of the entire endeavor. Consequently, they must be produced, used, and conserved judiciously. "Need to know" should be the overriding criteria in deciding on the what, how, why and who of written communication.

2. Regardless of the medium used, every written communication must

   a. Have a cogent rationale and purpose within the consultation process

   b. Be written clearly and contain valid information

   c. Be communicated in a timely fashion when the information is most useful

   d. Be directed only to those individuals who can use it on a "need to know" basis

   e. Be completely purged from the written record when the information is no longer useful or valid

3. Confidentiality of all written (paper and electronic) communication must be a continual priority for the counselor consultant. Even a brief note reporting the progress of a client will violate client and consultee confidentiality if it falls into inappropriate hands.

INTEGRATING: STAGES, PURPOSE,
AND COMMUNICATION SKILLS

Now that we have looked at the purposes of consultation and the communication skills required of the consultant in achieving those purposes, it is helpful to place both purposes and skills within the context of the consultation process. The following matrix (Figure 7.1) attempts to link the purposes, communication skills, and stages. Although the matrix can only provide a general overview of these connections, it should help you appreciate

Stages	Purposes	Skills
Preentry	Provide Information	Written/Verbal Directives
Entry	Provide Information Support & Reassure Persuade & Influence Empathy & Rapport Instruction	Written/Verbal Directives Open & Closed Questions All Reflective Listening
Exploration	Obtain Information Provide Information Affirm & Reinforce Empathy & Rapport Creative Data Gather Instruction	All Active Listening Tacting Leads Summarization
Goal Formulation	Obtain Information Affirm & Reinforce Persuade & Influence Creative Data Gather Instruction	All Active Listening Tacting Leads Summarization Written/Verbal Directives
Strategy Develop & Implement	Obtain Information Provide Information Creative Data Gather Persuade & Influence Instruction	All Active Listening Tacting Leads Written/Verbal Directives
Maintenance	Provide Information Obtain Information Affirm & Reinforce	All Active Listening Written/Verbal Directives
Termination	Affirm & Reinforce Obtain Information Instruction	All Active Listening Summarization Written/Verbal Directives

FIGURE 7.1 Communication Skills in Consultation Stages, Purposes, and Skills

that the communication skills of the consultant are varied, complex and always purposeful.

SUMMARY

Communication Skills in Consultation:

Intended Outcomes

School-based consultation is a purposeful process designed to help consultees, clients, and clients systems achieve goals and objectives. Whenever possible, the counselor–consultant facilitates collaboration throughout the change process. The consultant uses many skills in facilitating this process, but no skill is more important in achieving success than the communication skills that are demonstrated. Whether verbal, nonverbal, or written, these skills lay the foundation for the empathy, trust, rapport, and credibility that supports the collaborative relationship. As the consultative process proceeds, various communication skills will be employed to achieve the specific purposes of informing or providing information; obtaining information to formulate goals and solve problems, support and reassure, affirm and reinforce, persuade and influence, demonstrate empathy and build rapport; brainstorm; and teach knowledge and skill through instruction and directives.

Skills of Active Listening

Prior to employing the skills of active listening, the effective consultant will need to learn to fully attend to the consultee and to demonstrate to the consultee that she or he is attending. Attending or being with another requires both a physical attending and a psychological orientation. In addition to taking an actively receptive physical stance, the consultant must also be **psychologically active** in the communication exchange. Accurate empathy is best demonstrated by a consultant through reflective listening, minimal encouraging, and paraphrasing the consultee's communication.

Skills of Exploration

This process of exploration entails a real reconnaissance or exploration of the consultee's total experience so that all the relevant data can be gathered and processed. The consultant will attempt to gather data, not just on the client, but also relevant information about the consultee and the consultee's system. Questioning can be a very useful tool for a consultant to use to begin to gain a real understanding of the issues confronting the consultee. However, questioning, if done inappropriately, can do much to block a helping, facilitative consultation relationship. The effective use of questioning will be guided by the following principles: (a) be purposeful; (b) be clear, concrete, and simple; and (c) ask as few questions as possible.

Skills of Focusing

Following the initial exploration and facilitation of consultee's ventilation, the consultant needs to assist the consultee to begin to identify and define, in clear, specific, concrete terms, the nature of his/her concern, the desired goals and objectives, and the strategies for desired change. This process of focusing is facilitated through the proper use of **clarifications, tacting leads,** and **summarization.** The nature of these communications can be spoken or written.

IMPORTANT TERMS

Attending	Directives	Paraphrasing
Brainstorming	Empathy	Summarizing
Clarifying	Minimal encouraging	Tacting response leads
Closed questions	Open questions	Themes

SUGGESTED READINGS

Kampwith, T. (1998). *Collaborative consultation in the schools: Effective practices for students with learning and behavior problems.* Upper Saddle River, NJ: Prentice Hall.

Marks, E. (1995). *Entry strategies for school consultation.* New York: Guilford Press.

Parsons, R. D. (1996). *The skilled consultant.* Needham Heights, MA: Allyn & Bacon.

Pugach, M. C., & Johnson, L. F. (1995). *Collaborative practitioners: Collaborative schools.* Denver, CO: Love Publishing.

Sugai, G., & Tindal, G. (1993). *Effective school consultation, an interactive process.* Pacific Grove, CA: Brooks/Cole.

WEB SITES

Gorkin and Cook, Inc.: Provides individual and group training and coaching on interpersonal, leadership, and communication skills.
http://www.gorin-cook.com/index13.html

Self-growth: Communication skills information, plus links to various sites.
http://www.selfgrowth.com/comm.html

Change Dynamics: Information and training on effective and persuasive communication.
http://www.changedynamics.com/s136cs.htm

REFERENCES

Atkinson, D. R., & Hackett, G. (2004). *Counseling diverse populations* (3rd ed.). Boston: McGraw-Hill.

Brammer, L. M. (1994). *The helping relationship: A process of skills* (5th ed.). Englewood Cliffs, NJ:Prentice Hall.

Brown, D., Pryzwansky, W. B., & Schulte, A. C. (2001). *Psychological consultation: Introduction to the theory and practice* (5th ed.). Boston: Allyn & Bacon.

Caplan, G., & Caplan, R. (1993). *Mental health consultation and collaboration.* San Francisco: Jossey-Bass.

Carkhuff, R. R. (1987). *The art of helping VI.* Amherst, MA: Human Resource Development Press.

Delaney, D. J., & Eisenberg, S. (1972). *The counseling process,* Oxford, England: Rand McNally.

Egan, G. (1977). *You and me: The skills of communicating and relating to others.* Pacific Grove, CA: Brooks/Cole.

Friend, M., & Cook, L. (1992) *Interactions: Collaboration skills for school professionals.* New York, NY: Longman.

Ivey, A. E. (1994). *Intentional interviewing and counseling.* Pacific Grove, CA: Brooks/Cole.

Jones, S., & Sims, D. (1985). Mapping as an aid to creativity. *Journal of Management Development, 4*(1) 47–60.

Mehrabian, A. (1970). *Tactics of social influence.* Englewood Cliffs, NJ: Prentice Hall.

Pedersen, P., & Carey, J. C. (1994). *Multicultural counseling in schools.* Needham Heights, MA: Allyn & Bacon.

Ryan, K., & Cooper, J. M. (1988). *Those who can teach* (5th ed.). Boston Houghton Mifflin.

Schmidt, J. J. (2003). *Counseling in schools* (4th ed.). Boston: Allyn & Bacon.

Wilcox-Mathew, L., & Ottens, A. (1997, April) An analysis of significant events in counseling. *Journal of Counseling & Development, 75*(4), 282–292.

8

⤬

Working with Resistance

I don't get it. Dr. Jameson said that he wanted to work
with me, and I feel like I'm using all my communication skills,
but every time we get started, he seems to have something else
he has to do or some "Yes, but" kind of response. This is
getting really frustrating. If he wasn't my administrator,
I'd just as soon tell him to forget it!

ust as it was demonstrated that systems often respond to consultation in
a self-protective, somewhat closed, and defensive manner, so too may a
consultee. This is certainly what our consultant is currently experiencing
as he attempts to work with Dr. Jameson.

It may be hard for a consultant to accept that even though his intentions
may be pure, his ideas reasonable, and his communication clear, resistance may
still be encountered! And, like the frustration expressed by our illustrated consultant, counselor–consultants who are ill prepared to work with resistance
may simply choose to terminate the relationship or attempt to employ power
to push through consultee resistance. In either case, the outcome of the consult is doomed, and a future consultation relationship with that consultee may
no longer be possible. Although consultee resistance can be experienced as
frustrating, it need not be viewed as adversarial, something to overcome,
something to defeat. A consultee's resistance to consultation may be a direct
reflection of the nature of the consultative process, the characteristics of the
consultant, or the unique nature of the consultee. In either case, it may prove

to be an important element to the consultation dynamic and needs to be understood and embraced. Accepting and working with resistance can lead a consultant to better understand the consultee. Working with the consultee's resistance can result in the development of a more productive collaborative relationship. Therefore, to be effective, a consultant needs to maintain his emotional objectivity when confronted with resistance. The effective consultant needs to employ his understanding of the nature of resistance along with his skills to **work with,** rather than push through, consultee resistance.

CHAPTER OBJECTIVES

Because the knowledge and skill required to work with consultee resistance is so essential to effective consulting, they will be the foci of the current chapter. The information and exercises provided in this chapter will assist the reader to develop the understanding and consultative skills needed for effectively working with consultee resistance.

After completing this chapter, the reader should be able to

1. Recognize the existence and source(s) of resistance, including those originating with the consultee, the consultant, or the consulting relationship

2. Embrace resistance as part of the growth and change process (rather than as a personal attack)

3. See the consulting relationship as an invaluable resource to the consultation and as such accept the resistance as an opportunity for gaining increased clarity and direction in the relationship

4. Employ strategies to work with resistance, including assisting the consultee in identifying her emotional concerns or uncertainties that may be the foundation for her resistance

5. Develop preventive strategies aimed at reducing the risk of resistance

UNDERSTANDING THE SOURCES
OF RESISTANCE

Resistance may be defined as any behavior that thwarts the probability of a successful process or outcome (Cormier & Cormier, 1991). In consultation this is often manifested as a consultee's failure to actively engage in the problem-solving process (Piersel & Gutkin, 1983). Understanding the bases for a consultee's resistance is an important first step to the process of working with consultee resistance. Change (or desire to maintain status quo) is an intrinsic dynamic that produces resistance. All change carries anxiety about the unknown and fear of failure.

A number of authors have conceptualized and described the many causes for resistance (e.g., Brown, Pryzwansky, & Schulte, 2001; Dougherty, Dougherty, & Purcell, 1991; Friend & Cook, 1992; Margolis & McGettigan, 1988; Piersel & Gutkin, 1983; Powell & Posner, 1978; Randolph & Graun, 1988; Waugh & Punch, 1987). Although the specifics of these categorizations may vary, they all seem to suggest that resistance is an emotional response to a perceived or real threat. The source of that threat can lie within: (a) the consultee's own issues and concerns, (b) the consultant's style, or (c) the nature of the consulting relationship. It is important for the consultant to discern the source of this threat so that it can be best addressed.

Resistance: Often a Reasonable Response

As depicted in our opening scene, the consultant encountering consultee resistance may find himself quite frustrated. Feeling that resistance is nothing more than a block to productive outcome, the consultant may attempt to push through the resistance or in some way coerce the consultee's involvement. It is important to understand that sometimes consultee resistance may, in fact, be a reasonable response, one that needs to be understood.

Consultee resistance can be a protective response instituted when an individual feels that the perceived change is too risky, too dangerous. Under these situations, resistance to consultant recommendations may be appropriately self, and system, preserving. Consider the situation in which a teacher, as consultee, is directed to "confront" and "stand up" to the aggressive gang leader who is disrupting her class. The consultee may find such a suggestion threatening to her well-being and safety and thus resist the consultant's recommendation. Under conditions in which the health and well-being of the consultee or the consultee's system are threatened, resistance may be a rational response, a response that if understood could lead to more productive recommendations.

Resistance—A Response to Consultant Insensitivity

At a minimum, consultee resistance indicates that the consultee is feeling uncomfortable. Often this discomfort can be a direct result of the consultant's insensitivity. Consider the case of the overly "competent" consultant (Case 8.1).

As you most likely recognize, the problem was not in the plan, but in the planner; not in the product, but the process. The result of this consultant's style and approach was a consultee who felt insulted, unheard, humiliated, and angry. The consultant did experience the reality of resistance—but in this case it was a resistance, he truly deserved.

As is evident in this case, resistance is often an indirect way for the consultee to express discomfort with the consultant or the consultation process. The ability to be sensitive to this indirect expression of discomfort and discern the bases (either rational or ill-founded) on which the discomfort rests is an essential diagnostic first step to successfully working with the dynamics of consultation. The effective consultant will need to recognize

CASE 8.1   The Overly "Competent" Consultant

A counselor–consultant, new to a school and eager to demonstrate his competence, was thrilled to receive a request for assistance from a well-liked and respected first-grade teacher.

Ms. L. asked if the consultant to assist her with Timothy, one of her "troublesome" first graders. She noted that over the course of the last 5 weeks Timothy's behavior had become increasingly disruptive to the class. According to Ms. L., Timothy began by calling out in class (without raising his hand and waiting to be recognized), but has since escalated his disruptive behavior to the point where he now "throws books up to the front of the room!" After listening to Ms. L.'s brief description, the consultant thanked her for her confidence in him and asked if he could visit the classroom to observe Timothy in action.

The next day, the consultant stopped in to observe Ms. L.'s class. What he noticed was that Ms. L. was a very creative, animated, and apparently interested teacher. Her room was brightly decorated, and the children were working at one of five learning stations located around the classroom. The children appeared very involved and attentive to the particular tasks they found at each learning station. Ms. L. was enthusiastically "bouncing" from station to station, both lending support and providing extensive verbal reinforcement.

In this environment of active, cooperative learning, sat Timothy. He was isolated from the other children and the learning stations and was sitting at his own desk working on individual worksheets. Ms. L. stated that Timothy tended to be too disruptive in the small groups and thus was given individual seat work during these periods of cooperative learning.

As the consultant observed the class interaction, he noted that Timothy would wait until Ms. L. was engrossed in discussion or demonstration at one of the learning stations, and then he would reach under his desk and select a book, which he would promptly throw up to the front of the room. Needless to say, the loud sudden noise startled every one in the room and resulted in Ms. L. coming over to Timothy and reprimanding him for his behavior. The consultant observed this scene played out four more times in the span of 20 minutes. Feeling his observations confirmed his initial hypotheses about what needed to be done, the consultant excused himself and informed Ms. L. that he would provide her feedback at her lunch period (which was in about 30 minutes).

During the interim, the consultant went to his office, where he promptly typed a proposal for extinguishing this attention-seeking behavior, along with a detailed instruction on how to employ teacher attention to shape Timothy's positive behavior. The proposal was detailed, providing step-by-step instruction on the shaping process, along with a number of supportive references and recommended readings on extinction and shaping. It was truly a paper worthy of any graduate student.

The consultant met with Ms. L., handed her the paper, and suggested that after she read it she could contact him if she had any questions. However, he was sure that things would work out fine as long as she followed the recommendations. Fine!

The end result of this insensitive display of pomposity was that the recommended program failed miserably. Timothy became more disruptive in his attention-seeking behavior. Ms. L. became more frustrated with Timothy, stopped the implementation of the plan, and reported to her fellow teachers that "(the consultant's) plan made things worse!" Further, she swore to her colleagues that she would *never* consult with "that guy" again.

resistance in its many forms and identify the possible cause(s) for this resistance, if she or he is to work with this resistance.

Resistance—A Reaction to Consultee
Issues and Concerns

As noted earlier, resistance is at one level an emotional response to a perceived or real threat. Often the source of the threat, although initially placed on the consultant, the consultation relationship, or the specific recommendations or processes encountered, actually stem from the consultee's personal issues. Four such issues or concerns—(a) negative or conflicting expectations, (b) concerns regarding control, (c) feelings of vulnerability, and (d) anxiety around problem finding and/or problem solving—are discussed in some detail.

Negative and Conflicting Expectations   In addition to these less-conscious sources of resistance, a consultee may exhibit resistance as a direct result of her conscious, negative expectations about the need or potential costs of this consultation encounter.

The consultee may exhibit resistance because of differing perceptions and expectations (Randolph & Graun, 1988). The consultee may not agree with the consultant that a problem exists or that one exists at a level of severity necessitating this consultation (Piersel & Gutkin, 1983). Or, in those situations where there is agreement on the existence and nature of the problem, differing expectations regarding the strategies or even the goals to be achieved may serve as the source of resistance. Certainly, the more the consultant's expectations regarding the nature of the problem, the goal to be achieved, and the specific recommendations are compatible with that of the consultee, the less resistance will be encountered (Elliot, 1988a, 1988b; Kazdin, 1981; Witt & Elliot, 1985). It is important that the consultation contract clearly reflect the congruence of both consultant and consultee expectations regarding consultation process and outcome (Kurpius, Fuqua, & Rozecki, 1993).

Even with such agreement of need, goals, and strategies, the consultee may exhibit resistance as a simple result of his negative expectations regarding time, resource, and energy cost that may be incurred as a result of engaging in consultation (Parsons & Meyers, 1984; Randolph & Graun, 1988). This seems especially true for individuals who are overwhelmed or are experiencing burnout. These individuals may simply not have the energy to participate in the change that it is anticipated will result from consultation. They may see the consultation as one added burden to an already overburdened agenda (Friend & Bauwens, 1988).

In attempting to address this last point regarding potential costs, the consultant needs to keep in mind that the less change indicated and the more culturally (and personally) compatible the change, the less costly such change will be and thus the less resistance one should encounter. Further, the more rapidly the consultant can identify the consultee's motivations and needs and enter the relationship at a level that will satisfy at least one of these motivational states, the more payoff will be experienced by the consultee, and thus the less resistance encountered (Parsons & Meyers, 1984). For example, when working with a consultee who is experiencing burnout and/or crises around a particular client, a consultant can reduce or even prevent resistance by providing immediate relief through the provisional modality (even if it is short term). Stepping in with hands-on assistance or removing an extremely disruptive client may prove more useful in reducing resistance than would engaging the client in a lengthy data-gathering process. Requiring the over-burdened consultee to collect data or learn new observation or intervention techniques would increase the consultee's expectations that such a relationship will be too costly and thus should be resisted.

The counselor–consultant experiencing consultee resistance as a result of negative expectations regarding need–goal–strategies and/or value (i.e., cost–payoff benefit) will need to clarify and (re)establish specific elements of a collaborative consultation contract. Specifically, the consultant would need to

1. Provide or review for the consultee the rationale and potential benefits of using consultation highlighting the preventive value
2. Reemphasize the confidential nature of the relationship
3. Reiterate the consultee's right and responsibility to accept, modify, or reject the recommendations and the freedom to renegotiate and/or terminate the contract at any time
4. Clarify the goal and direction that is mutually acceptable.

Exercise 8.1 provides an opportunity for you to recognize and develop strategies for working through consultee negative and conflicting expectations.

EXERCISE 8.1

Recognizing and Working through Negative and Conflicting Expectations

Directions: Because there may be multiple approaches to working with resistance, it would be beneficial to work this exercise with a colleague, supervisor, or mentor. For each of the following scenarios you are to

1. Identify a possible negative and/or conflicting expectation that may serve as a source of consultee resistance
2. Suggest the specific strategy you may employ to reduce or prevent this potential source of resistance

Sample: The consultant, Ms. Eberly, is a counselor at a Senior High School. She receives a call from, Gail, the social studies department chair.

    Gail: (voice is cracking, shaking) I would like to talk with you. I could . . . (starts to cry) . . . could really use your advice.

I (long pause) . . . really have a situation with Helen, our new teacher. I am really worried (crying), I think I blew it! (in the background the consultant hears Helen, yelling about taking Gail to the union representative).

Recognizing the consultee was in crisis, the possibility that the consultee was feeling vulnerability and out of control, and the real press of Helen threatening the consultee, the consultant:

1. Decides to go to Gail's office, rather than having Gail come to her office (reduce cost) and reduces her feeling of vulnerability by not exposing her to others she may encounter coming to his office.

2. Entering Gail's office decides to ask Helen if he could speak with Gail and if she would be kind enough to sit in an outer office rather than attempting to mediate in the situation (hands on, meeting needs to reduce attack, serves as payoff).

3. Begins to speak to Gail, rather than asking Gail what happened (reduced costs of possible vulnerability and provides emotional support and consultation refocus, which serves as need satisfier).

Consultant: Gail, I can see you are very upset. And Helen sounded angry. Helen is in the outer office, she's calming down. I let her know I will talk with her and that we can probably resolve whatever it is. She seems to be okay with that. I know you are concerned that you blew it . . . but it may not be that bad. Together I am sure we can work something out. Look, let's talk about it.

4. Having reduced the immediate crises (separating Helen and calming Gail), the consultant begins the problem identifying and resolving processes.

Consultant: Perhaps you could tell me a little about the problem and what you would like to see happen. I feel that if we work together on this we probably can figure out what to do.

Practice Scenario 1: The principal (consultee) asks that you "consult" with Ms. Hopkins (client), the 10th-grade English teacher. Ms. Hopkins is in her last year of teaching and is scheduled to retire at the end of this year. The principal has had a number of parent complaints about her inability to manage her classroom. He is concerned that perhaps she is simply too old and may need to be removed. But he is hoping that you can assist her to develop some new classroom management techniques.

Prior to your contacting Ms. Hopkins, she approaches you and asks that you work with Drew, a "real problem child." From Ms. Hopkins' perspective, Drew is the source of all the problems in her class.

For Reflection and Decision

1. What are the possible negative and/or conflicting expectations that may serve as a source of consultee resistance?

2. What specific strategy might be employed to reduce or prevent this potential source of resistance?

Practice Scenario 2: Helen B. is a bright, conscientious, 33-year-old assistant principal. She had been at the school only 6 months when the sudden resignation of the building principal served to elevate her to that post. She is the first woman to have achieved this position in this school and has been in this position for only 3 months. You are the chair of the guidance department, and she requests a meeting with you.

At the meeting, Helen appears upset, but with great effort controls her emotions and explains that "she is feeling that the assistant vice principal and other department chairs (all men) show little respect and often make inappropriate comments, often quite sexually suggestive. They also seem to be teaming up to make me look bad. I want you to speak with them. Find some excuse to provide us a workshop on the changing laws regarding harassment, diversity, and so on. They'll get the message. But you can't let on that I requested it!"

For Reflection and Decision

1. What are the possible negative and/or conflicting expectations that may serve as a source of consultee resistance?

2. What specific strategy might be employed to reduce or prevent this potential source of resistance?

Concerns Regarding Control   Resistance often reflects the consultee's concern about losing control or at a minimal being perceived as without control. Block (1981) noted that control not only reflects on the person's level of competence and professional maturity but is also often the mark of success within the organization. The more control, responsibility, and authority an individual is able to obtain, the more she or he is perceived as successful (Block, 1981). From this perspective, enlisting the assistance of a consultant may be perceived (by self or others) as an act of surrendering control and thus a personal and organizational failure. As a result, a consultee may feel that maintaining the semblance of control is more important than increasing his own professional effectiveness. In this situation, the consultee may be willing to resist consultation and maintain control even if it results in poorer performance (Block, 1981).

Consider Case 8.1, the issue of extinguishing book-throwing behavior. The consultee feeling as if the consultant was demeaning and attempting to illustrate how much more competent he was, gained a sense of control by inappropriately employing the consultant's recommendations for extinction and behavioral shaping. The disastrous results not only justified her own inability to rapidly resolve the problem, because the consultant was also unable to resolve the problem, but she was also able to dismiss the consultant, take back control of her class, and suggest to the world, ". . . I'll simply have to do it myself!"

The more the consultant can enlist consultee's participation and thus ownership in the creation of the intervention plan, the more control the consultee will feel. With this increased sense of control, resistance will be reduced. The challenge for the consultant is to create a condition in which the consultee not only feels in control, but is in fact a coequal partner controlling the nature and direction of the consultation. This is not always easy.

The effective consultant, although interested in demonstrating his own value and effectiveness, will not compete for control over the recognition for the operation and success of the consult. Rather, it is important to allow the consultee to feel actively contributing and directing the process and outcome, while at the same time feeling as if he/she can share the work, the burden, and the responsibility for possible failure.

Feeling Vulnerable   Engaging in consultation, like any helping encounter, requires the consultee to disclose—to share—to reveal their professional (and perhaps personal) experience. In the process of such sharing, the consultee exposes her competencies and incompetencies, strengths, and weaknesses. Sharing with the consultant about her professional practices that have proven unsuccessful increases the consultee's vulnerability to recognition of imperfection and failures. In fact, the consultee may even be concerned that she will be blamed for the problem (Alderman & Gimpel, 1996).

This sense of vulnerability can often be compounded by the very fact that consultation often involves learning new behaviors. As a natural outcome of the learning process, the consultee will experience an increase in feelings of incompetency as he learns these new behaviors. This possible demonstration of reduced competence may increase the consultee's sense of vulnerability, especially if the consultee is unclear about the nature of the consultation or the role and function of the consultant and anticipates that the consultant may evaluate him/her, either personally or professionally (Parsons & Meyers, 1984).

Besides possibly experiencing a sense of personal vulnerability as a result of disclosing and demonstrating one's level of incompetence, many consultees experience vulnerability within the organization should they enlist the support of a consultant. The climates of many organizations are not conducive to asking for help. For example, Gutkin, Clark, and Ajchenbaum (1985) reported that teachers working in closed organizational climates, as characterized by administrators who were below average in consideration and structure, typically were less open to engaging in consultation. Further, organizations that tend to be quite competitive and in which asking for help may be viewed as a sign of weakness and something that may be used by others as a way of advancing over the individual seeking help would certainly inhibit a consultee's interest and willingness to engage in consultation.

Engaging in consultation can at some level place the consultee at risk and vulnerable to others who seek to get ahead (Block, 1981). It would not be completely out of the question for a new teacher to be concerned about how his or her reliance on counselor support may be viewed by a tenure or promotion committee. And it is not just teachers who can feel this sense of vulnerability as highlighted by the following case illustration (Case 8.2).

The manner in which Ms. Wilson made contact with the counselor–consultant (via phone) and the request to call her at home, rather than simply stopping into her office, suggests that there may be a little more behind this

---

CASE 8.2   Consultee Vulnerability

Ms. Anita Wilson, Assistant Vice Principal, called the counselor seeking some assistance. Rather than stop in at the counselor's office or invite the counselor to hers, she simply called and left the following message:

"This is Anita Wilson, I would like to discuss the possibility of you working with me on some in-service training I am preparing. The principal asked me to develop an in-service for the teachers around the issues of cultural diversity, sexual harassment, and racial tension. I would like to discuss with you the ways you may be of assistance to me. Please give me a call—at home—rather than here at school. My phone number is 555-5555."

---

request than initially suggested. It appears that Ms. Wilson would like to keep the meeting with the counselor–consultant somewhat private. Perhaps this desire was based in some political or organizational reality or may be truly a matter of her self-induced vulnerability. Regardless, the consultant who ignores such signs of vulnerability may also proceed in insensitive ways that increase that sense of vulnerability and result in increased consultee resistance.

Until a consultant is able to change the norms and values of a consultee and the system in which he is functioning, she must remain sensitive to the consultee's experience of personal and organizational vulnerability. To reduce this sense of vulnerability in the consultee, the consultant should remain descriptive and nonjudgmental in her communications with the consultee, demonstrate respect for the consultee, exhibit a belief in the value of discussing success and failures as a way of growing, and highlight the confidential nature of the relationship.

Anxiety About Problem Finding/Problem Solving   Block (1981) noted that a consultant is often perceived as forcing the consultee to face "difficult realities." These difficult realities are reflected in the existence of the problem to be discussed or in the requirements involved in implementation of the solution. This difficult reality may explain why Meyers, Friedman, Gaughn, and Pitt (1978) found that consultee anxiety and hostility increased with consultant entry. The consultee's discomfort and resistance may be a defense against the reality that they will have to make difficult choices, confront their reality, and change (Block, 1981). Identifying, embracing, and working with our problems can be painful and thus may be resisted.

A very subtle twist on this source of resistance comes in the form of the consultee who is eager to identify problems, but may be less than eager, and thus resistant, to finding solutions. Often the change signified by the process of consultation also suggests the potential loss of some vested interest or aspect of value to the consultee. While experiencing the difficult realities of a problem, the consultee may also be experiencing some personal gain or need satisfaction by the existence of that problem and as such may feel anxious that such a problem will be resolved. The positive or negative consequences of a behavior can be referred to as secondary gain when accompanied by undesirable consequences for the same behavior. The reinforcement value of the secondary gain will often outweigh the negative consequences, thus maintaining the problem behavior.

For example, there may be contingencies operating within the system that maintain the old approach while resisting the new (Piersel & Gutkin, 1983). Consider the situation in which a company rewards an efficient, effective teacher by placing most of the "problem students" in her class or by increasing her adjunctive work assignments. In this setting, the teacher having a problem may find that he is given increased support and reduced adjunctive work. Thus finding a solution to the problem could prove costly to this teacher.

Resistance—A Reaction to Consultant Style

As noted by Wickstrom and Witt (1993), consultants experiencing consultee resistance would do well to reflect on their own approach and style of consultation. Certain consultant thoughts, feelings, and actions can contribute to resistance or blockage experienced in consultation. Specifically consultants who restrict consultee freedom, exhibit abrasive characteristics, and lose professional objectivity may stimulate consultee resistance.

Restricting Consultee Freedom   According to the theory of psychological reactance (J. W. Brehm, 1966; S. S. Brehm, 1976) individuals are more likely to resist attempts by another to change them whenever they perceive their freedom to be reduced or eliminated. Thus the consultant who attempts to impose control over the consultee or employ power to coerce the consultee to embrace the recommendations may threaten consultee freedom and thus elicit resistance.

One simple directive aimed at reducing consultee resistance would be to always **ask** consultees to do something, rather than **tell** or **direct** them to do something. In addition to this simple step, a consultant can increase the consultee's perception of freedom and control by developing a **collaborative relationship** that: (a) emphasizes the consultee's freedom to accept or reject consultant recommendations, (b) encourages consultee participation, and (c) deemphasizes consultant contribution (see chapter 7).

Abrasive Personal Characteristics   We may all like to perceive ourselves as likeable, approachable, and credible. The truth of the matter may be that this may not be how our consultees experience us. The consultant's personal characteristics can impact the degree of consultant persuasiveness (Kenton, 1989) and thus influence the degree to which resistance will be experienced within the consultee–consultant relationship.

The consultant's manner of self-presentation, manifestation of helping attitudes and skills, and (mis)use of power can either increase or decrease the level of resistance encountered. Thus a consultant who is perceived by the consultee as inappropriately dressed, using unprofessional or inappropriate language, or manifesting distracting and distasteful personal habits will elevate the possibility of resistance. Further, consultants who are perceived as lacking dynamism, energy, and confidence or have limited verbal skills and ability to be flexible and adaptive are perceived as less credible (Kenton, 1989) and thus may experience more resistance.

Further, consultants who fail to exhibit essential helping attitudes and skills and thus appear nonauthentic or uncaring or lack effective communication skills will also experience increased consultee resistance. But perhaps it is the consultant's use and or misuse of power within the consultation relationship that may contribute the most to the resistance encountered.

As noted previously (see chapter 5), the consultant who can find the appropriate balance between expert and referent power may be able to reduce the amount of system resistance encountered; the same is true for the relationship with the consultee. Establishing oneself as an expert by way of demonstrating professional preparedness, experience, competence, and intelligence is important for the persuasive consultant (Kenton, 1989). Thus consultants who fail to be perceived as possessing specialized knowledge or ability may have greater chance of experiencing consultee resistance. However, consultants not only need to possess and employ expertise, but also must be perceived as approachable and able to empathize with the consultee. In addition to possessing and appropriately employing expert power, consultants need to be perceived as able to relate to the other and of concern in helping the consultee (and the client) rather than simply furthering her own personal goals (Tingstom, Little, & Stewart, 1990). Thus consultants who are unapproachable, who remain detached and/or aloof, even while possessing great expertise, may experience consultee resistance.

It would appear that by properly blending expert and referent power (French & Raven, 1959; Martin, 1978; Meyers, Parsons, & Martin, 1979; Parsons & Meyers, 1984) the consultant will elicit both perceptions of competence and willingness to help and as such reduced resistance.

Resistance—A Reaction to a Dysfunctional Consulting Relationship

Consultation as viewed from a social psychological perspective is first and foremost a social interaction, a relationship (Parsons, 1996). As a social interaction success and failure can depend in large part on the dynamics of the social encounter (Tingstrom et al., 1990). Consultee resistance is often an indication of dysfunction within the consulting relationship (Parsons & Meyers, 1984).

Specifically, consultee resistance may indicate that the consultation process is experienced as aversive or as incongruent to expectations.

Consultation as an Aversive Process   Abidin (1975) suggested that resistance was a reaction to the fact that the procedures and process required in consultation were experienced by the consultee as aversive (Abidin, 1975). In a similar line of reasoning, Piersel and Gutkin (1983) suggested consultation could be resisted if engaging in consultation was met with punishing contingencies initiated at the systems level. Clearly, if the consultation process is aversive, then it will be resisted.

It would appear that any time engaging in consultation is more costly, physically, socially, or psychologically, than it is rewarding, the consultee will find the interaction aversive and tend to resist it. This is somewhat indirectly supported by the findings of Tingstrom et al. (1990), who after reviewing the literature noted that resistance was reduced under the following conditions: (a) the more severe the problem and (b) the less time and resource required to implement the treatment.

The effective consultant will attempt to maximize payoffs within the consultation relationship and as a result of engaging in consultation, while at the same time reduce the costs associated with and experienced in consultation. Rewards include any aspect of the relationship that is enjoyable or satisfying. These payoffs may be those gratifying experience that come as a direct result of the interchange between the consultant and consultee (i.e., endogenous rewards) or those that result as a by-product of the interaction (i.e., exogenous rewards). Resolving the presenting complaint would be an example of the exogenous payoff, whereas feeling heard and supported by the consultant could be an endogenous payoff. Costs can also be of an exogenous (e.g., any requirements on the consultee to modify his style or to collect data) and endogenous (e.g., the anxiety felt disclosing one's inadequacies as the consultant–consultee analyze the problem at hand). Although there will always be costs in a relationship, be it as simple as the amount of energy one has to employ to meet and exchange with another, the important point is that the payoffs or rewards need to outweigh these costs for the relationship to be maintained, rather than resisted (see Exercise 8.2).

EXERCISE 8.2

Reducing the Aversive Nature of Consultation

Directions: This exercise is best accomplished by working in a small group or a dyad (with a supervisor, mentor, or colleague) to allow for brainstorming. Following you are presented a brief description of characteristics surrounding a consultation. After reading the description:

1. Identify three possible cost that could occur within the relationship (endogenous) and three costs that may be incurred as a result of the encounter (exogenous). Similarly, identify three exogenous and three endogenous rewards.

2. Be specific and concrete and generate strategies aimed at reducing each of the identified costs.

3. Generate strategies for adding as many additional payoffs as you (or the group) can generate.

Scenario 1: Because of recent school redistricting, Mr. Adams, a teacher with 33 years experience at the junior high level, has been assigned to teach third-grade social studies. Mr. Adams is 1 year away from retirement age, even though he hopes to continue teaching for at least 5 years past this point. Mr. Adams has been experiencing a lot of frustration and stress because of the "immaturity of his class." He approaches you informally at lunch one day and states: "Boy, kids are really different today. I don't know where they get the energy. Sometimes an old guy like me can feel pretty worn out at the end of the day. You have any magic tricks you could share with me?"

Scenario 2: Hector Henriques is a new teacher hired to work in the sixth-grade math and science department. Hector contacts you and asks you to reassign two students from his fifth-period math class. Hector, the first Hispanic American to work in the school district, stated that he observed some racial/ethnic slurs written in notes being passed by these two boys, and he is afraid that he will "loose his cool," with them if he catches them again. Hector made it very clear to you that he has a very hot temper, and he wants these students out. Further, Hector suggests that he is aware that there are people within the school that would like to see him fail, and that he "hopes that you are not one of them."

Model of Consultation as Incongruent to Expectations   The discomfort and dissonance experienced when the consultee and consultant have incongruent expectations about the nature of consultation and the roles to be played may serve as a primary source of resistance (Piersel & Gutkin, 1983). For example, a consultee expecting that the consultant will take a provisional or prescriptive role may resist the active, contributory role of consultee required by a collaborative approach. The consultee and consultant may also be in conflict over the focus of the problem. This may be a problem in situations in which the consultee targeted the source of the problem as resting with the client, whereas the consultant has identified the source as within the consultee or the system at large. The outcome goals and objectives of the consultation can also be a source of contention and thus resistance in a consultee. Finally, resistance may occur when the consultee and consultant disagree in terms of the intervention to employ (e.g., removal of the client versus modification of consultee style).

In order to avoid or reduce incongruent expectations, the consultant needs to be clear in defining the nature of the contract, the process to be employed, and the roles to be played by both the consultant and consultee (Caplan, 1970; Parsons, 1996; Sandoval, Lambert, & Davis, 1977). This clarification and definition needs to occur during the entry stage of the consultation and may need to be reiterated throughout the consultation contract. In addition to defining the role and parameters of the consult, the consultant needs to help the consultee to achieve clear agreement on the problem of concern, the outcomes to be pursued, and the strategies to be employed. This agreement on the problem to be addressed has been identified as the most critical step in the problem-solving process of consultation (Nezu & D'Zurilla, 1981).

RECOGNIZING THE MANIFESTATIONS
OF RESISTANCE

The first step in working with resistance is recognition. That is, the consultant must be aware of resistance when it is present. Too often, consultants get lost in the task of problem solving and fail to register or record the interpersonal cues that are conveyed by the consultee and that suggest that the consultee is not totally embracing this process. A consultant needs to remain sensitive not only to the progress of the problem solving but also to the health and well-being of the relationship. It is important for the consultant to be aware of the verbal and nonverbal cues that provide evidence of the consultee's experience in the consultation. The consultant must learn to not only recognize repetitive behaviors or verbalizations that are blocking the process, but also needs to be sensitive to the level of participation demonstrated by the consultee. Is the consultee attentive? Is the consultee enthusiastic and participative? Is the consultee demonstrating a sense of ownership, or is she exhibiting signs of discomfort?

In addition to looking for these subtle signs of potential discomfort or resistance, the consultant would be wise to ask directly about the consultee's level of comfort or feelings of apprehension or concern. This inquiry into the consultee's experience with the consultative process is not only a useful form of evaluation but is also a valuable means of involving and empowering the consultee throughout the consultation.

The ways a consultee can manifest discomfort and resistance are many and have been conceptualized in a variety of ways (e.g., Block, 1981; Friend & Bauwens, 1988; Karp, 1984). Regardless of the system employed or the label applied, consultee resistance involves an action on the part of the consultee that in effect thwarts the process of consultation. Some of the forms are quite obvious, as in the situation in which the consultee directly, explicitly, and perhaps even quite dramatically says NO to the process. But most often resistance is less obvious, less direct, and therefore less easy to assess.

Following are brief descriptions of some of the more subtle forms of consultee resistance. Readers interested in a more elaborate discussion of these and other forms of consultee resistance are referred to works of Block (1981), Friend and Bauwens (1988), and Parsons (1996). This list included here is not intended to be exhaustive, nor are the items necessarily exclusive of one another. It is simply a sampling of the various forms resistance may take, ranging from the more direct and obvious, to those forms that can be quite subtle. The intent is simply to provide a feel for the many faces of resistance in hopes of increasing the reader's ability to recognize the presence of resistance in his/her own consulting.

The Push Away

Sometimes a consultant may find that a consultee, who initially approached consultation enthusiastically, begins to find reasons within the dynamics of the relationship to push the consultant away and terminate the relationship. The consultee using this form of resistance will find an opportunity to become angry at the consultant. The consultee may blame the consultant for having imposed an overwhelming amount of work on the consultee. The consultee may complain that doing what the consultant requests is disrupting the normal flow of his/her work. Whatever the form of blaming, accusing, and fault finding takes, these are manifestations of the consultee's desire to resist consultation by pushing the consultant away. Consider the following dialogue.

> **Consultee:** I know I told you I was willing to work with you but I didn't realize you were going to come into my classroom and disrupt the class.
>
> **Consultant:** Disrupt the class? I am a bit confused. I thought we agreed that observing Tommy was a good way to begin to gather some information.
>
> **Consultee:** It may have been a good idea for you, but it was clearly disruptive for me! You saw how excited the children became. They were almost unmanageable. They kept looking back at you and not paying attention to the story being read. I mean, Tommy even asked if you were my boyfriend. That's all I need. This is making things worse, not better!

The consultee's attempt to push the consultant away by being annoyed, irritated, or stimulating a sense of guilt or responsibility onto the consultant can prove very effective should the consultant take it personally and counterattack or respond in a defensive mode. The consultant needs to be careful not to be seduced into the anger or accept the guilt. The consultant should avoid getting into a competition about what "we" agreed upon. Rather, the consultant will prove more effective if he increases his empathic listening skills, attempts to label the feelings being experienced by the consultee, and invites the consultee to work with the concern at hand. The scenario presented would not even happen if the consultant had followed the stages of the consultation process, collaboratively formulating goals and interventions.

For example, continuing with the preceding scenario, the consultant may suggest the following.

> **Consultant:** I can see how upset you are about the classroom visit. And even though I didn't experience the same degree of disruption in the class as you did, I respect how it may have impacted upon you. It certainly was not what I intended, nor what you or I anticipated when we discussed it yesterday. Although this is certainly something we didn't anticipate, it is something with which we can still work. Let's think of ways that we can gather the information we were seeking while being sure not to disrupt the class.

Yes, But . . .

A somewhat more subtle form of resistance and one that can prove extremely frustrating for a consultant is one that comes in the form of "agreement . . . but." The consultee, employing a "yes, but" form of resistance will demonstrate a willingness and even an enthusiasm for the process or direction of the consultation. However, this enthusiasm, this willingness, is quickly followed by a point of objection and concern that undermines the previous work. This form of resistance is especially noticeable when the prescriptive modality is employed using directives from the consultant.

For example, the consultee might suggest that other competing demands make the consultant's suggestion impossible.

Consultee: I think this is a great idea, but you know with all the things I have to do, it is simply going to be impractical.

Or, the consultee may attempt to deflect the consultant by suggesting that a newer crisis is making it difficult (if not impossible) to continue with the consult.

Consultee: I know you want me to gather baseline on Kathy's calling out behavior, but we were just informed that we are beginning Middle States Accreditation visits, and I am on the Governance Committee. So we'll have to get back to this at a later time. I really want to follow through on Kathy, because we had some really good ideas, but you know how it is!

The consultee may even attempt to displace the responsibility for the resistance onto others in the environment.

Consultee: I really like the idea, it is very creative, but you know the others in the work group are not going to go for this. I know it's frustrating. But it's not me, I simply don't have the authority or power to influence the rest of the faculty.

In the situations in which the consultee is exhibiting resistance through a "yes, but . . ." response, the consultant may be seduced into believing the consultee is cooperative and thus feel maximum frustration when the blockage occurs. When the consultant encounters repetitions of the "yes, but" consultee response, he should summarize the pattern and invite the consultee to discuss his/her own discomfort with the process or direction of the consultation.

Consultant: Tom, I really appreciate your enthusiasm and energy during this brainstorming session. We have come up with six pretty good ideas for working with Louise. However, I have noted that each time we get an idea that at first seems good, you identify some reason that it won't work. It is possible that you may be feeling some apprehension or concerns that we could talk about?

Again, as with all interventions with resistance, this form of confrontation will require all the helping attitudes and skills the consultant can muster. Change strategies that are linked to client goals that have been formulated by the consultee experience less resistance. After summarizing the client goal, the consultant might say,

> **Consultant:** Let's generate as many actions that we can that will help us to achieve your goal for Tommy. Then we can select those actions that can realistically be implemented.

Passive Aggression

Passive aggression refers to an indirect form of resistance expressed through such maneuvers as forgetfulness, procrastination, repetitive mistakes, and inefficiencies. Consider the resistance exhibited by the consultee in the following illustrations. The consultee had met with the consultant previously and was scheduled for a follow-up meeting, at which time they would discuss the data the consultee was to have collected. Rather than outright refusal, the passive-aggressive consultee will feign eagerness to perform, only to have been blocked by events beyond his/her control. Consider the following consultee responses and how you may feel as the consultant.

> **Consultee A:** I'm sorry about missing our meeting—I know third time (is it a charm?) but I simply have so much on my mind that I forgot. Oh, I know I was supposed to do something or prepare something for today but it really slipped my mind. I simply have to start writing things down.
> **Consultee B:** Hi, how goes it? Before you begin, I know I promised to gather that baseline data, and actually I started, but there has been so much other stuff going on, I just didn't get a chance to do it this week. I promise you, I'll complete it next time! So anything else I can do?
> **Consultee C:** I gathered the data you asked for, but I can't seem to find the file. It's here somewhere! I think I can remember what I wrote, because it was only five items, you know I counted how many times he was late following morning break. Oh, I'm sorry. I was supposed to record how many times he was late following both morning and afternoon breaks?

Although it is not suggested that this response style is reflective of a personality disorder, it is clear that such an indirect expression of resistance not only actively blocks progress but can also serve as a major source of frustration and irritation to the consultant. The danger is that the consultant may, in fact, be seduced into venting her own frustration and anger, giving the consultee justification for terminating the specific process, if not the entire relationship.

Requesting Counseling

An interesting form of resistance identified by Caplan (1970) was that involving the consultee's request for personal counseling. It is interesting in that as a mental health consultant one might be easily pulled into believing this is a profitable direction for the consultation to go. But the fact is that engaging in counseling is effectively terminating the consultation.

A request for counseling actually directs the focus away from the consultation. Such a request attempts to change the nature of the relationship. No longer is the focus on the client, but now on the consultee; no longer is the target a work-related issue, but now on the consultee's personal problem, and no longer is the relationship one of coequal problem solving but of a helper–helpee encounter.

Although the consultee may ask the consultant for counseling directly, often the consultant is seduced into this role shift by the consultee's expression of negative affect around their work performance (Randolph & Graun, 1988). For example,

> **Consultee:** You've been a godsend. If it hadn't been for you I would
> have quit long ago. I just can't take it. I can't do it anymore
> (starting to tear up). Look around, we don't have needed supplies.
> The administration couldn't care less that we are breaking our backs.
> You get absolutely no support . . . nor respect. You know it just isn't
> worth it. I can't cut it anymore. I really don't know what I'm going to
> do (crying).

In these situations, the consultant must remember that consultation *is not* counseling. What is needed in situations like this is for the consultant to provide the consultee with supportive refocus (Randolph, 1985). The consultant, while showing a level of empathic support, needs to draw the consultee and the relationship back to focus on the client or the consultee's skills, knowledge, and objectivity with working with the client.

> **Consultant:** Tom, I can tell you really feel like it is a lot to handle.
> Today is obviously not a good day for you, and you sound like you
> really feel overwhelmed and perhaps a bit unappreciated. But you
> and I had begun to develop some really interesting and useful ideas
> about getting Kevin and the rest of that seventh period back on
> track. So why don't we go grab a cup of coffee and I'll show you
> that information on building classroom teams that I was supposed to
> get. We could check it out together and see how it applies to Kevin
> and the other guys.

Quick Sell/Quick Buy

In discussing the process of entering a consultative contract Meyers et al. (1979) warned that "even when no reservations or concerns are raised, the consultant should raise typical concerns to be sure there are no problems" (p. 66).

These authors' experience negotiating contracts for consultation with a system has application when negotiating the more informal contracts with the consultee. Although it can be quite gratifying for the consultant to have the consultee immediately embrace his/her orientation and consultation delivery model, the reality is that often too rapid agreement and blind acceptance of the consultant's recommendation may be one way the consultee can avoid involvement in the process. Efforts to create and maintain collaborative consultation following the stages of the consultation process will go a long way in mitigating this form of resistance.

The consultee who actively nods agreement and provides verbal affirmation for the suggestions ("Oh yes . . . absolutely . . . etc.), may be dismissing the consultant and the consultation process. Quite often the rapid, "that's great, you bet, no problem" response reflects either a lack of understanding or an intentional decision not to follow through, even though providing whole-hearted verbal support.

Consultation involves change and resistance is to be expected. The consultee who expresses concerns, wants to problem solve together, and manifests some degree of anxiety about the process is most often actively engaged in the process and aware of the work it entails. The consultee who exhibits blind, rapid acquiescence may later demonstrate through his/her lack of follow-through or inappropriate application of the steps discussed that he was not truly aware or involved in the consulting dynamic.

If the consultation goals and objectives are based on the concerns brought by a consultee to a consultant and the interventions are collaboratively formulated, resistance will be minimal, though never eliminated. In collaborative consultation, one is to expect differing opinions and compromise. Blind total acceptance of the consultant's direction or recommendation is contraindicative of this type of collaboration. The consultant confronting such a situation would be wise to encourage discussion of reservations, objections, or concerns experienced by the consultee. The consultant, although not attempting to create problems, should be willing to raise typical concerns that could be discussed when the consultee fails to identify his own concerns. Consider the following.

Consultant: I feel really good about our meeting today and your willingness to work with me on this situation. I know that you initially expected me to work with Linda directly.

Consultee: No problem. I really hadn't considered the fact that I could be of assistance to you or that somehow we could combine our efforts with Linda. I am really looking forward to it.

Consultant: Me too. Your input into the goals and objectives with Linda was critical. They had to come from you. I would imagine that this idea of collaborating with me in the development and implementation of a behavioral modification plan for Linda that will achieve those goals and objectives is adding to your workload. Do you see any problems this may cause for you?

Consultee: No, I don't think it will be a big deal.

Consultant: Great. I just know that oftentimes learning a new technique or applying some new methods takes time and energy to learn and apply.

Consultee: Nope! Sounds great!

Consultant: Do you have concerns about our meeting regularly? I know for some it could be seen as an added burden in terms of time and energy.

Consultee: Well, obviously it would be nice if things were simply OK and I could use this time for preparation, but actually I am excited about some of the new techniques and feel that they will help me in the future.

Consultant: Super. I'm looking forward to it as well. You know it may even be a good idea for us to periodically review both how well we are doing with Linda and how well we are doing with this consulting process. That way if there are any issues or concerns that come up, we will be sure to address them.

WORKING WITH, NOT DEFEATING, CONSULTEE RESISTANCE

As noted in the introduction of this chapter, resistance to consultation on the part of the consultee need not be an adversary nor something to be subdued. The position here is that the effective consultant, who understands consultee resistance, can utilize that understanding to develop an effective, productive, collaborative relationship with the consultee. Once resistance has been identified, it is essential for the consultant to (a) invite the consultee to "own the resistance," (b) reframe the resistance as a source of valuable information, and (c) recognize and ameliorate the source(s) of resistance.

The Invitation

The invitation stage is intricately tied to the identification state in that the consultant is acknowledging resistance as a natural, normal part of any change process. Once consultee resistance has been experienced, a consultant may be tempted to attack or directly confront the consultee and the resistance. Although such a tendency may be understandable, given the consultant's frustration, such a strategy would most likely be ill fated. Block (1981) suggests that a consultant take on somewhat of a Zen quality to working with resistance. Rather than intensifying and buffering one's argument with more data and research, only to find the consultee more entrenched in her defense, it may be more fruitful to sit quietly following the identification step to allow the consultee to reflect and take ownership. This period of silence is not employed as a technique or tool to make the consultee uncomfortable or defensive, rather it is used as time to reflect, consider, and embrace what is being said. Expanding upon this peaceful defense is the practice of Aikido. Morihei Ueshiba integrated Zen and Buddhist philosophy into the Japanese concept of Bushido, the Japanese word for "stopping the spear" (Nitobe, 1905). This defensive martial art is called Aikido, which translates into "Harmony, Spirit and Path." Aikido's foundation is blending. Instead of confronting an attack, you blend in with the attack, accommodating, controlling, and ultimately resolving it. The attacker's own energy is absorbed and unbalanced, protecting both parties from harm. Blending, joining, and connecting with the person's energy leaves the attacker unbalanced and susceptible to harmonious compromise. The Aikido master uses minimal force to achieve a harmonious resolution in which the attacker is under control, the attack is stopped, and both parties are safe (Dobson, 1980). The school consultant practicing the art of Aikido will acknowledge the consultee's resistance, affirm the consultee's right to that resistance, and join them in their desire to overcome that resistance. Terry Dobson (1980), Thomas Crum (1987), and Koichi Tohei (1966) offer excellent applications of Aikido to resistance and conflict resolution in daily life.

The consultant seeking harmonious resolution of resistance will directly encourage the consultee to fully express his/her concerns, reminding him/her about the collaborative contract and the consultee's right to reject suggestion. The consultant needs to invite the consultee to share his/her experience with both the progress and direction of the problem solving and the process of the consultation and the relationship with the consultant.

The goal of this step is to move the consultee from indirect expression of concerns (i.e., resistance) to direct expression of concerns, which now can be addressed.

Reframe the Resistance

Once the consultee has taken ownership over his/her concerns and the expression of resistance, the consultant needs to assist the consultee to accept his/her concerns as valid and to reframe his/her apprehension and concerns so that they are viewed as important data to the process of the consultation. Rather than attempting to suppress these concerns or express them indirectly, the consultee needs to be encouraged to work with the consultant around these concerns as if they were naturally occurring concerns that were part of the consultation experience. Exercise 8.3 is provided to assist you in practicing this reframing process.

EXERCISE 8.3

Working with Resistance

Directions: Because resistance is experienced at different levels of awareness by different consultants and because the manner in which a consultant identifies, invites, and reframes varies from consultant to consultant, completing Exercise 8.3 is best performed with another person or in a small group. Additional cues will be identified, and alternative ways of inviting and reframing can be experienced by working within a group.

The task involves reading the consultative interaction to follow and responding to each by:

1. Identifying the specific point in the exchange that you became aware of the resistance. Identify what it was that specifically cued you to the resistance. Identify how you would feel as the consultant, up to that point. This awareness of your reaction may be useful diagnostic cues.

2. After recognizing the presence of resistance, write out the specific response that you would employ to "identify" and "invite" the consultee to embrace this resistance. Be sure to employ nonjudgmental, descriptive, empathic, and here and now responses.

3. After reading the entire exchange, identify how you would respond to the consultee's implicit concerns in order to reframe the consultation experience in a more positive and hopeful light.

> **Consultant:** Hi, Marie it is very nice to meet you. I understand through Dr. Morton (the principal) that you wished to speak with me regarding your third-grade student, Drew.
>
> **Consultee:** Yes. I am really grateful you had time to see me. Drew's been a real problem. I was hoping you would talk with him.
>
> **Consultant:** Well, that certainly could be a possibility, but I generally find that it is much more effective if I work along with the teacher to develop some problem-solving ideas. After all, you really are the expert when it comes to Drew and the work that he is failing to produce. So perhaps you could help me know what it is that Drew is doing (or not doing) that concerns you, as well as some of the things you have tried up to this point.
>
> **Consultee:** Oh, I thought you were going to simply take him out of my class and do counseling with him.
>
> **Consultant:** Again, Marie, if after discussing the situation, we feel that is the best strategy, it certainly will be considered. Maybe we could start by you telling me what you think is up with Drew and the kinds of things you have tried.
>
> **Consultee:** OK, but I only have 30 minutes free period now so we may have to do this another time.
>
> **Consultant:** No, really, I'm OK with at least starting on this if you are, and 30 minutes is really quite a bit of time.
>
> **Consultee:** Well, what is it exactly I should tell you?
>
> **Consultant:** Marie, there really isn't anything in particular that you should tell me but anything that could help me get a feel for what it is about Drew that is concerning you would be useful. Further, it might help both of us to understand the kinds of things you have found that work and those that haven't been as successful.
>
> **Consultee:** Did Dr. Morton seem to be concerned that I needed help?
>
> **Consultant:** No, she actually appeared impressed with your concern for Drew and your willingness to seek assistance.
>
> **Consultee:** Assistance! That's putting it mildly. You know, maybe I ought to be talking with you about me. I think I'm losing it.
>
> **Consultant:** I know it can feel overwhelming at times, but I feel confident that if you could help me understand a little about the situation with Drew, you and I could begin to work out some things that could help.
>
> **Consultee:** You know, I guess you are right, maybe working together will help, but right now I really have to prepare for class. I'll give you a call and set up an appointment so we can meet again.

Ameliorating the Source of Resistance

As has been emphasized throughout this text, the consultant who is employing a collaborative consultation following the stages of the consultation process will experience the least amount of resistance from their consultee. When resistance is encountered, the counselor–consultant needs to not only recognize the presence of resistance but also identify and eventually ameliorate its source.

It is possible that the goals and/or methods to be employed along with the consultant's approach to the problem may simply be inappropriate, and the consultee's resistance serves as a directive that an adjustment is needed. This would be the case when the consultant recommends interventions that are immoral, unethical, illegal, or simply beyond the values and culture of the consultee and his organization, or when the goal to which the consultant is working is antithetical to the original reason for the consultee seeking consultation. Under these situations, resistance is appropriate, and it is the consultant, rather than the consultee, who needs to adjust.

Assuming that no such adjustment is warranted, the consultant needs to elevate the consultee's awareness of his resistance by identifying or naming the resistance. In order to assist the consultee to become more aware and more responsible for the dynamics of the consultation, the consultant needs to describe his/her experience in the consulting process up to that moment. This is not a point of evaluation or personal judgment. It is a simple description of the apparent repetitiveness, difficulty, or blockage being experienced.

The consultant needs to employ appropriate helping skills and attitudes and present his/her experience in genuine, nonjudgmental, nonaggressive, and empathic language. It is also important to focus on the current, here and now experience, rather than reporting or describing something that has passed and for which our memories may be clouded. For example, consider the exchanges listed in Case 8.3.

REDUCING THE RISK OF RESISTANCE

Developing the knowledge and skill needed to recognize and identify consultee resistance and to invite the consultee into a reframing of his/her concerns in light of a positive view of consultation are essential to effective consulting. However, establishing conditions that reduce the risk of resistance may prove even more beneficial to successful consultation.

Social psychologist Jack Brehm (1966, 1972) proposed that when a person feels that his/her freedom has been threatened or abridged, he/she will engage in actions that help them regain control and personal freedom. The specific state of motivation that energizes their attempts to regain control he termed *reactance*. Consultee resistance has been viewed and interpreted within the context of reactance (Hughes & Falk, 1981). Thus from this perspective, a consultant who can develop a consultation relationship and dynamic that maximizes consultee control and personal freedom should reduce reactance and thus reduce the risk of resistance.

CASE 8.3   Identifying the Source of Consultee Resistance

Each of the following demonstrates one way in which a consultant attempted to unearth the possible existence and source of a consultee's resistance.

Situation 1: The "yes, but" form of resistance

Consultant: I am a bit confused. For the last 10 minutes I have been making suggestions and you seem to initially agree and support the suggestion. You have been nodding and saying, "Yes, that's a good idea." However, each time we can begin discussing how to implement the idea, you seem to offer a "but" as to why it won't work. There is something that perhaps I'm missing, something that may be very important to the formulation of strategies that we both can support.

Situation 2: Passive-aggressive—forgetting:

Consultant: I know you said that you were sorry that you forgot

about the assignment. I appreciate that you were apologetic for the fact that this was the third time in a row that you have now forgotten to do the assignment. As you told me you were sorry, you appeared to be annoyed or angry at something. Could we talk a little about how you have been feeling about working together around this issue?

Situation 3: The consultee employing, the quick sell/quick buy form of resistance:

Consultant: You certainly appear supportive. But it seems that everything I suggest is equally as acceptable to you. It may be useful if you could help me see what the possible costs or downsides to each of the suggestions may be. That way we could tailor the suggestion that fits best with your own thoughts and style.

As such the best means of preventing or at least reducing the risk of resistance would be to create a consultation relationship that is a truly collaborative working relationship (Caplan & Caplan, 1993; Friend & Cook, 1992; Parsons, 1996). The unique characteristics of a collaborative consulting relationship, including the creation of a coequal and mutual balance of power and ownership, stimulate a sense of freedom and control and thus reduce the need for reactance and resistance.

SUMMARY

Understanding the Sources of Resistance

Although resistance may be experienced as somewhat frustrating to a task-driven counselor–consultant, resistance needs to be recognized and addressed as a clear signal of consultee discomfort. It is important for the consultant to be sensitive to this indirect expression of discomfort and to be able to discern the bases (rational or ill-founded) on which the discomfort rests. This is an essential diagnostic first step to successfully working with the dynamics of consultation. The effective consultant will need to recognize resistance in its many forms and identify the possible cause(s) for this resistance if she is to work with this resistance.

Recognizing the Manifestations of Resistance

Regardless of the system employed or the label applied, consultee resistance involves an action on the part of the consultee that in effect thwarts the process of consultation. Some of the forms are quite obvious, as in the situation in which the consultee directly, explicitly, and perhaps even quite dramatically says NO to the process. But most often resistance is less obvious, less direct, and therefore less easy to assess.

Working with, Not Defeating, Resistance

Consultee resistance need not be an adversary, nor something to be subdued. The position here is that the effective consultant, who understands consultee resistance, can utilize that understanding to develop an effective, productive, collaborative relationship with the consultee. Once resistance has been identified, it is essential for the consultant to (a) invite the consultee to "own the resistance," (b) reframe the resistance as a source of valuable information, and (c) recognize and ameliorate the source of resistance.

Reducing the Risk of Resistance

It would appear that the best means of preventing or at least reducing the risk of resistance is to create a consultation relationship that is truly collaborative. The unique characteristics of a collaborative consulting relationship, including the creation of a co-equal and mutual balance of power and ownership, stimulate a sense of freedom and control and thus reduce the need for reactance and resistance.

IMPORTANT TERMS

Aikido	Negative/conflicting expectations	Requesting counseling
Collaborative relationship	Passive aggression	Resistance
Endogenous	Quick sell/quick buy	The push way
Exogeneous	Reactance	Ultimate resistance
		Yes, but

SUGGESTED READINGS

Brehm, J. W. (1966). *A theory of psychological reactance.* San Diego, CA: Academic Press.

Cowan, E. W., & Presubry, J. H. (2000). Meeting client resistance and reactance with reverence. *Journal of Counseling and Development, 78*(4), 411–419.

Crawford, M. T., McConnell, A. R., Lewis, A. C., & Sherman, S. J. (2002). Reactance, compliance and anticipated regret. *Journal of Experimental Social Psychology, 38*(1), 56–64.

Randolph, D. L., Wood, T. S., & Waldrop, D. G. (1998). Assessing consultant strategies for dealing with consultee resistance. *Psychology: A Journal of Human Behavior, 35*(3–4), 33–38.

Wynne, C. P. (2002). The explanatory value of psychological reactance and cognitive dissonance theory in mandated consultation in schools. *Dissertation Abstracts International Section A: Humanities & Social Sciences, Vol. 63*(1-A), 89.

WEB SITES

An APA fact sheet: Summarizing school-based interventions with successful academic outcomes. http://mirror.apa.org/ppo/issues/pschoolbased.html

CPP: Providers of products and services for professionals focused on meeting individual and organizational development needs. http://www.cpp-db.com/

Society for Industrial and Organizational Psychology, Inc.: Home Web page for the society and offers useful search engine. http://www.siop.org/

REFERENCES

Abidin, R. A., Jr. (1975). Negative effects of behavior consultation: "I know I ought to but it hurts too much." *Journal of School Psychology, 13,* 51–56.

Alderman, G. L., & Gimpel, G. A. (1996). The interaction between type of behavior problem and type of consultant: teachers' preferences for professional assistance. *Journal of Educational and Psychological Consultation, 7,* 305–313.

Block, P. (1981). *Flawless consulting.* San Diego, CA: Pfeiffer & Comp.

Brehm, J. W. (1966). *A theory of psychological reactance.* New York: Academic Press.

Brehm, J. W. (1972). *Responses to loss of freedom: A theory of psychological reactance.* Morristown, NJ: General Learning Press.

Brehm, S. S. (1976). *The application of social psychology to clinical practice.* New York: Wiley.

Brown, D., Pryzwansky, W. B., & Schulte, A. C. (2001). *Psychological consultation: Introduction to theory and practice* (5th ed.). Needham Heights, MA: Allyn & Bacon.

Caplan, G. (1970). *The theory and practice of mental health consultation.* New York: Basic Books.

Caplan, G., & Caplan, R. (1993). *Mental health consultation and collaboration.* San Francisco: Jossey-Bass.

Cormier, W. H., & Cormier, L. S. (1991). *Interviewing strategies for helpers* (3rd ed.). Pacific Grove, CA: Brooks/Cole.

Crum, T. F. (1987). *The magic of conflict.* New York: Simon & Schuster.

Dobson, T. (1980). *When push comes to shove: Handling problem people.* Burlington, VT: Workshop Materials.

Dougherty A. M., Dougherty, L. P., & Purcell, D. (1991). The sources and management of resistance to consultation. *The School Counselor, 38,* 178–185.

Elliot, S. N. (1988a). Acceptability of behavioral treatment in education settings. In J. C. Witt, S. N. Elliott, & F. M Gresham (Eds.), *Handbook of behavior therapy in education* (pp. 121–150). New York: Plenum Press.

Elliot, S. N. (1988b). Acceptability of behavioral treatments: Review of variables that influence treatment selection. *Professional Psychology: Research and Practice, 19,* 68–80.

French, J. R. P., Jr., & Raven, B. (1959). The bases of social power. In D. Cartwright (Ed.), *Studies in social power,* (pp. 150–167). Ann Arbor: University of Michigan Institute of Social Research.

Friend, M., & Bauwens, J. (1988). Managing resistance: An essential consulting skill for learning disabilities teachers. *Journal of Learning Disabilities, 21*(9), 556–561.

Friend, M., & Cook, L. (1992). *Interactions: Collaboration skills for school professionals.* New York: Longman.

Gutkin, T. B., Clark, J. H., & Ajchenbaum, M. (1985). Impact of organizational variables on the delivery of school-based consultation services: A comparative case study approach. *School Psychology Review, 14,* 230–235.

Hughes J. N., & Falk, R. S. (1981). Resistance, reactance and consultation. *Journal of School Psychology, 19*(2), 134–141.

Karp, H. B. (1984). Working with resistance. *Training and Development Journal, 38*(3), 69–73.

Kazdin, A. E. (1981). Acceptability of child treatment techniques: The influence of treatment efficacy and adverse side effects. *Behavior Therapy, 12,* 493–506.

Kenton, S. B. (1989). Speaker credibility in persuasive business communication: A model which explains gender differences. *Journal of Business Communication, 26,* 143–157.

Kurpius, D. J., Fuqua, D. R., & Rozecki, T. (1993). The consulting process: A multidimensional model. *Journal of Counseling and Development, 71,* 601–606.

Margolis, H., & McGettigan, J. (1988). Managing resistance to instructional modifications in mainstreamed environments. *Remedial and Special Education, 9*(4), 15–21.

Martin, R. (1978). Expert and referent power: A framework for understanding and maximizing consultation effectiveness. *Journal of School Psychology, 16*(1), 49–55.

Meyers, J., Friedman, M. P., Gaughan, E. J., & Pitt, N. (1978). An approach to investigate anxiety and hostility in consultee-centered consultation. *Psychology in the Schools, 15,* 292–296.

Meyers, J., Parsons, R. D., & Martin, R. (1979). *Mental health consultation in schools.* San Francisco, CA: Jossey-Bass.

Nezu, A., & D'Zurilla, T. J. (1981). Effects of problem definition and formulation on the generation of alternatives in social problem-solving process. *Cognitive Therapy and Research, 5,* 265–271.

Nitobe, I. (1905). *Bushido, the soul of Japan.* New York: Putnam's.

Parsons, R., & Meyers, J. (1984). *Developing consultation skills.* San Francisco: Jossey-Bass.

Parsons, R. D. (1996). *The skilled consultant.* Needham Heights, MA: Allyn and Bacon.

Piersal, W. C., & Gutkin, T. B. (1983). Resistance to school-based consultation: A behavioral analysis of the problem. *Psychology in the Schools, 20,* 311–320.

Powell, G., & Posner, B. Z. (1978). Resistance to change reconsidered: Implications for managers. *Human Resources Management, 17,* 29–34.

Randolph, D. L. (1985). *Microconsulting: Basic psychological consultation skills for helping professionals.* Johnson City, TN: Institute of Social Sciences and Arts, Inc.

Randolph, D. L., & Graun, K. (1988). Resistance to consultation: A synthesis for counselor–consultants. *Journal of Counseling and Development, 67,* 182–184.

Sandoval, J., Lambert, N., & Davis, J. M. (1977). Consultation from the consultee's perspective. *Journal of School Psychology, 15,* 334–342.

Tingstrom, D. H., Little, S. G., & Stewart, K. J. (1990). School consultation from a social psychological perspective: A review. *Psychology in the Schools, 27,* 41–50.

Tohei, K. (1966). *Aikido in daily life.* Tokyo, Komiyama.

Waugh, R. F., & Punch, K. F. (1987). Teacher receptivity to systemwide change in the implementation stage. *Review of Educational Research, 57,* 237–254.

Wickstrom, K. F., & Witt, J. C. (1993). Resistance within school-based consultation. In J. E. Zins, T. R. Kratochwill, & S. N. Elliot (Eds.), *Handbook of consultation services for children* (pp. 159–178). San Francisco: Jossey-Bass.

Witt, J. C., & Elliott, S. N. (1985). Acceptability of classroom intervention strategies. In T. R. Kratochwill (Ed.), *Advances in school psychology* (Vol. 4, pp. 251–288). Hillsdale, NJ: Erlbaum.

Consultation Foci

9

Client-Focused Consultation

The Student as Client

It certainly was helpful, being able to sit with Dr. Jameson and get a better feel for what may be going on with Ellen. His perspective and observations of Ellen certainly provide a unique angle—something that I wouldn't typically get by talking with Ellen.

I think that with both of us gathering additional information, we will be able to come up with a plan that helps Ellen and may even give us some ideas about what else could be done to prevent this kind of thing from happening again.

For most school counselors the thought of assisting a student conjures images of closed-door offices and face-to-face contact with the student. In this typical model of service delivery, the counselor, often in the isolated confines of her office, employs a variety of techniques, instruments, or approaches to assess the student and identify the depth and breadth of the presenting concern. With these data, the counselor then begins to implement steps to remedy the situation.

Although this one-to-one direct service can be quite effective, its effectiveness can be increased and the impact can be expanded if service to the student is conceptualized from a counselor-as-consultant model of service delivery. This is certainly true for our model counselor–consultant. His inclusion of Dr. Jameson, the consultee, into the mix not only broadens his own perspective on what may be going on with Ellen, but also it increases the number and types of strategies he (they) can now use to remedy this situation.

CHAPTER OBJECTIVES

Using consultation as mode of service delivery, even when the target of our interventions is the student, is the focus of the current chapter. After completing this chapter, the reader should be able to

1. Describe the differences between a restricted direct-service model and a consultation approach, which allows for direct contact
2. Expand goal focus to include goals for the student, the tasks the student is assigned, and the environment in which the student functions
3. Describe the application of a multimodal behavioral model as applied to a student-centered form of consultation
4. Describe the tenets of solution focus consultation

APPROACH STUDENT SERVICE
FROM A CONSULTATION PERSPECTIVE

In traditional counseling services, the school counselor would meet with the student and employ a variety of techniques or approaches to evaluate or assess the student's problems or concerns. Once these are identified, the counselor and student typically set goals and then begin to implement a plan of action to move toward the achievement of these goals. Quite often this entire process is carried out behind the closed door of the counselor's office, without input from or to the teacher or teachers who share a concern for that student.

To remedy this shortcoming, many counselors moved out of their offices and attempted to observe the student or to dialogue with the teacher to gather information from this new perspective. This extension of the problem-defining, goal-setting and intervention-planning process to include the input from the classroom teacher has not only increased the utility and validity of the data gathered but has also allowed both the teacher and the counselor–consultant to benefit from their unique perspectives and skills. The result of this joining forces is the development of a more effective plan for the student and the possibility of changes to the classroom that will positively impact all the students.

The inclusion of the teacher-as-consultee in this process of problem identification goals setting, and plan development is based upon the following rationale.

1. The teacher–consultee has knowledge about the client that may be difficult if not impossible to obtain in the brief focused encounter with the counselor.

2. Problems are to some degree situationally defined and thus are best understood within the context in which they occur. The teacher–consultee can provide information regarding the uniqueness of the classroom, its unique task demands, and its social environment.

3. Intervention plans will prove more effective if they can be applied both within the counselor's office and within the actual classroom or environment of concern. Such spread of intervention will be more accepted if the teacher–consultee was involved in its development.

4. The student's current level of functioning is assumed to be a result of the client interacting with a particular task and within a particular environment. Understanding and intervening with the task and the environment is best achieved with consultee involvement.

The counselor–consultant seeking to modify the behavior, attitudes and feelings of a student or students may gather needed information, directly (e.g. interviewing, testing, or observations) or more indirectly through dialogue with the consultee (i.e. teacher, parent, administrator). In either case, the focus of problem identification, goal setting and intervention planning processes is on the student, as client. Yet, it is a process that involves the mutual involvement of consultee and consultant.

FOCUSING ON THE ONE WHILE IMPACTING THE MANY

Client-focused consultation (Parsons, 1996) involves the full collaboration of consultant and consultee in problem identification, goal setting, and intervention processes. Such consultative collaboration provides a number of potential benefits. First, by incorporating varied perspectives (i.e., counselor–consultant and teacher or administrator–consultee) on data collection and interpretation, the potential bias intrinsic to either perspective is checked, and the validity of data collected may be increased. Second, by gathering data on the specific elements of the task and environment with which and in which the client is operating (e.g., the classroom) the possibility of achieving an assessment–intervention linkage has been increased. Finally, the collaborative exchange can serve an educative and thus preventive function for the consultee, increasing her knowledge of the influencing effects of task and environmental demands.

Through their collaborative efforts not only will the counselor–consultant gain better insight into the student's functioning but also the consultee will be assisted to use the experience with this case to improve her abilities to reduce the possibility of similar situations occurring in the future.

From this consultation frame of reference not only are the diagnostic and intervention planning processes expanded to include consultee collaboration, but also the approach has been expanded to ensure both remedial and prevention effects. This expanded approach is based on the assumption that behavior is a function of the interaction between the unique characteristics of the client, the task the client is asked to accomplish, and the environment in which this occurs (i.e., **Behavior** $= f$**(client-task-environment)**). Consider, for example, the case of Bennie, a 13-year-old Caucasian male who has just recently been diagnosed as having an Attention Deficit Disorder without hyperactivity. The identification of his ADD has helped Bennie to understand why he is and has been inattentive in school, is oftentimes accident prone, and has trouble remembering what his mother has asked him to do. A case can certainly be made for the fact that ADD is a result of Bennie's neurological functioning. Thus his behavior can be attributed to his internal conditions. However, the degree to which this behavior is manifested and problematic can be influenced by the nature of the task or the characteristics of the environment in which Bennie is asked to function. For example, it is fair to assume that Bennie may have greater difficulty staying attentive to a task that has low motivational value and is repetitive in nature than he would to one that is stimulating and of high interest. Similarly, one may expect that Bennie would have more difficulty attending to teacher directions if he is sitting next to an active gerbil cage than if he was sitting in the front of the class, near the teacher. Thus, the behavior of concern, which in the case of Bennie may be his turning around and playing with his pencils is a product of Bennie's unique makeup, which is interacting with the characteristics of a task he is assigned within the context of a particular social and physical environment.

This client-task-environment focus results in the identification of multiple points of intervention that are easily accessed by the consultant and consultee. These multiple interventions not only facilitate change in this student–client, but can also decrease the likelihood of future problems for that client (i.e., the preventive potential). Further, the analysis of the task demands and environmental presses and the way they can impact this client helps the consultee to begin to consider modification of these variables as a way of avoiding similar problems with other clients in the future. Efforts to intervene with one student can result in positive, preventive steps that impact many.

PROBLEM IDENTIFICATION

Collaboration of the consultant and consultee during the problem-identification stage can occur in a number of ways and at a number of points along the process. Clearly, the consultee has expertise concerning the nature of the situations (i.e., environments and tasks) in which the behavior of concern is most evident. Therefore, a teacher as consultee might be invited to sit in on the counselor–consultant's interview with a student, assuming that such cointerviewing would be both appropriate and acceptable to the client. If the counselor employs surveys or some form of evaluation tools, the consultee might even observe the testing process and share observations about the client's behavior while he is engaged in the testing. These observations can be compared to those of the consultant and used to illustrate the types of problems or behaviors encountered by the consultee in the classroom.

The importance of the role and contribution of the teacher as consultee becomes even more obvious as we attempt to understand the unique environmental factors and their potential impact on the client's level of functioning. Specifically, the teacher can help provide valuable information about the unique demands of the classroom tasks as well as the characteristics of the physical and social environment in which these tasks are performed.

Assessing the Specifics of the Task Demands

It is clear that the difficulty a client is exhibiting may be a result of some unique personal problem that she may be experiencing. For example, consider the case of Liz, a fifth-grade student. Liz's teacher reported that within the last month Liz's academic performance has deteriorated. Liz's teacher noted that Liz appears very stressed and is having difficulty concentrating. Further, Liz, while previously being an almost model student when it came to homework, now either fails to hand in any homework or if something is handed in, it is only partially complete. On further investigation, the counselor finds that Liz's parents are currently in a very heated divorce process. Liz is spending every other night either with her dad or her mother, in two different locations. In this situation, the source of Liz's work difficulty may be her physical and emotional exhaustion, which are the results of her current living situation and the stress of her parent's very hostile divorce process.

Now, consider Sally. Sally's English teacher also reported that Sally has shown a dramatic decline in the quality of her homework assignments. The teacher reported that previously Sally's homework assignments were often creative, descriptive, and quite elaborate, but they now were very brief, without full description. Further, she (the teacher) noted that many of these assignments were simply handed in without being complete.

In interviewing the teacher (consultee), the consultant discovered that this change in Sally's homework performance appeared to correlate with a change in the nature of the task. The teacher now required that all written homework should be completed using cursive writing as opposed to previously allowed word processing or block printing. With further investigation, it became clear to the counselor–consultant and the teacher–consultee that Sally was having difficulty with cursive writing. As such, she found this new requirement to be interfering with her ability to be creative, to elaborate, and to be fully descriptive in her writing. In this case, it was most likely that the unique demands of the task itself, rather than any personal problem, was the major contributor to Sally's poor work performance.

Thus although the difficulty a client may be exhibiting may be the result of some unique personal problem, it is also possible that the specific demands of the task with which the client is having difficulty may be augmenting the effects of the personal problem or perhaps may even be the primary source of the work-related problem. As such, it is important to include an assessment of the task demands as part of an expanded diagnostic or problem-identification process. It is in this arena that the consultee can prove to be a valuable resource.

The process of task analysis is far from new or novel. Task analysis was originally develop by R. B. Miller (1962) as a process aimed at facilitating the training of armed services personnel. The basic concept is that a task, be it performing rudimentary mathematics, computer skills, or running a sales meeting or supervisory session, involves a number of subtasks, each requiring specific abilities and skills. Further, it is assumed that successful completion of these subtasks is a precondition to the successful completion of desired final task. A task analysis gives a picture of the logical sequence of the steps necessary to take in performing some final process or achieving some ultimate goal. Further, the specific analysis of the task into subunits assists the consultant and consultee in identifying the unique demands placed on the client by each subtask, as well as the unique skills or knowledge required to successfully perform that task.

The A–B–C model previously discussed in chapter 6 provides one schema or algorithm for conducting a task analysis. Each discrete action (thought and operant behavior) in a complex task can be viewed as a link in a chain, with the completion of each action serving as the reinforcer for that behavior as well as the antecedent stimulus for the next behavior in the chain.

Such a microanalysis of the task may identify the source of the client's work-related problem. By analyzing the task that appears to be involved with the client's problem and reviewing the specific demands such a task places on the person attempting to complete it, the consultant and consultee can identify those areas mastered by the client, as well as those areas causing the most difficulty. Perhaps the client is having a problem because he lacks the necessary prerequisite skills. This could certainly be the case of a student who has been misplaced in an advanced mathematics class without having had the training in the prerequisites. The frustration experienced by the student, along with the potentially disruptive behavioral manifestations of that frustration, can best be understood and remedied by the realization of this lack of prerequisite skill acquisition.

But in addition to possibly lacking the skills required to successfully complete a particular unit or subtask of the task, perhaps there is something unique in the task demands that interacts with the client's own current psychosocial–emotional resources to produce or elicit an interfering response. Consider the case of Keith, found in Exercise 9.1.

EXERCISE 9.1

The Case of Keith—Focusing on the Task

Directions: In this exercise you will be given a brief statement of the problem, provided by Keith's teacher, Dr. Hagerstown, along with some background information on Keith. In Part I, you are asked to read the referral information. Your task is to identify the particular tasks causing Keith some problems. More specifically, you are to identify five factors involved in performing the task. In Part II, you are asked to identify five personal issues or experiences that may interact with these components of the task to inhibit Keith's performance. Through discussion of your response with a colleague, mentor, or supervisor, you will begin to see the value of task analysis to the diagnostic process.

Part I
Problem Statement

Dr. Hagerstown, Keith's creative writing teacher, has noted that "Keith's performance in class has become simply unacceptable. I am not sure what happened. He has been an excellent student up to this point, and he is certainly a compliant youth, but he is simply not producing the creative work that is required, and expected of one so talented. Since the beginning of the second marking period (Nov. 8th), his essays have been short and not descriptive, his personal journal writing has been sporadic, and his verbal contribution during our class creative round table are simply sterile! Keith is simply not putting himself into his work."

According to Dr. Hagerstown, his class is run like a college seminar. Students are assigned a theme at the beginning of each marking period. Their assignments (all of which will vary in form and genre) reflect aspects of that theme. The theme for this marking period has been "Family—Community—Belonging: Essential to Our Human Existence."

Students orally present their creations to their study group for peer feedback before correcting and presenting to the class as a whole. Students' presentations to the class are somewhat formal, with the presenter standing at a podium. Following each presentation the presenter will answer questions about the process they employed in producing this work.

Although other teachers have noted a drop in Keith's overall performance, most have attributed it to "senior-itis." Further, his math, science, physical education, and art teachers feel Keith is performing at expected levels.

Part II

In column A identify five separate task demands. In column B suggest five unique personal characteristics or experiences that may be negatively interacting with the task demand to reduce Keith's performance.

Column A Task Analysis (sample):	*Column B* Personal Characteristics
Knowledge and comfort with theme	Parents currently in divorce process
1. _____	_____
_____	_____
2. _____	_____
_____	_____

3. _____   _____

   _____   _____

4. _____   _____

   _____   _____

5. _____   _____

   _____   _____

Assessing the Environment

The setting or psychosocial–physical environment in which the client is functioning (or dysfunctioning) can serve an active role in eliciting and supporting this dysfunctionality. Thus an expanded model of problem identification involves the analysis of the environmental conditions potentially impacting the current problem. The following sections briefly discuss the nature of some of those environmental factors that have the potential to affect the client. For a more in-depth presentation, the reader is referred to the references cited.

Physical Environment   Research (e.g., see Dunn, Beaudry, & Klavas, 1989; Dunn & Dunn, 1987; Tharp, 1989; Torrance, 1986) suggests that an individual's learning and performance are impacted by the social–physical environment in which they are asked to perform. This research suggests that an individual's performance can be significantly affected by variables such as the amount of light, noise, temperature, formality, or mobility found within the performance or learning environment. Further, space utilization (Hall, 1966), the arrangement of materials, the physical layout, and forms of stimulation (e.g., noise, colors) have all been considered as environmental elements that can impact an individual's level of performance and thus should be considered when diagnosing a client.

Social/Cultural Climate   Research has demonstrated the potential impact of social/cultural elements on learning and performing. For example, Vasquez (1990) emphasized the family- and group-oriented view of the Hispanic culture and suggested that as such the Hispanic-American students would prefer a more cooperative learning environment than one promoting competition. This same author (Vasquez, 1990) noted that Navajo students sometimes show strong preferences for learning privately, through trial and error, rather than having their mistakes made public. Similar unique preferences to learning and performance environments were reported with African-American populations (Bennett, 1990) and Asian Americans (Park, 1997).

Others (e.g., Glasser, 1990; Johnson & Johnson, 1997; Slavin, 1991) have reported that individual academic performance is correlated with levels of group support and cooperation found within the classroom. Therefore, classrooms environments that employ intense competition goal structures and punitive management techniques may prove detrimental to a child's level of comfort and academic production. It is possible that the child who is reported to be nonparticipatory, failing to ask or answer questions, or volunteer to come to the board may simply be attempting to cope with a negative, fearful classroom environment. This same child may be actively engaged and contributory when observed in a more supportive and cooperative environment.

Thus it is important, when attempting to understand the nature of the problem as well as to set goals, to view the presenting concern in the context of the physical and social/cultural environment in which it occurs. This approach provides both an expanded framework for problem identification as well as added directions for intervention and prevention, which can be collaboratively pursued by consultant and consultee. Let's return to the case of Keith (see Exercise 9.2).

EXERCISE 9.2

Keith—An Environmental Analysis

Directions: As with Exercise 9.1, your task is to review the data provided. The additional data highlights a number of unique factors of the physical–social–psychological environment found in Dr. Hagerstown's classroom. After reading the five pieces of information provided, identify two possible ways these unique physical and/or psychosocial environmental factors could negatively impact Keith's performance.

Discussing your conclusions with a colleague, mentor, or supervisor will help you to expand your awareness of the possible interactions between environment and client.

Classroom observation: In observing Keith in his creative writing class, you collected the following observations:

1. Classroom arranged in major sections—what appears to be an area for small peer groups and one for large class discussion (20 students).

2. Classroom is very bright, cheery, many decorations—both commercial and student created. According to the teacher, the decorations reflect the theme of the marking period and therefore change four times throughout the year.

3. When students are working in their small groups, they review each others' written work, rough notes, and any graphics or pictures that accompany the work.

4. Keith's peer group (five students) includes himself and four females. There are eight other boys in class besides Keith.

5. Keith's group meets in the rear left corner of the room, and Keith sits in a seat facing the back of the larger room.

6. You understand from one of the students that the girl directly facing Keith (in his small group) is his ex-girlfriend.

Possible Impacts

(example):

#1. The pictures placed around the room show happy families, both commercial products and snapshots of the students' families on vacation, at home, etc. The pictures are very upsetting to Keith, and he has trouble focusing on his work, being pulled to fantasize about his "one-time happy family."

#2. _____

_____

#3. _____

_____

Assessing the Client

Our discussion of the client has been placed last to emphasize the extrapersonal focus of the consultation model employed. However, this is not to suggest a linear approach to assessment, that is, first assess the task, then the environment, and then the client. Clearly, in assessing each of the previous focal points for diagnosis (i.e., task and environment), consideration has been given to the client. Thus, assessing the client has already begun. Now we turn our attention to a fuller understanding of the client and the elements he brings to the task and to the environment. But before we do, it must be emphasized that this assessment, regardless of the model employed, is different than that typically employed within a direct-service form of counseling. The assessment of the client from a consultation model will continue to be triadic, employing the assistance of a consultee, and will focus on the interaction of unique client, environmental, and task characteristics as they take form in the presenting concern.

There are many interesting and varied models for assessing a client and his problems. The A–B–C model previously discussed in chapter 6 (Kahn, 1999) is an example of such a model. Another, and one we will use in this chapter, is the multimodal model of Arnold Lazarus (1989).

The essence of this multimodal approach is that a person's functioning or dysfunctioning can be defined as manifesting within seven areas, or modalities. These seven areas are **b**ehavior, **a**ffect, **s**ensations, **i**mages, **c**ognition, **i**nterpersonal relationships, and **d**rugs (or biological functions).

Using the acronym BASIC ID to represent these various modalities (i.e., behavior, affect, sensation, image, cognition, interpersonal relations, and drugs), Lazarus argued that a complete identification of one's problem must account for each modality of this BASIC ID. Because of the potential value of this model for the consultant, each modality along with the type of questions to be posed and considered by the consultant in attempting to define the client functioning are presented following.

B: Behavior For Lazarus (1981), it is important to be mindful of areas of behavioral excess (e.g., client drinks too much? interrupts too often?) and deficit (e.g., doesn't initiate conversation, fails to do homework). Thus it is important to begin to identify how the client acts. What does he *do* and what are the conditions under which they act or behave differently? This modality approximates the client's A–B–Cs.

In regards to the client's presenting concern, what behaviors does he exhibit or fail to exhibit, and which appear to a part of the problem experienced? Asking the client or the consultee questions such as: What would you (the client) like to do, or stop doing? or If you (the client) were performing the way you wished, what would you be doing that you are not doing currently? will help to identify habits or behaviors that need to be targeted for change.

Consider Keith's situation. Dr. Hagerstown suggested that Keith's performance has dropped off drastically. He describes the problem behaviors as:

1. Writing short essays
2. Not being descriptive in his journal writing
3. Not being personal in his classroom discussions

In looking at the client's behavior, we must also consider what events (antecedents) led up to his acting a certain way and similarly, what are the results (consequences) of his actions. Oftentimes, one's behavior is heavily influenced (if not caused) by these antecedents and consequences. For example, if every time Keith attempted to enter into the classroom discussion he began to cry and feel sick to his stomach, it may be hypothesized that lack of participation is a way of avoiding these painful consequences. Such an understanding not only clarifies the nature of the problem but also may help the consultant and consultee identify other ways of gaining Keith's participation in a way that results in less-noxious consequences.

Those interested in more fully understanding the relationships between behavior and antecedent and consequential events are referred to the work of cognitive behavioral theorists such as Cormier and Cormier (1991) and Kahn (1999).

A: Affect When most people think of helping another person, they generally envision someone asking the client, How do you feel about that? Feelings are important aspects of the human experience and thus need to be identified, especially as they are tied to a presenting complaint. However, identifying feelings is not sufficient. The consultant and consultee need to be attentive to both those feelings that are reported and those that are never or rarely noted. The consultee and the consultant will need to consider the degree to which the client's feelings appear appropriate to the situation, as well as the degree or intensity with which the feelings are experienced. Questions such as: Are these emotions overdone and the client too sensitive? Or, Are the client's feelings being blunted, somewhat insensitive, or underdone? need to be considered. Also, the consultant and consultee need to consider the degree of control (too much, too little) the client exhibits in the expression of his or her feelings.

Perhaps the sterility of expression exhibited by Keith is a reflection of his own grieving of his parents' marriage. It may be appropriate following such a loss, but is it proportional to the actual loss? Does Keith experience the loss in other ways other than sadness? Does he feel depressed, hopeless? Does he find any pleasure in the activities he felt pleasurable prior to the divorce? Finding the answers to these types of questions not only clarifies the depth and breadth of the problem but also begins to identify goals and outcomes desired.

S: Sensation　When considering the client sensations we are obviously concerned about their five major senses and the degree to which they are accurately receiving the signals around them, but we also need to listen to the degree to which their problem is presented in the form of body sensations (e.g., sick to the stomach, dizziness, headaches). For example, when Keith speaks of being upset, does he also mean that he feels sick to his stomach or has headaches or muscle tensions?

The sensations the client reports may be valuable for two reasons. First, as with the other modalities, identifying sensations associated with the concern more clearly defines the nature of the problem and how it is experienced. Secondly, the identifications of such sensations may even provide us with an earlier diagnostic warning system, as when a person experiences a muscular tension (in the neck) before becoming very angry. Such an early warning system could be useful in developing strategies for early intervention.

I: Imagery　For Lazarus, imagery involves the various mental pictures that seem to influence our life. For example, the student who sees himself as being laughed at may tend to withdraw from volunteering an answer in class. Or the person who may see him/herself as fat, even after losing weight, may still act and feel fat. Having a better understanding of the way the client sees him/herself and his/her world is useful information. It not only reflects a part of the client's concern but it can also suggest a helpful goal to be achieved. Questions such as: What bothersome dreams or memories do you have? How do you view yourself? How do you view your future? may begin to reveal such imagery. Again, consider Keith.

As noted, Keith has withdrawn from active participation in the classroom discussion. In fact, he reports feeling sick to his stomach when he attempts to participate (sensation). In interview with Keith, the consultant learns that he sees himself starting to talk about his family and completely losing control in class. The others in class he sees as being disgusted by his emotional outburst. He especially envisions his ex-girlfriend making fun of him. Further, Keith reports that he can hardly get the image of his mom crying out of his mind. This is especially difficult to do when surrounded by all the "happy family" pictures hung on the wall of the classroom.

These images play an important role in the overall problem Keith is experiencing. Further, helping Keith remove or reshape these images would be a very valuable goal for the consultation.

C: Cognition   The C in Lazarus' BASIC ID stands for cognition. Cognition is thoughts, beliefs, or ways of making meaning out of one's experience. Often, the way we interpret our experience is inaccurate. We need to learn to identify when our thinking is distorted and thus learn to correct it.

The effective consultant needs to unearth the client's cognitive patterns as a part of their overall experience of the problem. Seeking the answers to questions, such as: What does this mean to the client? What assumptions about him/herself, his/her world is he/she making? will provide a clearer picture of the client's cognitive orientation.

For example, although the loss Keith is experiencing is one that is both undesirable and disappointing, it is not unbearable, nor does it provide evidence of his failure. In reviewing Keith's journal, it becomes clear to Dr. Hagerstown that Keith blames himself for his parents' divorce, in fact in one section he wrote: "If I had been more like the son my dad wanted, he would never have left my mom! It is all my fault!" Concluding that his parents' divorce is his fault is certainly a distortion of reality. Such a distortion exaggerates both the importance of his role in the marriage and leads to an inordinate amount of guilt tied to a decision over which he had no control. Further, correcting such a distorted interpretation would prove to be a very useful and helpful goal and relieve much of what is most likely debilitating guilt.

I: Interpersonal Relationships   As social animals how we behave, or not behave, with others is an essential element of our human experience. We need to begin to assess how the client approaches others, responds to others, and communicates with others.

In assessing the interpersonal modality, the client may come to understand how this component both reflects the problem experienced and may in fact contribute to it. Again, in the case of Keith, we come to understand that he becomes overly withdrawn when emotionally upset. This tendency to withdraw from friends and family can certainly increase the experience of anxiety and concern over the demise of his intact family by removing him from other possible sources of support. Further, his social withdrawal in class has created a situation in which his grades are declining, and this in turn has compounded his feelings of guilt. Thus a useful goal for this consultation would be to assist Keith to learn to use appropriate disclosure and reliance on friends and family as way of adjusting to the emotional crises he is experiencing.

D: Drugs (Biology)   Although the D certainly does complete the acronym, it may be a bit misleading. Lazarus is not focusing only on drugs. He is suggesting that we consider the nonpsychological aspects of a person's experience. We need to consider the client's diet, general health and well-being, and general physiology (hormones, nervous system, etc.).

The consultant and consultee are most likely not trained to intervene with organic conditions, but they need to increase their awareness of the effect of substances (such as chemicals, food additives, or even natural substances such as caffeine) and physiology (e.g., hormones) in creating problems in our life.

In the case of Keith, the consultant and consultee need to consider whether Keith's reaction may be associated with his lack of sleep or change in eating (which may result from the disruption of the family patterns at home). Does Keith's emotional response pattern have any possible connection with any medicine he may be taking or has stopped taking? Again, seeking the answers to such questions not only gives the consultant and consultee a more complete picture of the depth and breadth of the problem but also begins to provide clarity about the goals to be achieved.

Although the purist may wish to define a client's problem in terms of each of these seven modalities, what is being suggested here is that the BASIC ID model is a useful template or guide for systematically assessing the client's situation. Whether the consultant or consultee employ seven or less modalities, such a model enables them to more specifically and more concretely define the nature and scope of the client's concern as the first step to formulating useful and achievable goals and outcomes. Once problematic modalities have been identified, a functional behavior analysis (A-B-C) can be employed to assess the relationship of the modalities within their environmental context.

Exercise 9.3 will help to demonstrate the use and value of problem defining using the model of the BASIC ID.

EXERCISE 9.3

Keith—Assessing the Client

BASIC ID

Directions: After reading the case material, use the BASIC ID to identify the various components or modalities involved in Keith's experience.

In interview with Keith the consultant discovered the following information. Since the beginning of the second marking period, he has found himself daydreaming a lot in class. He sometimes sees himself on a small boat like a dingy, and the big boat is going off in the sunset. He doesn't feel very energetic in creative writing (and says he seems and feels okay in other classes).

Keith admitted that he is not spending much time on his creative writing assignments; he seems to get distracted with thoughts about his mom and his dad, kind of thinking that ". . . I can't make it without them!" When he thinks like this, he finds it hard to concentrate on the various writing tasks. In fact, sitting down to write seems to make this daydreaming and thinking happen. As such, he simply avoids the tasks.

Keith also noted that he has split up with his girlfriend (Laura), who is in the same creative writing class. As a result, he just doesn't feel like he can talk to anyone.

Keith noted that he is losing weight and has some difficulty getting to sleep. He finds himself feeling sad—and nervous—like sometimes his body is tingling.

Analysis of the Client:

B - EHAVIOR: _____

_____

_____

A - FFECT: _____

_____

_____

S - ENSATION: _____

_____

_____

I - IMAGERY: _____

_____

_____

C - OGNITION: _____

_____

_____

I - NTERPERSONAL: _____

_____

_____

D - RUGS (DIET, ETC.): _____

_____

_____

GOAL SETTING AND
SOLUTION-FOCUSED CONSULTATION

Although there are many approaches and models that may help to guide goal setting and intervention planning, we have found that a solution-focused orientation or model (Berg & Miller, 1992; de Shazer, 1985; Kahn, 2000) serves as a useful framework from which to facilitate collaborative goal setting and solution implementation. As such, the basic tenets and specific considerations for school consultants' use of a solution-focused approach will be briefly discussed.

Basic Tenets of a Solution-Focused Model

The solution-focused model is informed by certain beliefs and assumptions about the structure of reality, the nature of problems, and the dynamics of change. Foremost among these assumptions is the belief that reality is a social construction created and maintained by each of us through our use of language (Guterman, 1994; Vygotsky, 1962). Through language we frame certain events as problematic, and we perpetuate and reify those experiences as problems in the way we think about them and describe them to others. A physical disability or a skill deficiency becomes problematic because it is framed (constructed) in the most negative, debilitating, and pessimistic manner. And through this construction the problem becomes an objective reality whose cause must be discovered and resolved for remediation to occur. The solution-focused approach suggests that just as we can construct our problems and frame our difficulties as obstacles to be overcome, we can also choose to think about (reconstruct or reframe) our difficulties in manageable and even positive ways. Or we could choose to disregard the difficulty or problem entirely and shift our focus to how we would like the issue or concern to be (the goal) and how we have approached that desired state in the past or present. The constructivist orientation replaces problem construction (and reconstruction as we explore the problem in detail) with a new, positive construction: the *absence* of the problem or, better yet, the presence of the desired state. Evidence (Bandura, 1997; Kanfer & Hagerman, 1987) suggests that focus on the desired condition or goal creates a positive reality that is reinforced by any evidence of movement toward that desired goal. This 180-degree shift in attention from the problem (and its continual reconstruction with each telling) to its goal and solution represents another basic assumption of the solution-focused model.

The solution-focused orientation accentuates the positive by helping individuals identify and use their strengths, resources, and past successes in formulating desired goals and constructing solutions to achieve those goals. Rather than using language to reconstruct the problem, the solution-focused consultant engages the consultee in a goal-directed and solution-focused conversation. This solution talk focuses on what is right and working, devoting primary attention to the goals of the consultee and, more explicitly, the objectives that will serve as evidence that the goals have been realized. Additionally, the solution-focused model assumes that there are exceptions to every problem that demonstrate times, places, and instances when the problem does not occur. Operating from this belief, the solution-focused consultant identifies and then builds on those exceptions to create practical solutions that are often already within the consultee's repertoire. Because change is dynamic and occurring all the time, small changes in the desired direction lead to more and larger changes. This ripple effect is enhanced as consultees draw on their own strengths and resources to achieve their own goals, resulting in a most self-reinforcing and empowering internal locus of control. As individuals gradually move toward their goal, the solution-focused consultant helps them realize the changes that are occurring and the role that the consultee is taking in creating the desired changes. The solution conversation revolves around questions leading to goal statements, exception identification, task or solution development, and positive reinforcement for any progress demonstrated.

A helpful goal statement question developed by de Shazer (1988) is the miracle question. A variation of this question is: Suppose that tonight, while you are asleep, there is a miracle and this problem is solved. How will you know? What will be different tomorrow? Questions that attempt to identify exceptions would be: When does the problem not happen? When was the last time (the goal) happened slightly? Task or solution development questions might include: What will the consultee be doing? What did you do to make that happen? How did you choose to do that? How would others describe the client and you when your goal is occurring? With each small change the solution-focused consultant processes and reinforces successes with such questions as: How were you able to do that? What benefits have you gotten from doing that? The consultant will also employ reinforcing statements such as: I am impressed with efforts you have made to stay on track and achieve your goal.

Throughout the consultation process the solution-focused consultant is practical, concrete, and encouraging of any and all efforts and increments of change. Although the counselor–consultant is always deferential to the consultee's choice of goals, the operational description of the desired goals and subgoals must be consensually validated. Goals of commission are sought as the consultee describes the thoughts and behavior that he or she will be doing.

Considerations for School-Based Consultation

For a solution-focused consultation model to operate effectively in the school, the consultant must espouse the basic assumptions of the model. In addition, the consultant must also:

1. Identify goals with increased utility and validity.
2. Select goals that are directed to both immediate and long-term change.
3. Expand the focus of change to include not just the client, but also the consultee, the program (classroom norms, curriculum, structure), or broader systemic factors existing within the school, family, or community. The broader the focus of intervention, the greater will be the influence on the client and others and permanence of the change.

Goals for Client, Task, and Environment

The utilization of task and environmental analyses along with the widespread view of the client (i.e., BASIC ID and A-B-Cs) will increase the utility and validity of the intervention processes in a number of ways. First, by the inclusion of the consultee as task and environmental expert, the consultant has not only increased her breadth of solution but has also tailored the understanding of the nature of the problem and the intervention steps to be taken to the specific needs of that client with that specific consultee.

Further, the focus on the specific task, which appears to be the primary arena in which the difficulty is manifesting itself, provides the consultant and the consultee the opportunity to develop specific remedial steps that are not only clearly relevant to the needs of the consultee but also are tied specifically to the client's task-related deficiencies. Together the consultant and consultee can use the data from the task analysis, environmental analyses, and client assessment to

1. Develop additional training or intervention processes to assist the client with developing the skills needed to perform the subtasks

2. Identify the components of the task or the environment that may be manipulated or modified to facilitate and cue the desired behavior or, at a minimum, reduce or eliminate those components that interfere with the desired behavior

Returning to our case of Keith, the linkage of assessment to intervention becomes clear. One point of problem definition was that Keith experienced a number of intrusive and upsetting images that interfered with his attending and concentrating on his class work. Understanding that these images, although being responses to his own personal fears surrounding the divorce of his parents, are also responses to the visual stimulation found around the classroom (i.e., pictures of happy, intact families).

In this situation the professional counselor may attempt to employ strategies such as rational emotive imagery training (Ellis & Grieger, 1986) to assist Keith to reduce the debilitating effect of his imagery. As a collaborating consultant, this professional counselor would not only employ such imagery training techniques but also assist the consultee to reconsider the posters and pictures that decorate the classroom. Through a collaborative dialogue, the consultee may choose to reduce the emphasis on dual-parent family photos and include additional happy single-parent images.

In addition to this form of intervention, the professional counselor, working with Keith, may employ a variety of Gestalt-type techniques, such as the empty chair technique (Perls, 1969) to assist Keith to identify and express his feelings of anxiety, anger, and guilt. This may be seen as the first step to problem solving. Although, such a strategy would not be appropriate within the classroom, the utilization of journal writing as a way to express feelings or even a project on creative problem solving would be appropriate to Dr. Hagerstown's class, and both may prove therapeutic for Keith.

Setting Priorities and Finding a Place to Start

The concern of the consultee for the functioning and well-being of the client must be acknowledged. Further, it is important to frame this concern as a sincere commitment on the part of the consultee to participate in the amelioration of the identified problem. However, the focus of attention must shift to goals, objectives, and solutions.

The analysis of the client, task, and environment will most likely lead to the generation of a wide variety of goals. It will become quite obvious to both the consultant and consultee that it may not be possible to pursue all goals equally or simultaneously. The consultant needs to facilitate the narrowing of the focus and prioritization of goals and strategies. In selecting both the goals and the nature of the intervention plan or solutions to be employed, the consultant should consider the following general guidelines.

Breadth of Impact One of the first points to be considered in selecting a point and process of intervention is the breadth of impact. The consultant and consultee should attempt to select goals and strategies that provide the broadest impact for the effort. Solution strategies that impact a variety of client modalities and/or task and environmental elements may have a greater chance of being successful and thus should be first considered for implementation. Further, because the goal of consultation is twofold (i.e., remediative and preventive), the consultant needs to consider the remedial and preventive value of each intervention in hopes of identifying the intervention with the broadest (both remedial and preventive) impact possible.

In our exercises, it becomes clear that expanding the subject matter of the pictures decorating the classroom will not only help Keith, but will also provide other students living in single-family conditions a point of personal reference. This single intervention would therefore not only impact Keith, but also all students distracted by the exclusion of their family experience in the models presented.

Address the Goals of Priority Strategies or solutions that achieve goals of greatest satisfaction will most likely be those embraced and accepted. These are the issues that the client and the consultee would be most motivated to do something about and thus be least resistant to the intervention process.

The desire to once again be able to elaborate within his writing appears to be a significant goal for Dr. Hagerstown and Keith. Given this valuing of that goal, solutions that are targeted toward that goal achievement will most likely met with acceptance by both the consultee (Dr. Hagerstown) and the client (Keith). Perhaps the degree of personal disclosure will increase if Dr. Hagerstown could assure Keith that his writing would not have to be presented publicly until he was ready. With such an assurance and sense of control, Keith may be willing to risk some vulnerability and personal disclosure with Dr. Hagerstown, thus enriching his written work.

Achieving Success The solution-focused consultant targets goals that appear achievable. This affords the consultee the experience of success. It is useful, therefore, to begin with a goal that is manageable. Thus it might be important to attempt to break the larger goal down into more manageable subparts, which can be addressed one at a time, starting with the step that appears to have the most likelihood of success. Goal scaling (Berg & Miller, 1992) is especially helpful in formulating immediate and attainable goals from those that are long term and more difficult to achieve.

Again, although it is desirable to have Keith expand on his formal writing projects, what might be needed is to assist Keith to first feel comfortable with elaborating on his journal writing.

Developing and Employing Solutions

Although breadth of impact of the solutions we select is clearly an important consideration, it needs to be tempered by the cost to the consultee of implementing such a solution. As noted throughout the text, consultation implies change, and change by its very nature is costly. For the solutions to have a chance of succeeding, they must be implemented and maintained. As such it is important to select solution strategies that cause least strain or costs on the consultee or the system's resources. For example, if a consultant can choose between an intervention that requires the consultee to learn new skills and acquire some additional resources (e.g., materials, supplies) versus an intervention for which the consultee has the ability and resources needed, it is generally more effective to consider the latter, as least costly.

One of the unique elements of a solution focus approach is that it directs the consultant and consultee to the identification of existing resources, past successes (especially exceptions to the presenting concern), expertise, and solution-focused ideas of the consultee. It is these successes and resources that represent the substance of the conversations surrounding the consult.

Further, as solutions are employed in an atmosphere of experimentation, the solution-focused consultant can keep the focus upon small increments of success. Continual assessment through observation (of desired change), self-report, and goal scaling can be employed not only to provide a measure of accountability but also to serve as evidence of consultee success. The part played by the consultee and other participants (stakeholders) in any success must be emphasized.

The solution-focused consultant is encouraging of any evidence of success and empowers the consultee with full responsibility for any effort and progress made. Although relapse is acknowledged and even expected, the solution-focused consultant helps the consultee to anticipate setbacks and formulate flexible strategies to stay on track and remain goal and solution focused. A good example of a solution-focused approach to consultation can be found in chapter 14, Case 2.

SUMMARY

Approach Student Service
from a Consultation Perspective

All consultation could be said to be client or, in the case of school counselors, student targeted. However, not all consultation involves direct student assessment and intervention. The student as focus offers a client-focused consultation form of consultation in which diagnostic and intervention efforts center on the client as he/she interacts with a specific task within a specific environment. In client-focused consultation, the counselor–consultant is free to interact directly with the student and/or gather diagnostic information and implement intervention strategies indirectly, using the consultee as the conduit for such activities.

Focusing on the One While Impacting the Many

Student-focused consultation involves the full collaboration of consultant and consultee in problem-identification, goal-setting, and intervention processes. Such consultative collaboration provides a number of potential benefits. First, by incorporating varied perspectives (i.e., counselor–consultant and teacher or administrator–consultee) on data collection and interpretation, the potential bias intrinsic to either perspective is checked, and the validity of data collected may be increased. Secondly, by gathering data on the specific elements of the task and environment with which and in which the client is operating (e.g., the classroom) the possibility of achieving an assessment–intervention linkage has been increased. Finally, the collaborative exchange can serve an educative and thus preventive function for the consultee, increasing his/her knowledge of the influencing effects of task and environmental demands.

Problem Identification

This chapter presented an expanded model for assessing and intervening with a student from within a collaborative consultation framework. As discussed within this chapter, the consultant can increase the validity and utility of the diagnostic information by expanding the focus to include not only specific information about the client, but also information regarding the nature and requirements of the task and the unique characteristics of the environment in which the task is performed. Such an expanded view not only expands the data available but also facilitates the linkage of assessment to intervention and changes that offer preventive value.

Goal Setting and Solution-Focused Consultation

A solution-focus approach to consultation was provided. The model follows the basic tenets of focusing on positive behavior, what is working, devoting primary attention to the goals of the consultee and identifying exceptions to every problem that demonstrate times, places, and instances when the problem does not occur.

With this model as the framework, the consultant will assist the consultee to: (a) identify goals with increased utility and validity; (b) set priorities and find a place to start; and (c) identify existing resources, past successes (especially exceptions to the presenting concern), expertise, and solution-focused ideas of the consultee.

IMPORTANT TERMS

Assessment–intervention
  linkage
BASIC ID
Behavior = f(client-task-environment)
Chain
Client-focused
  consultation
Direct-service model

Exception identification
Expand goal focus
Goal setting
Goal scaling
Miracle question
Multimodal behavioral
  model
Physical environment
Problem identification

Psychosocial–physical
  environment
Social construction
Social/cultural climate
Solution-focus
  consultation
Solution-focused
  model
Task analysis

SUGGESTED READINGS

Davis, T. E., & Osborn, C. J. (1999). *The solution-focused school counselor: Shaping professional practice*. Philadelphia: Accelerated Development.

Lazarus, A. A., & MacKenzie, K. R. (1997). *Brief but comprehensive psychotherapy: The multimodal way*. New York: Springer.

Metcalf, L. (1995). *Counseling toward solutions*. West Nyack, NY: The Center for Applied Research in Education.

Miller, G. (1997). *Becoming miracle workers: Language and meaning in brief therapy*. Hawthorne, NY: Aldine de Gruyter.

Rossett, A. (1999). *First things fast: A handbook for performance analysis*. San Francisco: Jossey-Bass/Pfeiffer & Co. Publishers.

WEB SITES

Brief Therapy: A not-for-profit training and research institution.
  www.brief-therapy.org

Solution Focus Links: Links to sites providing information on application of solution focus to business and oganizations.
  www.thesolutionsfocus.com/linksh.cfm

The Centre for Multimodal Therapy: An international training center that runs modular courses in multimodal therapy.
  http://members.lycos.co.uk/Stress_Centre/index.html.htm

REFERENCES

Bennett, C. I. (1990). *Comprehensive multicultural education: Theory and practice* (2nd ed.). Boston: Allyn & Bacon.

Berg, I. K., & Miller, S. D. (1992). *Working with the problem drinker: A solution focused approach*. New York: Norton.

Cormier, W. H., & Cormier, L. S. (1991). *Interviewing strategies for helpers* (3rd ed.). Pacific Grove, CA: Brooks/Cole.

de Shazer, S. (1985). *Keys to solution in brief therapy.* New York: Norton.

de Shazer, S. (1988). *Clues: Investigating solutions in brief therapy.* New York: Norton.

Dunn, K., & Dunn, R. (1987). Dispelling outmoded beliefs about student learning. *Educational Leadership, 44*(6), 55–63.

Dunn, R., Beaudry, J. S., & Klavas, A. (1989). Survey of research on learning styles. *Educational Leadership, 47*(7), 50–58.

Ellis, A., & Grieger, R. (Eds.). (1986). *Handbook of rational-emotive therapy* (Vols.1–2). New York: Springer.

Glasser, W. (1990). *The quality school: Managing students without coercion.* New York: Perennial Press.

Guterman, J. T. (1994). A social constructionist position for mental health counseling. *Journal of Mental Health Counseling, 16,* 226–244.

Hall, E. T. (1966). *The hidden dimension.* Garden City, NY: Doubleday.

Johnson, D. W., & Johnson, F. P. (1997). *Joining together: Group theory and group skills* (6th ed.). Englewood Cliffs, NJ: Prentice Hall.

Kahn, B. B. (2000). A model of solution-focused consultation for school counselors. *Professional School Counseling, 3*(4), 248–254.

Kahn, W. J. (1999). *The A-B-C's of human experience.* Belmont, CA: Brooks/Cole.

Kanfer, F. H., & Hagerman, S. (1987). A model of self-regulation. In F. Halisch, & J. Kuht (Eds.), *Motivation, intention, and volition* (pp. 123–135, 293–307), Berlin: Springer-Verlag.

Lazarus, A. (1981). *Behavior therapy and beyond.* New York: McGraw-Hill.

Lazarus, A. (1989). *The practice of multimodal therapy.* Baltimore: Johns Hopkins University Press.

Miller, R. B. (1962). Analysis and specification of behavior for training. In R. Glaser (Ed.), *Training research and education:* Science edition. New York: Wiley.

Park, C. (1997, March). A comparative study of learning style preferences: Asian-American and Anglo Students in secondary schools. Paper presented at the Annual meeting of the American Educational Research Association, Chicago.

Parsons, R. D. (1996). *The skilled consultant.* Boston: Allyn & Bacon.

Perls, F. (1969). *Gestalt therapy verbatim.* Lafayette, CA: Real People Press.

Slavin, R. (1991). Are cooperative learning and untracking harmful to the gifted? *Educational Leadership, 48,* 68–71.

Tharp, R. G. (1989). Psychocultural variables and constants: Effects on teaching and learning in schools. *American Psychologist, 44,* 349–359.

Torrance, E. P. (1986). Teaching creative and gifted learners. In M. Wittrock (Ed.), *Handbook of research on teaching* (3rd ed., pp. 630–647) New York: Macmillan.

Vasquez, J. A. (1990). Teaching to the distinctive traits of minority students. *The Clearing House, 63,* 299–304.

Vygotsky, L. (1962). *Thought and language.* Cambridge, MA: MIT Press.

10

Consultee-Focused Consultation

Dr. Jameson is certainly concerned about Ellen. In fact,
I'm worried that he may be a bit overly concerned
and overly involved with her.

My observations suggest that Ellen can use some
assistance, but he seems to be catastrophizing the situation.
Somewhere along the process I will need to confront
this and see if I can help him regain some professional
distance and objectivity about what's going on.

I n **consultee-focused consultation** (Caplan 1970; Caplan & Caplan, 1993;
Parsons, 1996) the counselor–consultant attempts to increase the work-
related functioning of the client by targeting changes in the professional
functioning of the consultee. As our consultant will soon find out, focusing on
the consultee as target for change is both delicate and complex. Consultee-
focused consultation employs many of the same observational and interpersonal skills previously discussed, but it will also rely heavily on self-monitoring
techniques, direct and indirect confrontation, and educational programming.
Consultee-focused consultation will most likely result in the consultee gaining
personal insight as well as gaining in skills and knowledge related to job performance. However, it must be emphasized that consultee-focused consultation is not intended to serve as personal counseling or psychotherapy for the
consultee. The consultant engaged in consultee-focused consultation must be

alert not to cross the boundary between consultee-focused consultation and personal consultee counseling. The knowledge and skills required for maintaining such a balance are the focus of this chapter.

CHAPTER OBJECTIVES

After completing this chapter, the reader should be able to

1. Describe the nature and value of consultee-focused consultation
2. Identify when the consultee's level of professional knowledge, skill, or objectivity are pivotal to the creation, maintenance, and eventual amelioration of a client problem
3. Employ appropriate confrontational skills as the base for intervention at the consultee-focused level of consultation
4. Describe techniques employed in consultee-focused consultation, including didactic information giving and theme interference reduction strategies.

THE CONSULTEE: A SIGNIFICANT EXTRAPERSONAL VARIABLE

In chapter 9 much attention was given to the fact that a client's behavior is assumed to be a result of the interaction between certain client factors, the task characteristics, and the environment within which the task is being performed. Clearly, an important factor operating within the client's environment and one having potential impact on the current problem and its resolution is the consultee's own professional style and interpersonal mannerisms.

It is possible that it is the consultee's own response to the client, which if not causing the current client-related problem, is exacerbating the situation. Consider the case of Tanisha, a bright, achieving, 17-year-old who has been referred to the counselor's office by her social studies teacher, Ms. Bias. Ms. Bias reported that Tanisha has been "giving her attitude" since day one of this academic year. Ms. Bias reported that Tanisha has this look of disdain each time she is called on in class and that when confronted about her attitude simply explains ". . . it's not (her) problem!" Tanisha is doing all her work and continues to be an A student in all her classes with the exception of social studies, where her level of performance and participation is significantly less than that reported in other classes. When interviewed, Ms. Bias stated that she really was confused by Tanisha's behavior. "I have tried everything with this girl. I know she is applying to Ivy League schools, and I remind her that her attitude is not going to serve her well in those environments. Further, when she hands in less than acceptable work, I have tried to motivate her by writing reminders like "Ivy League?" and "Valedictorian?" on the top.

The counselor–consultant interviewed Tanisha and found her to be a highly achieving and self-motivated individual. Tanisha shared with the counselor that since her mom's death 3 years ago, keeping up her schoolwork has been difficult. Tanisha's father works multiple jobs, and Tanisha helps out by assuming some responsibility for the care of her three younger siblings. When asked about her reaction to Ms. Bias, Tanisha explained that she doesn't appreciate Ms. Bias's demeaning tone of voice and her constant referral to Tanisha as "her little star." Tanisha continued that she felt Ms. Bias's comments of "Ivy League?" and "Valedictorian?" were sarcastic. Tanisha explained that although she was taught to respect her teachers, and as such would not say or do anything offensive in Ms. Bias's class, that she really didn't feel the need to "act nice and friendly" to someone so uncaring.

As the counselor–consultant reflected on the situation it became clear that what was intended as praise—my little star—and motivators—"Ivy League?"—were being received as sarcastic, devaluing, and demeaning commentary. Helping Tanisha to reframe Ms. Bias's comments as those originating from good intent would be one target for intervention. However, with the possibility that others may also misinterpret Ms. Bias's comments, a broader more preventive approach would be to increase Ms. Bias's awareness of the impact of her commentary. The consultant wondered aloud with Ms. Bias that "maybe Tanisha was interpreting Ms. Bias's best intentions as sarcastic and demeaning." This reframing question helped Ms. Bias to increase her understanding of Tanisha's concerns, and consequently she began to reduce her own attempts at using prods as motivators. More importantly, with this new understanding, Ms. Bias began to speak with Tanisha both about her own college experiences and the pressure she felt being the first female in her family to go on to higher education. This openness and personal sharing helped Tanisha to appreciate that Ms. Bias was truly trying to help and served as a basis for the development of a better relationship and the reduction of the inadvertent antagonism that had developed.

It certainly would have been possible and appropriate to focus on simply helping Tanisha become less sensitive to Ms. Bias's comments. However, given the broader desire of achieving prevention, a more efficient target and focus for consultation is to increase the consultee's (Ms. Bias) understanding of her own behavior. With this new awareness, Ms. Bias could make the needed adjustments in her approach, which not only helped reduce the negativity between herself and Tanisha, but also reduced the possibility that this scenario would be replayed with another student in the future.

In this example, the focus of the consultation was on increasing the consultee's level of understanding. Once accomplished, the consultee had the needed skills and professional level of objectivity to adjust her own style to more effectively motivate her student. There are times, however, when increasing the consultee's level of understanding and knowledge are not sufficient. The consultant working in a consultee-focused consultation will encounter situations in which the focus will go beyond increasing consultee knowledge, to increasing consultee skill and/or professionalism. Each of these targets for consultee consultation (i.e., knowledge, skill, and objectivity) present special opportunities and challenges for the consultant, and therefore each are discussed in further detail.

COLLABORATING ON KNOWLEDGE DEVELOPMENT

It is not unusual to discover that the steps employed by a consultee to remediate a situation are based on faulty information and as such not only fail to ameliorate the situation but in fact exacerbate it. Thus, for example, when Ms. Bias assumed Tanisha was becoming less involved because of her lack of motivation, she began to increase her use of "motivating comments" such as "Ivy League?" and "Valedictorian?" However, as we soon found out, these interventions did not achieve the intended outcome; in fact, they stimulated further withdrawal and reluctance to participate.

In such situations, it is not the lack of goodwill nor even professionalism that serves as the base for the consultee's involvement with the client's problematic behavior. Rather, it is simply the consultee's lack of a clear understanding about the nature of the situation. To further clarify this point, consider the case of Mrs. H.

Mrs. H. has been a teacher for the past 38 years. Her health, particularly her hearing and eyesight, is not as good as it used to be, and her speech is sometimes slurred. She is very afraid of losing her job through forced retirement and is very defensive about any suggestion that she may no longer be fit to teach. She has sent two boys to the guidance counselor's office writing: "Please counsel these two disrespectful, disruptive hooligans!"

After the consultant spoke with Ms. H. about her concerns they both decided that it would be helpful if the consultant spoke with the two boys. In speaking with the two boys, the counselor, contrary to the comments from Mrs. H., found that neither of the youths was disrespectful nor did either have any history of acting out in class. In fact, the direct opposite had been the case with the two in question. In reviewing the records, the counselor found that the boys had excellent academic histories and were very interested in pursuing careers in education. Further, it appeared that their talking to each other during Mrs. H.'s class was the result of their need to check their understanding of Mrs. H.'s lectures. They stated that they really have difficulty understanding her sometimes, and they check with each other to validate that what they heard was accurate. It appears that what Mrs. H. interprets as disrespectful is the fact that these two often ask questions of Mrs. H. that may appear off the topic. Through observations of the class interaction, the consultant soon realized that the questions asked were a result of the boys misinterpreting what Mrs. H. said, a misinterpretation created by Mrs. H.'s tendency to sometimes slur her words. It was clear, through the observation, that the boys were not intending to disrupt or embarrass Mrs. H., but were only seeking clarification.

The consultant working with this case could certainly assist the boys (the clients) to develop more effective styles of coping with this environment, but a better approach, both in terms of immediate remediation and potential prevention, would be to focus the consultant's efforts on providing Mrs. H. additional understanding of the nature of and motivation for the boy's behaviors.

In this situation, a fuller understanding of the dynamics of the classroom and the true motivation behind the boys talking with each other and asking questions may assist Mrs. H. to reduce her negative perception of them. Further, her increased understanding of the nature of the situation may result in her adapting her own style, for example, by employing lecture outlines and printed handouts. Such a change in her own teaching approach would not only reduce the boys' need to interrupt with questions or to dialogue with one another but would also prevent other students from needing to engage in similar actions.

The situation in which a consultee's lack of knowledge or understanding serves as the primary source behind the experienced difficulty is most clearly evident when the population with whom the consultee is called to work has changed, and the unique talents and needs of the client population may not be that for which the consultee was originally trained. Perhaps one of the clearest examples of this comes as a result of the movement to educate exceptional students in regular classrooms in a process referred to as full inclusion (Parsons, Hinson, & Brown, 2001). Exercise 10.1 provides an example of just such a situation. Exercise 10.1 also provides an opportunity for more fully understanding the impact that a consultee's limited knowledge can have a client work-related problem.

EXERCISE 10.1

Full Inclusion

Directions: Read the following case scenario. For Part I of this exercise, develop two hypotheses regarding the possible point of connection between the consultee's level of understanding and the referral problem. Further, identify ways you as consultant could develop the data required to support either of your hypothesized connections and engage the consultee in this validation process. You may find this exercise more effective if performed with another, such as a classmate, a colleague, or a supervisor.

Case Presentation
Referral: Timothy was referred to your office by his fifth grade teacher, Ms. Ellison. Ms. Ellison reported that Timothy, a new student to your school, is "constantly getting out of his seat, tormenting other children, and almost never on the page or the worksheet that he is supposed to be doing." Ms. Ellison reported that Timothy has been doing this "since day one, and it is only getting

worse each day." Further, she noted that she cannot tolerate it anymore and is truly "beginning to dislike this boy!"

Classroom Observations

In observing the classroom, you note that Ms. Ellison, a third-year teacher, is highly energetic and enthusiastic in class. She moves rapidly around the room, speaks loudly, and employs a lot of animation in her communication patterns. Ms. Ellison's is an activities-driven classroom. She has her class set up in learning stations that are very stimulating both visually and auditorially, and she has the children moving around the class, going from one learning center to another. The classroom is very active, very stimulating, and very energetic. It is clear that there is much opportunity for students to be engaged in the learning process.

Additional Information

In looking at Timothy's records, you find that he had been diagnosed as having Attentional Deficit Hyperactive Disorder. Timothy has recently transferred from a self-contained program for ADHD children where he spent the last three years. He is now enrolled in all of the regular education classes within the school.

Part I: Connecting Ms. Ellison's lack of information to Timothy's behavior.

Hypothesis 1:

Hypothesis 2:

Part II: Supporting your hypothesis.
What type of data would you attempt to gather to support either of your hypotheses, and how would you engage Ms. Ellison in this process?

As suggested by the example in Exercise 10.1, full inclusion could certainly create problems for both the regular classroom teacher and the child who is brought into the regular classroom if the teacher is ill informed or lacking in knowledge as to what to expect and how to respond to the child's special needs. In situations where the consultee is responding to people and processes without the proper understanding and knowledge, the consultant needs to serve as a source for informational dissemination and education.

Identifying the Problem

Interview and observational skills will prove invaluable tools in diagnosing the lack of consultee knowledge. In discussing the client, the consultant serving as content expert needs to be sensitive to the consultee's accuracy of understanding of the client's functioning and the interpretation of such client's behavior as compared to normative developmental or job-related behavior.

For example, consider the situation with Sr. Patrice an eighth-grade teacher at a local parochial school. Sr. Patrice had over 12 years of teaching experience, but prior to this year all of her experience was with first graders. Sister contacted the consultant extremely upset over the overly hostile behavior of one of her male students. Sister described Paul as "having some real anger toward women!" She noted that Paul liked to tease the girls in the class, but more importantly he liked to run up behind them in the playground and put them into bear hugs, sometimes picking them off the ground. Sr. Patrice thought it was important for the consultant to work with Paul. After observing Paul's behavior in the playground, it became apparent that what Sr. Patrice saw as hostility was actually adolescent sexual play. Paul, and many of the other boys and girls, would find ways to come into physical contact—touching, poking, grabbing, or even bear hugging each other. Although Sister may have identified an area in which some instruction might be useful, to approach it as if Paul had a serious problem would have only exacerbated the situation. What was needed was for Sister to become somewhat more familiar with preadolescent and adolescent behavior.

Sometimes it is not so much the consultee's comprehension of the client's behavior that is at issue. There are times when the consultee may need to develop a more accurate understanding of her own response style as well as the degree to which that style is congruent with standards of professional practice. Consider, for example, Helen, a teacher in a community day care center. Helen reported having an unusually difficult time managing one particular 4-year-old. Helen was very aware of what typical 4-year-old children like to do, and she was even knowledgeable about the use of reinforcement as a means of shaping behavior. She simply could not understand why she was unable to manage Theo, the 4-year-old in question.

The center had been used for some university research, and as such it was equipped with a one-way mirror and a video recorder. The consultant asked the consultee, Helen, if he could tape the children at play so that together they could attempt to understand what might be going on with Theo. As they observed the tape, Helen almost embarrassingly exclaimed, "Gads, look at me, I look so serious. I don't seem to be enjoying myself, and it has been 45 minutes and I have yet to provide any child with a word of praise!" It became apparent to both the consultant and the consultee that even though she was quite knowledgeable about child development and classroom management techniques, Helen was somewhat less knowledgeable about her own teaching style. As they continued to view the tape Helen quickly identified that Theo's behavior was really quite normative and that his limit testing appeared to be an attempt to gain her attention.

In diagnosing the existence of a consultee's lack of knowledge or understanding, the consultant will attempt to answer three separate questions (Meyers, Parsons & Martin, 1979). First, the consultant needs to identify the degree to which the consultee is aware of his professional behavior. The question to be addressed is, does the consultee possess accurate self-knowledge and reality-based perception on his behavior with the consultee? In order to answer this first question, the consultant needs to systematically observe the consultee in interaction with the client. The consultant needs to have the consultee estimate his behaviors and compare them against the data collected. The feedback provided must be objective and nonevaluative. In the previous case involving Theo and the preschool teacher, Helen, the availability of the videotape proved efficacious in that the data could be presented in objective and nonevaluative manner, and the incongruency between the way Helen thought she acted and how in fact she behaved was quite apparent.

Assuming that the consultee demonstrates an accurate awareness of his response style, the consultant proceeds to the second question. The consultant now needs to determine whether the consultee's observed and self-defined behaviors are congruent with the consultee's attitudes about how he should professionally function. That is, the consultant wants to be sure that what the consultee is doing is what the consultee desires to do. The final question to be addressed is whether or not what the consultee is doing and wishes to do is congruent with what is known to be the accepted form of professional practice. Clearly, discrepancies at any point of the questioning need to be confronted and accurate information provided as the potential remedial steps increasing knowledge and understanding.

Interventions

In the situation where the consultee lacks understanding, the intervention of choice is to provide the consultee with the information needed. As noted, the consultee may need specific information about the client, information about the developmental or theoretical principles operating, or even information about her own response style. Providing the consultee information may allow her to more accurately understand the client's responses and perhaps open for her a variety of options that were not apparent previously.

Interventions employed, although tailored to the specific needs of the consultee, in general involve two steps. The first step of an intervention aimed at a consultee's need for information is to confront the consultee with the need for more information. This delicate process of confrontation will be discussed later in this chapter. The second step would be for the consultant to serve as an informational resource and to collaboratively develop an educational program for the consultee. It is obvious that this form of feedback and didactic instruction requires the consultant to be both directive and confrontational. Because of the possible resistance encountered, it is important for the consultant to have developed a collaborative relationship with the consultee *prior* to implementing such consultee-focused consultation. Further, the consultant needs to remind the consultee of the confidential, nonevaluative nature of the relationship.

The goal for the intervention would be to provide the consultee with nonevaluative feedback about his current level of knowledge and the degree of congruence that knowledge has with that of current research or expert opinion. Further, the feedback needs to highlight the impact that this lack of information has had on the consultee's choices of response in working with the client and how these choices have contributed to (if not caused) the client's current work problem. Once the need has been identified and embraced by the consultee, the second phase of intervention would be to provide an educational program for the consultee.

The first step of developing an effective intervention is to establish concrete goals and learning objectives. Identification of the goals will help give shape to the specific form of information dissemination and education needed. It is essential that the consultant establish these goals in collaboration with the consultee. It is important that the consultee expresses clear ownership of both the goals and the process to be employed.

COLLABORATING ON CONSULTEE SKILL DEVELOPMENT

It is not usual to find a consultee who is very accurate in her self-observation and is also aware that her behavior is *not* that prescribed as professional practice. However, this same consultee may be having a great deal of trouble implementing the type of response or behavior she desires, simply because she lacks the necessary skills.

Consider the case of a teacher who understands the limited effectiveness of the use of mild reprimands and other forms of punishment as a form of classroom management and embraces the value of employing positive reinforcement within his classroom. However, this same teacher finds that his habitual style is to ignore the desired behaviors, simply being happy that the student is doing what is expected, and to reprimand the child when not performing. Although understanding the inefficiency of his classroom management style, the consultee in question is having difficulty shedding the old habit. In this situation it is skill development rather than information acquisition that is needed. This consultee needs assistance in increasing the habit strength and skill in using positive reinforcement within his classroom.

Facilitating Skill Development

Because specific professional practices may be more related to individual preferences and professional cultures than to theoretical models (Caplan & Caplan, 1993), full and complete agreement on both the need and the specifics is essential. Further because in most situations there are a number of behaviors, actions, regimens, or skills that can be employed, it is important for the consultant to collaborate with the consultee in identifying the skills viewed as desirable, reasonable, and possible to develop.

Although the specific skills to be developed will be unique to the individual consultee, the task with which they are engaged, and the environment and culture where they work, a number of general areas for teacher training have been identified in the literature as targets for ongoing skill development. Some of these generic areas for consultee skill development are problem solving (Zins, 1993), management (Bergan & Kratochwill, 1990), behavior modification (Anderson, Kratochwill, & Bergan, 1986), and group and interpersonal dynamics (Robinson & Wilson, 1987).

Program Development

When the goal involves increasing the consultee's skill, practice is essential. Skill development is not typically accomplished by one or two in-services but generally requires a system of practice and corrective feedback. Because of the need to be systematic in such skill training, the consultant should attempt to connect the consultee to any of the training programs or mechanisms (such as in-services, workshops, etc.) that are offered as part of the typical operation within that system. Connecting the consultee to the system's natural mechanism for training will ensure ongoing support for the consultee. In the absence of such a natural mechanism, the consultant along with the consultee will need to develop an individualized program of training and skill development.

It has been these authors' experience as well as that of others (e.g., Caplan & Caplan, 1993) that when programs have to be developed, it is best to attempt to offer such training on a group basis rather than on an individual basis. The use of a group training format has a number of pedagogical benefits (e.g., the availability of a variety of practice partners and alternative view points), psychological benefits (reducing the consultee's feelings of inadequacy by demonstrating the widespread need among his/her colleagues, with appropriate peer reinforcement), and consultation benefits (in that it helps to spread the effect and thus increase the preventive impact). This latter benefit establishes new skills as norms within the system.

Training Considerations

The specific form of the training program needs to be shaped by the nature of the skills to be developed, the unique needs and resources of the consultee, and the available resources of the consultant and training environment. However, even with this mandate to tailor the learning experience, a number of general rules can be applied.

1. Establish clear objectives. It is important that all participants understand what the purpose of the training experience is and is *not*. Establishing clear objectives will not only facilitate the learning process but will also assist in keeping the activities in line with the desired goals.

2. Specify evaluation procedures. It is important to ensure that the learning experience is for professional development and *not job evaluation*. All forms of assessment should be formative in nature and created with the purpose of remediating and prescribing rather than simply labeling. Using a number of clear, concrete criterion reference measures (Parsons & Brown, 2002; Parsons, Hinson & Brown, 2001) will help the participants know

when they are mastering the basic skills as well as to assist them in knowing which skills need continued development.

3. Design the specific learning activities. Because the focus is on the development of skills and not simply increasing the consultee's knowledge, a general guideline for learning activities is that they should employ demonstration or modeling (either in vivo modeling or video presentations), the opportunity for application and practice (e.g., role play opportunities), and the use of corrective feedback. It is important that the consultant and consultee approach this task of skill development as an opportunity for professional development and not one of job performance evaluation. With such an orientation, the consultee will approach the corrective feedback with more receptivity. For the training to come full circle, it would be useful for the consultant to observe the consultee applying the skills with the work setting and again provide the needed corrective feedback. From this point additional training could be considered. As an alternative to the use of actual practice when such hands-on practice is not possible, the consultant could use pencil-and-paper simulations. This simulation approach is less desirable because it may demonstrate a consultee's ability to know what to do, yet fail to increase his ability to do it (Parsons & Meyers, 1984).

REGAINING OBJECTIVITY
AND PROFESSIONALISM

There are situations in which the consultee, although both knowledgeable and skilled at efficiently managing the client and the client's work-related behavior, is currently ineffective. Often, such ineffectiveness is the result of the consultee's loss of professional objectivity or the fact that his own emotional needs and particular psychosocial history is interfering with the performance of his professional duties. The position taken here and elsewhere (e.g., Meyers, Parsons, & Martin, 1979; Parsons, 1996) is that extrapersonal factors play an important role in the creation, maintenance, and eventual alleviation of the client's related problem. One extrapersonal factor that can highly influence the client's functioning is the consultee and the manner in which the consultee approaches his role. For example, the client in our sample case may need assistance. However, it appears that Dr. Jameson's ability to provide his best professional insights may be somewhat compromised by his personal involvement with her and the resulting loss of professional objectivity that is occurring. It is even possible that the client's current behaviors are in direct response to Dr. Jameson's loss of objectivity and overinvolvement. Under these conditions, the most effective and efficient approach to remediating this client's difficulty may be to assist the consultee in gaining knowledge, skill, and/or professional objectivity. Consider the case of Ellen H.

Ellen is a third-grade teacher who is well liked by students, parents, and colleagues. She is recognized as highly effective, working very well with children with special needs. Recently, the principal has noted more noise and apparent disruption coming from her classroom. Observation reveals that Ellen appears disorganized, somewhat negative in her reactions to the children, and emotionally somewhat flat. One student, Jerome, appears especially affected by this new teacher style.

Jerome is a student who had developed a close relationship with Ms. H. and seemed to be highly motivated by her praise and words of encouragement. Now somewhat confused by her increased negativity and emotional distancing, Jerome appears to be acting out to gain attention. Sadly, his behavior only elicits more negativity from Ms. H., which in further stimulates Jerome to employ disruptive attention-seeking behaviors. Clearly, the added stress that Ms. H. is experiencing is interfering with her professional functioning and impacting the performance of at least one of her students, Jerome. From a systems perspective Jerome is the identified "client," but the root cause of the problem is the lack of objectivity in Ellen. Consequently, the "entry level" to the problem is through Jerome, but the focus of change is his teacher.

Working in the arena of loss of objectivity can truly tax the consultant's ability to maintain a collaborative relationship. The consultant will most certainly have to confront the consultee's loss of objectivity. It is important that the intervention attempt to keep the focus on the consultee's current level of professional functioning in relation to the client, while avoiding any in-depth discussion of the personal issues or experiences that may have contributed to this loss of objectivity.

Categorizing Loss of Objectivity

One model for understanding the different sources of loss of objectivity and the depth of impact has been developed by Caplan and Caplan (1993). Caplan and Caplan (1993) suggest that in most cases loss of objectivity can be classified into five overlapping categories: (a) direct personal involvement, (b) simple identification, (c) theme interference, (d) transference, and (e) characterological distortions. Each of the categories is discussed in some detail.

Direct Personal Involvement Although it is less than optimal, it would not be unusual to find a teacher who has both a professional and personal relationship with a student. This would happen in the situation where a teacher is also a student's aunt or next-door neighbor or even a good friend of the student's mother. In this situation, the personal relationship the consultee has with client outside the school environment could interfere with the consultee's objectivity and ability to respond professionally to the client within the school. For example, a teacher's ability to discipline a student may be compromised if that same student is the daughter of a person that teacher is dating.

The consultee whose objectivity has been compromised because of a personal relationship with the client may be aware of this distortion in her professional judgment and behavior. However, even with such an awareness the consultee may be unwilling to publicly admit this distortion of her professionalism because of her own sense of guilt or shame. Clearly, the consultant will need to foster a conscious awareness and acceptance of this distortion of professional objectivity prior to providing any strategies for assisting the consultee to separate her personal needs from those of her professional duties and responsibilities.

Interventions employed with this and all the various forms of loss of objectivity will involve confrontation. The goal of this confrontation will be to assist the consultee to not only regain her professional relationship with the client, but also to discover ways to replace the satisfaction of her personal needs with appropriate satisfaction found in professional goal attainment. Thus the consultee who is unable to reprimand the daughter of a friend may be helped to reframe this reprimand, not as punishment, but as an attempt to help this student perform and achieve to her potential.

Simple Identification   A second form of loss of objectivity occurs when the consultee relates or identifies with the client or one of the other significant individuals within the client's situation. Often, this process of simple identification is easy to recognize, in that the point of connection or similarity may be quite apparent. For example, the consultee and client may share physical similarity, ethnic backgrounds, unique behavior (e.g., tics, stutters), or common social experiences (e.g., recently divorced, moved out of the house, have an overbearing parent). The consultee's description of the client or client's current situation will often highlight these points of similarities. Further, it is not unusual for the consultee to refer to the client in very positive and sympathetic terms, speaking as if it were from personal experience. This was the case of Ms. Z.

Ms. Z. is a young, highly achieving, African–American woman who expressed concern over the social harassment and bullying experienced by one of her fifth-grade students, Aisha. Ms. Z. reported that the children were being cruel, taunting Aisha in the playground and actively rejecting her from all social interaction. The consultant observed Aisha and her classmates in the playground and at lunch and reported back to Ms. Z. The following dialogue ensued:

Ms. Z: Well, didn't I tell—they are cruel (very excited).

Mr. L.: I know how much concern you are feeling. So I observed Aisha in both the playground and at lunch . . . and

Ms. Z: (interrupting) Do you believe how they treat her?

Mr. L: Well, actually that is what I wanted to share. During the time I was observing, I noticed some teasing

Ms. Z: (interrupting) Some? Some? I bet you have never been on the receiving end of a cruel comment!

On further reflection and with supportive interaction, Mr. L. was able to have Ms. Z. disclose her own experience of being one of a very few

African-American children in her elementary school and the painful rejection and bullying she experienced. Further, in this dialogue, Ms. Z. was able to consider that perhaps her own experience was making her somewhat overreactive to typical fifth-grade teasing when it came to Aisha. Mr. L. reframed this overreaction, viewing it, rather, as being sensitive to the possible impact cruel comments can have on all children. The result was that Ms. Z. inquired about the possibility of providing a guidance lesson on teasing and bullying to her class, stating that all the children could benefit.

As with all forms of loss of objectivity, the consultant in this case needed to confront the consultee about her possible distortion and loss of professional objectivity. Using skills of confrontation, both direct and indirect forms (to be discussed later within this chapter), the consultant attempted to raise the consultee's level of consciousness around the emotional identification she felt regarding this particular client and client situation. Further, the consultant helped the consultee recognize the ways such identification may be distorting her professional judgment and behavior.

Theme Interference Theme interference (Caplan, 1970) can usually be recognized by the fact that the consultee who had typically worked both effectively and professionally now presents as unable to handle a particular work-related issue and as a result appears both confused and upset. The difficulty that the consultee is exhibiting is also confusing to those who supervise the consultee because it is the type of situation that she has both the knowledge and skills needed to professionally respond. The consultee experiencing theme interference appears blocked in her response to the work situation and may appear unaccountably sensitive to some facet or aspect of the work situation (Caplan & Caplan, 1993). According to Caplan & Caplan (1993), what happens is that a conflict related to the consultee's personal experience has not been satisfactorily resolved and now persists as an emotionally toned cognitive constellation, called a *theme*. A theme is some distorted or dysfunctional and rigid thinking that links two separate thoughts or interpretations without empirical bases. Caplan (1970) noted that a counsultee expressing theme interference was operating from a rigid, syllogistic form of thinking. The consultee had locked into the belief that **if** event **A** occurred, then **B** had to follow. Consider the case of Tom.

Tom, having previously taught for 6 years at the middle school, was now reassigned to teach 11th-grade social studies. Although being knowledgeable about content and pedagogy, Tom was experiencing a great deal of difficulty in managing his classroom, something that he had never previously experienced. In discussing the matter with the counselor–consultant, Tom emphasized that he hates having to discipline the students, he hates being mean, "a real ogre!"

It appears that Tom is making an inevitable link between one thought, "I need to manage my classroom" with a second thought, for example: "You have to be mean to discipline high school students and therefore nobody will like you." Assuming this is the case for our consultee, then finding himself in this position of now teaching high school stimulates the inevitable conclusions regarding the fact that everyone will dislike him. This conclusion is both unpleasant and unacceptable and thus blocks his utilization of effective classroom management techniques. The result is a classroom that is on the verge of being out of control.

The rigid, almost syllogistic thinking found in theme interference leads the consultee to jump to conclusions about the students. In Tom's case, that conclusion is that they would dislike him. As such, the consultee's own reaction, of failing to discipline the students, would be in reaction to this anticipated client response, rather than to any evidence in reality.

Caplan and Caplan (1993) suggest that typically the theme is adequately repressed or otherwise defended against but may become active when the consultee's equilibrium is upset. Thus even though our consultee has had this theme within his life, it has not been disruptive because he had not previously taught at the secondary level. However, once reassigned to a position requiring the exertion of more authority, the theme was aroused, and the disruptive conclusions began to influence his job-related responses and his perceptions of his students. Unresolved themes can lead the consultee to not only draw invalid conclusions about a particular client (e.g., that student is really angry that I corrected him), but also may lead the consultee to respond in an impulsive, nonfunctional way as an attempt to intervene with the perceived client problem. Exercise 10.2 is provided to further clarify this point.

EXERCISE 10.2

Theme Interference

Directions: Read the following case presentation, being especially sensitive to identify elements of the client's situation that appear to have an unusual emotional tone or charge for the consultee. Next, identify those consultee responses that appear to be an artifact of the theme rather than an objective response to the client's need.

Case: Ms. Roberts is a sixth-grade teacher. She is a recent college graduate, and this is her first professional teaching assignment. Ms. Roberts has invited the consultant to help her with one particular child in her class, Liz. According to Ms. Roberts, Liz needs to be watched very closely. Ms. Roberts stated that Liz is a child "just waiting to explode." Ms. Roberts is unable to point to anything specific that Liz is doing or not doing, but she wants the consultant (the school counselor) to begin to counsel Liz.

From her position as teacher, Ms. Roberts will keep a "tight control on Liz, giving her a lot of structure and be sure to check up on her daily." Ms. Roberts continued: "I have made time in my day where I can meet with Liz and let her know I'm available if she needs to talk, but I know she needs more than I can provide." "She is really a neat kid, it's a shame to see her throw it away and start to get out of control."

When the consultant questioned the need for the counseling and the extreme control, Ms. Roberts avoided the questions and turned the discussion to the fact that: "Liz's mom is newly divorced and has since returned to work. Liz is obviously going to be one of those latchkey kids, and you know what happens to them! You sometimes have to wonder why people like that have kids."

Questions

What possible theme or themes is operating to block Ms. Roberts' utilization of her skills as classroom manager?

Which responses appear tied more to Ms. Roberts' issues rather than client need?

Intervention with Theme Interference   Intervention with such theme interference can take two forms. First, the consultant can attempt to unlink the referral problem, or client behavior, from category A of the consultee's syllogistic thinking. Assisting the consultee to reexamine her perception of the client may help the consultee to understand that her perception of this particular client's situation was not accurate. Thus in the case of the latchkey child, helping Ms. Roberts understand that Liz's mother works at a local elementary school and that her schedule parallels Liz's may help her to reframe her initial impressions regarding Liz as a latchkey child. Similarly, providing the consultee with additional data regarding the client or the client's situation may facilitate the consultee's attempt at reframing the client's experience so that it can be unlinked from the inevitable conclusions drawn from the syllogism of the consultee's theme. For example, in the case of Ms. Roberts, providing her information regarding Liz's after school activities, such as her active involvement with girl scouts, peer tutoring, and church youth group and the very loving and close-knit relationship that Liz has with both her father and her mother, may help her to reduce the feeling that Liz will inevitably become a problem child. This form of intervention may assist the consultee to give up on displacing her own conflictual issues on the client because the client no longer is perceived as fitting the logic of the initial category.

This unlinking, while assisting the consultee to relate more objectivity to this one specific client, does little to reduce the possibility that linking may occur in the future. In order for this to occur the basic irrationality of the consultee's thinking must be identified and reformed. This is the aim of a second type of intervention that is to reduce or remove the theme.

Caplan (1970) recommends a process of theme interference reduction to test the logic of the consultee's thinking. One such method would start with the consultant accepting the client and/or the client's situation as fitting into category A. For example, Liz is a latchkey child. However, in so doing the consultant is attempting to set up a cognitive dissonance (Festinger, 1957), which will eventually lead to the reformulation of the consultee's logic. That is, if we accept the client or the client's problem as fitting the category A (i.e., Liz is latchkey), then we are to assume B (i.e., Liz will become a problem) to follow. The consultant needs to assist the consultee to gather objective data around the specific occurrence of B. For example, asking Ms. Roberts to gather evidence or point out data that would demonstrate Liz's problematic behavior may help her identify that her prediction, that Liz would be out of control as a result of the latchkey experience, is not supported by the data and therefore the connection between these two ideas is not supported. When, the existence of B is not evidenced by the data, the inevitable linkage is challenged and the validity of the logic questioned.

It is hoped that such dissonance will cause a reformulation of the consultee's thinking. Further, it is assumed that the weakening of the certainty of the linkage between the two events will result in a lessening of the interference due to the theme. Once the theme interference is reduced, the consultee will move from the crisis-oriented response pattern that has most likely aggravated, if not caused, the current client problem, and return to her effective level of professional functioning.

For those interested in developing more specific skills in the process of theme interference reduction, you are referred to chapter 8 in Gerald Caplan and Ruth B. Caplan's *Mental Health Consultation and Collaboration* (1993).

Transference   Transference is the fourth form of loss of objectivity discussed by Caplan and Caplan, (1993). The consultee who is acting out of transference will project onto the client a set of attitudes, expectations, and judgments that more accurately reflect the experience of the consultee (rather than the client's own experience) and that will distort the consultee's accurate and objective evaluation of the client and the client's life experiences. Under these conditions, the consultee will respond from their own transferred feelings. This is different than simple identification, in which at least some of the conditions to which the consultee is reacting do exist for the client.

Consider the case of Bernard, a high school science teacher. Bernard approached the consultant seeking assistance with one of his students. Bernard explained that Elsie, the student with whom he had concerns, was new to the school. Elsie, according to Bernard, just moved to this area, having previously lived in Georgia. Bernard noted that Elsie appeared to be a bright and capable student. Even though it was hard for Bernard to pinpoint his concerns he simply "felt that there was something just not right with Elsie" and he wanted the consultant to "check her out." After meeting with Elsie and having her assess her experience with the move and the new school, the consultant returned to Bernard. As he entered the second session with the consultee, Bernard met him at the door with a big smile and stated, "What do you think, a religious fanatic?" Caught somewhat off guard, the consultant was unsure how to respond. In the silence that followed, Bernard followed up by stating, "You got to watch these Bible Belt people, they'll jam it down your throat. You have a problem, well that's God's way of saying you are a sinner and damned. I can hear her now, tell her parents, we all need to repent!"

The consultant reflected Bernard's feelings and asked if he or the other staff had noticed any such behavior. Bernard responded: "Oh, no, I was just having a little fun, you know—the Georgia thing, the southern Bible circuit, just having a little fun."

In follow-up conversations with both the student, Elsie, and the consultee, Bernard, it became clear that there was no truth to his concerns. Elsie was raised as a Roman Catholic and although attempting to live a good, value-based life, was not very active in her church. Further, it became obvious that Bernard had some very old, unresolved issues regarding his own faith stance and in particular his own feelings of guilt surrounding some of his earlier choices in life. It appeared to the consultant that Bernard was allowing his own fears of condemnation and sense of guilt to interfere with his assessment of Elsie. Further, his concern regarding her talking to her parents about the teachers' need to repent appeared to be more a projection of his own fear of being discovered as a "sinner."

In most settings, transference, as a process, is discouraged by the very fact that the consultee and the client remain emotionally detached. In most situations, the consultee has separated his professional interactions from his private life, and thus the boundaries of the profession serve as a reality check to hold in place transferential distortions. The possibility of blurred boundaries can be a significant issue for teachers because they are responsible to maintain close observations and connections with those students, particularly, those who are having the most difficulty functioning. In these situations, the characteristic of the client (e.g., new to the school) can encourage the consultee to provide emotional support or guidance. Along with this invitation to provide emotional support comes the invitation to engage at a psychoemotional level with the client and thus become more vulnerable to the opportunities for transference.

The existence of a transference reaction can often be identified by the somewhat stereotyped prejudged nature of the consultee's reaction to the client. This was certainly the case with Bernard's assumptions about Elsie, simply because she relocated from Georgia. Once identified, the distortion must be confronted and the transferential issues elevated within the consultee's consciousness. Because transference typically reflects events or experience with significant personal relevance, working with a consultee around these transferential issues is extremely difficult if one is attempting to maintain a collaborative consultation relationship and avoid moving into a psychotherapeutic contract. Because of this delicate balance, it is often preferable for the consultant to employ less-direct forms of confrontation (discussed later) in order to allow the consultee the opportunity to retain a sense of personal privacy while at the same time making the connections between his own personal experience and the current distortion of the client's reality. There may be times when the consultee is so defended from his own awareness of the transferential issues that the best the consultant can hope for is to be able to successfully refer the consultee for additional therapeutic support and individual counseling.

Characterological Distortions   There are times when the work-related problem experienced by the consultee is not a result of the dysfunctionality of the client, but rather the enduring emotional problems of the consultee himself. A consultee exhibiting exaggerated distortions of reality or enduring psychological disturbance are most often easily identified and responded to through normal administrative and supervisory channels. As noted elsewhere (Caplan & Caplan, 1993; Parsons, 1996) it is not impossible for less than obvious disturbances to go unnoticed until they begin to significantly impact the functioning of the client population. Consider the situation of the junior high school teacher who was constantly sending his male students to the disciplinarian because of various "perverted sexual acts." When the consultant followed up on one such referral, she heard the consultee complain about the general immorality of these students. "Sex is the only thing on their minds. I have to watch them like a hawk. They are constantly touching themselves, placing their hands in their pockets and we know what that means." The consultee expressed his fear that if these boys were not identified and helped, they would end up "attacking and molesting some poor little girl!"

As might be assumed, the behaviors that the teacher was identifying were most often nonsexual, and those that might have some sexual overtone were well within the normal developmental limits for that population. Further, much of the consultee's behavior during the interview suggested to the consultant that the consultee was deriving some vicarious pleasure from discussing these incidents. The consultee, while voicing concern about the "perverted sexual acts," did so while smiling and inviting the consultant to share her own feelings about such actions. The consultee even appeared somewhat seductive in response to the consultee, making statements regarding her attractive blouse and flattering shoes. The consultee's comments were not only outside the context of the discussion but were also clearly inappropriate to the professional nature of the relationship.

It is not the suggestion here that the consultant become a clinical diagnostician after meeting with the consultee for only one or two times, nor is that an appropriate role for the school counselor. However, counselor–consultants must be aware that the possibility exists that work-related difficultly identified by the consultee may, in fact, be a reflection of the consultee's own emotional problems and not a response to a client's behavior.

Caplan and Caplan (1993) suggest that there are times where a brief consultative contract may be sufficient to enlist the consultee's adaptive controls in order to return the consultee back to a reasonable level of professional objectivity and job performance. Thus, in the situation previously described, it would be felt that a consultant who could provide the consultee with information that accurately described the client's behavior and the interpretation of that behavior within the boundaries of normal development would be sufficient to return the consultee to his performance of his professional duties. Sadly, this is not always the case.

Some consultees who, because of a complex and long-standing set of experience, have ongoing distortion of reality will require more direct intervention. And although the role of the consultant is *not* one of therapist, it is suggested that the consultant attempt to identify for the consultee the areas of intense personal concern that she may be experiencing and invite the consultee to seek out and contract for professional services so that they could regain the professional objectivity needed to perform their job. In addition to such a direct intervention, the consultant should provide appropriate feedback regarding the work functioning of the consultee (not the personal, emotional history) to those in direct responsibility for his supervision and work assignments. This reporting to a supervisor represents one of those exceptions to confidentiality that occurs within the consultation relationship. The goal here would be to provide the consultee with the support needed for controlling his emotional needs within the work setting. The consultee needs support in regaining professional distance from clients who arouse these distortions, and the client(s) deserves protection from the further deterioration of the consultee's professional objectivity.

CONFRONTATION: AN ESSENTIAL INTERVENTION

The specific forms and strategies for intervening with consultee-focused consultation will vary according to the unique needs of the consultee, the depth and nature of the consultation relationship, and the unique characteristics of the consultant. However, core to all interventions with a consultee is the element of confrontation. As such, the remainder of the chapter will look at appropriate methods of direct and indirect confrontation.

Methods of Direct Confrontation

When attempting to understand the value and use of confrontation in consultation, the consultant must overcome the general tendency to equate the word *confrontation* with that of a destructive, aggressive, hostile act. Confrontation, when used within a helping context, does not take the form of lecturing, judging, or punishing. These are examples of the abuse of confrontation rather than the appropriate use of confrontation.

Within the context of a helping relationship, confrontation represents an **invitation** by one participant to have the other participant look at, discuss, clarify, or reconsider some event occurring within the helping exchange. It is truly an invitation to explore all the facets of what is being presented. Such an empathic invitation to self-exploration has been found to facilitate the other's self-exploration (Pierce & Dragow, 1969)

For example, we have all had occasion, while talking with a friend, to question a point they made in relation to which we had contradictory information. Imagine the following dialogue between two teachers.

Ted: Gads, how will we ever get through this assignment for our accreditation visit, especially when we have to go on that training seminar this weekend?

Mary: Gee, I may be wrong, but I thought the memo said that the training seminar was next weekend!

The interaction, although not a hostile, attacking, or destructive exchange, is nonetheless confrontational. In fact, it reflects a particular type of confrontation called a **didactic** (informational) confrontation—a confrontation in which one member of the dialogue invited the other member to reconsider his/her position in light of this more accurate information. Because the confrontation addresses inconsistencies, these confrontations are referred to as **contrasting responses.** A consultant may find confrontation useful when she experiences

1. An inconsistency between what the consultee says and how she behaves. For example, perhaps the consultee states that she is excited about trying the new techniques discussed in the consultation, yet week after week the consultee notes that she forgot to use the strategy.

2. A discrepancy between what the consultee "knows" to be true and the evidence or facts as the consultant knows them. This was the case with the previous example regarding the training weekend.

3. A contradiction between the verbal and nonverbal expressions of consultee's emotions. This may be the case when a consultee states that he is fine with the recommendations of the consultant and yet demonstrates a frown and/or worrisome look.

4. An inconsistency between two pieces of information the consultee verbally presents. This would happen in the situation where a consultee states that he understands and values the use of positive reinforcement and yet notes that his primary technique for controlling the class is through verbal reprimand.

Although these are four situations in which a consultant should seek clarification of the inconsistencies, contradictions, or discrepancies, in reality, confrontation occurs anytime we call to question another's behavior, attitude, or feelings. Because confrontations are inevitable, the effective consultant will need to understand the elements that make a confrontation productive, facilitative, and relationship building, rather than destructive and attacking.

Guidelines for Effective Confrontation

In attempting to confront a consultee, the effective consultant will consider each of the following guidelines.

1. Present conclusion as tentative. In presenting our confrontation, we must present the apparent discrepancy or inconsistency in a tentative manner. The issue or discrepancy with which we wish to confront the consultee reflects our perception and may not necessarily reflect absolute facts.

As such, we need to present our confrontation as our tentative conclusions about the event. What appears to us to be an inconsistency may in fact be totally consistent from the consultee's point of view. This need to be tentative in our conclusions is especially important when confronting a consultee in the early stages of the consultation relationship. During the early stages, the consultant may not have a full grasp of the consultee's world and thus misread experiences they share. An excellent example of this technique was used by the TV detective Colombo when he would scratch his head and present a discrepancy as confusion on his part and solicit clarification from the guilty party. You do not need the raincoat to perform this technique effectively, however.

2. A motive of understanding. It is important for the consultant to keep a clear sense of the motive for his confrontation. Pointing out a discrepancy or an inconsistency in hopes of embarrassing or humiliating another will certainly be confrontational, but not helpful. The confrontation, to be helpful, needs to be presented from a helping, caring, supportive intention or motive. It should reflect the consultant's desire to clarify and understand rather than exhibit power or one-upmanship.

3. Use a descriptive, nonjudgmental style. The helpful confrontation is presented in language and tone that is descriptive, rather than judgmental and labeling. The consultant is not trying to evaluate the consultee. Rather, the consultant's goal is to describe her own experience and points of confusion with hopes that the consultee can provide clarification.

4. Be empathic. In presenting the confrontation, the consultant should consider how the confrontation will be received. The confrontation should be presented in a way that maximizes the consultee's ability to receive it. Although the preceding characteristics will assist in this process, it is also important to provide the confrontation from a perspective of empathy for the other. The consultant needs to consider how her confrontation will appear to the consultee. The consultant needs to consider how receptive or open she would be to receiving this confrontation if she were in the consultee's shoes at this time.

Keeping this perspective of the consultee as a guideline, the consultant may find that it is more helpful to present the confrontation in small specific steps, rather than to dump one large general blast of issues on the consultee.

The consultant who, from a perspective of empathy with the consultee, can **descriptively** and **tentatively** point out areas of consultee misinformation or mixed and confusing messages can constructively move the consultation relationship to a greater level of accuracy, clarity, and collaboration. For example, the confrontation presented in the example regarding the training seminar moved the interaction to more clear, accurate communication and common agreement. However that confrontation could have been less productive and much more destructive to the relationship if Mary had stated: "You are really a nerd! You never read anything. The memo said . . . the training seminar is NEXT weekend . . .WAKE UP!"

Even when we attempt to follow the guidelines to appropriate confrontation, our confrontation may be less than productive or effective. The real proof of effectiveness is not in the degree to which all the correct elements were present, but rather the degree to which the desired effect was achieved. If the consultee attempts to discredit the statement or attempts to argue the point or tries to devalue the importance of the confrontation, he may be giving evidence that the confrontation was too much for him to accept. Remember that the purpose of the confrontation is to move the relationship to greater clarity and accuracy. When this happens, the consultee is likely to openly accept and consider the confrontation, rather than deny or defend against it. So the proof of the effectiveness of the confrontation is in the response of the consultee! Exercise 10.3 will assist you in employing the previous guidelines while formulating your confrontation. As you formulate the confrontations, consider the possible impact your comment may have on the consultee.

EXERCISE 10.3

Effective Confrontations

Directions: Complete an appropriate confrontation to each of the following. As with other exercises, it is useful to compare your responses to those of a classmate, colleague, or supervisor. In writing a confrontation be sure to

- Consider the perspective of the consultee
- Use descriptive language
- Provide small steps of confrontation
- Have your tone reflect your helping intentions

1. **Consultee:** I really like what you are saying and I am sure it will help (looking anxious).
   Consultant: _____

2. **Consultee:** These students have a real bad attitude, I have to be on their backs every moment in the day.
   Consultant: _____

3. **Consultee:** I'm really going to develop a sense of team work in class, so I told them that they have to come to the class prepared next Friday—or else.
   Consultant: _____

4. **Consultee:** NO! There is NOTHING wrong! Get off my back!
   Consultant: _____

5. **Consultee:** I know Timmy called Alfred a name, but Timmy is so frail, I just know the bullies in the class are always picking on him.
   Consultant: _____

Methods of Indirect Confrontation

Prior to employing direct confrontation, the consultant must determine the degree to which this relationship is established as an open, honest, trusting helping exchange. The consultant needs to consider the extent to which the consultee has demonstrated openness to the consultant's inquiries, a willingness to be open to the consultant's ideas and feedback, and the degree to which the consultee has demonstrated a willingness to explore a variety of issues and topics. When the consultee appears to be somewhat closed and protected within the consulting relationship, indirect forms of confrontation may prove more productive.

Indirect methods of confrontation allow for the consultee to maintain her defenses and protective stance while at the same time becoming somewhat open to new and potentially conflicting material. The goal is to provide the consultee with enough psychic safety to enable her to be receptive to the confrontation.

Two forms of indirect confrontation to be discussed are (1) modeling and (2) talking around the issue and the use of the parable.

Modeling   One indirect form of confrontation occurs when the consultant acts as a role model of the consultee interacting with client or the client's situation using professional strategies that are conflictual to that anticipated as necessary by the consultee. Consider the consultee presented in scenario #5 of Exercise 10.3. Assume that Timmy is not as helpless or as fragile as the consultee may perceive. A consultant could indirectly confront this consultee belief by interacting with Timmy in a playful, yet somewhat challenging way. The experience of having Timmy hold his own with the consultant and possibly tease back would be an indirect confrontation to the consultee's perception that Timmy needed to be protected from such interaction.

The use of modeling as an indirect form of confrontation does not force the consultee to admit something that may be uncomfortable, while at the same time providing the consultee with an experience that will "force" him to reconsider his own perception and actions in relationship to the client.

Talking Around the Issue and the Use of Parable   Talking around the issue and the use of parable are additional forms of indirect confrontation. As is true for all indirect confrontation, these techniques when employed successfully will allow the consultee room to keep his personal ego in tack while at the same time providing information that may create enough personal dissonance to motivate a change in the consultee's perception and behavior.

Talking around is a technique in which the consultant describes similar situations in which she was involved. For example, rather than directly suggesting that the consultee has lost her objectivity, the consultant may simply share a story about a time when she misinterpreted a student's behavior because of having experienced a similar student in the past. Thus the consultant working with the case of Tommie may note for the consultee, "You know, Tommie is very tiny. He reminds of me of my next door neighbor's child. Rob is kind of small for his age, but is he quick. All the kids like him on their team when they play tag because he is so fast and elusive. But, you know he is quite a con—when he get's caught in tag, he often kids the bigger kids about picking on this little kid (referring to himself)."

A similar approach was suggested by Gerald Caplan (1970) and discussed as the use of parables. In using a parable, the consultant invents an anecdote that is similar to that currently experienced by the consultee. Embedded within the parable is the message of overinvolvement and the role it played in creating the situation experienced by that consultee. The elements of a parable are characters and situations that are possible identification objects and behavior and outcomes that convey a moral. The task for the consultant is to find a parable that, while portraying the essential features of the current case is sufficiently different so as to allow the consultee's defenses to remain intact. As such the consultee can risk accepting the moral of the parable and choose to apply it to his own experience or, if too threatening, can privately refuse to embrace the moral without risking admonition from the consultant. From this perspective, the parable must balance being far enough removed from the current situation so as to not be threatening, while at the same time having enough relevance and realness that it can prove instructional. Thus for a consultant to share a story about "Tina" who is pale and sickly looking and yet was always the instigator of the problems in the classroom, may be too obvious and direct for Tommie's teacher. Whereas, expanding on the neighbor's child, who on first perception appeared too small to keep up with the neighborhood kids, may provide enough distance that the consultee could dismiss the case as irrelevant to the classroom, but close enough to extract the moral—that the child may be more competent and responsible than first appears.

PUTTING IT ALL TOGETHER

The identification of the specific elements that need to be addressed within a consultee-focused consultation is not always easy. What may at first appear to be simply a lack of clear information and understanding may be a situation in which the consultee lacks the skill to implement her knowledge or is blocked emotionally for doing so. The accurate identification of the consultee's need is an essential step in the intervention process. The second most crucial element to a consultee focused consultation is the effective use of confrontation, both direct and indirect. Because of the value of these two processes, we close the chapter with Exercise 10.4.

EXERCISE 10.4

When Consultee-Focused Consultation Is Needed

Directions: For each of the following situations:

1. Identify the type or form of loss of objectivity exhibited by the consultee
2. Provide an example of a direct confrontation that could be used
3. Describe an example of an indirect confrontation that might prove useful

Situation A

Ms. H. is very concerned about Lisa's home life. According to Ms. H., Lisa appears to be uncared for, is often "tired looking," has only minimal lunches (a sandwich and a piece of fruit), and lacks personal hygiene ("She never does her hair up!"). Your observations and that of the social worker is that Lisa has a good yet modest home life. Lisa presents as both a happy and well-cared-for child. In discussion with Ms. H., you discover that as a child she was neglected and at the age of 7 was placed in a foster home. You sense that Ms. H. continues to have personal fears of abandonment.

Situation B

Henry is in his first year of teaching. Henry is currently teaching 12th-grade English. He came to you because he is having problems with controlling his seventh-period class. In discussing the situation with you, Henry notes that he doesn't understand it, "the guys in my seventh period are really cool—I don't know why they treat me this way. I really like them. I don't know what to do, after all I don't want to come across like some kind of ogre!"

Situation C

Paul is very upset with the way the kids are teasing Jerome and rejecting him, just because he is "Orthodox." Paul lets you know in no uncertain terms that he "just knows" how horrible it is for Jerome, after all he (i.e., Paul) "was also the only Jewish boy attending his public school." Your observations suggest that Jerome's interactions with his classmates are age appropriate, and Jerome appears quite accepted by his peers.

SUMMARY

The Consultee: A Significant Extrapersonal Variable

It is possible that it is the consultee's own response to the client that, if not causing the current client-related problem, is exacerbating the situation. In working with the consultee, the consultant may soon discover that the problem rests in the consultee's limited knowledge, lack of skill, or failure to maintain professional objectivity.

Collaborating on Knowledge Development

There are times when a consultee may simply lack the proper knowledge and understanding of the particular student or the general principles of human development, management processes, or even interpersonal dynamics. In diagnosing the existence of a consultee's lack of knowledge or understanding, the consultant will attempt to answer three separate questions: (a) Is the consultee aware of his professional behavior? (b) Are the consultee's observed and self-defined behaviors congruent with his attitudes about how he should professionally function? and (c) Is what the consultee is doing and wishes to do congruent with what is known to be the accepted form of professional practice?

Collaborating on Consultee Skill Development

When attempting to diagnose the specific consultee skill development, the consultant must be extremely sensitive to the need to maintain a collaborative relationship. Although the specific skills to be developed will be unique to the individual consultee, a number of general areas for teacher training have been identified in the literature. These include problem solving, communication, intervention techniques, management skills, and group dynamics.

Regaining Objectivity and Professionalism

There are situations in which the consultee's ineffectiveness is the result of the consultee's loss of professional objectivity or the fact that his own emotional needs and particular psychosocial history is interfering with the performance of his professional duties. The model used here to classify such loss of objectivity is that orginally presented by Caplan and Caplan (1993). The five overlapping categories are (a) direct personal involvement, (b) simple identification, (c) transference, (d) theme interference, and (e) characterological distortions.

The specific forms and strategies for intervening with consultee-focused consultation will vary according to the unique needs of the consultee, the depth and nature of the consultation relationship, and the unique characteristics of the consultant. However, core to all interventions with a consultee is the element of confrontation.

IMPORTANT TERMS

Characterological distortions
Consultee-focused consultation
Consultee knowledge
Consultee skill

Consultee objectivity
Contrasting responses
Direct personal involvement
Extrapersonal factors
Indirect confrontation

Modeling
Nonevaluative feedback
Simple identification
Theme interference
Transference
Use of the parable

SUGGESTED READINGS

Acheson, A., & Gall, D. M. (2002). *Clinical supervision and teacher development: Preservice and inservice applications.* New York: Wiley.

Caplan, G., & Caplan, R. (1993). *Mental health consultation and collaboration.* San Francisco: Jossey-Bass.

Cummings, C. B. (2000). *Winning strategies for classroom management.* Alexandria, VA: Association for Supervision & Curriculum Development.

Luborsky, L. & Crits-Christoph, P. (1998). *Understanding transference: The core conflictual relationship theme method.* Washington, DC: American Psychological Association.

Rossett, A. (1999). *First things fast: A handbook for performance analysis.* San Francisco: Pfeiffer & Co.

WEB SITES

TeAch-nology: Web portal for educators. Includes sites for stress management and burnout. www.teach-nology.com

Teacher Source. Search options for online professional development. www.pbs.org/teachersource

Teacher Burnout: Scale measuring teacher burnout. www.as.wvu.edu/~richmond/measures/burnout.pdf

REFERENCES

Anderson, T. K., Kratochwill, T. R., & Bergan, J. R. (1986). Training teachers in behavioral consultation and therapy: An analysis of verbal behavior. *Journal of School Psychology, 24,* 229–241.

Bergan, J. R., & Kratochwill, T. R. (1990). *Behavioral consultation and therapy.* New York: Plenum.

Caplan, G. (1970). *The theory and practice of mental health consultation.* New York: Basic Books.

Caplan, G., & Caplan, R. (1993). *Mental health consultation and collaboration.* San Francisco: Jossey-Bass.

Festinger, L. A. (1957). *A theory of cognitive dissonance.* Evanston, IL: Row, Peterson.

Meyers, J., Parsons, R. D., & Martin, R. (1979). *Mental health consultation in schools.* San Francisco: Jossey-Bass.

Parsons, R., & Meyers, J. (1984). *Developing consultation skills.* San Francisco: Jossey-Bass.

Parsons, R., Hinson, S., & Brown, D. (2001). *Educational psychology: A practitioner-researcher model of teaching.* Belmont, CA: Wadsworth.

Parsons, R., & Brown, K. (2002). *Teacher as reflective practitioner and action researcher.* Belmont, CA: Wadsworth.

Parsons, R. D. (1996). *The skilled consultant.* Boston: Allyn & Bacon.

Pierce, R. M., & Dragow, J. (1969). Nondirective reflection vs. conflict attention: An empirical evaluation. *Journal of Clinical Psychology, 25,* 341–342.

Robinson, E. H., & Wilson, E. S. (1987). Counselor-led human relations training as a consultation strategy. *Elementary School Guidance and Counseling, 22,* 124–131.

Zins, J. E. (1993). Enhancing consultee problem-solving skills in consultative interactions. *Journal of Counseling & Development, 72*(2), 185–189.

11

⤫

The Group as Client

From Team Building
to Mediation

It's amazing. We start off talking about Ellen and lately
we seem to end up talking about that damn parking lot! Dr. J. is really
annoyed with the teachers, as are the entire administration. He seems to
feel he's stuck in the middle. Even though he's an administrator, he
sympathizes with the faculty's concern about their parking lot.

The huge potholes, broken speed bumps, poorly marked parking areas,
and a dysfunctional drainage system have taken a severe toll on tires, cars,
and shoes. Although the principal and central administration have
scheduled to have the entire parking lot repaved next summer, with almost
seven more months of school left, the faculty are ready to revolt now.

This thing is adding lots of stress around here—or at least on
Dr. Jameson. Hmmm? I wonder if this tension between faculty and
administration is impacting the students? Affecting Ellen?

All too frequently, systems such as schools will experience conflict
between various groups or subsystems within it. It is also not that
unusual to find that this conflict spills over to affect others not directly
involved with the dispute. For example, it is possible that some of the faculty
<None>room style. Further, it is possible that a student such as Ellen could
be adversely affected by this change in the teacher's style or the increased negativity and tension in a classroom. Thus, what appears to be a single student's

problem may in fact represent a single symptom of a larger problem—group conflict within the system.

Why should subgroup conflict between students and teachers, teachers and parents, teachers and administrators, teachers and other teachers, administrators and parents, and so on be of concern to a school counselor? Why might a conflict over a parking lot have any relevance to a counselor? The answer lies in the primary charge of the school counselor and the social systemic forces that challenge that charge. National Standards for School Counselors (Campbell & Dahir, 1997) specify that the primary goal of the school counseling program is to promote and enhance student learning. Consequently, anything that interferes with student learning should be of concern to the school counselor. Interpersonal and subgroup conflict creates systemic stress that impairs job performance (Levine, 1998) and interferes with student learning. Clearly, students learn and develop best when their stakeholders cooperate and collaborate toward shared goals. When school counselors help stakeholders achieve this harmony, they are following their primary purpose in a school.

The existence of such subsystem conflict is not a sign of system failure. In fact, any dynamic, open system such as a school will quite naturally experience conflict as needs and interests (and positions) change over time. Policies, procedures, resource allocation, working conditions, curriculum design, and methodology are all potential sources of conflict between individuals and groups working in our schools. In general, these conflicts represent differences of opinion about how the system should operate.

It is only when these conflicts fester and the parties adopt rigid "win–lose" strategies of resolution that the morale and effectiveness of the entire system is compromised. It is when specific groups of individuals (i.e., subsystems) believe that their needs and interests have been violated. Their grievances center on formal or informal *norms* that violate their sense of well-being. The change that they seek, either assertively or aggressively, that will remedy the perceived violation is often framed as their **position** or solution to the problem. Once formed, that position solidifies and quickly becomes the criteria for winning or losing the conflict.

The prudent counselor consultant is frequently privy to the earliest stages of system conflict and can be instrumental in mediating conflict resolution for the betterment of the entire system. It is the models and mechanisms a consultant can use to achieve this that serves as the focus of chapter 11.

CHAPTER OBJECTIVES

In this chapter we will look at the nature of conflict within school systems and strategies that counselor–consultants can use to detect nascent conflicts. Our attention will then shift to consultation strategies that will bring the conflicting parties to win–win resolution of their grievances. The strategies employed in win–win conflict resolution can also be used in planning, program development, and team building, the essential ingredients in prevention and purposeful change. Systematic planning through force-field analyses and PERT charting will be offered as mechanisms for program development and change.

Because the consultant will be using group interventions to resolve interpersonal conflicts and build cohesive teams, it is helpful to be mindful of the member needs and interests while maintaining group norms to achieve group tasks. The three-legged stool model of group goals is an excellent schema for conceptualizing the purpose and function of any group; consequently, we will start with this paradigm.

After completing this chapter the reader should be able to

1. Describe the discrete and interdependent categories of goals that drive the work of every group

2. Describe the causes and manifestations of conflict in schools

3. Describe the elements of a conflict resolution model designed to produce win–win resolution of conflict

4. Describe strategies of decision making and planning that rely on consensus and team building

5. Describe procedures for assessing the restraining and driving forces that influence desired change

6. Describe procedures for planning and organizing the achievement of desired outcome goals

THE THREE-LEGGED STOOL

Imagine the situation in which you are invited into a sixth-grade classroom to observe a student, Barbara, who has been describe by one of her teachers as "extremely shy, withdrawn, and almost . . . 'autistic.' " Prior to your observation, you set up a meeting to discuss this student with her sixth-grade team of teachers. Shortly within the meeting, the discussion shifts from Barbara to a discussion over the right way to teach these "types of children." The discussion is lively, even heated, with the team splitting into two very clear distinct groups. As you observe the conflict, you question, whether it is possible that this conflict—this competition—over teaching methodology has resulted in undue stress on Barbara as each group of teachers goes about to prove their method works. If so, perhaps it is this stress from which Barbara is currently withdrawing, and thus the presenting concern would be but a symptom of this larger, intergroup conflict.

But how does one begin to approach such a conflict? How will you, as consultant, conceptualize this problem so that the groups involved have their needs and interests considered while the specific tasks of the group receive adequate attention? One way to keep in focus the discrete yet interdependent goals of a group is to use the prism of a three-legged stool (Kahn, 1988; Rose, 1972).

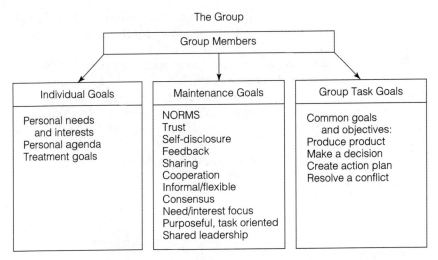

FIGURE 11.1 Group Goals

This conceptualization of group goals representing the three legs of the group can be seen in Figure 11.1. The oval represents the membership of the group, such as the various task groups cited previously. Every purposeful group that is comprised of two or more individuals will maintain three interdependent categories of goals. Each member's personal needs and interests comprise the first leg of our stool. Satisfying these **individual goals** constitutes each member's personal agenda. Being recognized and affirmed by the group, wielding power and control, deriving safety and security from the group, and experiencing a feeling of creativity are all examples of personal needs and interests that drive one's personal agenda. In a clinical counseling group these individual goals also include the idiosyncratic treatment outcomes for each member. Whether the group purpose is clinical or exists to achieve tasks, the members will passively or actively resist the work of the group if their individual goals do not receive their due attention. For this reason, the counselor consultant needs to be attentive to each member's individual goals while simultaneously building the group's **maintenance goals.**

Often referred to as process goals or the **norms** of the group, these maintenance goals represent the conditions or environment in which the group operates. As group norms, they prescribe the rules and regulations (implicit and explicit) for how members are to interact and work together. They inform the members which behaviors are acceptable or unacceptable in the group and what sanctions would be employed in maintaining those behaviors. Norms of sharing, active listening, constructive feedback, task focus, and consensus building are crucial for work groups to achieve their goals. The responsibility for maintaining those norms falls with the consultant as he purposefully structures activities and tasks that both support desired norms as well as address the needs and interests of individual members.

Group task goals might be the completion of a product such as an Individualized Educational Program (IEP) or a strategic plan or represent a decision that resolves a conflict or recommended course of action. In either case, group task goals are achieved through the collaborative effort of all members and dictate the formal agenda of each group meeting. The agenda of a group meeting comprising structured activities, tasks, problem solving, and decision making should always be made with careful attention to the needs and interests of each member and the norms that will enable the group to do its work. By conceptualizing a group as comprising these three interdependent categories of goals, the counselor–consultant has a practical framework for addressing the many groups that seek his or her help.

SYSTEMIC CONFLICT: UNFULFILLED NEEDS AND INTERESTS

Before the counselor–consultant can begin to resolve conflicts that occur in his school, he must understand the source and manifestations of conflict. *Webster's Encyclopedic Unabridged Dictionary* (1996, p. 428) defines conflict as "to come into collusion or disagreement; discord of action, feeling or effect; antagonism or opposition, as of interests or principles; incompatibility or interference, as of one's idea, desire, event, or activity with another." Conflicts exist when an action taken by one person or group prevents, blocks, or interferes with the occurrence or effectiveness of another (Deutsch, 1973). The word *conflict* is derived from the Latin *conflictus,* meaning a "striking together with force" (Johnson & Johnson, 2003).

At its source, conflict occurs when one's wants, needs, goals, and interests are perceived or experienced as being threatened or blocked by others (Johnson & Johnson, 2003). These authors define **wants** as our individual desires for something whereas our **needs** represent those things such as food, water, and oxygen that are necessary for survival. From our wants and needs we formulate **goals** that describe the conditions under which our wants and needs are achieved. Achieving our goals occurs within a social context. We form cooperative relationships with those with whom we share mutual goals and competitive relationships with those who oppose our goals. The benefits that we gain by realizing our goals constitute our **interests** (Johnson & Johnson, 2003).

As you can see, personal **needs and interests** are at the core of our values and goals. The solutions and positions that we formulate and embrace so strongly as "our way" of meeting our needs are only a means to an end, that end being the satisfaction of our needs and interests. Most of our conflicts revolve around defending our positions and solutions when the focus should be on the underlying needs and interests that are served by the positions that we maintain (Fisher & Ury, 1991). Strategies for facilitating this shift in focus

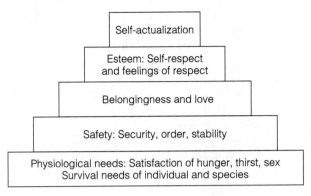

FIGURE 11.2 Maslow's Hierarchy of Needs (Turner & Helms, 1987, p. 61)

from positions and strategies to needs and interests will receive considerable attention later in this chapter.

To understand the essential nature of conflict, we must have a clear and practical definition of **need.** One conceptualization of the diversity and complexity of human needs can be found in the work of Abraham Maslow (1962). Drawing on his extensive research (Maslow, 1954, 1970, 1971), Maslow formulated a five-layered hierarchical model of human needs in the form of a pyramid (Figure 11.2). The base of the pyramid constitutes our physiological needs such as food, water, oxygen, tactual stimulation, and sex, those things that enable us to survive individually and as a species. Satisfying these physiological needs is a continual effort, challenge, and source of pleasure throughout our life. When these needs are unsatisfied and threatened, we immediately mobilize our every resource to restore their satisfaction. It should not be surprising that our most intense conflicts occur when others are perceived as blocking or even diminishing our satisfaction of these survival needs. If, on the other hand, our survival needs are satisfactorily met, we can begin to focus our energies on meeting the next level of need, that of safety. Establishment of a secure sense of safety enables us to shift our priorities to each successive (and successful) layer of the hierarchy and ultimately to the experience of self-actualization at the top of the pyramid.

One author (Kahn, 1981) has used Maslow's basic hierarchy of needs (Figure 11.2) as a diagnostic tool in school consultation. This self-report survey (Figure 11.3) extrapolates from Maslow's pyramid to assess the extent to which the respondent's needs are satisfied within a school or work environment. Employing a Likert scaling of each level of need, the *Job Wellness and Satisfaction Survey* helps identify those needs that are most neglected and thus sources of conflict and low morale. Case 11.1 presents the application of this survey to resolve a conflict within a middle school.

A. Physiological Needs:	Met Always	Met Usually Most of Time	Met Occasionally Sometimes	Seldom Never Met
1. To get enough food/water	1	2	3	4
2. To get enough sleep.	1	2	3	4
3. To get enough clean air.	1	2	3	4
4. To get enough physical activity.	1	2	3	4
5. To work in a healthy environment.	1	2	3	4
6. To maintain my basic physical health.	1	2	3	4
B. Safety Needs:				
7. To feel safe from threat & danger.	1	2	3	4
8. To feel safe from fear of unknown and unexpected.	1	2	3	4
9. To feel secure in the future.	1	2	3	4
10. To feel in control of actions that affect me.	1	2	3	4
C. Social and Belonging Needs:				
11. Affiliation—To feel like I belong.	1	2	3	4
12. Nurturing—To feel like others care and watch out for me	1	2	3	4
13. Acceptance—To feel like my ideas/views are welcome.	1	2	3	4
14. Acknowledged—To feel that my work is valued & recognized.	1	2	3	4
D. Esteem Needs:				
15. To feel self-respect & self-confident.	1	2	3	4
16. To feel important & accomplished.	1	2	3	4
17. To feel independence and self-control over my work.	1	2	3	4
18. To feel that my work makes an impact on others.	1	2	3	4
19. To feel that my work carries status and prestige.	1	2	3	4
E. Self-Actualization Needs:				
20. To feel that I am reaching my full potential.	1	2	3	4
21. To feel challenged with a variety of stimulating tasks.	1	2	3	4
22. To feel that I am growing and developing in positive ways.	1	2	3	4

FIGURE 11.3 Job Wellness and Satisfaction (Wallace J. Kahn)

CASE 11.1   SPECIALS WHO DON'T FEEL SPECIAL

The principal of very affluent, suburban middle school noticed that those teachers who taught the "special" subjects of music, art, physical education, emotional support, etc. were angry and antagonistic toward the "regular" subject area teachers as well as the principal. These "special" teachers expressed their unhappiness by avoiding school functions and only passively attending faculty meetings. As their morale plummeted the principal sought advice from a veteran counselor in the school. The counselor was aware that there was some dissension in the ranks of these teachers but was unaware of the reason. After a brief consult the principal and counselor agreed to schedule a faculty meeting for "special" teachers only, to be conducted by the principal and counselor. The meeting opened with the principal expressing concern about the dissatisfaction and poor morale evidenced by these teachers. All of the teachers present were reluctant to disclose their grievances directly to the principal, but they were all willing to complete the Job Wellness and Satisfaction Survey anonymously for the counselor. After the surveys were completed and given to the counselor the meeting was adjourned with the understanding that a subsequent meeting would be scheduled to review the results of the survey.

The survey results revealed that the teacher's physiological and safety needs were always or usually met. However, social and belonging, esteem, and self-actualization needs were more problematic for these teachers. Most of the respondents reported high scores (i.e., low need satisfaction) for numbers 11 (affiliation), 13 (acceptance), and 14 (acknowledged) of their social and belonging needs. Their esteem needs were also uniformly reported as

seldom or never met. It was obvious from this survey that this cohort of teachers felt left out, ignored, and unappreciated by the principal and the other teachers in this school. The counselor asked the principal to call another meeting with these teachers to uncover the substance of their dissatisfaction. In order to reduce any intimidation that the teachers might be feeling the principal requested that the counselor conduct the meeting in the principal's absence. After the grievances were unearthed the principal would join all subsequent meetings.

Displaying anxious curiosity the teachers found seats and waited for the meeting to begin. The counselor summarized the results of the survey and conveyed the principal's desire to remedy their dissatisfaction. With this reassurance and the undisputable empirical data evidenced by the survey the teachers expressed how they were ignored, undervalued and disempowered over the past year. Throughout the current year the school (and district) was preparing for a Middle States evaluation to be conducted the next year. The planning model consisted of a number of strategic planning task groups that would draft the elements of the school's strategic plan. None of the "special" teachers were invited to join these task groups, even though some of the groups included parents and other members of the school community. The school also published a monthly newsletter that was mailed to all of the parents and posted on the school's website. The "special" teachers were not asked to submit announcements or articles for this newsletter, and their occasional submissions were edited to "incoherence." Additionally, when students were required to leave a class for any extended period of time

---

CASE 11.1   CONTINUED

they were always removed from their "specials." The norm of the school was that students could not miss their critical regular classes, but they could miss a special class without dire effect. To add to the insult, students would often cut or leave one of these classes with a permission slip from another adult without even notifying the "special" teacher.

It was abundantly clear that these teachers did not feel "special" in this school. Their needs for belonging and esteem were consistently ignored. Through subsequent meetings including these teachers, the principal, a secretary and the counselor, measures were taken to add volunteers to the strategic planning groups, to devote a prominent section of the newsletter to "Special Happenings," and to establish a policy that no student could miss any part of *any* class without permission of the teacher. The aggrieved teachers all acknowledged that these solutions would satisfactorily meet their needs and interests.

To apply this survey to the case scenario opening this chapter complete Exercise 11.1.

EXERCISE 11.1

Assessing Needs and Interests

Directions: In the opening scenario of this chapter (11) the counselor becomes aware of considerable dissatisfaction expressed by the teachers about the conditions of the school parking lot. If the dissatisfied teachers were to complete the Job Wellness and Satisfaction Survey, answer the following questions:

1. How might their dissatisfaction be reflected in their responses to the survey?

2. How might these survey results be used to address the conflict between the teachers and administration?

INTRASYSTEM CONFLICT:
CONCEPTUALIZING THE TRIAD

With our understanding of basic needs and interests, we can now expand our perspective to ways in which needs and interests receive appropriate consideration in resolving conflicts, planning, making decisions, and building cohesive teams. We start by looking at the consultation triad when the parties comprise groups. As we have said previously, the fundamental relationship that defines consultation is the triad of client, consultee, and consultant. In the majority of school-based consultations, the three roles within the triad constitute individuals: student, teacher, counselor; student, parent, counselor; parent, teacher, counselor; and so on. A more expansive role for the school counselor as consultant finds the counselor working with groups of consultees or clients to resolve conflicts, solve problems, make decisions, and enhance teamwork. These group consultations are often initiated when an aggrieved group brings a conflict to the attention of the counselor–consultant for remediation. In most cases, the individuals initiating the referral are experiencing conflict with another subsystem group of individuals within the system. For example, in our opening scenario, we saw how a student, identified as having or if you will being a problem, may merely be one symptom of the existence of an intense subsystem conflict. In this case, the student experienced the effects of the conflict in the form of teachers who were angry and frustrated over the deterioration of their parking lot. Although the target of their dissatisfaction was the administration and in particular the school principal, who refused to repair the parking lot in the timely manner desired by the teachers, the impact of this conflict could be felt by others not directly involved (e.g., students).

When groups (subsystems) are in conflict, such as teachers with other teachers, teachers with administrators, teachers with parents, students with teachers, regardless of which party initiates the referral, it is most helpful to view the conflicting parties as consultees and the system itself as the client. With this conceptualization, the consultant will address the needs and interests of the disputing parties collaboratively to resolve their differences satisfactorily and ultimately restore harmony and efficiency within the system. An African proverb says, "When elephants fight, it is the grass who suffers" (Elephant Country, 2002). So, too, when subsystem groups are in conflict, it is the system that suffers. For the consultant to remain neutral and objective, she must be perceived and experienced by all parties as a free broker, advocating for the needs and interests of everyone. In application to our opening scenario, Mr. Thomas, the school counselor, might invite a representative group of teachers, the school principal, and an administrator responsible for "buildings and grounds" to form a Parking Improvement Task Force. Certainly both groups (teachers and administrators) will enter the negotiation embracing their own position. By advocating for each consultee group, it will be the consultant's job to facilitate a win–win solution in which the needs and interests of all parties receive primary consideration. In so doing, the counselor consultant will help the conflicting parties relinquish their pet solutions and staunchly defended positions in favor of new solutions that attempt to satisfy the needs and interests of everyone. The steps leading to win–win solutions have been developed and empirically tested by Roger Fisher and William Ury (1991).

FACILITATING WIN–WIN SOLUTIONS:
GETTING TO YES

In our opening case scenario, our counselor–consultant faced a dilemma and an opportunity, as he considered the conflict over the parking lot. His dilemma was that both parties had settled on their solution or **position** and were already building their case to defend that position. The teachers wanted the parking lot repaired *now* and the administration wanted it repaired *next summer*. Both parties were at an impasse because for one side to win, the other side had to lose. The opportunity that this conflict presented was for both sides to experience a principled negotiation in which the shared needs and interests would drive the solution and the integrity of the relationships would be maintained and even enhanced.

To expedite this principled negotiation Mr. Thomas employed a conflict resolution and negotiation model that passed its greatest test in directing the successful Middle East peace negotiations at Camp David in 1978. Known as the Camp David Accords, this peace treaty between President Sadat of Egypt and Prime Minister Began of Israel was brokered by President Jimmy Carter using the model of principled negotiation developed at the Harvard Negotiation Project by Roger Fisher and William Ury. As the title of their book (Fisher & Ury, 1991) implies, principled negotiation led historic rivals to a solution in which both parties could say "yes."

This peace negotiation succeeded in moving the parties from their positions to their shared needs and interests. Here is a sketch of how they did it.

> Israel had occupied the Egyptian Sinai Peninsula since the Six Day War of 1969. When Egypt and Israel sat down together in 1978 to negotiate a peace, their positions were incompatible. Israel insisted on keeping some of the Sinai. Egypt, on the other hand, insisted that every inch of the Sinai be returned to Egyptian sovereignty. Time and again, people drew maps showing possible boundary lines that would divide the Sinai between Egypt and Israel. Compromising in this way was wholly unacceptable to Egypt. To go back to the situation as it was in 1967 was equally unacceptable to Israel.

> Looking to their interests instead of their positions made it possible to develop a solution. Israel's interest lay in security; they did not want Egyptian tanks poised on their border ready to roll across at any time. Egypt's interest lay in sovereignty; the Sinai had been part of Egypt since the time of the Pharaohs. After centuries of domination by Greeks, Romans, Turks, French, and the British, Egypt had only recently regained full sovereignty and was not about to cede territory to another foreign conqueror.

> At Camp David, President Sadat of Egypt and Prime Minister Begin of Israel agreed to a plan that would return the Sinai to complete Egyptian sovereignty and, by demilitarizing large areas, would still insure Israeli security. The Egyptian flag would fly everywhere, but Egyptian tanks would be nowhere near Israel.

Reconciling interests rather than positions works for two reasons. First, for every interest there usually exist several possible positions that could satisfy it. All too often people simply adopt the most obvious position, as Israel did, for example, in announcing that they intended to keep part of the Sinai. When you do look behind opposed positions for the motivating interests, you can often find an alternative position which meets not only your interests but theirs as well. In the Sinai, demilitarization was one such alternative. (Fisher & Ury, 1991, pp. 41–42)

With the needs and interests of security and sovereignty at the focal point, both leaders could replace irreconcilable positions with creative solutions. Let us take a closer look at the basic tenets of the model.

The model of principled negotiation developed by Fisher and Ury offers four principles for effective negotiation. The authors view a good agreement as wise, fair, efficient, lasting, leading to satisfactory "wins" by all parties involved, and improves the relationship. In sharp contrast to positional bargaining in which the parties enter the negotiation with a favored position and try to convince (or bully) the other party to accept their position, this model excavates the needs and interests that underlie and motivate the positions. As shared needs and interests are revealed, brainstorming is used to create new solutions that meet the criteria for good agreements.

Positional negotiation is so common that we naturally believe that it's the only way to meet our needs and interests. "I refuse to work any overtime!" "We insist on adopting this textbook." "We won't consider eating anything but turkey for Thanksgiving dinner." "The temperature in this room must be kept at 68 degrees." All of these are positions that unconditionally announce "My way or the highway!" Even when your position prevails, there are strong disadvantages to positional bargaining. It perpetuates blinders on the parties, only allowing them to see and defend their position, and thus restricting creativity. Because each position calls for an elaborate rationale and explanation it is inefficient. Positional bargaining provokes anger, fear, and stubbornness as each party pressures the other to yield. At its conclusion, positional bargaining leaves both winners and losers. Finally, its most deleterious and long-term effect is that it does harm to the parities' relationship. The conflict is seldom over for the loser.

Fisher and Ury follow four principles as they facilitate the negotiation process: (a) separate the people from the problem, (b) focus on interests rather than positions, (c) generate a variety of options before settling on an agreement, and (d) insist that the agreement be based on objective criteria.

Separate People from the Problem

As the parties in a dispute become personally involved with the problem and their side's positions they tend to take responses to those problems and positions as personal attacks. People become identified with the problem and a potentially threatening position. Separating the people from the problem and their preconceived positions reduces stereotyping and increases an objective approach to the people and the problem. Actions may contribute to a problem, but people are not the problem. People problems can occur, however, for a variety of reasons. First are the different perceptions and interpretations of the facts that the disputants hold. It is crucial for all sides to hear and understand the other's viewpoint. By putting themselves in the other's place they will better understand the problem, the positions that are taken, and most importantly, the shared needs and interests that will be crucial to solution generation. Negative emotions dissipate as people feel that they are being heard and understood, even if agreement is not expressed.

Emotions can also contribute to people problems. People often react with fear, anger, and frustration when they feel that their needs and interests are threatened. A norm in negotiation should be that all emotions are acknowledged and respected. When emotions are expressed, even negative emotions that seem unreasonable, they should be recognized and explored to understand their source. Ignoring or criticizing the expression of emotions in a negotiation will only intensify that emotion. Rather than giving an emotional response to someone's expression of feeling, as natural as that is, an empathic paraphrase or summarization of that feeling will enhance the relationship and the quality of the communication between the parties. Employing active listening through the use of paraphrasing and summarizing will also help to deal with a third source of people problems, the presence of poor communications.

It is usual for disputing parties to enter a negotiation with their own perspective, position, and agenda. Consequently, they feel that they have little investment in hearing and understanding the other side. In fact, they may feel that to even acknowledge or empathically reflect what the other side is saying or expressing will be viewed as weakness and concession. Helping the parties to actively listen to each other is one of the most daunting challenges for the consultant in a negotiation. Rather than listen to another, some disputants may be grandstanding for their respective constituencies or listening for a lead so that they can get their own points in. Misunderstandings can occur even during the best active listening. The consultant can model, encourage, and reinforce active listening (chapter 6), however, by giving the speaker their full attention by paraphrasing and summarizing the speaker's comments to confirm their understanding. The consultant needs to remind the parties that active listening to another does not mean agreeing with them. Speakers will need to talk with the other parties as they direct their speech to each other, keep focused on the issues being discussed, and use "I" statements when they are talking about themselves. All the potential people problems that we discussed can be avoided or minimized if the parties think of each other as partners in the negotiation, rather than adversaries, and maintenance of good relationships as a primary goal of the negotiation.

Focus on Interests

As we have already discussed the differences between needs, interests, and positions, we will just highlight this second principle. Fisher and Ury define a position as something that you decide on, whereas interests are the needs and motivations that caused you to make that decision. For example, meeting any of the needs in Maslow's hierarchy provides a motivation for action. When we are very hungry and our blood sugar level is very low, the need for nourishment increases, stimulating our motivation to eat. If we typically grab for food that is high in carbohydrates, such as cookies and donuts, we are deciding how to relieve our hunger, and by making this decision, we are taking a position about the importance of carbohydrates in our diet. Likewise, if our job is dull, repetitive, and unchallenging, we feel that our self-actualization needs are severely unmet, even though the paycheck may meet our other needs adequately. Fulfilling this unmet need becomes a strong interest that motivates us to decide to take another job. The job that we decide on reflects our position about how we (and others) can find stimulation and challenge in the workplace. As you can see, as needs increase, or their satisfaction is lessened or threatened, fulfilling those needs becomes our interests. Each of our interests offers myriad solutions and positions from which to decide. To fixate on any one position without accurate identification of its underlying needs and interests severely restricts our creative problem solving and our capacity to adequately meet our needs and interests.

Most of the time parties in conflict come to the negotiation with much clearer positions than their underlying needs and interests. As each party describes the problem they will usually offer their own solutions or positions about how to fix the problem. Although a description of these problems and their presumed positions should be acknowledged, they should receive as little attention as possible before exploring their needs and interests. If problem and position description is all that you have at the start of the negotiation, then that is where you begin. With their stated position as a reference, the consultant will help the parties to identify their respective needs and interests. This can be done by asking them why they hold the position they do, what that position does (or will do) for them (i.e., the payoffs, benefits), and even why they don't hold some other possible position. If they can understand the link between their position and its needs and interests, you can just ask them to identify those needs and interests. Ultimately, this is the linkage that you are working toward. Each party usually has a number of different needs and interests underlying their positions. Likewise, interests may differ among the individual members of each side. Brainstorming should be encouraged as a strategy for identifying all possible needs and interests. Once the common needs and interests have been exhausted, the process of finding shared or common needs and interests is undertaken. It is only when members agree on the accuracy of their shared needs and interests that this composite of shared interests will form the basis for the next principle.

Generate Options

The two questions that must drive the generation and ultimate selection of creative solutions are, "Have we exhausted every possible solution through creative brainstorming?" and "Which solution(s) will meet the greatest number of shared needs and interests?" Without attention to these questions, the parties are liable to decide prematurely on a solution or fail to consider other alternatives. They may be intent on narrowing their alternatives to a single solution. They may define the problem and its solution in win–lose terms, assuming that one side must win and therefore the other side must lose. Lastly, one side may withdraw from the negotiation, believing that the other side is responsible for creating a solution.

To overcome these obstacles to solution creation and selection, the consultant can employ a number of strategies. Throughout the generation and selection process the parties need to separate the invention of options from their evaluation. The invention process must employ all of the elements of brainstorming that were described in chapter 6 to generate all possible solutions to the problem. Diverse, creative, and even outrageous ideas are encouraged and listed **without** positive or negative reactions from others. Even partial solutions can be offered, as they can be expanded during the analysis and evaluation stage of the process. Once our first question has been answered in the affirmative, the parties will move into the analysis and evaluation stage.

At the outset of the evaluation stage, each of the solutions generated must be reviewed for their clarity. Vague and incoherent solutions must be clarified and reworded so that everyone understands their meaning. Parties may also begin to refine and improve their solutions as they move into the analysis and evaluation stage. The evaluation of each solution is then undertaken by matching each solution to the needs and interests that were previously identified by each party. The most promising solutions to remain for consideration will be those that link to the most significant (in number and intensity) needs and interests. In evaluating each of the most promising solutions, the parties should be encouraged to invent ways to make it better, more realistic, and attractive to everyone involved. The *best* qualities of each solution should be highlighted and built on or merged with other solutions. Fisher and Ury suggest that your Best Alternative to a Negotiated Agreement (BATNA) serve as the standard for measuring the value of each solution. Essentially, your BATNA is the degree to which a negotiated solution is better for each member than the current conditions or the results of discontinuing the negotiation. To maximize the BATNA for everyone, it is helpful for each party to look for solutions that are of low cost to them and high benefit to others. The key is to select solutions that are appealing to all sides and the easiest to agree on. As the most promising solutions emerge, additional criteria for evaluating their merit should be their legitimacy within the culture of the system and the precedent offered by that solution. The final test in selecting the most acceptable solutions (Fisher and Ury suggest that at least two solutions be put forward for trial and experimentation) is to subject them to objective criteria, our fourth principle.

Use Objective Criteria

Few solutions will meet all of the needs and interests of disputing parties, thus the final selection to be tried can be marred by dissention, threat, and sabotage. Decisions made under this cloud of distrust and animosity will never result in successful solutions and will always tarnish the relationship. Decisions that are based on objective, empirically based, and reasonable standards will make the final decision making easier, increase the likelihood of success, and preserve the relationships. In developing objective criteria for selecting the solution with the best BATNA, we can start by identifying fair standards that apply to the unique features of the solution and are acceptable to all the parties. There will usually be multiple criteria for each solution, but at a minimum, criteria employed must include practicality, legitimacy with the system, and independence from influence by either party and allow for empirical assessment of success or failure of the solution. Fisher and Ury (1991) offer examples of criteria that meet these standards: "Market value, Precedent, Scientific judgment, Professional standards, Efficiency, Costs, What a court would decide, Moral standards, Equal treatment, Tradition, Reciprocity, Etc." (p. 85). Criteria that may be especially appropriate in school negotiations might include school district policies and procedures; collective bargaining agreements; school law; curriculum; impact on students, parents, and community; and standardized testing.

The objectivity of your criteria is usually acceptable when all parties agree to use them as the standard for selecting a solution. Only by agreement and consensus in the generation of criteria will the criteria actually be used as the measure for deciding on workable solutions. Whatever the criteria chosen, they must be viewed as objective, independent of the will or influence of any one party, fair and reasonable. Fisher and Ury (1991) suggest the following three points in discussing and selecting the final criteria to be used.

1. Frame each issue as a joint search for objective criteria.

2. Reason and be open to reason as to which standards are most appropriate and how they should be applied.

3. Never yield to pressure, only to principle. (p. 88)

If the consultant is viewed by all parties as a neutral, objective, and reasonable broker, she can proceed to help the parties apply the selected criteria to the remaining solutions. The prospects of a successful solution will be significantly influenced by the commitment made by every member for that solution. And each person's commitment will be a function of their agreement and ownership of that solution. Consequently, the consultant does not want to bring the final decision to a vote in which a majority wins. Even a minority of one is enough to diminish a solution's chance for success. Moreover, bringing decisions to a vote usually (unless you are sure of unanimous agreement and want to officially record that unanimity) results in a win–lose decision, which violates the very premise of principled negotiation. Instead, the consultant wants to move the parties to consensual agreement.

The dictionary (*Webster's Encyclopedic Unabridged Dictionary*, 1996, p. 433) defines consensus as "general agreement or concord; harmony." In order to close negotiations with win–win solutions *every* participant must feel that the solution is acceptable and that they had ample opportunity to say all that they wished to say about the solution. Very seldom do all the parties in a dispute enthusiastically and unconditionally embrace a given solution. Individuals often have reservations about a solution but are generally willing to give it a try. In order to reach the outcome of unanimity, if somewhat reserved agreement, consensus building requires that every solution be discussed until everyone has had their say and every question has been thoroughly answered. Concerns and disagreements are given full disclosure and respectful discourse. Sometimes an objection or concern is assuaged by modifications in the solution, but when concerns cannot be remedied, individuals will be reminded of their BATNA and asked to support a trial run of the solution. By approaching solution implementation as a collaborative experiment instead of a final and absolute decision, the more reluctant and skeptical members will be inclined to agree. This willingness of these reluctant agreers is the product of the four principles of negotiation just described. Their agreement is based on their belief that the negotiation was handled with fairness, honesty, openness, and respect for the needs and interests of every participant. And that belief translates into trust that the final solution will ultimately be in their best interest, and thus their BATNA.

Principled negotiation has been shown to produce agreements and solutions that work and last. Obviously, it works best when parties negotiate in good faith and honesty, respectfully, and commited to win–win solutions. Unfortunately some disputants choose to ignore principled negotiation in favor of power plays and dirty tricks. Fisher and Ury (1991) describe negotiations in which one party is much more powerful than the other, stubbornly uses positional bargaining in lieu of principled negotiation, or uses dirty tricks to gain an advantage. The authors advise weaker parties in a negotiation to keep their BATNA as a clear, firm base from which to negotiate. The weaker party should also try to estimate and use the other side's BATNA. Finally, the weaker party should reject agreements that leave them worse off than their BATNA. When disputants are stuck in positional bargaining, the consultant should continue to use the principled strategies and refuse to respond to positional bargaining. When positional bargainers assert their position, the other party can respond by asking for the reasons (needs and interests) behind that position. When they attack another side's ideas or people, the consultant can reframe the attack as constructive criticism and redirect the attack to the presenting problem. Unprincipled disputants will sometimes resort to dirty tricks such as good cop/bad cop routines, uncomfortable seating, deception of the facts, scheduling of meetings when parties are unable to attend, distorting the minutes of meetings, personal attacks, and even blatant threats. These tricks are all designed to increase the stress and discomfort of the negotiation and decrease the confidence and assertiveness of the other parties. The best way to respond to these dirty tricks is to explicitly bring evidence of the tricks to the negotiation table and use principled negotiation to establish procedural ground rules for the negotiations. When all else fails, the positional bargainers may simply refuse to negotiate, making their willingness to negotiate contingent on concessions made by the other party. The principled negotiator will expose the trickster's needs and interests that underlie their refusal to negotiate. All

PROBLEM	POSITION	NEED & INTEREST	OPTIONS/ACTION IDEAS
An unmet NEED Or INTEREST	SOLUTION, STRATEGY MEANS to end	How it will be different when the problem is not present	BRAINSTORM options for meeting needs & interests
Gap Between: Current Desired State State		Desired END state	Work toward CONSENSUS

EXAMPLE:

| Ruts, holes, mud in parking lot Cars, tires damaged | Teachers: "Pave the lot NOW!" | Place to park undamaged car Safety for car, self | All parking at local high school stadium lot with shuttle bus service for four weeks |
| | Admin.: "Pave lot in summer!" | At least four weeks To repave lot | |

FIGURE 11.4 Principled Negotiation

concessions and sidebar agreements should be strongly discouraged before the principled negotiation has followed its course. Although we have only high-lighted some of the machinations of unprincipled disputants, the reader is encouraged to peruse the many strategies that Fisher and Ury describe for dealing with foul play in conflict negotiation.

Figure 11.4 offers an illustration of how principled negotiation could be used in our opening case scenario. First, notice how incompatible the two positions are. However, when the need and interest of each party is identified, the option chosen is satisfactory to everyone.

Exercise 11.2 describes a problem that one counselor education program experienced with the introduction of distance learning into the course delivery medium. Formulate a principled negotiation that would realize the needs and interests of students, faculty, and the university.

EXERCISE 11.2

Conducting a Principled Negotiation

Directions: You are a consultant to a counselor education department that trains school counselors. Many of the courses are conducted using Web-based technologies (using Blackboard platform with chat rooms, discussion boards, and other distance learning features), PowerPoint, and videoconferencing. No course has been designed or delivered using total distance learning. The university has strongly urged all departments to deliver courses through distance learning as frequently as possible to cut costs and reach more students. The faculty in this department is split between three different *positions:*

1. The *total techies* want every course in the entire curriculum to be taught through distance learning.

2. The *status* quo group wants to continue the partial use of technology in most courses that already employ it.

3. The *nontechies* want all Web-based technologies and PowerPoint presentations to be eliminated, contending that counselor education requires face-to-face interaction in all courses.

As the consultant, describe the steps that you would take in facilitating a principled negotiation between these three groups. Specifically, what would the final Options/Actions Ideas be, and how would you create them?

THE FORCES THAT INFLUENCE CHANGE

Now that you have negotiated a solution that everyone can live with, successful implementation of that action idea needs careful planning. In any purposeful change there are forces that support that change and forces that resist all or part of it. For example, in order for the parking lot to be repaved while the school was in session the teachers needed an alternative location to park their cars. The existence of a large parking lot at the local football stadium just a mile away was a **driving force** that supported the action of repaving the lot immediately. Unfortunately, transportation from the stadium lot to the high school did not exist for the teachers. This **restraining force** had to be addressed for the solution to have any chance of success. Another driving force that would counterbalance this restraining force was the timely coincidence of a contract renewal between school district and a local bus company. With the presence of competitive bids by other companies, the Acme Bus Company (ABC), the district's current carrier, wanted favorable consideration. With a renewed contract the ABC agreed to provide a continual shuttle from the stadium to the high school from 6:30 to 8:30 A.M. and reversing direction between 3:00 to 5:00 P.M. Stopping the restraining force with an effective driving force was as simple as ABC when the **force-field analysis** (Hustedde & Score, 1994) was conducted.

Force-field analysis is a planning technique developed by Kurt Lewin (1951) that systematically identifies forces that restrain desired change and then identifies forces that counteract those restraints as well as other forces that will drive the change in the desired direction. All purposeful change requires driving forces such as incentives, timing, leadership, competition, and even degree of pain (remember, "Move in a crisis"?) that will initiate change and keep it going in the desired direction. Restraining forces such as the lack of resources, apathy, hostility, fear, incompetence, complacency, and secondary gain act to restrain or decrease the driving forces and resist attempts at desired

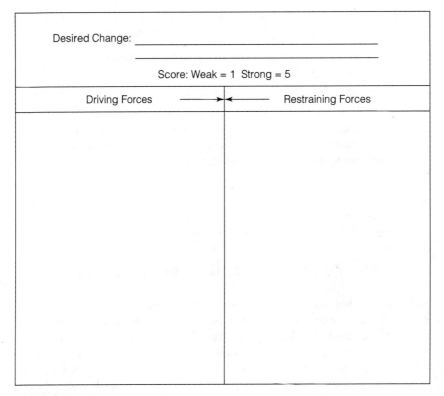

Desired Change: _____

Score: Weak = 1 Strong = 5

Driving Forces ——→|←—— Restraining Forces

FIGURE 11.5 Force-Field Analysis

change. Successful solutions require that on balance, driving forces outweigh the power of restraining forces, and that the most powerful restraining forces be met with more powerful driving forces. For change to occur, the driving forces must ultimately outweigh the power of the restraining forces. Otherwise, if the two forces simply match each other's influence, **equilibrium** will result and maintain the status quo. Just strengthening the driving forces without reducing or eliminating a restraining force will not lead to desired change. Moreover, strengthening the driving forces can sometimes have the unexpected result of strengthening or even creating new restraining forces.

Once a well-defined solution or action option is selected, a force-field analysis can be conducted. Figure 11.5 shows the basic elements of a force-field analysis and Figure 11.6 reveals a sample of a force-field analysis applied to help the students at Joe Buck Elementary School learn conflict resolution skills. The process calls for the following steps.

1. Start by writing the solution or desired change. In the case example, the staff wanted to teach conflict resolution skills to grades K–3 using the Second Step curriculum.
2. Collaboratively brainstorm all existing or possible restraining forces in the right column. Six restraining forces were identified in our example.

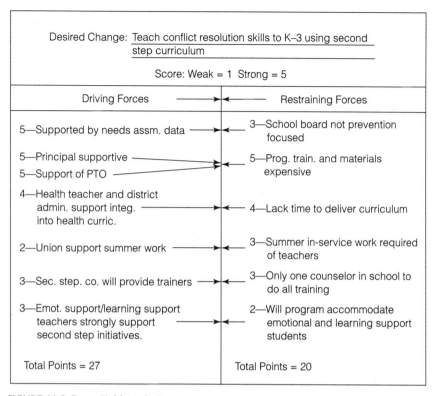

FIGURE 11.6 Force-Field Analysis

3. Draw arrows from each restraining force to the center line.

4. Assign a score from 1 (weak) to 5 (strong) for each force identified. The score reflects the strength of the force and the degree to which it can be resisted. The cost of the Second Step Program training and materials was beyond the existing budget of the school, causing it to receive a score of 5. Other forces received lesser scores.

5. Follow steps 2–4 in identifying and scoring your driving forces. It is very important that you brainstorm driving forces that will reduce or eliminate identified restraining forces. In response to the cost of training and materials, two driving forces were identified. Because the school principal was highly supportive of the initiative, she agreed to redirect computer upgrade funds to subsidize the training. Secondly, the school Parent Teacher Association agreed to hold a bake sale and silent auction to obtain funds for the purchase of materials.

6. In reviewing all your forces, make sure that each restraining force is met with an equally powerful driving force, and that the aggregate score for the driving forces exceeds that of the restraining forces. Note that the in-service training required of the teachers would have to occur over the summer. Although the teachers' union supported summer work for their

teachers, they would still have to volunteer to participate in the training. Getting volunteers was not assured, and incentives would have to be found.

In general, the driving forces outweighed the restraining forces in total score, and with only one exception, the restraining forces were all addressed. Now that you have seen a force-field analysis in action, see what you can do with Exercise 11.3.

EXERCISE 11.3

Conducting a Force-Field Analysis

Directions: With a student colleague you are asked to use Case 11.1: Specials Who Don't Feel Special to formulate a force-field analysis for **each** of the three action options that resulted from their negotiations. The solutions that were recommended were

1. To add volunteer special teachers to the strategic planning groups

2. To devote a prominent section of the newsletter to "Special Happenings"

3. To establish a policy that no student could miss any part of any class without permission of the teacher

---

PLANNING AND ORGANIZING
SOLUTION IMPLEMENTATION

So far we have identified needs and interests, formulated solutions, and addressed the restraining and driving forces that will influence our solutions. Now we are ready to organize, schedule, and coordinate the tasks that will bring our solution to reality.

There is a very wise proverb that says that, "Nothing succeeds like a deadline." This proverb is especially pertinent to the manner in which we organize our plan of action into the outcomes (**Events**), tasks (**Activity**) leading to those outcomes, over a designated period of **Time**. Integrating these three variables of events, activity, and time is critical for solutions to be implemented successfully. Fortunately, we have planning and organizational models to guide us in organizing activity to achieve events over reasonable time lines. The model that we will use to direct our implementation effort is referred to as the Program Evaluation Review Technique (Cook, 1978) or its acronym, PERT, charting.

The PERT methodology for planning and organizing change was first developed by the U.S. Navy in the 1950s to organize and coordinate the submarine missile program. Other organizing systems developed for the private sector such as the Critical Path Method and the Time Event Charting (TEC) method use essentially the same methodology as PERT. These models view all planned change as having a starting point (i.e., baseline), a measurable end point (i.e., outcome objective), tasks (i.e., activities) that need to be performed in attaining subgoals, and a specific time frame for all this to occur. In other words, complete implementation of a solution can be viewed as a **chain** with each link representing the subgoals and the tasks and time required to achieve those subgoals. Thus, complex activities are broken down into their discrete, interconnected and sequential parts.

Figure 11.7 presents a simple PERT chart for planning the solution of a new parking lot at Kirkwood High School. In this PERT chart, you will see all the components necessary for planning and organizing the replacement of the parking lot. We begin creating the chart by framing the ends of the horizontal line with the present state on the left and the end state (outcome goal) on the right. The sequence of subgoals (products or events) is then placed below the line. This chain of contingent events can be built from either end of the continuum. If we start at the baseline level dated January 20, 2003, we would identify the next subgoal that would have to be accomplished that would show progress toward our outcome goal of "the lot fully repaved and ready for parking." This first subgoal would have all the staff parking in the stadium and using the shuttle bus to and from their high school. We next ask the same question with the answer being the "removal of all broken asphalt from the lot." Each succeeding question asks for the next subgoal of the next link in our chain. In this way we proceed from left to right using **forward chaining.**

An alternative to forward chaining is to start at our outcome goal and build our event line from right to left. Through **backward chaining** we would identify the event that would precede but directly lead to our desired outcome goal. In this case, having all the lines painted would be the last event before the lot was completely ready for parking. We would then identify each preceding subgoal event until we reached our current condition on January 20, 2003. The advantage of backward chaining is that we can use each subgoal event as the reference for determining the immediate antecedent condition. Regardless of which chaining direction we use, the end product should be the sequence of subgoal events leading from baseline to outcome goal. With these subgoal events entered under our time line, we are then ready to identify the tasks or activities that will need to be done in order to accomplish each subgoal. These specific tasks are represented by capital letters placed between each subgoal. For example, the letter *A* between our baseline and first subgoal indicated that at least five tasks will have to be done for the next subgoal to be achieved. Tasks listed under *B* will next ensure that "removal of all broken asphalt" will be achieved, and so on, with subsequent tasks leading to each succeeding subgoal.

Once all our subgoals and tasks have been placed below our time line, we are ready to identify deadlines for our outcome goal and all preceding subgoals. Again, we can determine our deadlines from either direction on our time line. If we are firm about the deadline for our outcome goal, then we need to start there and work backward. The advantage of backward dating is that it provides a firm deadline from which to work. However, the disadvantage is that it can result in too little or too much time designated to accomplishing specific tasks.

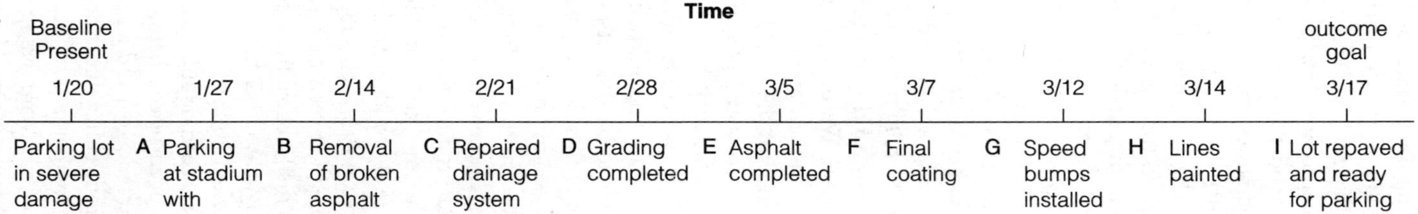

Baseline Present										outcome goal
1/20	1/27	2/14	2/21	2/28	3/5	3/7	3/12	3/14		3/17
	A	B	C	D	E	F	G	H		I
Parking lot in severe damage	Parking at stadium with	Removal of broken asphalt	Repaired drainage system	Grading completed	Asphalt completed	Final coating	Speed bumps installed	Lines painted		Lot repaved and ready for parking

Event

Tasks

A = 1. Get police clearance to park at the stadium.
2. Locate alternative parking for central administration and staff.
3. Ensure that no other activities are scheduled at stadium during period.
4. Schedule drivers for shuttle buses.
5. Issue temporary parking permits for stadium parking.
6. ?????????

FIGURE 11.7 PERT Chart of Paving the Parking Lot

Forward dating allows us to realistically assess the time necessary to accomplish the tasks leading to each subgoal. Because the teachers wanted the parking problem resolved as quickly as possible, the administration agreed to a final deadline of March 17, 2003, to fully achieve their desired outcome goal.

Although the six weeks required for the entire project was a few weeks longer than the teachers wanted, by PERT charting the project they appreciated the time and effort that would be required. PERT charting is a concrete, realistic, practical, and collaborative method for bringing principle negotiated solutions to fruition. It allows everyone to experience ownership over the process as well as the outcome. Using the guidelines of PERT charting, see what you can do with Exercise 11.4.

EXERCISE 11.4

PERT Charting a Solution

Directions: In Exercise 11.3 you conducted a force-field analysis for each of the three action options negotiated in Case 11.1. Select either one of the three action options for which you did your force-field analysis and construct a PERT chart for that solution. Use the format that is presented in Figure 11.7.

This chapter has looked at the nature of group problems, needs and interests, and strategies that the school counselor–consultant can use to mediate conflicts, build cohesive teams, negotiate agreements, and successfully plan and implement solutions to achieve group goals. In short, problem identification to resolution. The final exercise (Exercise 11.5) in this chapter asks you to select a need or problem that was identified from your system's analysis in chapter 3, Exercise 3.3, and describe the process that you would undertake to resolve that need or problem using the principles and strategies of principled negotiation, force-field analysis, and PERT planning and charting.

EXERCISE 11.5

Groups in Conflict: From Problem
Identification to Solution Planning

Directions: In chapter 3, Exercise 3.1, you were asked to conduct a systems analysis. From your analysis of that system, identify one problem that exists in that system in which two or more groups are in conflict. Such conflict might occur between any of the groups (teachers, students, parents, administrators, staff, counselors, community members) and be expressed in minor disagreement, positional bargaining, or even open warfare. In most of the conflicts that you will discover, the needs and interests of one group have been threatened or violated. Examples abound but could include: a group of students may object to a disciplinary procedure; some teachers might feel that some tasks assigned to them are unreasonable; parents might feel that a redistricting plan disadvantages their children; local homeowners surrounding a college or university might contend that student residents are "trashing" their community; and some teachers might believe that the principal is discriminating in his allocation of resources.

Once you have identified the groups and their concern, your job as counselor–consultant within that system is to answer the following six questions.

1. What is the presenting problem?
2. What position do the various parties in the dispute seem to be taking?
3. What are the needs and interests that lie beneath those positions?
4. How would you conduct a principled negotiation with the disputants and what solution may come from those negotiations?
5. What would a force-field analysis for that solution look like?
6. What would a PERT chart of the implementation of that solution look like?

SUMMARY

Conceptualizing the Triad and Their Goals

In this chapter we focused on the school counselor's consultation with groups of consumers seeking redress of grievances, resolution of interpersonal conflicts, and some form of systemic change. The first consideration in working with these groups is to be attentive to their individual needs and interests while establishing group norms and formulating viable task goals. It was further suggested that the consultant view the parties in dispute as consultees and the system as the client in the triad.

Facilitating Win–Win Solutions and Getting to Yes

This model of conflict resolution helped the disputing parties shift their attention from their positions and solutions to the underlying needs and interests motivating those positions. Through recognition of the common or shared needs and interests, the disputing groups can creatively formulate solutions and action plans that will lead to win–win outcomes.

The Forces That Influence Change

With win–win solutions generated by brainstorming and consensus building, the consultant can then help the groups to subject their solutions to force-field analysis. By careful analysis of the driving and restraining forces in the implementation of a solution, the parties can mobilize resources and actions that will minimize resistance to change and maximize the probability that desired outcomes can be achieved.

Planning and Organizing Solution Implementation

The final step in solution implementation is in the planning and organization of the desired change. The Performance Evaluation Review Technique (PERT) method was offered as a clear and practical approach to the dissection of an action plan into manageable outcomes and tasks along an explicit and reasonable time line. Such planning follows the basic tenets of shaping, chaining, and task analysis, offering clarity, collaboration, and accountability to the experience of group problem solving, decision making and outcome goal realization.

IMPORTANT TERMS

Activity

Backward chaining

Best Alternative to a
Negotiated
Agreement
(BATNA)

Brainstorming

Conflict

Consensual agreement

Driving force

Equilibrium

Events

Force-field analysis

Forward chaining

Group task goals

Individual goals

Interests

Job wellness and
satisfaction survey

Maintenance goals

Needs

Norms

Positional bargaining

Principled negotiation

Program Evaluation
Review Technique
(PERT)

Restraining force

The three-legged stool
model

Time

Win–lose outcomes

Win–win conflict
resolution

SUGGESTED READINGS

Lee, J. L., Pulvino, C. J., & Perrone, P. A. (1998). *Restoring harmony: A guide for managing conflicts in schools.* Upper Saddle River, NJ: Prentice Hall.

Levine, S. (1998). *Getting to resolution: Turning conflict into collaboration.* San Francisco: Berrett-Koehler.

WEB SITES

Alliance for Mediation and Conflict Resolution, Inc.: Source for training seminars, including e-learning and hands-on instruction, customized to fit the needs of your particular organization. www.we-mediate.com

CADRE, The National Center on Dispute Resolution: It is funded by the U.S. Department of Education and provides technical assistance for implementation of the mediation requirements under '97. Provides support for parents, educators, and administrators to benefit from the full continuum of dispute resolution options that

can prevent and resolve conflict and ultimately lead to informed partnerships that
focus on results for children and youth.
www.directionservice.org/cadre/cr-education.cfm

Conflict Resolution, Research and Resource Institute: A nonprofit corporation that
provides programs and publications to help people and organizations deal with
conflict. www.cri.cc

Mediate.com: Provides information, technology and education. Everything about
mediation and mediators and conflict resolution, including articles and resources.
www.conflict-resolution.net

Pert Chart Expert: Project planning and project management software. Assist in planning
and manage project using a PERT. It is a Windows-based project management
software application that is used to create PERT charts.
www.criticaltools.com/pertmain.htm

REFERENCES

Campbell, C. A., & Dahir, C. A. (1997). *The national standards for school counseling programs.*
Alexandria, VA: American School Counselor Association.

Cook, D. (1978). *Program evaluation and review technique.* Lanham, MD: University Press of
America.

Deutsch, M. (1973). *The resolution of conflict.* New Haven, CT: Yale University Press.
Elephant Country. (2002). www.elephantcountryweb.com

Fisher, R., & Ury, W. (1991). *Getting to yes: Negotiating agreements without giving in*
(2nd ed.). New York: Penguin.

Hustedde, R., & Score, M. (1994). Force-field analysis: Incorporating critical thinking in
goal setting. *Community Development Practice 4,* 2–6.

Johnson, D. W., & Johnson, F. P. (2003). *Joining together: Group theory and group skills*
(8th ed.). New York: Allyn & Bacon.

Kahn, W. K. (1981). *Job wellness and satisfaction survey.* Unpublished survey.

Kahn, W. K. (1988). Cognitive-behavioral group counseling: An introduction. *The School
Counselor, 35,* 346.

Levine, S. (1998). *Getting to resolution: Turning conflict into collaboration.* San Francisco:
Berrett-Koehler.

Lewin, K. (1951). *Field theory in social sciences.* New York: Harper & Row.

Maslow, A. (1954). *Motivation and personality.* New York: Harper & Row.

Maslow, A. (1962). *Toward a psychology of being.* Princeton, NJ: Van Nostrand.

Maslow, A. (1970). *Motivation and personality* (2nd ed.). New York: Harper & Row.

Maslow, A. (1971). *Motivation and personality.* (2nd ed.). New York: Harper & Row.

Rose, S. D. (1972). *Treating children in groups.* San Francisco: Jossey-Bass.

Turner, J. S. & Helm, D. B. (1987). *Lifespan development* (3rd ed.). New York: Holt,
Rinehart & Winston.

Webster's encyclopedic unabridged dictionary of the English language. (1996). New York:
Random House.

12

⁓◦⁓

The System as Client

System-Focused Consultation

Despite of an hour and a half of resource room support each day, Ellen continues to struggle in math. I know that she hates going to the resource room, but it's the only special accommodation that was written into her 504 Service Plan. In a school this large, I can't believe that only four students use the resource room for support. Ms. Blue seems like a caring and conscientious teacher, but she lacks real clout in this school, especially with Dr. Jameson.

When I came to this school, career counseling was almost an afterthought, and then only for students not pursuing postsecondary education. I knew that Ellen has expressed some interest in music, but I haven't had the chance to talk with her about her plans after high school. This is not a school that prides itself on diversity, either in learning or vocational interest.

Our counselor–consultant is realizing the impact of a system's culture—and resources—on his ability to function effectively. Hopefully, his knowledge of the basic components of the system, as well as his ability to discern the unique dynamics in this particular system, will provide him with the needed information to begin a well-thought-out plan for system change.

In chapter 3 we introduced the basic components of a system, emphasizing the interaction of system population, consumer need, desired and obtained outcomes, process, and input. These structural elements of a social system such as a school organize our thinking about the purposes, processes, and accountability characterizing the system. We turned to the dynamic, evolving nature of these systems in chapter 4. Natural and purposeful change were discussed as enlightened individuals struggled to keep their system open in response to the natural forces of entropy and disintegration. Chapter 11 looked at the various subsystems (i.e., groups of teachers, students, parents, administrators, other stakeholders) that might be in conflict. Contention over positions, needs, and interests between these groups can impair student learning and system functioning. In this chapter we synthesize our knowledge of system structure and dynamics to ameliorate systemic problems that may be creating or maintaining client or consultee problems. To accomplish this we maximize our perspective by looking at interventions that will impact all levels of the system: client, consultee, classroom, grade level, school, district, and even community. Without a full grasp of the system within which the counselor–consultant is operating, a consultant may provide approaches that are not only counter to the culture of that organization but also may in fact provide inadequate assessment and result in short-sighted, ineffectual, and incorrectly targeted interventions (Schein, 2003). Consequently, we broaden our focus to include the special demands and unique opportunities of system-focused consultation.

CHAPTER OBJECTIVES

In addition to providing an increased awareness of the value and need for system-focused consultation, the chapter will provide guidelines for implementing such a system-focused approach and highlight the unique skills required for system-focused consultation. Specifically, after completing this chapter, the reader should be able to

1. Describe the various manifestations of the character or culture of a system
2. Explain a model for organizing diagnostic focus as system analysis
3. Employ diagnostic skills—including observational skills essential to system-focused consultation
4. Explain a model for introducing innovation and change within systems

SYSTEM-FOCUSED CONSULTATION:
WHEN THE SYSTEM IS THE PROBLEM

When a system-focused consultation is targeted, the consultant explicitly attempts to consider the multiple contexts of the manifested problem and from this viewpoint consider the options available for problem resolution (Wynn, McDaniel, & Weber, 1986). Consultation focused on the system has several purposes. First, the consultant hopes to increase awareness of those within the system of the current nature and status of their organization. Second, the consultant attempts to assist system members to identify and highlight those factors maintaining the current form of operation and to enumerate alternative natures or statuses for the system to consider. Third, the consultant will help the members articulate and implement the means of achieving this alternative form. And finally, the consultant will facilitate the system's capacity to continue this process of self-awareness and renewal (Parsons & Meyers, 1984).

When Client Symptoms Reflect System Problems

Historically, those involved with the study of organizational development have suggested that many of the problems found within organizations are the result of the ever-increasing bureaucratic machine model of organization (Meyers, Parsons, & Martin, 1979). That is, the highly specialized and fractionated organization of roles isolated the workers from the success of working on the whole and thus reduced their sense of accomplishment and achievement. Further, this same research suggests that the increased layering of authority generally resulted in decision making and prescriptive communication becoming one way, top down. Such structural impacts have resulted in a sense of worker disenfranchisement and what one author (i.e., Argyris, 1970) termed adaptive antagonistic activities on the part of the worker. These activities took many forms such as workers exhibiting passive aggressive behaviors (e.g., damaging equipment, " 'forgetting' important details," etc.), general apathy, and feelings of alienation toward the school. Argyris (1970) suggested that all such client behavior is more accurately attributed to the disenfranchising structure of the system as a whole, rather than a manifestation of a person's internal dynamic. As such, focusing on the client, in the absence of system change, would prove fruitless.

SYSTEM DIAGNOSIS

Although there may be a variety of models, approaches, and techniques to be employed in system diagnosis, it appears that there are some commonly agreed-upon activities that are needed to ensure an effective diagnostic process. It is typically agreed (Beer & Spector, 1993) that the diagnostic process:

1. Is most often triggered once the system or members note that a problem exists

2. Involves data collection by a combination of internal and external agents attempting to identify the problem source

3. Is targeted to data perceived by organizational members to be valid

4. Concludes with the results being fed back to organizational members

System Analysis: A Demanding Process

This process of system analysis is a time-consuming, demanding process that requires a number of unique talents and skills on the part of the consultant. Prior to beginning such a system-focused appraisal, the consultant would be wise to be apprised of the following observations.

1. **System analysis requires multiple skills.** As Kuh (1993) noted, system analysis demands a biographer's discipline, perseverance, an eye for detail, and the therapist's insight, intuition, and interpersonal skills. The consultant involved in system-focused consultation will need to perform content analysis of written materials as well as clinical interview of the system's "historians." The consultant will certainly need to develop collaborative relationships and be able to employ and maintain a team approach to the evaluation process.

2. **System analysis is both time and energy consuming.** Because of the wide array of units and focal points that need to be evaluated, as well as the many forms of data to be collected (e.g., material to be read, events to be observed and interpreted, people to be interviewed), system-focused consultation is time and energy draining. Further, because appraisal of the system's character cannot be conducted by outsiders alone (Kuh et al., 1991), collaboration is essential. The development and maintenance of such collaborative relationships will also take time, energy, and skill on the part of the consultant.

3. **System analysis will incur resistance.** Although the system may wish to grow and respond to the input of the consultant (its open orientation), systems are also self-protecting and self-maintaining (closed orientation) and thus may resist change. Because it is a critical process, it may be perceived as threatening to the current state of the system and thus be a serious violation of the self-preservation cultural norms (Kuh, 1993).

4. **System analysis is more than data gathering, it is intervention.** Diagnosis is a process of gathering information about the various subsystems of an organization along with the processes and patterns of behavior that take place within that organization (Beckhard, 1969). But system diagnosis is not simply for identification or data gathering only. System analysis as a diagnostic step is done for the purpose of mobilizing action on a problem (Block, 1981). It is not only essential as the first step of problem solving but it may also, in fact, be the first step of intervention. System analysis can actually be part of a process of large-scale organizational revitalization (Beer & Spector, 1993). It is a process that can serve to motivate organizational members to engage in change (Aldefer & Brown, 1975). When done effectively, system diagnosis is a process that can assist an organization or, in our case, the school by:

   1. Enhancing capacity to assess and change the culture of the organization

   2. Providing opportunity for members to acquire new insights into the dysfunctional aspects of their culture and patterns of behavior as a basis for developing a more effective organization

   3. Ensuring that the organization remains engaged in a process of continuous improvement (Beer & Spector, 1993)

Steps in the Diagnostic Process

According to Beer and Spector (1993) the effectiveness of the diagnostic process as a source of mobilizing change is influenced by the manner in which the diagnostic or intervention process is conducted. We have found the process articulated by Peter Block (1981) to be effective. Block (1981) provides a number of steps the consultant needs to go through in moving from the identification of a problem through to the implementation of the intervention. A slight modification of the process is presented next. The process is presented and discussed as being linear and sequential. Although articulated as a linear process, it must be highlighted that it is a process that focuses on collaboration and mutual ownership and as such may go back and forth across these steps to ensure that the consultant and the consultee are fully collaborative and in tune with one another. The specific diagnostic steps are described and illustrated with our ongoing case of Ellen.

1. *Identify the presenting problem.* Any diagnosis begins with a description of the problems. Systemically, it can be suggested that the presenting problem is usually only a symptom of the real problem, and the purpose of data collection is to elaborate and broaden this initially identified issue. The presenting concern offered in Dr. Jameson's referral casts the focus of the problem on Ellen's poor academic performance. Data collection will reveal more systemic faults.

2. *Make a decision to proceed.* The consultant needs sanctioning to proceed in the diagnostic process. This sanctioning is one way of removing a possible source of later resistance. It is important for the consultant to collaborate with the consultee's system when proceeding. Furthermore, this sanctioning must be done with the system's understanding that the process in which the consultant is engaged is ultimately for the purpose of impacting change. Dr. Jameson's initial expectation was that Mr. Thomas would immediately and directly diagnose and treat "Ellen's problem." Mr. Thomas delicately challenged this expectation by requesting to meet with Dr. Jameson first and then agreeing to assess and ameliorate the problem collaboratively. As principal, Dr. Jameson's legitimate power provided the systemic authority to proceed.

3. *Select the dimensions to be studied.* Although using a broad brush, it is important to restrict the number of areas that will be analyzed so as to not overwhelm the consultant or the consultee with too much data. At their very first consultation, Mr. Thomas directed assessment procedures that would address the client, task, and environment.

4. *Decide on who will be involved.* Involving people in the data collection also implies that they will be informed as to the findings. The system-focused consultant needs to identify the levels and types of representatives to be involved in the actual collection as well as those who will provide the data to be collected. Questions regarding whether the entire staff of a unit, subsystem, or organization will provide the data need to be resolved.

Mr. Thomas and Dr. Jameson shared in the process of assessing the client, task, and environment. Whereas the consultant reviewed Ellen's cumulative record and interviewed Ellen's resource room teacher, the consultee agreed to observe Ellen's interaction with others. These assessments were manageable yet thorough enough to reveal client, consultee, and system deficiencies.

5. *Select the data collection method.* The selection of the data-collection method is usually dependent on the scope and nature of the consult. The methods employed should not only fit the problem, but should also reflect the resources of the system, the time available, and the motivation and abilities of those involved. To minimize the perceived threat of such data collection, the consultant may want to proceed from less-structured forms of data collection (e.g., unstructured observations and individual interviews) to the more structured methods employing surveys and questionnaires. With Dr. Jameson's initial reluctance to participate in the process, the consultant decided to review existing data (i.e., cumulative records) and employ unstructured observations and individual interviews. In this way the cost to Dr. Jameson was minimal.

6. *Collect the data.* At this step it is important that the consultant *not* overcollect data. That is, it is important to reduce redundancy where possible. The data-collection phase can prove highly motivating (Nadler, 1977) and a way of initiating a desire to move from the status quo. The consultant does not want to loose this enthusiasm through overburdening or redundancy. The assessment of the client, task, and environment was dispatched with speed and specificity. A meeting was scheduled for only 3 days later to share results and formulate a plan of action. Under such tight deadlines, assessment directives receive high priority and are reinforced by quick action and substantive data.

Involving organizational members in the data collection will not only increase commitment but can also serve as a training process (e.g., teaching observation and interview skills) and a way of including data collection as an ongoing process to the culture of that organization.

Focusing the Diagnosis

A system is a complex entity with many dimensions, structures, processes, and elements. Each of these many components could be an appropriate target for the diagnostic process. Thus a consultant interested in system-focused consultation would be ill advised to enter the process without an understanding of the difficulty to be experienced and a model to guide the process. There are a number of excellent models or frameworks that can help the consultant organize data and diagnose organizational functioning (e.g., Gysbers & Henderson, 2000; Parsons & Meyers, 1984; Waterman, Peters, & Phillips, 1980; Wittmer, 2000).

The scope of the diagnostic process can either be narrow, involving a quick look at the easily identified trouble spots in an organization, or a more in-depth analysis of the intricate workings of the system. If change is to be long term and permanent, then a more systematic review of the interactivity and interdependence of the various system components will be necessary. It is important to understand that multiple interactive elements are operative within and without a system, which may impact its functioning. It is important for the system consultant to understand each of these components because they are interrelated and interdependent and thus play some part in the system's presentation.

In diagnosing a system, the consultant must, at a minimum, identify the consumers, needs, outcomes, processes, and inputs. In addition, the consultant needs to consider the impact of the specific processes employed by the system as it attempts to reach its particular goals. These processes include such things as specific programs implemented, organization structure and methods of communication, decision making, and evaluation. Finally, the system-focused consultation should consider the system output. What is the mission of the system, and how is it reflected in the outcomes it achieves? How successful is the system at attaining its goals, and do these goal meet the needs of those whom the system wishes to service?

Using the interaction of these five system components as your framework, consider Exercise 12.1.

EXERCISE 12.1

The Tale of Two Schools

Directions: As with most of the exercises presented, this exercise is best completed either with another or in a small group. Read the brief descriptions of two neighboring schools. As you read the descriptions, attempt to identify the unique inputs, process, and desired outputs present in both schools. Finally, answer and discuss the questions that follow the presentation.

"School on the Right": Constructed in 1965, the "School on the Right" is a private, religious-sponsored elementary school, grades K–8. The school is staffed by clergy and members of a religious community. Values teaching, by instruction and by model, is keystone to the curricular experience. The school is financially supported by the Archdiocesan Dept. of Education, the particular parish in which the school is located, and tuition paid by parents who send their child(ren) to the school.

"School on the Left": Constructed in 1982, the "School on the Left" is the public elementary school (grades K–5) for this local community. The school is one of four elementary schools in this district, which is directed by a single elected school board, a superintendent, three assistant superintendents, a principal, vice principals, and a host of support personnel (including guidance staff, nursing staff, crisis interventionist, and drug and alcohol counselors). The school receives funding through local taxes and a number of federally funded programs. The professional staff members are all certified, and the district is a union shop district. Academic excellence and social responsibility are the driving values for the curriculum.

Reflections:

1. Identify the unique demographics for each system. How would these demographics influence the needs and desired outcomes?

2. How would the identified needs and desired outcomes impact the internal processes and structures for each system?

3. Identify one unique demand placed on a student in each of the systems. On a teacher in each system. On an administrator.

4. Describe the relationship of the system to its consumer population. What limits to power—interactive influence—unique opportunities or limitations exist?

5. For each of the following behaviors, discuss how each system would (a) respond to it or be impacted by it, and (b) contribute to its creation. Stealing, fighting, requests for special Saturday makeup days, preadolescent sexual concerns, parent advocacy groups, faculty–staff input.

Analyzing the Systems— Elements, Forces, and Culture

One broad-based model for conceptualizing the many forces and potential targets for system-focused consultation appears in chapters 3 and 4 as well as other texts (Parsons, 1996). That model, in a somewhat elaborated and adapted form, will serve as the foundation for the discussion to follow.

The model to be presented focuses the system diagnostic process on the identification of the system's salient elements, impacting forces, and unique organizational culture, as they independently and interactively contribute to the system's current level of functioning and dysfunctioning.

The System's Elements

In analyzing a system, the system-focused consultant needs to consider the unique characteristics and impact of the **people** involved, the **physical environment,** and the **product** the system is attempting to produce. Each of these elements plays an essential role in the function and possible dysfunction of a system.

In assessing the people composing the system, the consultant needs to consider the unique values, skills, and orientations presented by these individuals. Whether the consultant is targeting the client(s), staff, or administrators, the unique values, skills, and orientation they bring to the system can prove significant to system functioning. Consider the values and religious community affiliation of the staff and faculty of "School on the Right" (see Exercise 12.1). Consider how those unique characteristics of the people element of that system will impact the consumer (i.e., student) and product (i.e., curriculum). Understanding both the uniqueness of this people element and its impact is essential for effective system-focused consultation.

In addition to describing the individuals, the system-focused consultant will identify the unique grouping of individuals and the specific nature, character, and influence each group has on each other and the system as a whole. Consider, for example, the potential impact of group affiliation of either union or nonunion on the day-to-day atmosphere and functioning of the "School on the Left," especially during a time of contract discussion.

A second class of elements operative within a system would be all those facets of the physical environment in which the people of the system function. Considered under this dimension would be the system's physical layout (including the use of space), the arrangement of various departments, units, resources, and the overall condition and feeling of the physical work space. One very real example for the authors is that this chapter was being written at a time when our geographic area was under a heat and humidity wave, with temperatures and humidity well into the 90s. How different our attitude, our focus, our productivity would be in an environment *without* air-conditioning or an overabundance of people. The physical environment is a significant variable in the overall operation of a system. Clearly the experience of facility convenience or crowding can enhance efficiency or result in frustration, which in turn can impact behavior and attitudes of those involved.

The final class of elements to be considered is the product or output desired by the system, as reflective of its mission. The mission of a system, that is, its "broad, overall long-term purpose of the institution" (Welzenbach 1982, p. 15), has or should have a profound influence on its culture, its style, and its character. As the rationale for what the system aspires to be, the mission represents the ends that the system hopes to attain. These ends are driven by consumer needs but also reflect the values, beliefs, and aspirations of the providers of the system's inputs and those employees who are delivering the processes. The mission of an institution would therefore guide institutional priorities and practices.

Assessing both the product desired and the product produced will not only provide insight into the special character, structure, and process of the system but also some of the unique demands placed on the system and system resources. In assessing the system product, the consultant needs to consider questions such as: Does the obtained outcome reflect the needs and mission defined as the desired outcome? What unique structures and processes have been instituted to facilitate the system's achievement of these goals? What are the indicators and processes employed to demonstrated outcome achievement? Exercise 12.2 will give you practice in assessing the impact of mission on structure and process of a system.

EXERCISE 12.2

The Impact of Mission on Structure and Process

Directions: For each of the contrasting organizational missions, assess the subtle or perhaps not so subtle influence of the organization mission on the development of system structures and processes for day-to-day operations. Further, consider the resources needed to fulfill the mission and the unique demands placed on the members operating within that system. It would prove useful to share and discuss your perspective with a colleague, mentor, or supervisor.

System	Mission (Outcome)	Impact
Set 1: A: A large, affluent suburban high school		
B: A small, rural high school operating in an agriculturally based community		
Set 2: A: An inner-city public school		
B: An inner-city private preparatory school		
Set 3: A: A social service agency such as a community mental health clinic		
B: A stockbrokerage firm		

Assessing Forces Impacting the System

In addition to knowing where the system wishes to go (i.e., mission- or needs-based outcome) and the physical and personnel resources it has available, the system-focused consultant needs to understand the forces that may be affecting its current level of operation.

June Gallessich (1974) differentiated among the many forces that may prove significant to the understanding and assessment of a system. She identified classes of forces as internal, trajectory, or external. The internal forces are those operating within the climate or culture of the organization. These would be forces created by the structures and processes existing within the organization (i.e., the system of authority, the rewards employed, decision-making processes), and these will be discussed in more depth in the next section.

In addition to internal forces, Gallessich (1974) noted that a system is impacted by its own history and developmental direction (i.e., trajectory). The trajectory of a system reflects both its history and its trend. Although it is not suggested that the projection of movement need be a predeterminer of system function, it is clear that past trends, as reflective of current and future realities, can impact the nature, character, and performance of a system and thus should be considered by the system-focused consultation.

The final class of forces that Gallessich (1974) discussed are those external to the system. The consultant must be careful not to limit system analysis to the internal operations of the system. Rather, to be inclusive and effective the system-focused consultant needs to be mindful of the powerful force and resources that the suprasystem offers (Ridley & Mendoza, 1993). In analyzing the external forces impacting the system, the focus is on both the adversarial and supportive roles played by the external environment.

The system-focused consultant needs to understand both the individual characteristics of the population (community) that may support the system via input of resources (e.g., tuition, taxes, purchases) as well as the unique characteristics of those who will consume the services of the system. In addition to understanding the individual characteristics of the population, the consultant needs to be sensitive to significant trends (e.g., economic, political, social–cultural) that may impact the system. Aplin (1978) noted a number of external trends that could impact a system's operations, such as:

1. Economic pressures leading to downsizing or rightsizing that organization
2. Business trends pushing for decentralization of authority and the use of total quality management
3. Technological innovations and increasing government regulations
4. Social political pressures for increased egalitarianism, diversity, and equity within the workplace

Beyond simply identifying the external forces operating, the effective consultant needs to assess the organizational capacity to collaborate and build supportive networks and healthy interdependencies with other systems in the external environment. At times of economic downturn and recession, family stress increases and family support for academic achievement is compromised as parents work harder and cut back on educational inputs. Furthermore, as economic bifurcation separates the financial haves and have-nots, technology will be less accessible to those consumers who are most in need.

Unless the organization is both aware of the changing environment and able to respond, it will be hard to be effective.

Assessing the System Character and Culture

Perhaps one of the most difficult yet most salient components of a system to assess is that of the system culture. A system's culture could be defined as the unique collective, mutually shaping patterns of institutional history, mission, physical settings, norms, traditions, practices, and beliefs that influence the behavior of individuals and groups (Kuh & Whitt, 1988). It provides a frame of reference within which to interpret the meaning of events and actions within and without the system (Kuh & Whitt, 1988). A system's culture is reflected in its explicit and implicit norms and would include, yet not be limited to, such things as job definitions, roles, structures and processes of communication and decision making, and general rules for behavior operating within a system.

Kuh (1993) provided an interesting illustration in describing a consultant offering a debriefing session to a representative body of a college. The membership at the meeting included the president of the college, the academic and student affairs deans, four faculty members, and three students. Kuh (1993) noted that the consultant, after exchanging pleasantries, reminded those in attendance of the purpose of the meeting (i.e., to solicit feedback on the report) and then asked for comments. As described by Kuh (1993), the consultant's request for comments was followed by 3 minutes of absolute silence. Following this extended silence, the president finally began to speak.

Many of us may have felt uncomfortable with this apparent lack of response to the consultant's invitation to ask question. We may have been tempted to interrupt the silence as a means of stimulating exchange and dialogue. However, in this instance, the consultant was familiar with the culture of the system and as such expected a protracted period of silence. The system that Kuh (1993) was describing was a Quaker college. It was a system where people listened at meetings, reflected, and thought carefully before speaking. This process of listening–reflecting–considering and responding was a reflection of the Quaker philosophy, which assumed that such a process allows "the light of truth" to emerge (Krehbiel & Strange, 1991). Thus the period of silence is part of the cultural process and need not, nor even should be, interfered with by the consultant. But a consultant without an understanding and appreciation of the culture that was operative may have missed this point and indirectly interfered with the process that was required by the system.

Various researchers have articulated concepts and approaches that are useful in the analysis and intervention within an organizational culture (e.g., Borum & Pedersen, 1990; Gagliardi, 1990; Hatch, 1993; Pederson, 1991; Turner, 1990; Young, 1989). However, Edgar Schein (1981, 1983, 1984, 1985, 1990) developed perhaps the most enduring and comprehensive conceptual framework from which to analyze and intervene in organizational cultures. Schein's framework will be used as the framework for the discussion to follow.

Schein saw the organization's culture as: "(a) a pattern of basic assumptions, (b) invented , discovered or developed by a given group, (c) as it learns to cope with its problems of external adaptation and internal integration, (d) that has worked well enough to be considered valid and therefore (e) is to be taught to new members as the (f) correct way to perceive, think, feel in relationship to those problems" (Schein, 1990, p. 111). According to Schein (1985), organizational cultures exist on three simultaneous yet separate levels—artifacts, values, and basic assumptions. Each of these levels can serve the system-focused consultant as targets for assessing the climate and culture of an organization.

Artifacts　　On the surface of any organization are the visible, tangible, or concrete manifestations of the organizations varied activities. These products Schein termed **artifacts.** Artifacts can be divided into three groups—physical (i.e., those things that surround people such as space, architecture, technical machinery), verbal (e.g., stories, written and oral histories, special words), and behavior (e.g., rituals, ceremonies). Artifacts would include items such as an organization's symbols, logos, slogans, images, and metaphors in addition to its formal organizational charts, rites, and rituals (Kuh, 1993). To understand or "know" a system, therefore, a consultant must be somewhat of a cultural researcher or anthropologist. It is in analyzing the system's shared symbols, ideology, values, myths, rites, rituals, customs, language, legends, logos, design, and even architecture that the system's culture begins to be known (Kuh et al., 1991).

Values The second level, according to Schein (1985), below that of the artifacts, is the **values** or social principles, philosophies, and standards of the organization. The philosophy of the system is the manifestation of widely shared values and assumptions, many of them tacit, about human nature and the process of doing what it is the system is created to do (e.g., for education systems, to teach, to promote learning). The values of a system present the system's view of the importance of certain goals, activities, relationships, and feelings (Kuh & Whitt, 1988). By reviewing the way those within the system traditionally and continually address specific problems posed by the situations they face in common, the system-focused consultant can begin to understand the system's values (Van Maanen & Barley, 1985).

The values, which are often in the form of some assertion about how the system should function, can be different than those observed. Often it is enacted values, that is, the way people and the system actually prioritize and function, that shapes policies, decision making, and so forth. As such, the system-focused consultant must be mindful of both the espoused and the enacted values along with the possible impact of any discrepancy between these two forms.

Basic Assumptions The final level of a system's culture, according to Schein (1985), is the **system's basic assumptions.** The system's basic assumptions reflect the organization's taken-for-granted beliefs about reality and human nature. These assumptions form the unquestioned, nondebatable truths and reality of people within the system. As Schein (1985) noted, when a solution to a problem works repeatedly, it comes to be taken for granted to the point where what was once only a hunch starts to be treated as a reality as if this is the way nature really works. These basic assumptions then serve as the foundation from which the system defines structures and processes to guide its operations.

It is this deepest level, the level of basic assumptions, that Schein felt held the key to understanding and thus changing the culture of an organization. What organizational members assume to be true shapes what they value and the form these values take. Thus if the assumption is that human beings are lazy and resist work, managers will have the expectations of laziness, which will color their perceptions of workers. Thus a teacher who is taking a deserved break or taking time to contemplate a task will be perceived as avoiding his responsibility of work. These assumptions will also shape administrative procedures and evaluation. For the system in which teachers are assumed to be lazy and resistant to work, administrative procedures or evaluation processes that reward sustained effort, activity, and restriction of teacher autonomy (because lazy people would use freedom to goof off) will be evident, and artifacts of administrative control (e.g., time clocks, daily productivity reports, various forms of accountability measures) will be plentiful.

The Linkage of Artifacts, Values, and Assumptions

The links among a culture's artifacts, values, and assumptions are central to the organization's operations. To understand the systemic influence of the culture of an organization, one must analyze the nature and interaction between the systems artifacts, values, and assumptions (Kuh, 1993; Kuh & Whitt, 1988; Schein, 1985). A number of procedures have been suggested for accomplishing these tasks.

For example, Schein (1991) suggested the use of interpretation of the artifacts and values as they reveal basic assumptions. It is also important to listen to the stories of the system about heroic figures and critical events. Such stories can offer insights into the morale of staff, as well as those behaviors that are valued or negatively sanctioned. Reviewing rituals and ceremonies along with traditions and celebratory events can also provide a look at the means through which a system's character is not only formed but also perpetuated (Whitt & Kuh, 1991).

The authors have found that clinical interviewing of the school employees to be a useful approach to understanding the basic operating assumptions of the system. Through such an interview process, the consultant can identify how work is conducted, which in turn reveals the basic assumptions guiding the organization. Identifying the rules of behavior or the norms of the system can assist the consultant in knowing the underlying values and assumptions operative within that system. But beyond facilitating the consultant's own understanding, the interview process can also be used to elevate the conscious awareness of these assumptions for organizational members. See if you can apply your knowledge of artifacts, values, and assumptions to Exercise 12.3.

EXERCISE 12.3

A Look at One System's Culture

Directions: To make the discussion that is to follow more meaningful and understandable, it is suggested that you attempt to apply the concepts, as they are discussed, to one of the specific systems in which you are involved. This could be your work environment, or if you are a student, it could be the educational institution in which you are enrolled or the specific program. It could even be your family.

It is suggested that you follow the steps provided to gain a full appreciation for the power of a system's culture.

Step 1: Briefly identify the system that you have targeted. As you describe, attempt to identify the mission, purpose, and global goals for that system.

Step 2: After observing your system, identify the unique physical artifacts, special spaces; and special stories, myths, logos, rituals, and ceremonies.

Step 3: Identify the widely shared values and assumptions, many of them tacit, about human nature and the process of doing what it is the system is created to do. These values will be reflected in the system's view of the importance of certain activities, relationships, and goals.

Step 4: Review the artifacts identified in Step 2 and interpret the basic assumptions—the taken-for-granted beliefs about human nature and reality—which they reflect.

Step 5: Structure and processes: This final step requires the participation of a colleague, mentor, or supervisor. Ask your cohort to review Steps 1 through 4 and now attempt to identify two specific organizational structures (e.g., positions, groupings, organizational chain of command) and processes (e.g., communication, decision making, evaluation) that he/she assumes would be a consequence of the basic assumptions in listed in Step 4. Discuss the accuracy of his/her prediction. It would be helpful for you to complete Step 5 using the data provide by a cohort reflecting his/her system.

Diagnostic Tools and Techniques
for System-Focused Consultation

The diagnostic process is an essential first step in system intervention. As part of an intervention strategy, the diagnostic process can elevate system members' awareness of the current level of system functioning and can also serve as a model for a process of ongoing open communication and nondefensive appraisal. As such, it is important that all the techniques employed, be they interview, survey forms, or observations methods, respect the appropriate privacy of those within the system while at the same time encouraging open dialogue and collaborative ownership. Involving system members in the diagnostic process can reduce resistance and educate the members on the value and nature of ongoing evaluation and system adjustment. This last point is essential if the intervention is to continue to impact the organization with a preventive payout.

Although data can be collected through a variety of methods (e.g., survey, interview, content analysis), the one technique that the authors feel is essential to system-focused consultation is naturalistic observation.

Naturalistic Observation   Through unstructured observation the consultant can develop a sense of the unique structure, dynamics, and feel of a system. Such naturalistic, participant-observation procedures require special consideration to maximize the validity of the data observed (see Parsons, 1996; Parsons & Brown, 2002). For example,

1. *Distinguish fact from interpretations.* The consultant needs to clearly delineate what is truly observed from what she feels is meant by that phenomenon.

2. *Observe from a perspective of the system.* The consultant should attempt to place himself in the perspective of those involved, rather than imposing his values and perspective on the analysis.

3. *Separate supported from unsupported hypotheses.* The consultant needs to keep conclusions that are supported by the data separate from conjectures or unsupported hypotheses.

4. *Employ extensive record keeping.* It is useful for the consultant to attempt to observe and record everything. What might at first appear to have minimal relevance or significance may prove key to the understanding of some other important facet of the system's operations. As such, the consultant should take extensive notes on all that is observed.

5. *Concretize data.* The consultant should gather quotes, examples, work samples, products, and other artifacts that appear to clarify and support her observations and conclusions.

6. *Be respectful.* As a visitor to the system, it is important that the consultant demonstrate respect for the privacy of those she observes and therefore treat all data collected with appropriate professional sensitivity and consideration of confidentiality. Operating as an ethical, respectful observer should take precedent over data collection.

SYSTEM-FOCUSED CONSULTATION: INTERVENTION AND PREVENTION

With a systems approach it is very likely that the consultant may discover numerous places in which intervention could prove useful. Selecting the target(s) to approach and the technique(s) to employ must take into consideration the specific characteristics of the system. The selection of the intervention target and approach must be guided by the unique needs, requirements, and resources of the part of the system targeted for intervention (e.g., personnel, policy, structure).

General Guidelines

With the realization that all intervention needs to be system specific as a backdrop to the following discussion, the consultant operating within a system-focused model may find the following general guidelines useful in the development of an intervention plan.

1. **Use diagnostic data as an intervention step.** Interventions that maximize diagnostic data should be used first when the situations are not completely known to the consultant or consultee.

2. **Interventions need to be understandable and acceptable.** It is important that the consultee or the parties responsible for implementing and maintaining the intervention understand the intervention and embrace the potential value of this intervention.

3. **Consider the success potential.** Although research is still needed to validate the effectiveness of the various techniques, strategies, or interventions that are possible, some interventions do have empirical support for their effectiveness in particular situations. It is prudent to

employ these proven approaches rather than unproven or untested approaches. Interventions should be prioritized in terms of expected effectiveness or to maximize effectiveness.

4. **Consider the efficiency potential.** Interventions should be ordered in a way to better use the current organizational resources (e.g., time, money, energy). From this perspective, interventions should be ordered in a way to maximize the speed with which the system attains organizational goals.

5. **Consider the cost of intervention.** All other things equal, the approach that requires the least expenditure of resources (personal and system) should be considered. Because resistance may be increased as a function of resource expenditure, the system-focused consultant would be wise to select the appropriate and least-disruptive form of intervention. The position taken here is that interventions that minimize psychological and organizational strain should take priority.

6. **Consider the cost of impact.** The interdependence of the various components of a system means that impacting one will surely affect others. As such, the selection of an intervention should also be done with consideration to the possible impacts on other parts of the system (Davis & Sandoval, 1991). The consultant must attempt to be mindful of this potential for multiple affects and where possible inform those involved within the system of this possibility. The consultant needs to be concerned that improvement in one area does not have a negative effect in another area. Interventions that minimize such cost of impact should be considered first.

7. **Seek longevity and spread of impact.** Again, all things equal, an intervention of choice is one that will have a great spread of effect. Priority should be given to interventions that not only impact this client or consultee but also may impact other and future such individuals or lead to preventive changes.

Using these guidelines as a backdrop, the following three classes of system intervention will be presented.

1. The use of data gathering and feedback, as intervention
2. Fine-tuning current system structures and processes
3. Changing the system's character and culture

Feedback: The First Level of Intervention

Often the problem presented by the consultee has not been resolved simply because those involved really do not have a clear picture of the nature of the problem. This lack of clarity may be a function of their limited or biased perspective on the nature of the problem or the very fact that they lack the information needed to clearly understand the problem and thus the possible resolutions. Therefore, an essential first step to system intervention is for the consultant to provide a clear, focused view of the nature of the problem and its likely causes. Often this first step is sufficient in and of itself to be remedial.

This was the situation at a high school when student medical records suddenly disappeared from the central office files. Those teachers who needed access to those records to ensure accurate student accommodations were perplexed and angry. When the principal was asked for an explanation, he embarrassingly informed the teachers that he forget to inform them of the new Health Insurance Portability and Accountability Act (HIPAA) regulations that required all student medical records to be private and secured. As a result of these regulations, the school nurse had moved all the records to locked filing cabinets in the school infirmary. Teachers who required access to this information on a "need to know" basis would have to get prior parental consent. The teachers were glad to comply with the new procedures as long as they could still retain access to important student information.

Simply identifying the disparity of documentation approaches and communicating the reason for the change was sufficient to reduce the negativity and strain encountered. No additional interventions were required.

Under these types of situations where a particular subgroup or unit of a system is in crises simply because it lacks the information and knowledge about a process or practice within the system, the provision of feedback can be a sufficient form of intervention. Even in those situations where data collection is but the first step of a more elaborate intervention plan, it does still mark the beginning of an action phase of consulting.

Preparing for Feedback   Once the data is collected, its value as both an informative and formative (in terms of facilitating the system's effort to adjust) vehicle is dependent on the consultant's ability to convey these data to those empowered to take action. The process of data feedback is therefore a very important and sensitive part of the system-focused intervention process.

The primary goal for data feedback is to reach consensus regarding those components or aspects of the organization that appear to be interfering with goal achievement. Once such consensus has been achieved, the consultant needs to facilitate the members' commitment to action. The last phase assists those in power to provide feedback of the discovery process and the plan of action to all organizational membership who have participated in the process (Beer & Spector, 1993). This feedback not only encourages additional validation and provides support for the process (closure) but also strengthens commitment via public disclosure.

In structuring data collection so that it can be useful as an intervention process, the system-focused consultant should consider each of the following guidelines.

1. **Keep it focused.** The consultant should narrow the diagnostic process, condensing the data to what is both important and usable by those within the system.

2. **Employ everyday language.** To be useful, the data collected needs to be translatable into action by those within the system. Using language understandable to those within the system can facilitate this process.

3. **Collaborate in design and implementation.** Joint ownership will prove essential if the consultant expects the members of the system to accept the implications and direction provided by the data.

4. **Include data on the specific problem and system response.** Block (1981) noted that if adjustments are to be effective, they should consider not only the nature of the problem itself, but also how the system is functioning or managing the problem.

5. **Avoid collusion.** The role of the consultant is to remain an objective reporter of the data. It is important for the consultant not to support a stance that reduces the system's ability to solve the problem. As Block (1981) noted, if the issues are essential—even if they are sensitive and to this point avoided by the consultee—it is important that the consultant not collude with their resistance by failing to focus on them as well.

6. **Confirm and confront.** The skilled consultant will present the data in ways that reduces consultee resistance and maximizes the consultee's ability to productively respond. This requires a skillful blending of feedback that is both confirming and confronting.

   The consultant should provide data that confirms those things the system is doing well. While confirming those aspects of the system that are functional, the consultant needs to also point out those things within the system that are self-defeating. The consultant must avoid protecting the consultee from the reality reflected in the data.

The Process of Providing and Managing the Feedback   Feedback of the data can be handled exclusively by the consultant, and there are times when such feedback may, at least initially, need to fall within the domain of the consultant. However, to maximize system involvement and ownership, it is useful, when possible, to engage a system representative (supervisor, administrator, master teacher, etc.) in copresenting the feedback. One process, the waterfall procedure, has been used to facilitate such involvement and has been presented by this author and others (Meyers, Parsons, & Martin, 1979). In this procedure the data is presented to small groups consisting of a top administrator and his/her immediate subordinates, proceeding from top of the organizations structure to the bottom. The waterfall procedure would have those people who were subordinates in the first meeting provide feedback to their subordinates in the second meeting and so on until all members have received feedback (Meyers, Parsons, & Martin, 1979).

Regardless of the method employed, it is essential that the consultant maintain a level of control over the feedback. For the data to prove useful, it needs to be structured and delivered in a clear, cogent, and focused manner. One sequence of presentation that has been found useful is the following.

1. Restate the original reason for the consultant's involvement.

2. Set the tone for this feedback session by structuring the meeting agenda.

3. Provide data descriptively (not interpretatively).

4. Provide data interpretation (referring back to summarized data for support).

5. Present recommendations referring to the specific data points addressed.

6. Solicit reaction to data. Keep control and focus on the data, not the interpretation or recommendation that will be discussed later.

7. Seek reaction to recommendations. It is important to have those attending consider the implications to their own unit or their own role and functioning.

8. Review purpose (originally) and seek feedback if the process is meeting the consultee's needs and specification of the original contract.

9. Discuss decision to proceed and develop initial next step(s), having each of those attending consider the steps they can and/or need to take.

10. Plan follow-up and provide support and encouragement for what they are doing and what they can do.

Fine-Tuning: A Second Level of Intervention

A second level of intervention involves making adjustments to the existing structures and processes within the system. There are situations in which the system has the processes and structures needed for effective functioning. However, it is possible that these structures and processes may for some reason not be operating optimally. Under these conditions the consultant will attempt to facilitate system members' understanding of how and why the system is not working optimally and initiate steps to bring all system processes up to running order. For example, consider Case 12.1.

CASE 12.1   Fine-Tuning the Systems

A large suburban middle school was proud of its new technological advances. All the classrooms were wired for Internet and PowerPoint presentations. Those teachers who were trained in PowerPoint development and presentation began to use the new technology in their teaching. Shortly after PowerPoint presentations began to replace the traditional "chalk and talk" lectures, the teachers experienced behavior management problems with their students, especially those seated in the rear of the classrooms. Prior to this new instructional technology the teachers had effectively moved around the classroom, providing stimulus control over their students' behavior. The PowerPoint technology required the teachers to remain in the front of their classroom, unable to maintain and control the activity occurring in the back of the room. As some teachers abandoned this expensive, cutting-edge technology, the principal sought help from the district's director of technology. After the problem was explained, the director informed the principal about portable remotes that could be used by the teachers to control their electronic presentations from anywhere in their classroom. At a reasonable cost, each teacher could monitor and control their students' behavior while continuing to employ some of the newest instructional technology. A simple device fine-tuned a significant methodological advance.

The introduction of the remote into the technological armament of the teachers was a simple solution that fine-tuned the system to operate more effectively. When fine-tuning a system, there are many possible targets for such fine-tuning. Some of these targets require only minor adjustment, such as that of distributing electronic remotes, whereas others require a bit more preparation and energy, such as might be the case in developing electronic and Web-based curriculum materials that will actively involve students in the learning process. Even though the target for fine-tuning will be situation specific, three general areas (i.e., role definition, communication, and skill level) are often involved in the system's dysfunctionality and as such will be discussed as arenas for fine-tuning interventions.

Role Confusion/Role Conflict   As a system grows, it is possible that additional duties and responsibilities are either informally assigned to system members or simply fall through the cracks and are not assigned. Without clear lines of authority and responsibility, members may inadvertently cross role boundaries and either fail to perform needed functions, duplicate efforts, or more seriously offend another by operating within the realm of another's authority. The resulting frustration, inefficiency, or experienced antagonism will drain energy from system functioning. Thus, role confusion and/or role conflict, when it occurs, needs to be a target for a fine-tuning intervention.

A review of job definitions and delineation of responsibilities may be needed in situations where there is conflict over domains of authority or confusion about responsibilities and areas of accountabilities. In this situation role-defining and clarifying activities would be useful. For example, in a meeting comprising all the members involved in role confusion or conflict, the members may be invited to introduce the other members to their role title and responsibilities. Specifically, they are asked to identify and share: (a) one aspect of their current role that they find satisfactory and that they wish would remain the same, (b) one aspect of their role that is good but needs to be implemented in a different manner or to a greater extent, and finally (c) one aspect of their role that they would like to reduce or eliminate. The consultant's role is to facilitate the discussion, with the primary goal being to educate one another about the role each plays within the system. However, a secondary goal, depending on the nature of the conflict, would be the refining or, if needed, the redefining of the roles, with responsibilities shifting to make them more efficient and enjoyable to those occupying the roles.

Communication Processes   In reviewing the communication processes, the focus for the consultant is on how information flows within the system and between the system and the external environment (suprasystem). The goal for such a review would be the identification of the internal communication network and the communication network between the system and suprasystem. It should include a look both at the formal mechanisms (i.e., line and staff, organizational chart, and chain of command) as well as the informal processes by which information and feedback are exchanged and decisions made.

There are times when the system's method and/or mode of communication (e.g., via newsletter, morning announcements, memo, staff meetings) and/or the competency of those developing and delivering the communication is simply inadequate. Under these conditions, the consultant will attempt to introduce alternative modes of communication and/or increase the current level of communication skills through staff training. Exercise 12.4 can help to further clarify the way method and mode of communication could serve as a target for system-focused consultation.

EXERCISE 12.4

Fine-Tuning Communication Processes

Directions: This exercise is best completed with another or in a small group. For each of the following brief scenarios (a) identify the way in which the mode or method of communication is contributing to the manifested problem and (b) discuss how the communication processes can be fine-tuned to alleviate the problem.

Scenario I: Morning Announcements

In Marion Elementary School the announcements of activities and schedules for the day are presented immediately after the bell rings signifying the beginning of school. The announcements are read by a student and presented over the public address system. Students have complained about missing club meetings and sporting events because they "never heard the announcement," and teachers have noted the disruptive influence of some readers.

Scenario 2: The Weekly Meeting

A small mental health clinic has weekly meetings of all clinical staff and supervisors. The original purpose of the meetings had been to staff cases, receive supervision, and discuss therapeutic procedures. However, because of a number of organizational changes and the addition of many new clinical staff meetings, most of the weekly meetings goes to providing information about administrative details around telephone usage, procedures for completing insurance forms, reviewing staff schedules, and so on. Staff have complained about the lack of supervision and case staffing opportunities.

In addition to fine-tuning the communication processes so that they convey accurate information with relative ease and efficiency, as might be the need in each of the scenarios presented in Exercise 12.4, the system-focused consultant should also attempt to maximize the degree to which the system's communication is characterized by each of the following.

1. **Congruency of action to message.** The focus here is on the degree to which administrative actions parallel the official messages conveyed.

2. **Communication as dialogue.** The consultant assisting the system in its effort to fine-tune its communication processes may focus on the degree

to which internal communication is a two-way process. Assisting the system to engage in a dialogue with administrators trained in feedback techniques as well as techniques that encourage upward communications will facilitate the quality of communication.

3. **Face-to-face in form.** In order to increase accuracy of communication while also conveying messages of employee value, methods of face-to-face communication—especially between top administration and employees—should be emphasized. This may entail the inclusion of more face-to-face meetings rather than relying on printed forms of communication.

It is the authors' suggestion that consultants attempting to improve a system's communications serve as a facilitator, rather then simply providing a packaged program on communication. As a facilitator, the consultant would assist work teams and administrative groups to identify their difficulties with the communication processes and solve the various problems identified. The process nature of this intervention increases the likelihood of member ownership and motivation for implementation.

Sometimes the system's philosophy of decision making and communication needs to be challenged, and the mechanisms and processes supporting this philosophy need to be revamped. Under these conditions, the consultant is seeking a more involved form of intervention than that included here as fine-tuning. The goal under these conditions is not to simply fine-tune the delivery system but to reframe a new philosophy about communication and to develop or reconfigure the processes and mechanisms employed in the communication process. Such a major revamping will be discussed later, as a third level of intervention.

Skill Acquisition and Development The changing nature of education along with the impact of technological or regulatory shifts may require system members to develop new knowledge and/or skills. Similarly, the changing character of the internal population of the system as a result of expansion, retirement, or new hiring practices may place those in educational roles in which their teaching or classroom management skills may be inadequate. Under these conditions, training programs targeted to the development of specific competencies would be useful.

The consultant in this situation can take on a provisional role by directly offering the training experiences or operate more prescriptively directing those within the system responsible for such staff development to the resources available and the programs needed. A number of companies and professional organizations offer prepackaged training materials, but the use of such materials should be done with the following caveat.

For a program of skill development to be effective, it is important to identify the specific skills needing development and match the didactic and experiential material presented with that particular skill need. In addition to this obvious matching of program-to-audience need, the consultant should also attempt to match the program-to-audience resources.

Once the topic or area of skill development has been identified, it is useful for the consultant to attempt to assess the current level of competency as the entry point from which to provide the program of development. Without such a tailoring to the competency and needs of the audience, the consultant risks the possibility of underestimating the competency of those in attendance and presenting what is already known and practiced, rather than what is needed. Conversely, without an accurate understanding of the current level of competence, the consultant may overestimate audience entry-level skills and thus begin training at a level too advanced to be useful.

In addition to providing programs that are tailored to audience need and skill level, the consultant needs to employ principles and practice of good pedagogy.

As a general guideline, programs aimed at skill training should include each of the following elements.

1. *Learning objectives:* Provide objectives that will help the participants focus on the purpose of the training.

2. *Overview:* Provide an overview to the presentation, highlighting steps or stages to be followed.

3. *Didactic presentations:* Basic information should be organized and presented clearly and simply. Use familiar terms, relevant examples, and illustrations.

4. *Modeling:* The principles and skills presented should be modeled—either via film, PowerPoint presentation, or in vivo demonstration—and analyzed and discussed.

5. *Guided practice:* In order to move beyond simple comprehension to skill development, a sequence of guided practice exercises need to be employed.

6. *Corrective feedback:* For the practice to be effective, the participant needs to have available a coach or mentor to monitor the practice response and give clear, concrete, corrective feedback when needed.

7. *Independent practice and self-monitoring techniques:* Participants need to be encouraged to apply the new skills on their own within the work setting. In addition to practicing the skills, the participants need to develop methods for self-monitoring the adequacy of their application as a method for maintaining the learning and skill development outside the formal training program.

Changing the Character and Culture of a System: The Third Level of Intervention

It is possible that the problems experienced within the school are a direct reflection of the basic character and culture of that system. As noted previously, patterns of behavior found within a system arise from the underlying culture (i.e., values and assumptions) of that organization. Therefore, when problematic patterns are noted, it may be the basic values, assumptions, or culture of the system that need to be addressed (Beers & Spector, 1993). Opening a system and moving a system to change its fundamental character is far from an easy process and requires much knowledge and skill on the part of the consultant.

Opening a System to Change When improving an organization's effectiveness necessitates changes to the system's structure, processes, basic character, and configuration, resistance is to be expected. As we pointed out in chapter 4, organizations are geared to avoid, deflect, and defend the culture and the patterns of behavior embedded within its culture (Argyris, 1996) and as such resist change. Also it should be noted that this resistance to change increases as systems age and move toward entropy. Knowing what to expect and how to work within a system's reaction to change may assist the consultant in his level three intervention. A somewhat classic model that can be used to guide this process of opening a system is that offered by Kurt Lewin (1958).

Lewin (1958) suggested that change occurs in three phases—unfreezing the system, moving the system (change), and refreezing the system. Each is discussed next.

Unfreezing the System A system's fundamental character and culture is perceived by the members as a valid condition of the organization, created and maintained by those currently operating within the system. As such, the first task that a consultant needs to address when attempting to change the culture of a system is to reduce system resistance by getting the system to accept both the diagnosis and the need for such a level of system intervention.

The consultant can reduce resistance and begin to "unfreeze" the system by assisting the members of the organization to see that although the way things "were done" was useful, the reality is that the environment (internal and/or external) has changed dramatically, and these ways are no longer as useful to providers or consumers. An essential first step in unfreezing the system is to heighten the members' awareness of their current form of functioning and the ineffectiveness of this approach. To achieve this heightened awareness requires that the consultant gain and maintain the system's commitment to the diagnostic process and outcome and provide appropriate data collection and feedback. The goal is to sensitize the system to the need to change, a need to modify its current structure and processes, to more effectively achieve its goals and fulfill its mission.

Quite often the role of the consultant during this unfreezing stage of system change is to be somewhat countercultural. The process of asking questions and collecting data around issues that others within the system had taken for granted is the beginning of this counterculture response. It is as if the consultant is willing to both ask questions about the "emperor's new clothes" and report the data that suggest the clothes are nonexistent. Although such data reporting will not automatically change the character or culture of the organization, it is the beginning of the introduction of new observations, ideas, suggestions, or values not reflective of the operative culture.

Beyond the introduction of these new observations, ideas, suggestions, or values, for change to occur, the consultant, through collaborative dialogue, needs to move those empowered within the system to embrace these new views. To facilitate this process, it is important for the consultant to assist those in the system to see that adjustment in the way the system operates can lead to increased efficiency in this changed environment.

This last point (i.e., increasing efficiency) is essential to the process of reducing resistance and unfreezing the system. Beer, Eisenstat, and Spector (1990) noted that motivation to change is increased when the change process addresses the critical strategic tasks of the organization. That is, the consultant attempting to adjust the character or culture of a system needs to employ as his starting point the demonstration of the possibility of increased effectiveness once system adjustment has been made. Resistance will be reduced by increasing the organizational dissatisfaction with the status quo and the increased awareness of the connection between current behaviors and reduced effectiveness. Similarly, Schein (1985) suggested that assumptions can be altered by the introduction of new values (usually by top administration) and the experience of success attributed to them. Schein (1985) argued that if new values lead to successful outcomes then they will be maintained, and over time they will be taken for granted—thus becoming a core assumption and system norm. But this process is not conflict free. Hatch (1993), for example, noted that this process is fraught with conflict and dissonance. That is, if the new values take hold, they will at first be at odds with existing assumptions, and thus it could be assumed resistance will be experienced. But as success is experienced, the dissonance will diminish, and the new will become the standard.

Moving the System The second step in this process is the actual introduction of changes in the system's way of operating. This may involve the introduction of new expectations, job definitions, or skill applications at the level of the employee. It also could mean the development of a new structure or set of operating procedures. In some rare circumstances it may even involve the development of an entirely new system of operation.

Refreezing The final step in the process is what Lewin (1958) termed *refreezing*. This refreezing involves institutionalizing and thus stabilizing these changes. The institutionalization of these changes takes root when the organization's recruitment, training, and evaluation processes have been modified to reinforce the new philosophy and values. With these changes, support structures and processes will also be modified to reflect and service the new values and assumptions.

Refreezing begins with the public acceptance of the new structure and processes and continues through the inclusion of these changes into the formal documents of the system (e.g., including new organizational charts, job descriptions, procedures).

The process of moving from unfreezing through change to refreezing a change in a system's fundamental character and culture is exemplified by Exercise 12.5.

EXERCISE 12.5

A High School in Need of Change

Directions: The following exercise is most effectively completed by working either with another person or in a small group. Although many of the concepts and variables discussed within this chapter are present within the brief description of the case of the high school in need of change, your task is to focus on the following questions and concerns.

1. How did the systems trajectory contribute to the current experience of dysfunctionality?
2. How did the external environment contribute to the current problem?
3. Where did unfreezing start, and what stimulated the unfreezing?
4. Where is refreezing being evidenced?
5. What else do you feel could be done to move this system in the direction of increased adaptability and openness?

Case Description   The consultant was invited by the principal of a large metropolitan high school to come in to work specifically with one grade level that, according to the principal, was experiencing "extensive bickering, back-stabbing, and general infighting." Through discussion with the principal, the original focus of the problem was expanded to include all the teachers in the school.

The principal stated, "I know that the problem is most notable in the ninth grade, but really there is and has been for some time now increasing tension and antagonism among all the teachers across grades. In fact, I think there is a real significant overall drop in teacher morale and motivation. I am also very frustrated by the reduction in the quality of their teaching as well."

Through a process of direct interviews of the teachers, the consultant began to understand that the organization had been experiencing a number of significant changes in terms of staff composition and responsibility. Because of their declining enrollment and school budget, the system had reduced its instructional staff by 20% and its support and clerical staff by 30%. This reduction forced a realignment of task assignments, with instructional staff required to not only cover more hours but also perform some duties that had previously been assigned to other teachers or the support personnel. In some cases, teachers and even counselors were assigned to cover classes outside the boundary of their discipline. The increased workloads, the redefinition and blurring of instructional/staff lines, and the anticipation that things might get worse resulted in the identified symptoms of tension, hostility, and low morale.

After gathering additional data regarding the internal environment of the system, including information on its mission, philosophy, and previous modes of operation, the consultant gathered data regarding the external environment, providers, consumers, and their needs. What emerged from these data was that the current symptoms of those in the system, although directly attributable to the changes within the system, were actually a response to the system's inability to adapt to a changing external environment.

The history and current mission of this high school could be best described as providing a rigorous academic curriculum that prepares students for postsecondary educational success. Historically, well over 70% of this school's graduates went on to college, receiving significant financial support from their affluent, upper-middle-class parents. The strong academic orientation that emphasized educational success leading to a professional career reflected the cultural norm and values of this school.

In reviewing the population demographics, it became evident that the community had changed significantly over the past decade. As manufacturing and businesses moved to suburban and rural locations—or to other countries—employment followed suit, leaving only unemployment and low-wage jobs. Families and neighborhoods disintegrated into poverty, with desperation and pessimism replacing pride and the expectation for upward mobility. A culture so recently imbued with strong family values, diligent work ethic, high regard for education, and opportunity for all had been prostrated by poverty, drugs, violence, and decay. Racial and ethnic minorities constituted the diverse demographic that attended this high school. Although some students, such as those recently emigrated from Korea, still viewed academic success as the engine for upward mobility, far too many students placed education at the bottom of their priorities. With this high school clutching its historical mission, it daily confronted a culture that characterized the antithesis of that mission.

The most glaring challenge for the teachers was the delivery of academic processes (curriculum, support services) that were suitable to student achievement and motivation. With high rates of truancy and poor homework completion, many students were unable to meet even modest academic achievement. Moreover, with the mandate for full inclusion, special needs students were sitting in classrooms lost, bewildered, and defeated. Teachers reported that custodial care was the best that they could offer these students. As teacher turnover rates increased and more teachers exercised their sick and personal days, the principal was forced to reassign teachers and increase class sizes. This problem was particularly acute in the ninth grade due to the larger number of introductory and general education requirements.

In reviewing their systems-analysis data, it became very clear to the consultant and school principal that the difficulty currently experienced was not simply the result of some disgruntled and adversarial teachers. The principal encapsulated the problem best when he said, "Our problem is that we are too damn rigid and nonadaptable. Our kids are vastly different then they were, and yet we expect to teach and motivate them in the old ways that worked in the past." This rigid, inflexible school, with many of the symptoms of a system in entropy, was not responsive to its changing environment. If not addressed soon, it would cause the demise of the school. The most efficient approach (while at the same time perhaps the most difficult) was for the consultant to assist the system to open its boundaries to the demands and opportunities presented by the new external environment and to adjust its own internal environment (i.e., structure and processes) to be responsive to this changing consumer population.

The intent of the data feedback was not to force the system to change its original mission but rather to invite those within the system to consider the relationship between their current mission, history of previous practice, and the needs of the consumers and providers. Using the data collected, the consultant and principal formed a task force of educators and interested parents with the following.

1. Identify the specific ways the mission of the organization is manifested in its structures and day-to-day processes.

2. Review the demographics and needs of its existing consumer population.

3. Identify those areas within the system's culture, as reflected in the structures and processes operating, that appear no longer useful or efficient, given the changing external environment.

4. Identify those aspects of the organization's mission, philosophy, structures, and processes that remain useful, even in light of the changing external environment.

This process of data feedback and analysis provided the School Improvement Task Force with a clear understanding that maintaining the current approach would lead to further increases in academic failure and teacher dissatisfaction and as such, lead to dismantling or takeover by the government or private sector. This awareness helped the members accept the need for fundamental change and increased their willingness to undergo the draining process that such change would entail.

As a result of the data collected, the ad hoc task force was expanded into a strategic task force with inclusion of representatives from the key consumer and provider groups. The charge for this task force was to begin to identify strategies for improving the school's efficiency and effectiveness. The consultant introduced a force-field model (see chapter 11) for identifying

1. The system's goals

2. The forces (internal and external) that would facilitate achievement of those goals

3. The forces (internal and external) that would inhibit achievement of those goals

4. Specific strategies for maximizing the facilitating forces and reducing the inhibiting forces.

With the realization that the current curriculum, teaching methodology, and student and teacher support services needed to be reevaluated and reconfigured, the task force took on its charge.

Committing to the change based on empirical data on their "new" consumer population, their needs, values, and culture resulted in a number of significant structural and process changes. Class sizes were reduced and wrap-around services were contracted for special needs students both within and outside the classroom. Attendance policies were clearly communicated and strictly enforced. Referent community leaders were enlisted to serve on specific task forces that addressed parental involvement in education, student motivation and discipline, and the establishment of a realistic vocational counseling program. Teachers were teamed to work on specific subjects with specific students with the authority and resources to tailor their curriculum and teaching methodology to the needs and abilities of those students. And finally, academic assessment and promotion were based on criterion-referenced testing instead of the norm-referenced assessment used previously.

The consultant in this case believed that he should not only assist the consultee by addressing the presenting problem (i.e., tension and low morale) but should also do so in a way that would leave the consultee better able to cope in the future. With this preventive focus in mind, the consultant assisted the system to institute and formalize the School Improvement Task Force. Moving the system from a long-range planning model to a more responsive, strategic planning focus would keep the system more open to the changing character of the internal and external environment and provide a structure and process that would facilitate ongoing adaptation to these changes.

SUMMARY

System-Focused Consultation:
When the System Is the Problem

The need to understand the nature and dynamic of the system within which a consultant is working is a given, if for no other reason than to ensure that the recommendations and or interventions proposed are compatible to the culture of that system. However, this chapter attempted to demonstrate that the need to understand the role and influence of the system extends far beyond this concern for treatment compatibility. In this chapter, situations in which what was identified as the client's problematic behavior was only a symptom of a larger, more pervasive system problem were highlighted. It was proposed that under these conditions all attempts to remedy the client behavior will prove ineffective unless the system problem is identified and remedied.

As should be obvious from this chapter, it is the authors' belief that system-focused consultation, although serving as the vehicle for a consultant to have the broadest remedial and preventive influence, is also one of the most demanding and time-involving forms of consultation. It is a focus for consultation that requires special diagnostic and intervention knowledge and skill. To assist the consultant seeking to increase his/her ability to engage in system-focused consultation, this chapter provided a review of the unique dynamics of a system's culture, offered a model for organizing the diagnostic information essential to understanding a system, and suggested a general model of introducing change to a system.

System Diagnosis

Specifically, the position presented here is that diagnosis can either be narrow, involving a quick look at the easily identified trouble spots in an organization, or a more in-depth analysis of the intricate workings of the system. The bias presented within this text, however, is that for change to be long term and permanent, a more systematic review of the interactivity and interdependence of the various elements, structures, processes, and forces will be necessary. The model offered allows for multiple foci for analysis and multiple skills and techniques to be employed. But regardless of the focus or the technique, system analysis requires that the consultant have a biographer's discipline, perseverance, and an eye for detail, as well as the therapist's insight, intuition, and interpersonal skills.

System-Focused Consultation:
Intervention and Prevention

In closing the chapter, a model and detailed explanation of three classes or levels of system intervention was presented, including (a) the use of data gathering and feedback as intervention, (b) fine-tuning current system structures and processes, and (c) changing the system's character and culture. Although the depth of change required varied across the three levels, for each the task of the consultant remained the same. Through a process of opening the system to change (unfreeze), introducing the innovation (movement), and attempting to institutionalize or stabilize the change (refreeze), the system-focused consultant was attempting to not only remediate the presenting problem but also assisting the system to increase its adaptability and flexibility, thus making it more responsive to current and future internal and external demands.

IMPORTANT TERMS

Artifacts

Basic assumptions

Bureaucratic machine model

Community-oriented programs environment scale

Corrective feedback

Culture

Feedback

Fine-tuning

Guided practice

Independent practice and self-monitoring

Learning objectives

Moving the system

Naturalistic observation

Overview

Refreezing the system

System

System-focused consultation

System's elements

Unfreezing the system

Values

SUGGESTED READINGS

Bogler, R. (2002). Changing schools in changing times: Implications for educational leadership. *International Journal of Educational Reform, 11*(3), 216–227.

Coglan, D. (2002). Facilitating learning and change: Perspectives on the helping process. *Organization Development Journal, 20*(2), 116–120.

Good, T. L., Wiley, A. R., Thomas, R. E., Stewart, E., McCoy, J., Kloos, B., Hunt, G. D., Moore, T., & Rappaport, J. (1997). Bridging the gap between schools and community: Organizing for family involvement in a low-income neighborhood. *Journal of Educational & Psychological Consultation, 8*(3), 277–297.

Leithwood, K. (Ed.). (2000). *Understanding schools as intelligent systems.* Stamford, CT: JAI Press.

Parsons, R. D., & Brown, K. S. (2002). *Teacher as reflective practitioner and action researcher.* Belmont, CA: Wadsworth.

Williams, W. W. (2003). Altering the structure and culture of American public schools. *Phi Delta Kappan, 84*(8), 606–616.

WEB SITES

Center for Strategic Management: Experts in business leadership, strategic planning, organizational development, strategic change, systems thinking/learning, and leadership development using our systems thinking approach. www.csmintl.premierdomain.com

Organizational Development: Publishers' clearinghouse for organizational development tools, all based on systems thinking resources. Focusing on the concepts and tools in the development and strategic management fields. www.systemsthinkingpress.com

School Change Collaborative: National association in support of school change. www.nwrel.org/scpd/natspec/coldev.html

Building School Capacity: Providing districts with systemic support for the process of change. www.ed.gov/pubs/turning/capacity.html

REFERENCES

Alderfer, C. P., & Brown, L. D. (1975). *Learning from changing: Organizational diagnosis and development.* Beverly Hills, CA: Sage.

Aplin, J. C. (1978). Structural change versus behavioral change. *The Personnel and Guidance Journal, 56,* 407–411.

Argyris, C. (1996). Unlocking defensive reasoning. *Across the Board, 36*(3), 18–19.

Argyris, C. (1970). *Intervention theory and method: A behavioral science view.* Reading, MA: Addison-Wesley.

Beckhard, R. (1969). *Organization development: Strategies and models.* Reading, MA: Addison-Wesley.

Beer, M., Eisenstat, R. E., & Spector, B. (1990). *The critical path to corporate renewal.* Boston: Harvard Business School Press.

Beer, M., & Spector, B. (1993). Organizational diagnosis: Its role in organizational learning. *Journal of Counseling & Development, 71,* 642–650.

Block, P. (1981). *Flawless consulting.* San Diego, CA: Pfeiffer & Comp.

Borum, F., & Pedersen, J. S. (1990). Understanding the IT people, the subcultures and the implications for management of technology. In F. Borum, A. L. Friedman, M. Monsted, J. S. Pedersen, & M. Risberg (Eds.), *Social dynamics of the IT field: The case of Denmark* (pp. 105–120). Berlin: Walter de Gruyter.

Davis, J. M., & Sandoval, J. (1991). A pragmatic framework for systems-oriented consultation. *Journal of Educational and Psychological Consultation, 2*(3), 201–216.

Gagliardi, P. (Ed.). (1990). *Symbols and artifacts: Views of the corporate landscape.* Berlin: Walter de Gruyter.

Gallessich, J. (1974). Training the school psychologist for consultation. *Journal of School Psychology, 12,* 138–149.

Gallessich, J. (1978). Consultation training program for school counselors. *Counselor Education and Supervision, 18*(2), 100–108.

Guzzo, A., Jette, R. D., & Katzell, R. A. (1985). The effects of psychologically based intervention programs on worker productivity: A meta-analysis. *Personal Psychology, 38*(2), 275–291.

Gysbers, N. C., & Henderson, P. (2000). *Developing and managing your school guidance program* (3rd ed.). Alexandria, VA: American Association for Counseling and Development.

Hatch, M. J. (1993). The dynamics of organizational culture. *Academy of Management Review, 18*(4), 657–693.

Krehbiel, L. E., & Strange, C. C. (1991). "Checking the truth": The case of Earlham College. In G. Kuh & J. Schuh (Eds.), *The role and contributions of student affairs at involving colleges* (pp. 148–167). Washington, DC: National Association of Student Personnel Administrators.

Kuh, G. D. (1993). Appraising the character of a college. *Journal of Counseling and Development, 71,* 661–667.

Kuh, G. D., Schuh, J. H., Whitt, E. J., Andreas, R. E., Lyons, J. W., Strange, C. C., Krehbiel, L. E., & MacKay, K. A. (1991). *Involving colleges: Successful approaches to fostering student learning and development outside the classroom.* San Francisco: Jossey-Bass.

Kuh, G. D., & Whitt, E. J. (1988). *The invisible tapestry: Culture in American colleges and universities.* (AAHE-ERIC/Higher Education Report, No. 1). Washington, DC: American Association for Higher Education.

Lewin, K. (1958). Group decisions and social change. In E. E. Maccoby, T. M. Newcomb, & E. L. Hartley (Eds.), *Readings in social psychology* (pp. 459–473). New York: Holt, Rinehart & Winston.

Meyers, J., Parsons, R. D., & Martin, R. (1979). *Mental health consultation in schools.* San Francisco: Jossey-Bass.

Nadler, D. A. (1977). *Feedback and organization development: Using data based methods.* Reading, MA: Addison-Wesley.

Parsons, R. D. (1996). *The skilled consultant.* Needham Heights, MA: Allyn & Bacon.

Parsons, R. D., & Brown, K. S. (2002). *Teacher as reflective practitioner and action researcher.* Belmont, CA: Wadsworth Publications.

Parsons, R., & Meyers, J. (1984). *Developing consultation skills.* San Francisco: Jossey-Bass.

Pederson, J. S. (1991). *Continuity and change: Central perspectives on organizational change and transformation in information technology firms* (Ph.D. Series 2.91 Samfundslitteratur). Copenhagen, Denmark: Copenhagen Business School, Institute of Organization and Industrial Sociology.

Ridley, C. R., & Mendoze, D. W. (1993). Putting organizational effectivenss into practice: The preeminent consultation task. *Journal of Counseling & Development, 72*(2), 168–177.

Schein, E. H. (1981). Does Japanese management style have a message for American managers? *Sloan Management Review, 23*(1), 55–68.

Schein, E. H. (1983). The role of the founder in creating organizational culture. *Organizational Dynamics, 12*(1), 13–28.

Schein, E. H. (1984). Coming to a new awareness of organizational culture. *Sloan Management Review, 25*(2), 3–16.

Schein, E. H. (1985). *Organizational culture and leadership*. San Francisco: Jossey-Bass.

Schein, E. H. (1990). Organizational culture. *American Psychologist, 45*, 109–119.

Schein, E. H. (1991). Process consultation. *Consulting Psychology Bulletin, 43*, 16–18.

Schein, E. H. (2003). Five traps for consulting psychologists: Or, how I learned to take culture seriously. *Consulting Psychology Journal, 55*(2) 75–83.

Turner, B. A. (Ed.). (1990). *Organizational symbolism*. Berlin: Walter de Gruyter.

Van Maanen, J., & Barley, S. R. (1985). Cultural organization: Fragments of a theory. In P. Frost, L. Moore, M. Louis, C. Lundberg, & J. Martin (Eds.), *Organizational culture* (pp. 31–54). Beverley Hills, CA: Sage.

Waterman, R. H., Jr., Peters, T. J., & Phillips, J. R. (1980). Structure is not organization. *Busines Horizon, 23*, 14–26.

Welzenbach, L. F. (Ed.). (1982). *College and university business administration*. Washington, DC: National Association for College and University Business Officers.

Whitt, E. J., & Kuh, G. D. (1991). Qualitative research in higher education: A team approach to multiple site investigation. *Review of Higher Education, 14*, 317–337.

Wittmer, J. (Ed.). (2000). *Managing your school guidance program: K–12 developmental strategies* (2nd ed.). Minneapolis, MN: Educational Media Corp.

Wynn, L. C., McDaniel, S. H., & Weber, T. T. H. (1986). *Systems consultation: A new perspective for family therapy*. New York: Guilford Press.

Young, E. (1989). On the naming of the rose: Interest and multiple meanings as elements of organizational culture. *Organization Studies, 10*, 187–206.

13

◦~◦

Ethical Concerns
and Considerations

I know Dr. Jamison is dying to know more about Ellen's
home situation, and actually some of this information may help us
to work more effectively with Ellen, but I don't know if . . .

The hesitancy expressed by Mr. Thomas, the consultant in our opening scenario, reveals not just a question but an ethical concern that confronts many school counselor–consultants as they decide what and to whom information may be revealed. Issues of confidentiality, client informed consent, professional competence, and boundaries are not new to those in school counseling. However, these issues, along with all of those issues involved in the practice and delivery of counseling services within the school, take on an added dimension when viewed from the triadic relationship found in consultation.

Consider the issues and concerns confronting the consultant depicted in the following brief scenario of a first-grade teacher seeking some assistance from the school counselor. Pat, the school counselor, was requested to assist Bob with one of his first-grade students, Alice. According to Bob, Alice is quite an active child and appears to be either unable or unwilling to follow the classroom rules. Bob was very concerned about coming to Pat because he was a first-year teacher and was afraid that perhaps his needing help may be perceived by the principal as a sign of incompetence. In discussing the situation further, Pat, the counselor–consultant, discovered that Bob employed his form of time-out. According to Bob, anytime Alice misbehaves, he would have her stand in the back of the room facing a blank wall. Bob has noted that even if he has her stand for an hour, it doesn't appear to change her behavior, and he is at his wit's end.

Asking for assistance on a classroom management issue appears to be straightforward enough, but with more information, what appears to be a simple matter is revealed to be packed with a number of issues that should raise a counselor–consultant's ethical concerns. In responding to the request and the information ascertained about the previous methods employed, the consultant will need to make a number of ethical decisions around issues, such as: Who is the client? What is the responsibility of the consultant to the child's welfare and safety? What is the consultant's responsibility and ethical response to the use of this form of time-out? What are the limits of confidentiality? What values and possible value conflicts may exist between the consultant, the consultee, and the system (i.e., the principal), and how will these impact the consultant's response?

As is suggested by the brief scenario, school counselors working from a consultation mode of service delivery can face numerous ethical issues in their delivery of services. Further, the unique nature of consultation and the consultation relationship often makes the resolution of these ethical concerns somewhat more complex than might be the case in the more traditional direct-service model of helping. The triadic nature of consultation, the possibility of multiple clients, and the issues surrounding advocacy and innovation offer many unique ethical challenges for the consultant (Dougherty, 1992).

This chapter will highlight a number of these unique ethical challenges for the school counselor functioning in the role of consultant. However, it should be noted that the discussion that follows and the concerns raised are not intended to be the definitive, all-inclusive statement on the issue of ethics in consultation practice. What follows is simply one attempt to sensitize the counselor–consultant to the unique ethical challenges potentially encountered in the practice of consultation in the schools.

CHAPTER OBJECTIVES

After completing this chapter, the reader should be able to

1. Describe the need for the ethical consultant to: (a) be competent and skilled, (b) be aware of his/her own operative values, and (c) demonstrate cultural awareness and sensitivity
2. Explain the ethical concerns and considerations involved with: (a) establishing and maintaining confidentiality, (b) gaining informed consent, (c) maintaining professional boundaries, and (d) utilizing influence and power within the consultation relationship

3. Describe the ethical issues involved in: (a) the identification of the client in a consultation process, (b) the utilization of efficient and effective treatment procedures, and (c) the need for consultants to demonstrate accountability

ETHICS AND STANDARDS OF PRACTICE: GUIDES, NOT FIXED DIRECTIVES

As a first guide to the ethical practice of consultation, it is recommended that the reader become familiar with the principles of practice and codes of ethics put forth by the American Counseling Association (ACA) (1995, 1998). As you review these codes of practice, it is important to remember that they are developed as guidelines for practice. They are not written as, nor intended to be, clear-cut absolute recipes or directives for action. The guidelines are provided so that each individual can regulate her own behavior. Because of the generality of these guidelines there may be instances and experiences encountered by the counselor–consultant that do not neatly fall into any one guideline. As such, decisions regarding one's professional behavior will ultimately depend on the personal values and ethics of the individual counselor–consultant.

A second general recommendation for the ethical consultant, therefore, is for the counselor–consultant to have and maintain access to updated professional literature, information, continuing education, peer interaction, and supervision. It is through the ongoing professional dialogue around issues of common concern, that judgments become articulated and clarified and professional practice standards take shape. Resources that will help you in your efforts to keep current within the profession will be found at the end of this chapter.

Beyond these two very general guidelines are a number of more specific concerns addressing issues tied to the characteristics and training of the consultant, the nature of the consultation relationship, and the who and how of consultation. Each will be discussed in some detail.

BASIC ETHICAL ISSUES TARGETING THE COUNSELOR AS CONSULTANT

Consultant Competence

A fundamental ethical principle with which all professional groups agree is that a helper must be aware of the limitations of her own professional competence and not exceed those limitations in the delivery of his/her service. For example, the American Counseling Association's *Code of Ethics and Standards of Practice* (1995) notes: "Counselors are reasonably certain that they have or the organization represented has the necessary competencies and resources for giving the kind of consulting services needed and the appropriate referral resources available" (ACA, 1995, D.2.b.).

The school counselor–consultant needs to guard against engaging in areas of service for which he is ill prepared. Working in a school counseling office, the counselor–consultant may find herself free of mentors, supervisors, or even peers. In this environment, with the pressing request for service, it may be difficult to either say no to the request or to seek support and assistance as one moves into new areas of practice. When the problem is beyond the scope of the counselor–consultant's competency, saying "no" and/or seeking support is the only ethical response.

This concern over professional competency is one that is felt and expressed in many areas of the helping professions. However, it is perhaps even more of an issue in the area of consultation because the specific activities, skills, and competencies deemed essential to consultation are simply not universally defined. The school counselor–consultant needs to conscientiously seek ongoing appropriate education, training, and supervision, and to practice within defensible ethical parameters. Given this guideline of competence, it can be suggested that the ethical consultant will

1. Know and embrace the limits to her competence

2. Seek ongoing training and supervision

3. Know when to seek support and consultation from a colleague

4. Make referrals to another counselor–consultant when the needs of the consultee and client will be best served through that referral

Consultant Values

According to Warwick and Kelman (1973), ". . . ethical responsibility requires a full consideration of the process and probable consequences of intervention in the light of set of guiding values" (p. 416). And although it could be argued that the guiding values referred to are those explicated in the professional code of ethics, it is also true that the professional counselor–consultant needs to be aware of the impact that his own personal values have in the professional decisions he makes (Parsons, 2001). Younggren (1993), for example, found that helper value systems can influence the helper's choice of goals, strategies, and even topics discussed.

Because the counselor–consultant is entering a situation in which numerous parties (consultee, client, system-units) will be involved, conflict of values is to be expected. In being sensitive to the value of the diversity to be encountered, a consultant must first be aware of his own operating values and how these operate to influence his decisions as a consultant. To assume a consultant can be value free or to simply attempt to ignore the role played by values within the practice of consultation could be "naive at best, and from an ethical perspective, dangerous" (Newman, 1993 p. 151). Further, to ignore the possibility of the imposition of these values would be in direct violation of the American Counseling Association's *Code of Ethics* (ACA, 1995, A.5.b). Thus, for Pat, the consultant in the brief illustration, her personal values regarding the use of inappropriate time-out as an approach to motivation need to be identified and clarified, as these may influence her own thinking and decision making within this consult. It is an ethical imperative that the practicing consultant clarify and where possible articulate his personal and professional values and the role these may play in the consultative process.

Although the specific values to be clarified will most often be defined from within a specific context, a first step to such clarification may be to simply begin to identify the values that motivate one's desire to be a counselor–consultant. Exercise 13.1 provides as a first step to such clarification.

EXERCISE 13.1

Identifying Operative Values

Directions: Although it may be hard for you to anticipate the type of consultee problems you will be invited to work with and thus hard to determine how your values may help or hinder your effectiveness, Exercise 13.1 is provided to assist you to at least begin this process of self-awareness of values and bias. As with each of the exercises, it is suggested you respond to the items presented and discuss your response with your colleagues, mentors, or classmates. This will be a two-part exercise.

Part 1: For each of the following identify your belief, your attitude, or your value about the issue presented.

- Equality of genders
- The need and value of unions
- Children's rights
- The recreational use of drugs
- The use of the "carrot" and/or "stick" as motivators
- The Horatio Alger viewpoint of pulling yourself up by your bootstraps
- The trustworthiness of people
- Inclusion (of those with special needs into the workplace and/or classroom)
- Alternative lifestyles
- The absolute right of privacy
- The value of competition versus cooperation
- The importance of power

Part 2: Through personal reflection and discussion of your responses to Part 1, identify those items in Part 1 for which you have strong opinions, attitudes, or values. Next identify types of consultee problems or consultee systems for which some of these values may hinder your ability to remain objective, nonjudgmental, and collaborative. For example, how might a consultant, who has very strong opinions about a women's need to place the role of mother and wife before that of her professional career, work with a young, bright senior in high school who is sharing her plan to not only have a family someday but be the CEO of a major corporation? Or what impact might the consultant's strong belief in inclusion of children with special needs into the regular classroom have on his ability to collaborate with a regular classroom teacher who is expressing having difficulty adapting her curriculum to a student with special needs?

The existence and impact of personal and professional values cannot be ignored. And although the counselor–consultant does not have the right to impose her values on the consultee, it needs to be noted that the consultant should not abdicate her values and attempt to present herself as totally value free. A discussion of the operative values, to the extent that they are identified and understood, prior to formal engagement in the consultation relationship, may be the most effective, responsible, and ethical way to handle the potential impact of differing values. As an individual with expertise, called into assist the consultee, the ethical consultant needs to

1. Understand the range of options available
2. Identify those options most in line with his/her own value structure
3. Attempt to help the consultee and consultee system to identify their own operative values and the relationship each options has in light of that value structure
4. Through collaboration determine both the intervention goals and strategies to be employed that are most aligned with the operating values of the consultee, the consultee's system, and the consultant's orientation.

The one value consistently expressed wtihin this text is that of collaboration. Following on the aforementioned, it is important to note that as an operative value, collaboration needs to be explained to the consultee prior to engaging in the diagnostic and intervention processes. Assuming the acceptance of this mode of operation and guide for decision making, collaboration would be employed throughout the consultation process and would then allow for the mutual resolution of future value conflicts.

Although it would be ideal to find the system and the consultee for whom the consultant's values are absolutely compatible, such universal agreement is not necessary. However, where significant incompatibility exists or the values of the system or consultee are clearly unethical in light of the consultant's personal and professional standards, contracts, when initiated, should be terminated or, better yet, not initiated nor consummated.

Consultant Cultural Sensitivity

Counselors have clearly been directed to *not* condone or engage in acts of discrimination (ACA, 1995, A.2.a). Counselors have also been directed to actively attempt to understand the diverse cultural backgrounds of the clients with whom they work (ACA, 1995, A.2.b). As noted throughout this text, the counselor operating from a consultation frame of reference is quite aware that any form of helping will occur within a cultural context. Within the chapters of this text it has been emphasized that a counselor–consultant must be sensitive to the culture and values of the system and the specific consultee. It is a prerequisite for effective consultation from point of entry through problem definition and intervention implementation. For a counselor–consultant to view individual concerns or a personal problem as separate from social, cultural context is to misunderstand them.

Beyond the practical implications and value of being sensitive to the cultural context in which one consults, the ethical requirement of providing for the care of those to whom we serve, demands that the consultant be sensitive and valuing of another's culture. The ethical consultant is one who engages in consultation for the care of the client, consultee, and consultee's system. This care demands that the consultant become sensitive to the cultural makeup of the system in which she is consulting and the role this cultural element plays in the creation and resolution of the problem presented.

In addition to being sensitive to the unique values and cultural influences impacting a client's life, being culturally sensitive is an essential ingredient if we, as consultants, hope to understand the true nature of the client's problem. To see what the client, consultee, or member of the system sees and experiences as a result of his cultural lenses, rather than to simply assume that his viewpoint is the same as our own, is both a challenge and an ethical responsibility. Being insensitive to another's worldview and imposing one's own cultural meaning on the experience of another and believing that what is needed is the same, regardless of tradition or heritage, is not only ineffective, but also an unethical demonstration of our lack of care for the client and consultee.

Perhaps it could be suggested that the solution to a consultant's ethnocentrism is to ensure that all consultants only consult to clients, consultees and systems with similar cultural backgrounds. Such an approach is simply unrealistic. Rather, it is incumbent on all of us to increase our own cultural sensitivity and to develop the skills and the attitudes needed to effectively and ethically work with a culturally diverse population.

It has been suggested (e.g., Sue, Arrendondo, & McDavis, 1992) that a culturally sensitive consultant will (a) be aware of her own culture and its influence, (b) understand the limits of a single-culture, "mainstream" approach, (c) be sensitive to alternative worldviews, and (d) employ approaches that reflect the respect and sensitivity for other cultures. Because of the practical and ethical importance of each of the aforementioned, they will be discussed in some detail.

1. *Awareness of one's own culture and its influence:* In addition to being sensitive to the unique value and culture of those to whom we consult, a consultant must also be aware of his own worldview and the impact that such a worldview may have on his consultative interactions. The effective and culturally sensitive consultant is aware of how his own cultural background and experiences, attitudes, and values influence his definitions of normality and abnormality and his approach to the process of helping. The culturally

sensitive and competent consultant understands and accepts that his worldview is but one (of many) valid and valuable sets of assumptions, values, and perspectives from which a person may effectively function.

2. *Awareness of the narrowness of a single "mainstream" perspective:* The ethical and culturally sensitive consultant is aware of the limitedness and narrowness of any one single cultural perspective, even if, and perhaps especially when, that perspective represents the cultural mainstream. The ethical and skilled consultant is aware that the truth is culture colored. The ethical and culturally sensitive consultant needs to be sensitive to a larger worldview. She needs to understand and appreciate how relative and nonabsolute any one cultural view may be, including her own, and thus avoid functioning from an ethnocentric perspective.

3. *Understanding and valuing an alternative worldview:* It is not the intent to suggest that the each consultant must be totally skilled and knowledgeable of all cultures or that one abandon her own cultural perspective. It is suggested that the ethical consultant will accept and **value** as legitimate the culturally diverse perspective presented by those with whom she works. Further, as was suggested throughout the text, the effective and ethical consultant will allow this sensitivity and valuing of the other's unique cultural circumstances to color her decisions at each stage of the consultation process.

4. *Employ culturally sensitive approaches to diagnosis and intervention:* Although it may be argued that there are few human universals, the one universal is that variation exists. People, although similar, are also clearly different. The cultural medium in which we operate and develop affects our values, our goals, our behaviors and as such will also affect the decisions we make or should make within the consulting context.

The ethical and skilled consultant continues to assess the goals and consulting strategies to ensure that these are relevant and appropriate to the culture in which the consulting occurs and are in line with the values of the consultant, consultee, and system. Problem definitions and goals occur within cultural context. For example, the assessment of desirable behavior in one cultural context may be diagnosed as undesirable in another. This point should not be lost on the culturally sensitive consultant.

The consultant must be aware and accepting of the fact that there can be wide variation of cultural definitions of normative and normal. As such, the consultant in attempting to define what is dysfunctional needs to be sensitive to the culture of the system in which he is working and how that culture defines acceptable, desirable, normal, or functional. As the professional help provider, the consultant may have assumptions about what constitutes conflict and problems as well as what defines solutions and health. However, the ethical consultant will be mindful that these definitions are culturally impacted and as such will place his goals and concerns within the context of the client, consultee, and system's culture. Exercise 13.2 is provided to further highlight this influence of culture.

EXERCISE 13.2

Events in Multicultural Context

Directions: Following you will find a number of variables that may be important to the consultation process. For each variable you will be provided a specific culture's response. Your task is to identify your perspective on that variable.

When your perspective varies from that presented, identify the potential impact of these varying cultural viewpoints on your consultation relationship with a consultee who presents that cultural perspective.

Variable	Cultural View	Personal View
1. Time:	Time is *not* linear, time is when something is happening, thus lunch is when our work is at a good point to stop or work begins when you get here. On time is when the events dictate rather than according to predetermined schedule.	
2. Contracts:	A verbal contract, a handshake are more important than written structured contracts. Organizations are personally and informally structured, not driven by organizational charts.	
3. Responsibility:	The top individual shoulders all the responsibility for positive and negative outcomes, regardless of where the action was initiated.	
4. Values:	Values cooperation, respect, and interdependence, rather than individual achievement and autonomy.	
5. Listening:	Shows respect and attending by listening without giving acknowledgment (not even a nod or an "uh huh") and with eyes downcast.	
6. Learning Style:	A global, visual preference in learning. When hearing a story prefers to receive the entire picture all the way through to the end before asking questions.	

7. Sociolinguistics: After providing feedback or
asking a question, the presenter
may experience no immediate
response from the listener; in fact,
a delay of up to a few minutes
may occur before the listener
responds.

BASIC ETHICAL ISSUES
TARGETING RELATIONSHIPS

At its most fundamental root, the process of consultation is a form of helping in which the professional consultant attempts to offer a service of caregiving to the client, the consultee, and the consultee's system. As a caregiver, the consultant must remember that the consultation relationship exists for the benefit and care of the client, consultee, and consultee's system and *not* for the personal needs or benefits of the consultant.

It is in placing the rights and needs of the client, the consultee, and the system as primary that a consultant begins to establish the general framework for ethical practice. The ethical consultant enacts this principle of professionalism, ensuring that any one consultation relationship is characterized by: (a) informed consent, (b) confidentiality, (c) professional boundaries, and (d) the ethical use of power.

Informed Consent

The ethical consultant must demonstrate a respect for the rights of the consultee to be fully informed. Consultees need to be provided with information to enable them to make informed choices. However, undertaking this can be quite delicate and difficult.

Providing the information needed for informed decision making at a time and in a manner that the client and consultee can understand and optimally use can be a real challenge. Too much information, too soon, can prove overwhelming, anxiety provoking, and even destructive to the consultation process. The goal of informed consent is to promote cooperation and participation of the client and consultee in the consultation process. As such, the ethical consultant will attempt to provide the consultee and client with information that can assist them to decide if they wish to enter, continue, or terminate the consultation relationship.

When working with the consultee it is essential that the consultant assist the consultee to understand both what consultation *is*, and *is not*. The consultant should inform the consultee about the nature and responsibilities of collaborative consultation. The consultee needs to understand the role the consultant is to play, the role the consultee is to play, and the anticipated nature and character of the relationship as it unfolds through the various stages of the consultation process. Further, it is important for the consultant to highlight as much as possible the projected impacts (both positive and negative) of engaging in consultation.

In addition to these general concerns, the consultant needs to continually update the consultee on the process and progress of the consultation, the anticipated steps to be taken next, and the unfolding consequences of each action so that the consultee can actively engage in the process of consultation from the perspective of understanding.

Similarly, the client needs to be fully informed that the approach being employed will involve a coordination of information and efforts on part of the counselor–consultant and the consultee, who referred the client. The client needs to be assisted to understand the benefit of this triadic approach and helped to understand the limits to which personal information will be shared.

Confidentiality

In seeking help, both the client and the consultee should be able to expect a relationship that is trusting, honest, and safe. For consultation to be effective, consultees must feel free to disclose and share their private, professional concerns. For such a sense of freedom to exist, both the client and the consultee need to feel that the interaction is one that is characterized by a respect for privacy.

The American Counseling Association's *Code of Ethics and Standards of Practice* (ACA, 1995, B.6.a) states that information obtained is discussed for ". . . professional purposes only with persons clearly concerned with the case." Further, this principle directs the counselor–consultant to make every effort to ". . . protect client identity and avoid undue invasion of privacy."

As with other guidelines for practice, the issue of confidentiality is not absolute nor are decisions to hold in confidence always black and white. The use of confidentiality requires professional judgment.

Although there has been elaborate discussion on the limits of confidentiality when applied to the more traditional, directive forms of helping, less clarity has been offered to those working within a consultation relationship. For example Newman and Robinson (1991) highlight the difficulty encountered by the practical limits on the consultant's ability to protect the confidentiality of information gathered. Modifications of the suggestions made by these authors (i.e., Newman & Robinson, 1991) to assist with this difficult issue of confidentiality are presented following. It is felt that the consultant concerned with his limited ability to protect the privacy and confidentiality of those engaged in the consultation should

1. Remember that in organizational contexts, maintenance of confidentiality depends not only on the consultant but also on the cooperative efforts of perhaps many organizational members as well.

2. Engage in information disclosure on a need-to-know basis. Because levels of participation by members are often variable, so, too, must access to information be variable.

3. Explain and negotiate the limits of confidentiality with each new consultation contract because these limits are situationally defined and not inherent in any given consultation relationship.

4. Publicly delineate these boundaries and limits to ensure that all parties know who has access to what information.

5. Encourage all parties involved to be respectful of the rights of all others engaged in the consultation and request that all information be treated appropriately.

The ethical consultant, while attempting to instill a sense of trust in the client and consultee along with creating an atmosphere conducive for disclosure, must accept the limits to her ability to maintain total privacy and protect confidentiality. Further, these limits *must* be conveyed to all involved in the consultation.

In addition to informing the client and consultee as to the limits with which the consultant may be able to protect confidentiality, the client and consultee need to understand the conditions under which the consultant will, in fact, break confidentiality. Although the situations under which confidentiality must be broken can vary, as a function of many variables (e.g., state laws, organizational procedures, age of participants), it is generally agreed that within a direct-service relationship, such as counseling, the counselor *must* break confidentiality when it is clear that a client might do harm to himself or to another, as might be the case in suicide, child or elderly abuse, or homicide. The determination of when a person is in clear and imminent danger to himself or to another is a professional judgment and is not always absolutely clear.

When viewed within the consultation relationship the conditions of clear and imminent danger to the client or others (consultee or system) may be even harder to detect. Nonetheless, the principle should still be employed. Although responsible to protect, the consultant must remember the multiple levels of persons (i.e., client, consultee, and system) for whom he is responsible. Thus when the issue of a consultee's privacy conflicts with the protection of the client or others within the system, confidentiality may have to be breached. Under these situations it would appear that open discussion of concerns with those empowered within the consultee system appears to be the most warranted response, with additional responses considered in light of the costs and benefits to be accrued (Newman, 1993). When the consultant is uncertain whether confidentiality should be maintained, she should consult with colleagues whenever possible to assist in that determination. Exercise 13.3 will help to highlight some of the difficulty in maintaining confidentiality in consultation relationships.

EXERCISE 13.3

Maintaining Confidentiality?

Directions: Following you will find a number of consultation scenarios. With a colleague, mentor, or supervisor, identify the specific factors in the scenario that may make confidentiality difficult to maintain or require that confidentiality be broken. Discuss the specific steps you, as consultant, would take in response to each situation.

Situation 1: As the school counselor, you have been invited to provide organizational consulting to a large high school. The principal of the school has two specific agendas: (1) he wants you to identify the teachers' needs for in-service training, and (2) he wants you to identify which teachers may have drinking and drug problems, sexual hang-ups, and problem marriages.

Further, he wants you to provide him with a written report on your findings, including names and specific quotes from the teachers.

Situation 2: As a counselor in the university counseling center, you have been invited to work with the R.A.s (residence assistants) in-servicing them on the identification of drug and alcohol abuse. You begin working with the director of the R.A.s in developing the program to be delivered. As you work with the director, you discover that he is having an affair with one of the R.A.s, and he is concerned that this may "blur boundaries" and make it hard to supervise her like the other R.A.s. The director is 38 years old and married with two children. The R.A. is a 19-year-old sophomore.

Situation 3: You have been requested by the school's instructional support teacher to work with her team. Apparently their work has been becoming increasingly less professional (e.g., poor record keeping, incomplete IEPs) with evidence of much interpersonal conflict among the six members. Through interviewing the team members, you find out that two have been pursuing other employment and have no interest in IST work. On more than one occasion they left meetings early and came unprepared. They ask that the consultant give them some time to settle their employment situation rather than tell the principal.

Situation 4: You are an elementary school counselor who was invited to work with a fifth-grade boy because of his "irritating, disrespectful behavior in class." In gathering additional information from the consultee (his science teacher), he states the following: "I need you to do something immediately! I have had kids like this before—in fact, I lost my last job because a kid like him got me so mad, I beat the kid up. Hey, this is confidential, nobody knows about that, you are *not* allowed to tell anybody. But I'm telling you, you got to get this kid to straighten up—he's *really* getting to me!"

Establishing and Maintaining
Professional Boundaries

It is generally agreed that someone seeking help has a right to expect a **professional** relationship with the helper. In fact, the *Ethical Standards for School Counselors* (ACA, 1998), section C.1.a., makes it perfectly clear that the relationship a counselor develops with faculty, staff, and administration is one that is professional and aimed at facilitating the provision of optimal counseling services. This principle can be violated with personal relationships, rather than professional ones, and guides the counselor–consultant's interaction within the workplace.

The opportunity to cross professional boundaries, although perhaps not as seductive as that found within the intimate confines of a therapist's office, can and does exist in consultation. The ethical consultant, therefore, needs to be able to recognize her own personal feelings and needs and distinguish those feelings from the professional needs and concerns of her consultee. It must be remembered that the purpose of this relationship is to assist the consultee and *not* meet the consultant's own personal needs.

Each of the professional organizations specifies the need to keep clear boundaries as a way of ensuring that the relationships remain professional. In considering this principle, in light of the nature of consultation, two possible threats to this professional relationship need to be considered.

First, professional boundaries and objectivity may be compromised when the consultant and the consultee are engaged in relationships outside that of the consultation. Situations in which a dual relationship exists between consultant and consultee (i.e., when the consultant and consultee have another type of relationship outside the work setting) threaten the principle of professional contact. Such dual relationships can impair the consultant's level of objectivity and professional judgment and thus need to be avoided whenever possible. The reality, however, especially for those functioning as internal consultants, as is most likely the case with the school counselor, is that it is sometimes impossible to avoid consulting with a consultee with whom other professional and personal relationships have been formed. Under these situations, the consultant must be sensitive to threats to professional objectivity that may exist and even share these concerns with the consultee. Further, under these conditions it may be helpful to discuss the situation with other professional colleagues or supervisors to develop ways to monitor the professional relationship and identify strategies that may help ensure that professional boundaries are maintained.

A second possible threat to the professional boundaries of the consultation contract is that involving the crossing into personal counseling with the consultee. As noted throughout this text, consultation is a process that focuses on work-related issues and not the personal, psychological needs and concerns of the consultee. The clear, work-related boundaries must be articulated and agreed on. Further, it needs to be made clear that this is *not* counseling for the consultee and as such personal, non-work-related issues will *not* be addressed. When such personal needs are interfering with the consultee's performance of his/her work responsibilities, than the consultant will attempt to refer the consultee for personal counseling, but will *not* offer to provide that counseling.

Assisting the consultee to understand these boundaries, as well as maintaining the integrity of the boundaries, is an ethical responsibility of the consultant.

Power

In discussing the issue of entry and the development and maintenance of a collaborative relationship, emphasis was given to the value of the use of expert and referent power to influence the nature of the relationship. As should be evident, the role of consultant is by its nature a role of potential power and influence.

The power to influence another's attitude or behavior is a natural consequence of interpersonal dynamics. The reality is that all consultants by the definition of having expertise and being requested to assist another to reach a heretofore unachieved goal have power and are in the business of influencing. Thus it is not the reality of power nor its use that is at issue; it is the potential for misuse or abuse that needs to be considered. The National Board of Certified Counselors (NBCC) states very clearly in its *Code of Ethics* (NBCC, 1997, E.4) that "certified counselors in consulting . . . encourage and cultivate client growth toward self-direction and do not create future dependency on the consultant."

The focus of this text has been on developing a collaborative relationship in which the consultee has the right to accept or reject the consultant's suggestions and recommendations at any time. This right includes the right to terminate the relationship any time. Thus consultation as presented within this text is a voluntary decision on the part of the consultee, and the consultant's actions to fully inform and collaborate should be geared to protect this voluntary nature of the relationship.

The right to voluntarily participate can be jeopardized by the consultant who unethically employs threats or sanctions to manipulate the consultee or even who unethically employs the various forms of interpersonal influence or power to restrict the consultee's freedom to choose. It is hoped that the techniques suggested within this text are used to balance the distribution of power between the consultant and consultee, moving the relationship to true collaboration. The development of a truly collaborative, informed, and voluntary relationship may be the best means to ensure that power is *not* abused.

PROCESS ISSUES

Identification of the Client

The characteristic of consultation as a triadic relationship raises a number of unique ethical concerns. Albeit the roles of consultant, consultee, and client may be clearly defined, the question for the consultant of who is in fact the client may remain an ethical concern. Is the consultant's client ultimately the system, as suggested by some (e.g., Fannibanda, 1976) or may it be the specific consultee with whom the consultant works, or the client for whom the consultee expresses concern? How does the consultant address the special need to "know," when often the specific client is excluded from the consultation processes

(Robinson & Gross, 1985), as may be the case in system-focused or consultee-focused consultation? Although many agree that the consultant shares responsibility for the welfare of the client (Brown, Pryzwansky, & Schulte, 1991; Newman, 1993; Newman & Robinson, 1991), what are the ethical limits to that responsibility when that client is most often not included in the deliberations of the consultation process (see Robinson & Gross, 1985, Snow & Gersick, 1986).

The ethical consultant must consider the impact of his presence and structured interventions on all those potentially involved, as well as all those specifically targeted for intervention. The welfare of members of each level of problem identification, be it the client, the consultee, and/or the system, needs to be protected. One way this protection of the welfare of those to be impacted may be achieved is for the consultant to expand the involvement and informed understanding of the processes to all those (or their representatives) who may be impacted by the consultation.

Efficacy of Treatment

Consultants are professional service providers. They present themselves as having particular expertise that they provide to others in need of that expertise. Implicit in this definition of a professional service provider is that the service provided is both valid and effective.

Granted, no one professional can guarantee success in each and every situation, but as an ethical practitioner, the consultant should, where possible, ensure that the services she provides have both technical and ethical adequacy (Newman, 1993).

The fact that the consultant is competent is the first step in ensuring this efficacy of treatment. But beyond the ethical requirement that one provide services for which one is both knowledgeable and competent, the consultant needs to provide those services for which some research (empirical and/or clinical) has been found to support its efficacy.

Although there is an ever-increasing empirical database across multiple disciplines that can be used to assess the relative efficacy of differential approaches and techniques for consulting, no one set of efficient, effective operating procedures has been identified. As directed by the ACA standards (ACA, 1995, C.2.f), counselors need to take steps to increase awareness of the current scientific and professional information in the field and maintain competency in the skills they use. The ethical consultant, therefore, needs to be alert to update his own professional knowledge and skill, as well as to keep abreast of the ever-increasing research supporting specific intervention strategies. The ethical consultant needs to incorporate these research findings into her own decisions regarding intervention strategies.

Because the existing research on the efficacy of various intervention strategies is still somewhat lacking, the consultant needs to not only be informed of these findings, but also function as his/her own practitioner—researcher. In order to insure efficacy, the consultant needs to both employ empirically validated forms of intervention when known and possible *and* employ outcome and process evaluation measures as part of his/her own consultation process. This need to monitor and evaluate intervention progress is not just a good idea; it is an ethical mandate (see ACA, 1995, C.2.d).

Evaluation—a Stage of Consultation
and an Ethical Consideration

Evaluation of the consultation relationship and its impact is very often viewed by practicing consultants as superfluous or as only tangential to the primary function of consulting. However, given the position of the American Counseling Association's *Code of Ethics and Standards of Practice* (ACA, 1995, C.2.d) it appears that knowing how to monitor and evaluate one's consulting activities is not only an essential step in the consulting process, but it is also an ethical requirement used to ensure accountability and effectiveness.

Having a system of evaluation in place serves a number of valuable and ethical functions. A system of evaluation can

1. Serve as ongoing reminder that the consultation relationship is not one on which the consultee can remain dependent
2. Provide the criteria needed for knowing when decisions and actions need to be reconsidered
3. Provide a means for monitoring and adjusting the nature of the relationship
4. Provide a rationale base from which to determine if and when closure is appropriate
5. Provide the means to justify the consultant's expense and market his/her value—for the client, the consultee and the system

Forms of Evaluation

Evaluation, as an ongoing part of consultation, takes two forms: formative and summative evaluation.

Formative evaluation is used at strategic points throughout the consultation to assist in the ongoing decisions to continue or modify the action plan and to check on the perceived level of collaboration and mutual satisfaction with the process. The overall purpose of such formative evaluation is to gather data that expedite decision making about the upcoming steps, procedures, and processes to be implemented in the consultation relationship. Such evaluation provides the basis on which to better "form" the process for attaining desired outcomes.

Formative evaluation can often be achieved by simply setting aside time for the consultant and the consultee to process or discuss the relationship and the procedures employed up to that point (Parsons, 1996; Parsons & Meyers, 1984). Often an informal procedure such as asking the consultee for her feelings about the plan or the progress they have made to date will serve the purpose of formative evaluation. Informally, the consultant can assess progress by the oral response of the consultee. Having the consultee discuss her feelings about the nature of the relationship and the consultation interaction, the strategies employed, and the problems they experienced are ways to gather soft information about the consultation process.

As a formative process, this type of evaluation should begin with the first session.

Summative evaluation addresses the issue of goal attainment. The specific intent of summative evaluation is to show that the action plan has reached its original objectives. A summative evaluation may attempt to answer the following questions.

1. Were the objectives/goals attained?

2. What factors in the action plan contributed to goal attainment or inhibited it?

3. What is the value of this action plan in contrast to alternative plans?

On a more structured or formal level, the consultee can be assisted to actually collect data that would be used to assess the degree to which progress has been made toward his goal. In addition to providing encouragement about progress, a summative evaluation can also be used to define the point at which the consultation can terminate. When the initial problems have been eliminated or sufficiently reduced, and the consultee is currently coping better with these problems, then termination appears appropriate, and the closure process can begin. Similarly, when the data reveal that the terminal goal has not been achieved, closure to the original contract may be appropriate and the need to reenter may be signaled.

As noted throughout the earlier chapters, there are numerous ways to establish such summative/outcome evaluations, especially if during the problem-identification stage and goal-setting stage the goal was specified in concrete, quantifiable terms. Readers seeking additional assistance with this process are referred to Parsons (1996), Parsons and Brown (2002), and Greshman (1991).

SUMMARY

Ethics and Standards of Practice: Guides, Not Fixed Directives

The unique characteristics of the consultation relationship and dynamic make the identification and resolution of the typical ethical concerns encountered by others in the helping professions even more complicated. As such, those intending to work as professional consultants must be aware of and employ a set of standards for guiding the ethical practice of their trade. As a first step toward such ethical practice, each consultant must be familiar with the ethical standards created by their own specific professional organization. Further, those working as consultants must be constantly alert to the articulation of specific principles of ethical practice that may be unique to the role and function of the consultant.

Specific guidelines to the ethical practice of consultation will continue to evolve and develop. It is imperative for effective, ethical helpers to keep abreast of these developments.

Basic Ethical Issues Targeting the Counselor as Consultant

- Ethical consultants are aware of their own needs and how these may be active in the consultation relationship.
- Ethical consultants do not meet their own needs at the consultee's or client's expense.
- Ethical consultants are aware of their own biases and cultural orientations and are sensitive and respectful of diverse cultural orientations.
- Ethical consultants employ techniques, models, and frameworks of consultation that are recognized and accepted as effective and efficient.
- Ethical consultants seek to increase their competence and contract to provide services only in those areas for which they are competent.
- Ethical consultants continue to develop their professional skills and knowledge through formal training, professional memberships, and peer consultation and supervision.

Basic Ethical Issues Targeting Relationships

- Ethical consultants are aware of their own needs and how these may be active in the consultation relationship.
- Ethical consultants do not meet their own needs at the consultee's or client's expense.
- Ethical consultants are aware of their own biases and cultural orientations and are sensitive and respectful of diverse cultural orientations.

Process Issues

- Ethical consultants employ techniques, models, and frameworks of consultation that are recognized and accepted as effective and efficient.
- Ethical consultants seek to increase their competence and contract to provide services only in those areas for which they are competent.
- Ethical consultants continue to develop their professional skills and knowledge through formal training, professional memberships, and peer consultation and supervision.
- Ethical consultants appreciate the power of the consultation relationship and use it for the benefit and care of the consultee.

- Ethical consultants protect against the possible misuse of power by developing a voluntary, collaborative working relationship with the consultee, one characterized by informed consent.

- Ethical consultants are concerned with issues of accountability and efficacy and as such employ formative and summative evaluative methods.

IMPORTANT TERMS

Accountability

American Counseling
    Association *Code
    of Ethics*

Boundaries

Confidentiality

Competence

Informed consent

*Ethical Standards for
    School Counselors*

Formative evaluation

National Board of
    Certified Counselors
    Code of Ethics

Need to know

Summative evaluation

SUGGESTED READINGS

American Counseling Association. (1995). *Code of ethics and standards of practice.* Alexandria, VA: Author.

American School Counselor Association. (1998). *Ethical standards for school counselors.* Alexandria, VA: Author.

Herlihy, B., & Corey, G. (1996). *ACA ethical and legal issues in school counseling* (5th ed.). Alexandria, VA: American Counseling Association.

Parsons, R. D. (2001). *The ethics of professional practice.* Needham Heights, MA: Allyn & Bacon.

WEB SITES

American Counseling Association homepage: Professional organization offers its news, journal abstracts, and membership information. www.counseling.org

American Counseling Association: Code of Ethics online. www.iit.edu/departments/csep/PublicWWW/codes/coe/ACA–CoE.html

American School Counselor Association: Contains publications, services, highlights, and events for counselors. Review early warning signs, violence-prevention resources and programs. www.schoolcounselor.org

REFERENCES

American Counseling Association (ACA). (1995). *Code of ethics and standards of practice.* Alexandria, VA: Author.

American School Counselor Association (ACA). (1998). *Ethical standards for school counselors.* Alexandria, VA: Author.

Brown, D., Pryzwansky, W. B., & Schulte, A. C. (1991). *Psychological consultation: Introduction to theory and practice* (2nd ed.). Needham Heights, MA: Allyn & Bacon.

Dougherty, A. M. (1992). Ethical issues in consultation. *Elementary School Guidance and Counseling, 26,* 214–220.

Fannibanda, D. K. (1976). Ethical issues in mental health consultation. *Professional Psychology, 7,* 547–552.

Greshman, F. M. (1991). Moving beyond statistical significance in reporting consultation outcome research. *Journal of Educational and Psychological Consultation, 2*(1), 1–13.

National Board of Certified Counselors (NBCC). (1997). *Code of ethics.* Greensboro, NC: Author.

Newman, J. L. (1993). Ethical issues in consultation. *Journal of Counseling & Development, 72*(2), 148–156.

Newman, J. L. & Robinson, S. E. (1991). In the best interests of the consultee: Ethical issues in consultation. *Consulting Psychology Bulletin, 43,* 23–29.

Parsons, R., & Meyers, J. (1984). *Developing consultation skills.* San Francisco: Jossey-Bass.

Parsons, R. D. (1996). *The skilled consultant.* Needham Heights, MA: Allyn & Bacon.

Parsons R. D. (2001). *The ethics of professional practice.* Needham Heights, MA: Allyn & Bacon.

Parsons, R. D. & Brown, K. S. (2002). *Teacher as reflective practitioner and action researcher.* Belmont, CA: Wadsworth P.

Robinson, S. E., & Gross, D. R. (1985). Ethics of consultation: The Centreville ghost. *The Counseling Psychologist, 13,* 444–465.

Snow, D. L. & Gersick, K. E. (1986). Ethical and professional issues in mental health consultation. In F. V. Mannino, E. J. Trickett, M. F. Shore, M. G. Kidder, & G. Levin (Eds.). *Handbook of mental health consultation.* (pp. 393–431), Rockville, MD: NIMH.

Sue, D. W., Arrendondo, P., & McDavis, R. (1992). Multicultural counseling competencies and standards: A call to the profession. *Journal of Counseling and Development, 70,* 477–486.

Warwick, D., & Kelman, H. (1973). Ethical issues in social intervention. In G. Zaltman (Ed.), *Processes and phenomena of social change* (pp. 417–477). New York: Wiley Interscience.

Younggren, J. N. (1993). Ethical issues in religious psychotherapy. *Register Report, 19*(4), 1–8.

14

Applying What
We Know

That was certainly quite an experience. Between juggling the
other things that I have to do—and working with Dr. J's issues—
there were times when I wondered if I picked the right profession.
But it is funny—things turned out really well—with Dr. J and I not only
working through the Ellen thing, but now brainstorming about some
possible in-service for the faculty around the concept of the resource
room. That has real potential to reduce the stress everyone has been feeling.

I'm sure it will get easier—actually—I know it is!
The more I do this, the more natural it feels.

As the story is most often told, a young child, interested in gaining
directions asks a man: "How do I get to Carnegie Hall?" The man
responded: "Practice, Practice, Practice!"

Perhaps the same prescription applies to each of us wondering how to
ever feel comfortable and competent with consultation as a paradigm for
school-based services. We need to practice, practice, practice! The model of
consultation presented throughout this text may at first feel somewhat artificial, even alien, when you attempt to apply it. However, with continued use it
will become a more natural, comfortable part of your professional identify.

This text will conclude by providing opportunities to practice. Two somewhat detailed cases are presented for your consideration and guided practice.
As you read the cases, you are invited to mentally superimpose the stages of

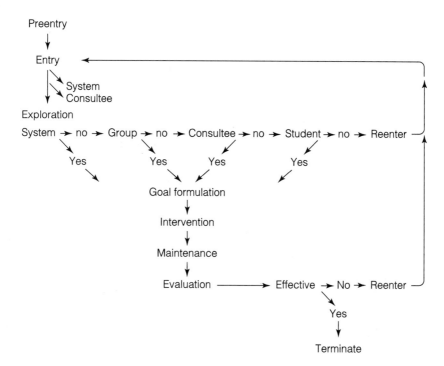

FIGURE 14.1 Stages of Consultation

consultation (see Figure 14.1) and the tasks and concerns to be accomplished at each stage (see Table 14.1). In an attempt to assist with this application of the model, the first case is accompanied by a number of consultant reflection questions, which may assist you in viewing the data through an integrated, multidimensional collaborative consultative paradigm. As with many of the previous learning exercises, it is suggested that you not only work through these cases on your own, but also that you share your conclusions, your insights, and your experience with a colleague or a mentor to benefit from the insight and experience of another. In Case 14.1, we will revisit the case presented at the beginning of each chapter, the case of Ellen, Dr. Jameson, and our consultant, Mr. Thomas.

As you read through Case 14.1 you will note that interspersed throughout are questions and reflections that Mr. Thomas considered as he processed the information gathered. You will be able to observe how he draws conclusions about the data, which in turn guides his decisions and actions. It is this process of questioning, hypothesizing, and testing that should guide your own practice of consultation.

Case 14.2 is offered without these introjections and consultant reflections. However, you will note places where you are reminded to reflect and consider what you have learned and begin to anticipate what should be done. It is hoped that you will be able to utilize the information provided and filter it through your understanding of the consultation process to anticipate the consultant's next steps.

CHAPTER OBJECTIVES

The intent of this chapter is to help you move from being a reader of consultation to a doer of consultation. As such, the chapter provides case illustrations to guide you in this process.

After reading this chapter, you should be able to do the following.

1. Apply the stages of consultation from preentry to termination
2. Identify a number of significant challenges to be addressed at each stage
3. Describe the unique tasks that need to be achieved and supported through each stage of the consultation process
4. Describe the actions to be taken by a consultant to create and maintain a successful collaborative consultation relationship through each stage of the consultation process
5. Describe the unique features of a solution-focused approach to collaborative consultation

A REVIEW OF THE
CONSULTATION PROCESS

Before we begin applying what we have learned, it may be helpful to quickly review the stages of the consultation process. As you most likely remember, consultation, as with other forms of helping, is a process. It is a process in which the nature of the interaction and the specific focus of the task change over the course of the consultation. In chapter 6 we detailed the stages of this process. Starting with the preentry stages in which specific processes and procedures are put into place to expedite efficient referral, the tone for a successful collaborative relationship is set. The second stage of entry is one in which permission to employ consultation as a mode of service delivery and a specific "contract" with the consultee have been established. The third stage in this developing process of consultation is exploration, in which consultant and consultee come to consensual agreement about the nature of the problem. Once the area of concern has been articulated and agreed on, the consultation moves to goal formulation and intervention planning. From this point, the consultation proceeds through a maintenance stage, then to evaluation and termination.

Although the stages were presented as discreet components, occurring in linear sequence, consultation in practice is a dynamic process. The consultant may at times experience the stages as occurring in neat, linear order, whereas at other times she may experience the consultation process as cycling in and

Table 14.1 The Specific Considerations and Tasks for Each Stage of Consultation

Stage	General Focus	Tasks
Preentry	Creating systemic norms that encourage, facilitate, and reinforce consultee referral for consultation.	1. Identify what is envisioned, desired, and sanctioned by the highest level administrator to whom you will be responsible (when negotiating the formal contract). 2. Identify culture, frame of reference, and points of resistance. 3. Create optimal conditions for consultee referral.
Entry	Establishing the consultative relationship concerning roles, functions, and expectations.	1. Explain the collaborative, expanded, integrated model of consultation in order to surface mixed feelings and concerns and to educate as to the rationale and value of such an approach. 2. Remedial and Preventive Focus: Present a contract that addresses immediate felt needs, while at the same time providing freedom to operate in a more preventive manner. 3. Role Definition: Describe the specific roles to be played (i.e., consultant and consultee), the nature of the relationship (i.e., collaborative).
Exploration	Identifying and defining the consultee's presenting problem. The operational definition of the consultee's concern should consider the A-B-Cs of the client, the requirements of the client's task, and the specific environmental factors influencing the problem. The consultant needs to look beyond the consultee's original conceptualization of the problem and solution to test whether other, more indirect and thus more preventive, approaches could be employed.	When attempting to identify the level of focus that is possible, the consultant needs to consider a number of factors such as: (1) the level of immediate crises (system, consultee or client); (2) the nature of the system's culture, structure, processes, and history; and (3) the consultee's expectations and openness to the collaborative exchange.
Goal Setting	Operationalize the desired goal(s) to be achieved. The model	1. Expanding the focus to include: client, task, and environmental elements.

(Continued)

Table 14.1 (CONTINUED)

Stage	General Focus	Tasks
	employed assumes that the client's behavior is a function of interaction between the unique characteristics of the client's A-B-Cs, the task requested, and the environment in which the client is to function. Thus all attempts to define the desired goals should include components of each of these factors (i.e., the client, the task, the environment).	2. Treat goal setting as primary opportunity for collaboration.
Intervention Planning	Identification of strategies that will achieve consultation goals and objectives. Although presented here as a separate stage in the consultation process, it must be noted that interventions and intervention planning have been an essential thread in the fabric of entry, problem identification, and goal setting.	1. Provide a multiplicity of strategies. 2. Maximize payoffs, minimize costs. 3. Mutual agreement. 4. Evaluation plan. 5. Task assignment.
Maintenance	Monitor the efficacy of change strategies and modification of strategies (and outcome objectives) as needed. In light of the preventive goal and the collaborative nature of the relationship, the consultant needs to resist the temptation to jump in and take on more responsibility for intervention implementation. Sharing equally in the process of implementation, as well as its success or failure, is still a goal for this collaborative process.	1. Work with resistance: Recognize that resistance occurs even at this stage. 2. Maintain collaboration throughout implementation. 3. Provide support: Be aware of the possible need to recycle through the process of redefining the problem or goals and generating alternative strategies, should a blockage be encountered in the intervention plan.
Evaluation	This evaluation should target both the degree to which the desired	1. Establish multiple criteria to assess the success of the outcome and process of the consultation.

Table 14.1 (CONTINUED)

Stage	General Focus	Tasks
	goals were achieved as well as the degree to which the collaborative process was maintained.	2. Employ some measures that will allow the consultant and consultee to recognize the positive impact of the relationship even if the terminal goals or outcomes were not achieved.
		3. Target measures that will help the consultant and the consultee to identify the value (to both the consultee and the consultee's system) of the consultation model.
		4. While focusing on the practical utility of the evaluation process, the consultant should consider employing simple structured designs that would increase the validity of the conclusions drawn from the evaluation (see, for example, Parsons & Brown, 2002).
Termination	Although termination of the consultation relationship can occur at any time throughout the process, closure as an anticipated stage occurs at the completion of the entire process of consultation.	*Closure when successful* 1. Review original contract. 2. Share view of experience. 3. Invite consultee disclosure. 4. Reinforce the consultee's valuable involvement. 5. Help the consultee to identify his/her current needs and the way the consultant might be of continued service. 6. Establish availability. *Closure when unsuccessful* 1. Convey a sense of hopefulness. 2. Resist the temptation to simply modify the intervention plan. Step back and reconsider the situation, given this new information. 3. Recycle (see Figure 14.1).

CASE 14.1 A View from a Counselor's Window: The Case of Ellen

The following case, "The Case of Ellen," will serve as the first of the two culminating case illustrations. As you read through the case material, note the consultant's reflections on the case. These reflections will highlight the manner in which this one consultant has attempted to incorporate the various principles, theories, and strategies discussed throughout the text to this one case.

The Original Referral

As the counselor for all 10th-grade students, our counselor–consultant, Mr. Thomas, was given a referral by Dr. L. S. Jameson, the assistant principal. The referral requested that he see Ellen, a 10th grader for whom Dr. Jameson had some serious concerns. The referral read as follows.

> "Please see Ellen M. immediately! I am very concerned about her safety. I worked with Ellen quite a bit last year (because of her tendency to inappropriately talk out in class), and I thought we had a good relationship. Well, yesterday I bumped into her in the hall after school. I began to talk to her and noticed she looked upset. She wouldn't look me in the eye. When I asked her if something was wrong, she looked down said "No" and then stated she had "to get home, right away!" Physically she looked fine to me, in fact she has lost some weight and looked as if she was giving more time to her hair and makeup. I know I don't have a lot to go on, just a feeling, and therefore I don't want to do anything official yet, but I think, maybe, she is being abused or doing drugs or something pretty serious. You need to check this out!

Consultant Reflections

- I don't know Ellen, other than seeing her in the hall. This is potentially very serious. I need to respond quickly and see her.
- It appears that Dr. Jameson anticipates a provisional, direct-service approach from the counseling office. That is a bit surprising because he and I previously talked about a collaborative consultative approach to counseling. I thought he understood and agreed. (preentry issues).
- Well, I will need to see Ellen, but I don't want to reinforce this direct-service provisional model expected by Dr. J. This is a good opportunity to reintroduce the collaborative, triadic nature of consultation.

Entry Considerations

- I need to reduce the cost of talking with me. Dr. Jameson is always on the move, so rather than formally invite him to the office or schedule to meet with him, I think I'll go roam the halls to see if I can spontaneously connect with him.
- If he's expecting direct service, he may feel frustrated or disappointed with me seeing him first. I need to give him some immediate payoff (thank him for his concern and let him know about the meeting I scheduled with Ellen today) and highlight his "expert power" and value to the process.
- I must remember Dr. Jameson's tendency to want to probe into students' personal issues and watch for boundaries and confidentiality issues.
- I must remember that the entire school just went through extensive training on the laws and responsibility governing child

CASE 14.1   Continued

abuse reporting, and there is a real heightened sensitivity right now both regarding professional duties and anxiety regarding litigation issues. I wonder if that is what is happening here?

- I know Dr. Jameson at a professional level only. He seems to be a concerned educator. I have heard he seems to want to step into the role of counselor when working with the students—I wonder if he will be challenged working with me?

- Without any other indications (e.g., physical changes, behavioral changes, other teachers' reports), I wonder if Dr. Jameson is overreacting or responding to something else (perhaps lack of information or loss of objectivity).

(Entry) Initial Session with Dr. Jameson

Dr. Jameson: You are going to see Ellen right away aren't you?

Mr. Thomas: I know this is very concerning to you and I will see Ellen as soon as possible. But I really wanted to get your insight on the situation. As we talked about before, it really is a lot more productive when I can collaborate with someone who has a lot of experience with the client. In fact I really would like to see if we can come up things that we both can do to help Ellen. Is that okay?

Dr. Jameson: Sure . . . I know the consultation thing . . .

Mr. Thomas: Great. It would help if you could tell me what you have been seeing with Ellen. I know we all have been under a lot of stress these past few weeks, so maybe whatever is

affecting Ellen is impacting others. It would be nice to head it off at the pass if it is.

Consultant Reflections

- Dr. Jameson appears somewhat resistant to this approach. I need to keep the costs down and get some type of immediate payoff for him.

- I know he understands the consultation approach and even the benefits in terms of prevention as well as providing intervention, but I'm not sure he's bought into it.

- I've heard that he enjoys playing the counselor with the students and in fact knows a lot about the community and their families. That's the expertise he brings to this consult; I need to point that out, while highlighting my own experience with working this way.

In the meeting with Dr. J., the consultant agreed to talk with Ms. Blue (Ellen's resource teacher) and to review her records before meeting with her. Dr. Jameson agreed to collect some observations about Ellen's interaction with others, such as her peers at lunch or other teachers in the hallway. The two agreed to meet in three days to discuss these data.

Exploration (Looking at Client, Task, and Environment)

In attempting to explore the depth and breadth of the problem, the consultant begins to collect data on the client, the tasks that appear problematic, and the environment in which the client is functioning. This last component, the environment, includes exploration of the consultee's knowledge, skill, and objectivity as well as the culture, processes, and structures that characterize the school.

(Continued)

CASE 14.1   Continued

Consultant Reflections

- I know my predecessor used a direct-service approach, and that seems to be the expectation of everyone in the school. I need to respect that expectation and start by gathering information about Ellen. But I need to continue to introduce the idea of expanding our view of the "problem" by including information on the task and environment. Plus, even though Dr. Jameson is used to simply sending the students, I need to keep him involved.

The Client

The consultant, approximating a direct-service model, gathered information through review of the cumulative record, interview with Dr. Jameson, and Ms. Blue (the resource room teacher) and even the client, Ellen. The data collected present the following picture of Ellen.

Ellen is a 15-year-old student in the 10th grade. She has a Full Scale IQ WISC IV Score of 78 (Verbal IQ: 84; Performance IQ 76). The school espouses adherence to the values and practice of inclusion (that is providing all students with the needed education in the least-restrictive environment). And as such, there are no special education classes within the school, although a resource room is available and some students are programmed into the room for individual assistance, as recommended by their subject teachers. Ellen has struggled through school since first grade. Up to this point her grades have generally been Ds and Cs. She has not failed any courses up to this point and is in fact on track to graduate. It has been very difficult, however, for her to keep up with the work, and it appears that it is getting harder as she progresses through high school.

In the ninth grade, after a review of her progress, she was assigned to work in the resource room for mathematics. Ellen was very upset with that decision and hated being assigned to what she called "the dummy room." However, through discussions with Dr. Jameson, she finally agreed, noting that although it may help her now, "she would get out of it—real quick!"

Ellen lives with her mother (an accountant), father (an elementary school teacher in a neighboring system), and younger sister (age 8, grade 2). The family has been in this school district for 8 years, having moved from a neighboring state when Ellen was in second grade.

The Consultee (meetings with Dr. Jameson)

Dr. J.: Well what did you find?

Mr. Thomas: Well, it is clear how much you care about Ellen and have worked with her through this resource room placement.

Dr. J.: That was a real bear. I was battling everyone, even Ellen.

Mr. Thomas: You know, it is funny you should say that. Maybe some of the reaction you received from Ellen is a reflection of her unhappiness about being in the resource room. I think you said she called it the "dummy room"?

Dr. J.: No, it's more than that . . . that's a good placement for her . . . did you see Ellen?

Mr. Thomas: She's coming down after fourth period today.

Dr. J.: Good, you need to talk with her.

Mr. Thomas: But before I do, I really would like to tap your expertise. What did you observe over the past few days?

CASE 14.1 Continued

Consultant Reflections
- Dr. J. seems very sensitive about the resource room placement. I wonder if something is blocking his objectivity here?
- It is clear that Dr. J. wants me to see Ellen, so I will, and I will get back to him in hopes that seeing her will be some sort of payoff for him. He really didn't want to do anything else until I saw her.

Meeting with Client
Being new to the school this year, the counselor–consultant has had only superficial contact (e.g., saying "Hi" in the hall) with Ellen. The initial contact with Ellen was somewhat strained. She presented as somewhat guarded and stated that "everything is fine—except for that dummy class!"

Ellen stated that school is going okay, with the exception of resource room, which "(she) really hates." She stated that she feels like she is wasting her time in that "dummy room" and is totally embarrassed when she has to go there. In the interview Ellen stated that she "is not very popular and has only a very few good friends." Although she noted that she "would like more friends," it isn't really bad because most of the students in her class seem to treat her in a friendly manner.

Ellen, while appearing guarded in her disclosure, maintained appropriate eye contact and generally demonstrated mature social behavior. When asked about home and her parents, she was quick to respond that "Everything is fine." Ellen went on to share that she and her mom and dad had recently become members of the church choir, and she is real excited about singing in the choir and even began to think that she would like to go to college to become a music teacher. When questioned about drug

or alcohol use, Ellen shared her feelings about how she believes that God gave her a body that she must care for and that drugs or "excessive" drinking or even smoking cigarettes damages the body, and as such she feels it is wrong. Her response appeared natural and genuine. She shared with the counselor that her mom and dad were going to come in to talk with the principal about moving her out of the resource room, and she wanted to know if (the counselor) could help her with that.

Consultant Reflections
- Overall, although being a private person, Ellen appeared nondefensive about her family, her Christian values and church involvement, and her antidrug stance. Further, she appeared healthy, well cared for, and gave no evidence of physical abuse.
- Her church involvement appears to be developmentally appropriate and is nonsupportive of drug involvement or family abuse.
- I am concerned about the issue of friends. I need to find out more about the extent of her social isolation both in school and perhaps at home to see if that is something with which I could be of assistance.
- I need to get a better feel for the resource room and the appropriateness of this placement. This may be the thing I can connect and contract with Ellen.
- I wonder if the culture here is one that promotes the perception of the resource room as a "dummy room"? If it does, it will eventually impact other kids negatively.
- I need to try to establish a relationship with Ellen to help her develop realistic career goals.
- I wonder if Ellen's reaction to Dr. Jameson had something to do
(Continued)

CASE 14.1   Continued

with the resource room? Was she angry at him? Maybe she was embarrassed knowing he knows she's in the "dummy class"?

- I need to try to share my observations with Dr. Jameson and get his insights about the resource room and how it is perceived.

Feedback to Consultee (continued Exploration)
Although Dr. Jameson made the referral and was willing to meet with the consultant, he continued to push for direct service. In sharing his observations, the consultant was aware of Dr. J.'s "disappointment" with the feedback. He assumed a negative physical stance toward the consultant, crossing his arms and appearing to be ready to walk away, not squaring his shoulders. When presented with the counselor's observations, he responded by saying "Boy, you are green. She's got you snowed. I know her, and there is definitely something serious going on here!" When informed that Ellen's mom and dad wanted to come in for a conference, Dr. Jameson appeared to become more agitated stating: "You really don't expect that they are going to come in—they don't care." When asked to explain what he meant, Dr. Jameson simply stated, "I know their type."

The counselor found out that what appears to be an antagonistic or belligerent style by Dr. J. has been experienced by others (e.g., Ms. Blue) but appears to be more noticeably directed to the counselors. Although he is fair with the kids, he is generally perceived by students and faculty as not very approachable or personable. According to Dr. Jameson, he worked with Ellen off and on throughout her ninth-grade experience. He expressed a sense of pride with the work he did, noting: "If it wasn't for me she

probably wouldn't have made it through the year." From Ellen's perspective, Dr. Jameson always treated her fairly, and although she has no interest in spending time with him, states that she does like him and he did help her. She feels that sometimes he gives her "too much attention," however.

Consultant Reflections
- Dr. Jameson appears to be defensive around the counselors and manifests that defensiveness by becoming abrasive and antagonistic.
- It appears that Dr. Jameson becomes defensive when directly confronted; I will need to continue to build referent and expert power and use indirect forms of confrontation.
- Dr. Jameson appears to have success with Ellen both in terms of assisting her with a classroom problem and in developing a personal relationship.
- I wonder if Dr. Jameson has lost some professional objectivity in relationship to Ellen and is overly involved with being her caretaker? Or perhaps even concerned that if "she doesn't need his help" she won't call on him or continue to relate to him?

Exploration (continued . . . exploring the System)
Resource room (task and environment): Information about the resource room was gathered from consultation with Dr. J. and observation of Ms. Blue's classroom. The data collected suggested the following.

Ellen has always had particular difficulties in math. She barely got Ds in her mathematics classes, and although she might be expected to do better in the resource room setting, she is struggling just as much. Ellen is

CASE 14.1   Continued

teamed with three other students in the resource room. They are doing word problems. The tasks for doing these problems entail: (1) Converting the written word into mathematical symbols and equations, (2) going to the board with answers, and (3) group work.

Ellen spends 90 minutes a day in the resource room with three other students. The teacher uses a token economy to keep the kids on task. Although Ellen is able to function without this high level of external motivation, she is comfortable with it. The lighting in the room is dim, it is fairly noisy, and Ellen sits on the side of the class away from the window. She stated that she is accepted by the others in the class and is in fact somewhat looked up to as one of the smarter kids.

Ellen's teacher, Ms. Blue, is the only resource room teacher in the school. She is generally liked by her students, but she is viewed as ineffective by parents and her peers. Most believe that although she is supportive and enthusiastic with the students, she lacks the skills to focus her students on task behavior. The implementation of the token economy came at the suggestion of the principal as a way to assist Ms. Blue in keeping the students on task. However, Ms. Blue feels that setting up and maintaining the economy has taken more energy than she suspected, and she hasn't been able to attend to teaching the students as much as and the way that she should. Ellen is not particularly close to Ms. Blue. In fact, she is not very trusting of most of the adults at school.

Ms. Blue did state that Ellen is active in class and is the best student in the resource room. In fact, Ms. Blue was questioning the value of Ellen's placement in the resource room. She felt that perhaps hooking Ellen up with a tutor would be a more effective way to help her with the mathematics. Ms. Blue also noted that she was considering returning Ellen to her regular math class at the end of the marking period, although Dr. Jameson seems to be resistant to that idea. Ms. Blue noted that each time she approached Dr. Jameson with the idea, he would insist that Ellen needs additional support.

Consultant Reflections
- Ellen's concerns about the inappropriateness of her placement seem supported by Ms. Blue.
- Ms. Blue's suggestion about returning Ellen to her regular classroom with the additional support of a tutor appears appropriate.
- What is Dr. Jameson reacting to? Does he know something I am still missing? Is it something going on within him, perhaps interfering with his level of objectivity?
- Does Ellen know Dr. Jameson has been resisting her return to the regular class? If so, maybe that explains her reaction to him in the hall.
- Why is Ms. Blue unable to help Ellen get placed back into the regular classes? What is her role? Power?

School Culture, Structure, and Organization (exploration continued)
The high school is in a supportive, white, middle-class, rural community. The school is rather small (300 students for four grades), with a low teacher-to-student ratio. With so few in the school, most students know each other and each others' families. Most of the families whose children are in the school have lived in this community for generations. Further,

(Continued)

CASE 14.1   Continued

most of the teachers and staff live in the community, with many having attended this school. The counselor and Dr. Jameson are the only two professional staff members who are not originally from this area.

The consultant is the first and only full-time counselor the school has had. Two teachers also work in the counseling department as 25% of their load. Prior to hiring the full-time counselor, the counseling was performed by the part-time teacher–counselors and Dr. Jameson.

Although the economy of the community is primarily agricultural, the mission of the school is to prepare students for postsecondary education. Most of the students go to college, and most return to this environment to work and live.

Consultant Reflections

■ As an outsider (to this community) I need to go slow and be sensitive to their cultural ways of doing things. Maybe being an outsider may elicit system and community resistance.

■ Because I am the first full-time counselor, the faculty and administration are unclear about how the counselor should function. But being a small school, they are used to collaborating. So a collaborative approach may be acceptable, even though Dr. Jameson sent Ellen for direct service.

■ To be effective I need to develop referent power with Dr. Jameson. Perhaps working on the issue of being outsiders and how difficult it is to connect with a closed, somewhat private community may give us some point of common reference.

■ With Dr. Jameson's limited connections within the community

at large and within the school community, is it possible he is using his relationship with Ellen as a way of establishing himself or meeting his own needs for relationship?

■ With the focus on post-high-school education, is Ellen feeling additional pressure to get out the resource room? Is it possible that the resource room is a social stigma as suggested by Ellen? If so, that may be an area for future systems-focused consultation.

■ I would like to enter at the consultee-focused level of consultation working with Dr. Jameson around possible loss of objectivity, while at the same time assisting him to find a balance between being the disciplinarian and the supportive administrator by demonstrating increased approachability to all students (and staff). I'm not sure if this will be possible.

Goal Setting

Consultant Reflections

■ Working directly with Ellen on the issue of abuse and/or drug involvement appears to be unnecessary. But with Dr. J. expressing a real concern, I will need to be sensitive in redefining the goal. I will try to reenter with Dr. Jameson around the new issue of Ellen's resource room placement and redefine the service to be collaborative working at the level of a client-focused consultation.

■ This may be a good way to reinforce the collaborative nature of consultation and keep Dr. J. central to the process. Refocusing our efforts on working with Ellen around the issue of the resource room should help because

CASE 14.1   Continued

he has been so involved with that and therefore has expert power in that area.

- As we work, we can observe Ellen's response in the resource room, and we can also be gathering more data to test for the possibility of any drug involvement or abuse.
- Further, by working with him around Ellen's resource room concern, I may be able to provide some indirect confrontation (via modeling and parable presentations) to confront Dr. Jameson's perceptions of Ellen as needing to be rescued from a much larger issue.

Meeting with Dr. J.

Dr. J.: Well, what's our plan?

Mr. Thomas: I've been thinking quite a bit about this. As I mentioned to you, Ellen is really annoyed about this resource room thing.

Dr. J.: Hey—we've been through this—she needs it.

Mr. Thomas: Well—I agree we have been through this, and you certainly are much more the expert when it comes to the resource room then I am. But, I was wondering. Do you think it would be of any value in building a better relationship with Ellen and therefore being able to see if anything else is going on in her life if we could establish some measure or criteria for her to meet in order to move out of the resource room?

Dr. J.: I don't understand.

Mr. Thomas: You know how you have experienced Ellen as somewhat hesitant to speak with you?

Dr. J.: Yeah—that's what initially concerned me.

Mr. Thomas: Well, I thought if we showed that we were working on something that she valued—like setting a plan for her moving from the resource room—that she would then see us as allies and would once again be more open. This would allow us to see if anything else, like your concerns about possible drug use, is an issue.

Dr. J.: I see. You know, maybe it would be best if I came up with the "measure" and shared it with Ellen.

Mr. Thomas: Because Ms. Blue has been working with her in the resource room, I wonder if it would help to have her on board. Perhaps both of you could come up with criteria that Ms. Blue could observe and then report on?

Dr. J.: Sure! She sees Ellen every day. I'll meet with her to formulate some reasonable criteria for Ellen to meet.

Mr. Thomas: That sounds like a good idea. I wonder, though, if I could join you and Ms. Blue when you present this to Ellen? I'd love to see the smile on her face.

Dr. J.: Oh, yeah . . . sure.

Consultant Reflections

- Well, with the goal to set a standard or set of criteria for moving out of the resource room, I'm hoping that not only will Ellen begin to feel more hopeful, but maybe developing these criteria will help Dr. J. to more objectively see for whom and when such

(Continued)

CASE 14.1   Continued

resource assignment is needed. (**redefining the task**)
- If Dr. J.'s judgment is being distorted by a lack of objectivity, working on this standard should not only confront that but also serve as a means for preventing it to influence his decision about retention in the resource room. (**consultee-focused consultation**)
- Involving Ms. Blue in the development and monitoring of the criteria for Ellen will empower her and bring her into a better working relationship with Dr. J. It will certainly help to clarify the role of the resource room and its teacher. (**System-focused consultation**)

Intervention Planning

Dr. J.: I reviewed the original mission and purpose of the resource room. In fact, I had to go to Ms. Blue for it because I couldn't find my copy.

Mr. Thomas: Great idea—that's where we should start. I'm glad you included Ms. Blue in the process. If this is going to work, not just for Ellen, but for all the students using the resource room, we will need her on board.

Dr. J.: Well, here's what I did (handing Mr. Thomas a paper).

Mr. Thomas: Great job. Wow! I like how you even created a goal statement for each student in the resource center. That certainly gives us the base for creating a measurable outcome. You can tell you were once a teacher.

Dr. J.: I guess those skills don't fade.

Mr. Thomas: How about if the three of us meet with Ellen to tell her the plan.

Dr. J.: Sounds like a plan. What do you think about the idea of asking Ms. Blue to use this format to develop objectives and outcome measure for the other students?

Mr. Thomas: That would certainly prevent this type of problem from occurring again! Great idea.

Consultant Reflections
- It appears that Dr. J. really feels empowered and valued for his expertise.
- I like the fact that he is using inclusive language with "us" and "our" plan.
- The fact that he is generalizing the process to include other students is fantastic, really hitting the preventive goal that I was hoping for.
- I'll need to reinforce his efforts as well as encourage Ms. Blue to continue her collaboration with Dr. J.
- I can't wait until we meet with Ellen. I know she will want to "get out" immediately, but if we can get her to look at the performance criteria that we have set, she will be surprised to find that she can demonstrate these things already, and therefore she will be out soon.

Maintenance

Consultant Reflections
- I've been very impressed with the work that Dr. J. and Ms. Blue have been doing to establish specific learning contracts for the students in the resource room. I have made a special effort to not only tell them, but also to ask that I sit in on some of their meetings to learn from them.

CASE 14.1   Continued

- I have noticed how Dr. J. has been visiting the resource room and encouraging the students by asking them if he could see their work. I told him how valuable it was for him to be verbally reinforcing the children for their work. I also told him how his presence and support has really energized Ms. Blue.
- As I suspected, Ellen was initially disappointed because she did not immediately get out of the resource room. But my follow-up with her seemed to help her see the concrete steps she needs to take and even project a time line for moving out of the resource room. I've encouraged her to share with Dr. J. what she is doing, what she has accomplished—pointing out that this is a great way for her to let him know she's ready to move on.

Termination

Mr. Thomas: Well, we've certainly come a long way in a short three weeks.

Dr. J.: I really appreciate what you've done.

Mr. Thomas: What we've done! I know the initial concern was Ellen, but with you sharing your insights and working with Ms. Blue, we not only were able to help Ellen achieve her goal, but we also have reestablished that supportive relationship that you have had with her. But I guess the real surprise for me was that we've developed a new process for resource room placement. I think with the learning contracts that you and Ms. Blue developed that other students, including some gifted students, may start to be referred.

Dr. J.: If that happens it would be great—really a way to change

that image of it being a "dummy room"!

Mr. Thomas: You know, maybe that's something you and I could talk more about. I mean I wonder what steps we could take to change the culture and perception of the resource room around here?

Consultant Reflections

- Well, Dr. J. appears satisfied with the outcome, as does Ellen.
- I feel really good that we not only addressed the immediate concern with Ellen but also were able to make some adjustments to the system that should reduce the possibility of similar problems in the future.
- I am really happy that Dr. J. seems enthused about discussing my ideas around changing the culture of the school and the perceptions around the nature and value of the resource room. He is truly an opinion leader, and with his help we may be able to make some significant system changes. I'll have to set up a meeting (**entry**) to see if we can explore this.

Case Postscript

The relationship was redefined from one of counselor provisional service to collaboration, and the focus of service was redefined to be one of indirect consultation intervention at the client-focused level. The consultant in this case was able to educate the consultee (Dr. Jameson) to the extended focus for the service being one of prevention and intervention and thus focusing on the role played by extrapersonal factors (including Dr. Jameson, the school environment, curriculum, etc.). This redefinition and recontracting required that the consultant be extremely sensitive to the points of

(Continued)

CASE 14.1   Continued

resistance both within the system and those emanating from Dr. Jameson and be attentive to developing a reduced cost, immediately gratifying relationship with a balance of referent and expert power. The end result was not only a solution for the original presenting concern, but also a system modification that should serve an ongoing preventive value.

CASE 14.2   A Solution-Focused Approach: Benny—A Picture of "Energy"

The second case, the case of Benny, proceeds from prereferral considerations through exploration, goal setting, and intervention planning and implementation. Although the stages of the consultation process are once again presented as almost linear, it will become apparent that the process cycles back and forth across these stages. You will also notice that the counselor–consultant is employing a solution-focused approach to this case. As you read and reflect on this case, see if you can recognize the aspects of the consult that are uniquely solution focused.

As you read the case data, you are reminded to practice "thinking like a consultant." Although the actual reflections of the consultant are not listed, you will note spots where reflections are indicated, and hints are provided to help you focus on the issues that may need to be addressed. It may be helpful to discuss your response to these points of consultant reflection with a colleague or supervisor to benefit from their perspectives. Further, as you read through the case consider each of the following guiding questions.

1. What are the expectations regarding the consultant role and job definition? Do the expectations—the job contract— place limits on the things the consultant is free to do?

2. What unique system factors must be considered as a means of reducing system resistance?

3. What unique consultee variables or factors must be considered and responded to in order to reduce consultee resistance to collaborative consultation? What special relationship considerations should I be aware of to develop and maintain a collaborative consultee relationship?

4. What appears to be the optimal level for consultation intervention (i.e., client focused, consultee focused, group focused, or system focused)?

5. What is the feasible level of consultation at this time? If different from the optimal, what elements prevent from operating at the optimal level? What steps can be initiated to move to re-contracting at the optimal level at a later time?

6. What is the specific focus for consultation intervention (i.e., goals)?

7. What intervention techniques or strategies appear appropriate and possible for this problem?

8. How will you know that the consultation was successful—both

---

CASE 14.2   Continued

in outcomes and process—and how could you demonstrate that success to the consultee or others?

Case Background

The school counselor, Mary Lou Dobbins, has been able to develop strong collaborative working relationships with all the teachers at Westview Elementary School. Through her 6 years of service at the school, she has worked hard to develop the teachers' expectation that they are referring themselves for assistance when initiating a teacher referral. Moreover, the teachers fully expect that they will be active participants throughout the remediation (i.e., consultative) process.

Stage 1. Preentry

The groundwork for this step has already been laid, as the consultant has established clear expectations for the role and function of each party in the consult, an efficient mechanism for teacher–counselor communication, and provided a timely response to the teacher referral. Ms. Dobbins requested that the teacher complete a referral form when initiating a consult. The form emphasizes the goal and solution-focused approach used by Ms. Dobbins by having the teacher provide, in addition to a brief description of the presenting concern, information on the student's (i.e., client's) strengths, successes, and exceptions to the presenting concerns. Instances (the most recent the better) when the teacher was successful with Benny are also solicited. To cast the consult in a positive, success- and future-oriented frame, the teacher is asked to note evidence that would indicate that the consult was successful.

The current case referral was sent by Ms. Carolyn Fox, one of three fifth-grade teachers at Westview Elementary School. Ms. Fox was seeking some assistance with one of her students, Benny, whom she described as "a very energetic boy."

Entry

Ms. Carolyn Fox, the consultee in this case, has spent the past 7 years teaching fifth grade at this relatively affluent, suburban school comprising 583 students enrolled in grades K–5. Teaching 23 students in one of three fifth grades, Ms. Fox employs a student-centered teaching methodology with frequent use of cooperative group activities, computer technology, and creative expression. Her classroom is usually boisterous, alive, and energetic with students actively engaged in projects. Through her frequent opportunities to formally and informally interact with her students, Ms. Fox has displayed strong encouragement, nurturance, and patience with her students. But of late, she has been exasperated by the hostile and aggressive behavior displayed by Benny, and she sent the following request for assistance.

Mary Lou, I really could use your assistance. Benny, while only 10 years old, has already established a long history of bullying his peers. Ever since entering first grade, he has used aggression to meet his needs and maintain power over the other children. Hitting, pushing, threatening, and verbally abusing others have characterized his peer interactions, while oppositional defiance is frequently directed toward the adults in his life.

Benny has a keen intelligence and special talent for drawing. These qualities have helped him prove successful academically. Through my discussion with colleagues I have found that other

(Continued)

CASE 14.2   Continued

teachers are as baffled as I by the fear and anger that he evokes in others.

According to our principal, Dr. Hanson, they wanted me to work with Benny because he felt that my style of engaging the students in a positive manner might lead him to a path of civility. But to be honest with you, I've been less than successful. By November, Benny had been well into his old aggressive ways. To be honest, I'm a little down on myself for not being able to work this out, but know that two heads are better than one, so I would love to discuss this case with you!

Counselor Reflections (Entry concerns and issues? Hint: Issues of confidentiality, role clarification, building collaboration, etc.)

Exploration

The information included on the solution-focused referral form lead naturally to stage three of the consult. Although a solution-focused approach emphasizes success, strengths, and positive indicators of goal attainment, with problem exploration the antithesis of solution formation, the consultee's experience of the concern must be acknowledged and respected. As mentioned previously, consultees will often seek help after persistent failure, rendering feelings of frustration, inadequacy, anger, and even shame. Their request for help includes a strong desire for understanding, recognition of their efforts and affirmation of their efficacy as teachers. Only in telling their story to an empathic, concerned colleague can they feel understood and view the consultant as a competent collaborator. In recognition of this consultee need, the consultant uses her reflective listening and empathy skills as Ms. Fox

describes her frustration and crisis of confidence in her failed attempts to bring civility to Benny's behavior.

Counselor Reflections (Hint: From solution focus framework, reframe concerns to focus on consultee and client strengths?)

While Ms. Fox shares her story, Mary Lou, our counselor–consultant listens for any indication of consultee and client success and consultee resources that can be employed in successful solutions. The counselor–consultant attempts to reframe her pronouncements of failure, disappointment, and frustration as patient, diligent, and even creative efforts to help a very challenging student to succeed.

As the dialogue continues, the consultant begins to recognize that Benny seems to like Ms. Fox and values her nurturing attention. Unfortunately, it appears that much of her attention has been directed to his misbehavior.

Consultant Reflection (Hint: Consider questions to identify if this is a function of consultee knowledge, skill, or objectivity limitations?)

Throughout Ms. Fox's revelations, the consultant acknowledges her story and affirms her feelings while simultaneously emphasizing her strengths and successes. Even the smallest evidence of success (with Benny as well as other students) is identified and emphasized. Attributions and expectations based on labels, absolutes, and hopelessness are reframed as situational behaviors that can (and probably already have) occurred in desirable ways. Defining those desirable ways in explicit, operational terms becomes the task of our next stage.

Goal Setting

The consultant is aware that a solution-focused approach would have the

CASE 14.2   Continued

consultee (teacher) describe what she would like to do differently or more frequently. Quite often, however, the consultee, frustrated with her inability to remedy the situation, needs to vent about the client. As such, Ms. Fox was encouraged to describe her desired goals for the client (student) first. Once goals for the client are formulated, the focus quickly shifts to the consultee's behavior: what she will be doing differently in support of and response to the desired changes in the client.

In response to the counselor–consultant's goal-oriented questions Ms. Fox indicates that she would like Benny to "get along with his peers and follow classroom norms of civility and cooperation." Ms. Fox's initial goal for Benny provided the foundation for the real work in solution-focused consultation, creating different ways of thinking and behaving for both client and consultee.

Consultant Reflections (Hint: Consultation has both remedial and preventive goals—do you see what they may be?)

Goals of civility, cooperation, and compliance, although certainly noble, needed to be much more clearly and concretely defined. It was important to describe these "goals" as behaviors (and their concomitant thoughts) that Benny will be doing. Mary Lou posed

the following questions as a way of moving the consultee to more concretely define what it was she desired. "What will Benny be doing when he is being civil and cooperative? What behaviors has he already done (i.e., exceptions) in your class or at any other time that are civil and cooperative?"

Consultant Reflections (Hint: A "Miracle Question," the value of scaling)

As Ms. Fox and the consultant continued to identify even the smallest increments of behavioral change that would be desired (i.e., objectives), the counselor–consultant posed the following: "Carolyn, if Benny were completely civil and cooperative what would that look like? How would he be behaving?" After gaining that description, the consultant asked the consultee to consider the following: "If this very best behavior was represented by 10 on a scale, and his very worst behavior a one on that scale, where would you score his current (i.e., baseline)?" To which the consultee responded "4."

By asking Ms. Fox such questions as: "What will Benny be doing at each level? What will you see, hear, and experience at each level?" the resulting collaborative goal scaling reveals the following:

WORST			BASELINE						BEST
1	2	3	4	5	6	7	8	9	10

WORST	BASELINE	BEST
bullies others	helps others in art	shares, cooperates
throws tantrums	lines up for lunch, recess	complies with requests
ignores requests	plays UNO with Tim	smiles and laughs
pulls desk apart	kind to class hamster	volunteers to help
		listens to others
		plays constructively
		expresses feelings appropriately

(Continued)

CASE 14.2   Continued

Expanding the scope of the consultation in an attempt to address extrapersonal factors and ensure that both prevention and remediation result, the consultant refocused the discussion to those behaviors (and thoughts) of Ms. Fox that will support Benny's behaviors at each succeeding level from his current baseline of four. In so doing, a goal scale is formulated for Ms. Fox that reflects what will support Benny's progress and reveal what she wants to be doing at each level leading to a 10.

Consultant Reflections (Hint: Importance of appropriate confrontation and factors involved in consultee-focused consultation, consensual validation of outcome and subobjectives).

Intervention Strategies

As the consultant helped Ms. Fox consider her own behavior in relationship to Benny's functioning at the 10 level, she began to identify that she will be directing her nurturing attention to Benny's "good" behavior rather than attending simply to his "bad behavior."

Consultant Reflections (Prevention value? Question of knowledge or skill? Future opportunity for system intervention?)

The consultee felt that if she focused on his natural strengths and ability to help others, she could begin to delegate more responsibilities and opportunities to Benny. This would help him develop more positive ways to interact with his peers and gain appropriate status. Further, she hoped that this would provide her with much more energy and time to devote to other students, and she will feel more competent and satisfied in her teaching. Rather than make a separate goal scale for Ms. Fox, these goals were incorporated into Benny's goal scale so that the relationship

between Benny's progress and Ms. Fox's goals are clearly understood and appreciated.

In order to more concretely identify intervention steps that would help move both Benny and Ms. Fox up on the goal scale, the consultant invited Ms. Fox to work on formulating subgoals that described what she and Benny would be doing at each level extending from baseline (4) to outcome goal (10). With data from levels 4 and 10 as references, Ms. Fox proposed the following goals for level 5: Benny will help her create a bulletin board on the Westward Movement, with drawings and maps of his own creation; and for his help she will give him special time to play UNO with Tim and even take the hamster home for the weekend. In addition, Ms. Fox will ignore his disruptive behavior as much as possible and instead focus on any behavior indicative of movement toward a 10. Unruly behavior requiring attention will be dispatched through a time-out procedure or administrative intervention.

Consultant Reflections (Hint: Is the intervention possible? What role for the consultant at this stage? How might the system support this strategy?)

As these subgoals were incorporated into the composite client and consultee goal scale, the consultant moved into the maintenance stage of the consulting process.

Consultant Reflections (Hint: What solutions does the consultee currently possess for moving through the scale, and how does the consultant assist?)

Maintenance

You may have noticed that the specific behavioral changes identified by the consultee emanated directly from her goals for Benny and herself.

CASE 14.2   Continued

These behavioral changes are already in her repertoire and constitute the strategies and solutions of this consultative intervention. Once Ms. Fox determined how she wanted Benny and herself to be, it remained only for the consultant to help her to redirect already existing strengths and resources to the task. What Ms. Fox will do at the five, six and subsequent levels she has already done successfully and with confidence. The consultant redirects Ms. Fox to her past successes and their translation into new solutions. The consultant discusses Ms. Fox's behaviors that she will exhibit when at level five.

Consultant Reflections (Hint: Understood, need for rehearsal? Support? Obstacles?)

Ms. Fox's motivation stemming from concrete and attainable goals is enhanced by the consultant's encouragement and commitment to her success. To this end, the consultant scheduled an additional meeting with her to review her (and Benny's) progress and help her to identify goals (behaviors and strategies) appropriate for each succeeding level of the goal scale.

Consultant Reflections (Hint: Termination? Criteria?)

Subsequent meetings were scheduled. A focus in each of these session was to reinforce the consultee's sense of a positive trajectory and its consultee-centered locus of control. For example, the consultant was highly supportive and reinforcing each time Ms. Fox reported situations, such as: a time when she and Benny drew a map of the Oregon Trail or a time when she gave him a warm "Thanks" when she actually "caught him" standing patiently in line at the water fountain. In addition to reinforcing her behavior, the consultant asked her: "How did **you choose** to do that?" The intent of this solution-focused question was to keep the locus of control for choice and change within the consultee. This consultee-focused processing of even the smallest increments of success is critical to the ultimate success of solution-focused consultation and leads naturally to termination.

Termination

In one of the meetings, Ms. Fox expressed her feelings that the attainment of level 10 was not required to define success. She felt that she had currently attained the level of success (8 on her scale) for which she was satisfied. Thus, the current consultation contract was terminated.

Consultant Reflections (Hint: Desire to spread the effect, seek additional referral)

Before terminating, the consultant reviewed with the consultee the various steps and activities in which they engaged. The consultant highlighted the specific steps the consultee has taken—the behaviors she has employed—to move up the scale. The consultant complimented the consultee for successes and efforts. Complimenting will enhance the consultee's internal locus of control for specific behavioral accomplishments and what the consultee did to foster these successes. Before ending, the consultant thanked the consultee for the opportunity to work together and reiterated her availability should the consultee seek assistance in the future.

Postscript

Upon completion of the case, the consultant reflected on her experience in hopes of identifying ways to improve her consultative skills. She also began to consider the potential value of providing a schoolwide in-service on the issue of "catching them at being good," a point she felt may have some prevention value.

out of various stages almost simultaneously. Figure 14.1, depicts an integrated view of the stages of consultation. The graphic highlights the stages of a consultation and will serve as a reference point for the cases which follow. Further, Table 14.1, provides a listing of the types of tasks to be accomplished at each stage.

A CONCLUDING THOUGHT:
NOT AN END, BUT A BEGINNING!

Throughout the text, various methods and strategies for diagnosing problems, establishing goals, engaging in consultation relationships, and implementing intervention strategies have been discussed. It must be emphasized, however, that as with other forms of helping, it is the quality of the person of the helper, or in this case the consultant, that is far more important than any skill or strategy. As a skilled, effective counselor–consultant, it is essential that one be first and foremost an authentic, ethical, and caring helper.

Although this is the end of this text, it is really only the beginning of an ongoing and continuing process of becoming a skilled, effective, and ethical consultant. We hope this was a good beginning, and we wish you well as you continue your development.

REFERENCE

Parsons, R. D., & Brown, K. S. (2002). *Teachers as Reflective practitioner and action researcher.* Belmont, CA: Wadsworth.

Index

A

A-B-C model (cognitive–behavioral)
    model, 123–25, 200, 204, 205, 211
Academic counseling, 3
Academic placement, 54
Accountability, 77, 78, 324–26
    of consultant and consultee, 11–12
    in job performance criteria, 80, 82
    of school guidance programs, 57, 58
Accurate empathy, 119, 139, 145,
    183, 239
Action researchers, 24
Active listening skills, 119, 121, 142–49,
    180, 259
Activity in solution implementation, 268
Administrations
    as consumers in school systems, 52
    and organizational structure, 76–78
Administrative coaches, 24
Administrators, 75
Adversarial relationships, 88, 165
Advocating for client and system,
    87–89, 310
Affect in BASIC ID model, 205–6
African Americans, 202
Agent for change, 76
    See also Change; Consultant as agent for
        change; System dynamics

Aikido, 185–86
Alcohol abuse, 4, 5
Alienation, 277
American Counseling Association (ACA),
    Code of Ethics and Standards of Practice,
    311, 312, 319, 322, 325
American educational system, 89
American School Counselor Association, 7
Antecedent stimulus in A-B-C model, 123
Anxiety, 124, 166, 184
    about problem finding/problem solving,
        174–75
Apathy, 277
Applications of consultation. *See*
    Consultation applications
Artifacts of the system, 286–87, 288
Asian Americans, 202
Assessment procedures, 133, 214
    See also Evaluation
Attending
    as a physical response, 143–44
    as a psychological response, 144–45
Authentic helpers, 352
Authority, 277, 285
    in job performance criteria, 80, 82
Autonomous problem solving, 125, 133
Aversive consequences, 124
Awards and citations, 102

B

Backward chaining, 269
Balance of power threats, 90–91
Baseline, 129
Basic assumptions of the system, 287, 288
BASIC ID model, 204–9, 211
    affect, 205–6
    behavior, 205
    cognition, 207
    drugs (biology), 207–8
    imagery, 206
    interpersonal relationships, 207
    sensation, 206
BATNA. *See* Best Alternative to a
    Negotiated Agreement
Behavior = *f*(client-task-environment), 198
Behavioral consultation, 23–24
Behavioral theory, 23–24
Behaviorally disordered students, 72
Behavior in BASIC ID model, 205
Behavior modification, 227
Beliefs of consumers and providers in
    systems, 47–48
Benny's case, 346–51
Best Alternative to a Negotiated
    Agreement (BATNA), 261, 262, 263
Blaming, 180
Block, Peter, 279
Body orientation, 143–44
Boundaries
    personal, 235
    professional, 322–23
    in systems, 51, 69, 71, 76, 77
Brainstorming, 141, 330
Breadth of impact continuum, 33–36
Brief approach to consultation. *See*
    Solution focused consultation
Buddhist philosophy, 185
Bullying, 4, 230
Bureaucratic machine model of
    organization, 76, 277
Burnout, 169, 170
Bushido, 185
Businesses, 23, 50

C

Camp David Accords, 257
Caplan, Gerald, and Ruth B. Caplan,
    *Mental Health Consultation and
    Collaboration,* 234
Career development services, 7, 54
Caring helpers, 352
Ceremonies, 286
Chain of command, 75, 76
Chaining in solution implementation, 269

Change
    reaction and resistance, 89–93
    resistance to, 70, 71, 81
    shaping/change in small steps, 97–99
    strategy development and
        implementation, 129–32
    in systems, 78–79
    See also Agent of change; Planned change
        principles; System dynamics
Characterological distortions, 236–37
Clarification, 154–55
    in questioning, 150
Classroom environment, 202–3
Client-focused consultation, 35, 195–217
    BASIC ID model, 204–9, 211
    benefits of, 197–98
    client assessment, 204–9, 211–12
    developing and employing solutions, 214
    focusing on one while impacting many,
        197–98
    goal setting and solution-focused
        consultation, 209–14
    physical environment, 202, 211–12
    prioritization of goals and strategies,
        212–14
    problem identification, 198–209
    social/cultural environment, 202–3,
        211–12
    student service from a consultation
        perspective, 196–97
    task analysis, 199–202, 211–12
    See also Students
Clients
    assessment of, 204–9, 211–12
    direct personal involvement with,
        229–30
    identification of, 323–26
    See also Students
Clinical model of school counseling, 117
Closed questioning, 152–53
Closed systems, 70–71, 76, 81
Closure, 134
Code of Ethics, National Board of Certified
    Counselors (NBCC), 323
Code of Ethics and Standards of Practice,
    American Counseling Association
    (ACA), 311, 312, 319, 322, 325
Codification in schools, 72
Codified protocols, 116, 120
Coequals in consultation, 15–16, 23, 103,
    173, 183, 189
Coercive power, 102
Cognition in BASIC ID model, 207
Cognitive-behavioral (A-B-C) model,
    122–25

Cognitive/behavioral theories, 24
Collaboration continuum, 32–33
Collaborative mode of consultation, 26, 117, 170
Collaborative relationships, 8, 12, 15–16, 20, 38, 76
  in consultation, 175, 178, 180, 189
  in open systems, 77, 82
Committee work, 99
Communication
  miscommunications, 91
  patterns of, 25
  in systems, 69, 76, 77, 90
  top down, 277
Communication in consulting, 138–64
  active listening skills, 142–49
  attending as a physical response, 143–44
  attending as a psychological response, 144–45
  clarification, 154–55
  exploration skills, 149–53
  focusing skills, 153–59
  integrating consultation stages, purposes, and skills, 160–61
  minimal encouraging, 145
  paraphrasing content, 145–47
  purposes and outcomes, 139–42
  questioning art and styles, 149–53
  reflection of feelings, 147–49
  summarizations, 157–59
  tacting response leads, 154, 155–57
  written communication, 160
Communication process, 295–97
Communities
  as consumers in school systems, 48, 52
  life cycle of, 55
  needs of, 54
Community-based services, 4, 23
Competence
  of consultant, 311–12
  in job performance criteria, 80, 82, 86
Competition, 202
Confidentiality, 119, 140, 160, 170, 174, 237, 319–21
Conflict resolution, 248, 257
Conflict theory, 78–79
Confrontation as intervention, 225, 230, 231, 237–42
Consensual agreement, 262–63
Consensual validation of consultee's perspective, 121, 125
Consequences in A-B-C model, 123
Conservatism in school reform and expansion, 52
Constructivist orientation, 210

Consultant as agent for change, 85–111
  adversarial relationships, 88
  advocating for client and system, 87–89
  balance of power threats, 90–91
  goal conflicts, 88–89
  increasing value and power as consultant, 100–105
  miscommunications, 91
  moving in a system crisis, 105–8
  promoting innovation (change), 93–108
  protecting tradition, 92–93
  reaction and resistance, 89–93
  self-preservation, 90
  selling services as consultant, 101
  sunk costs, 91
  See also Agent for change; Change; Planned change principles; System dynamics
Consultants
  accountability and responsibility of, 11–12
  competence of, 311–12
  cultural sensitivity of, 314–18
  decisions in form and focus, 37–39
  incongruent expectations of, 178–79
  increasing value and power as consultant, 100–105
  insensitivity of, 167–69
  interpersonal marketing skills, 22
  personal characteristics of, 175–76
  professional orientation of, 39
  role in consultation, 11
  self-disclosure of, 119
  style of, 175–76
  values of, 312–14
  See also Consultant as agent for change; Counselors
Consultation, 9–17, 312
  as an aversive process, 176–77
  and change, 86–87
  defined, 9–10
  dimensions of, 10–11
  dual focus, 16
  interaction mode, 11
  mutual and voluntary, 15–16
  as paradigm, 9–10
  point of focus, 10–11
  problem-solving focus, 14–15
  professional orientation and skills, 10, 16–17
  role of consultant, 11
  systemic level of entry, 11
  theory employed, 11
  triadic relationship, 11–14

Consultation (*continued*)
  See also Communication in consulting;
    Consultant as agent for change;
    Consultation process stages;
    Consulting model of service
    delivery
Consultation applications, 330–52
  Benny's case, 346–51
  Ellen's case, 336–46
  stages of consultation process, 115–37,
    331–35, 352
Consultation process stages, 115–37,
  331–35, 352
  entry, 115, 118–21
  exploration, 121–25
  integrating consultation stages,
    purposes, and skills, 160–61
  maintenance, 132–35
  outcome goals and objectives, 125–29
  preentry, 116–18
  strategy development and
    implementation, 129–32
  termination, 134–35
  See also Consultant as agent for change;
    Consultation; Consulting model
    of service delivery
Consultee-focused consultation, 35, 218–46
  categories in loss of objectivity, 229–37
  characterological distortions, 236–37
  confrontation as intervention, 225, 230,
    231, 237–42
  consultee as an extrapersonal variable in
    consultation, 219–21
  direct personal involvement with
    student, 229–30
  full-inclusion, 222–23
  interventions, 225–26
  knowledge development, 221–26
  problem identification, 223–25
  professional objectivity, 228–37
  simple identification, 230–31
  skill development, 226–28
  theme interference, 231–34
  transference, 234–35
Consultees
  accountability and responsibility of, 11–12
  anxiety about problem finding/problem
    solving, 174–75
  and consultant insensitivity, 167–69
  control concerns of, 172–73
  in entry stage, 118–21
  expectations of, 169–72
  experience/expectations/style of, 39
  as extrapersonal variables in
    consultation, 219–21

freedom of, 175
  incongruent expectations of, 178–79
  issues and concerns, 169–75
  professional functioning of, 218
  rapport with, 103–4, 139
  requesting personal counseling, 182–83
  subjective perspective of, 121
  and system change, 87
  vulnerable feelings of, 173–74
  See also Resistance in consultation
Consulting model of service delivery, 20–43
  breadth of impact continuum, 33–36
  collaboration continuum, 32–33
  consultant orientation, 39
  consultee experience/expectations/
    style, 39
  content–process continuum, 30–31
  contract in consulting, 37, 38
  felt need continuum, 29–30
  form and focus of consultation, 37–39
  integrating perspectives, 28–37
  nature of problem and goal, 38–39
  See also Consultant as agent for change;
    Parsons's model of consultation
Consumers in systems, 51–52
Content analysis, 289
Content–process continuum, 30–31
Content or process expertise in
  consultation, 24–25, 30–32, 103
Continuing education, 311
Continuous improvement, 278
Continuums in consultation, 28–37
Contracts in consulting, 37, 38, 116, 120,
  160, 169, 170, 178, 183
Contrasting responses in confrontation, 238
Cooperative learning environment, 202–3
Coordinators, 25
Corrective feedback, 298
Cost–payoff benefits of consultation,
  170, 177
Costs
  of consultation encounters, 169
  psychological, 91
  sunken, 91
Counselors, 75
  job performance criteria, 80, 82
  and system dynamics, 79–82
  See also Consultant as agent for change;
    Consultants
Covert behaviors in A-B-C model, 123
Creative problem solving, 212
Creativity, 69, 75, 76
Crisis or developmental nature of
  consultation, 21–22, 29–30, 35
Crisis intervention, 7–8, 35, 57, 118

Criterion reference measures, 227
Critical Path Method, 268
Cultural norms of nonverbal behavior, 143
Cultural sensitivity of consultant, 314–18
Culture of a system, 94–97, 169, 188, 298–304
Current behavior, 128
Current state of need, 53

D
Data, conflicting, 91
Data gathering and organization, 122–25, 140, 141, 278–80, 289–90
Data results in need assessment, 58
"Dead Person" standard, 127
Decision-making, 25
Demographic features of consumers in systems, 53, 54
Desired state of need, 53, 54, 55, 58
Developmental model of service, 7, 16, 57
  See also Preventive model of service
Developmental nature of consultation, 21–22, 29–30
Diagnosticians, 26, 197
Didactic (informational) confrontation, 238
Direct confrontation, 218, 237–38
Direct instruction, 131
Directives in consultation, 141–42, 181, 225
Direct personal involvement with student, 229–30
Direct-service model, 7–8, 24, 132, 310
  one-to-one, 195
  versus indirect service, 14, 35
Disenfranchisement of workers, 277
Distorted thinking, 231
Diversity, 285
Divorce, 4
Documentation, 160
Downsizing, 285
Driving force, 265
Drug abuse, 4
Drugs (biology) in BASIC ID model, 207–8
Duty to Warn, 119
Dyadic relationship, 14

E
Ecological–systems theories, 24
Ecology, 16
Education, advanced, 102
Education for All Handicapped Children Act, 89
Educational planning services, 7
Educational programming, 218, 225, 226
Educator/trainer, 23, 24, 25
Effective helpers, 352

Efficacy of treatment, 324–25
Egalitarianism, 285
Electronic communications, 160
Ellen's case, 336–46
Emotional impairment, 4
Emotions, reflection of feelings, 147–49
Emotions or affective labels in A-B-C model, 123–24
Empathy, accurate, 119, 139, 145, 183, 239
Employees, 75
  morale of, 76
Empty chair technique, 212
Endogenous rewards, 177
Entropy, 71–72, 77
Entry stage in consultation process, 115, 118–21, 331, 333
Environment, 16, 23, 47
Equilibrium, 266
Equity, 285
Ethical helpers, 352
Ethics, 119, 140, 309–29
  client identification, 323–26
  competence of consultant, 311–12
  confidentiality, 319–21
  cultural sensitivity of consultant, 314–18
  efficacy of treatment, 324–25
  evaluation, 325–26
  guides versus directives for, 311
  informed consent, 318–19
  multicultural context, 317–18
  power, 323
  professional boundaries, 322–23
  values of consultant, 312–14
Evaluation, 38, 57, 325–26
  of job performance, 80
  in skill training, 227–28
  See also Assessment procedures
Events in solution implementation, 268
Evidence that goals have been achieved, 127–78
Evolution of systems, 70–72
Exceptions to problems, 210, 214
Exogenous rewards, 177
Expectations in consultation, 116–17, 118
Experimentation, 214
Expertise in content areas, 103, 119, 176
Expert power, 102–3, 119, 176
Exploration skills, 149–53
Exploration stage in consultation process, 121–25, 331, 333
External consumers in school systems, 52–53
Extinguishing behavior, 124
Extrapersonal factors, 16, 87
Extrinsic reinforcement, 124
Eye contact, 143

F

Facilitators, 23, 25
Fault finding, 180
Faulty information, 221
Fear of failure, 166
Feedback, 38, 78, 106, 225, 291–94
  in learning activities, 227, 228
Feelings, reflection of, 147–49
Felt need continuum, 29–30
  See also Parsons's model of consultation
Fight or flight responses, 124
Fine-tuning, intervention and prevention in
  system-focused consultation, 294–98
First meeting in consultation, 115, 118–21
Fisher, Roger, 256, 257
Flexibility, 37, 69, 76
Focus group, 55
Focusing skills, 153–59
Force-field analysis, 265–68
Forgetfulness, 182
Formal needs assessment, 55–56
Formal social activities, 99
Formal systems, 72–76
Formative evaluation, 325–26
Form and focus of consultation, 37–39
Forward chaining, 269
Frontline educators, 73, 76
Full-inclusion, 222–23

G

Gap between desired and current state of
  need, 53–54, 57
General adaptation syndrome, 124
Generalists, 77
Generalization, 16, 23
Gestalt-type techniques, 212
Goals, 251
  conflicts in, 88–89
  in consultation process, 125–29, 331,
    333–34
  definition in consultation, 22
  of groups (three-legged stool), 249–51
  and objectives, 126–27
  prioritization of goals and strategies,
    212–14
  of systems, 57–58
Goal scaling, 21, 129
Goal setting and solution-focused
  consultation, 209–14
Governmental agencies as stakeholders in
  school systems, 51, 52, 72
Group dynamics, 25
Group-focused consultation, 35–36
Group interventions/counseling, 3, 7,
  11, 54

Groups as clients, 247–74
  force-field analysis, 265–68
  goals of groups (three-legged stool),
    249–51
  intrasystem conflict, 255–56
  Job Wellness and Satisfaction Survey (Kahn),
    252, 253
  Maslow's hierarchy of needs, 252
  needs and interests, 259–60
  objective criteria, 261–64
  option generation, 260–61
  separate people from the problem,
    248–59
  solution implementation, 268–71
  systemic conflict: unfulfilled needs and
    interests, 251–55
  win-win solutions, 248, 257–65
  See also System dynamics; Systems
Group task goals, 250, 251
Group training, 227
Guided practice, 298
Guilt, 180

H

Habit strength, 226
Hands-on assistance, 170
Harvard Negotiation Project (Fisher and
  Ury), 257
Health Insurance Portability and
  Accountability Act (HIPAA), 292
Here and now experience, 188
Hierarchies, 76
Highlighting in questioning, 150
HIPAA. *See* Health Insurance Portability
  and Accountability Act
Hispanics, 202
Homelessness, 4
Homeostasis, 76, 78, 79, 90
Human potential, 21

I

IEP. *See* Individualized Educational
  Program
Illegal behaviors, 88–89, 188
Imagery in BASIC ID model, 206
Independent practice, 298
Indirect confrontation, 218, 241–42
Indirect versus direct service, 14, 35
Individual goals in the group, 250
Individual interventions/counseling, 3, 7,
  11, 54
Individualized Educational Program
  (IEP), 251
Individual needs, 54
Industrial institutions, 23, 50
Industrial revolution, 50

Informal assessment, 57
Informal gatherings, 99
Informal processes in closed systems, 75–76, 78
Informal settings, 103, 104
Informal systems, 72–76
Informational power, 102
Information exchange in systems, 69, 76, 77
Information gathering and analysis, 27
Informed consent, 318–19
Innovation, 69, 75, 76
Input in systems, 49, 50, 71
In-service training, 227
Instruction in consultation, 141–42
Integrated model of service delivery in consulting, 20–43
Integrated systems, 75–76
Integrating consultation stages, purposes, and skills, 160–61
Interdependence, 77
Internal consumers, 52, 72, 78
Internal locus of control, 125, 133, 211
Interpersonal cues, 179
Interpersonal relationships in BASIC ID model, 207
Interpersonal skills, 16, 22, 24
Intervention and prevention in system-focused consultation, 290–304
    changing character and culture of a system, 298–304
    feedback, 291–94
    fine-tuning, 294–98
    general guidelines, 290–91
    moving the system, 300
    refreezing the system, 300
    unfreezing the system, 299–300
    See also System-focused consultation
Interviewing, 133, 223, 289
Intrapersonal factors, 16, 87
Intrasystem conflict, 255–56
Intrinsic reinforcement, 124
Invitation stage in resistance, 185–86
Involuntary, physiological-biochemical responses, 124
Isolated workers, 277
"I" statements, 259

J

Job descriptions, 48, 77
Job evaluation, 227–28
Joblessness, 4
Job performance criteria, 80, 82
Job security, 77
Job Wellness and Satisfaction Survey (Kahn), 252, 253
Journal writing, 212, 214

K

Kahn, Wallace J., *Job Wellness and Satisfaction Survey,* 252, 253
Knowledge development for consultees, 221–26

L

Labeling, 239
Language and reality, 210
Lazarus, Arnold, 123, 204
Leaders
    formal or informal, 99
    opinion, 99–100
Leadership styles, 25
Learning disabilities, 5
Learning disabled students, 72
Learning objectives, 298
Learning principles, 23
Lewin, Kurt, 299
Likert-type scale, 55, 252
Linear relationship, 12–13
Line authority, 75, 82
Listening skills, active, 119, 121, 145, 180, 259
Lock-down procedures, 106
Loss of objectivity, 229–37

M

Maintenance goals in the group, 250
Maintenance stage in consultation process, 132–35, 331, 334
Manuals, 72
Marketing research, 72
Maslow, Abraham, 252
Maslow's hierarchy, 252, 260
Mediation, 3
Mediational mode of consultation, 26–27
Mental health consultation, 23
Mental Health Consultation and Collaboration (Caplan and Caplan), 234
Mental health issues, 4, 5
Mentors, 24
Miller, R. B., 200
Minimal encouraging responses, 145
Minority populations, 50
"Miracle question," 211
Mirroring, 143
Miscommunications, 91
Mission of institution, 14, 50, 52, 53
    and system change, 88, 89, 90, 94, 283
Modeling in learning activities, 228, 241, 298
Modes of consultation, 25–27
    collaborative mode, 26
    mediational mode, 26–27

Modes of consultation (*continued*)
  prescriptive mode, 26
  provisional mode, 25–26
Motivation in job performance criteria,
    80, 82
Moving the system, 300
Multicultural context, 317–18
Multicultural sensitivity, 8

N

National Board of Certified Counselors
    (NBCC), *Code of Ethics,* 323
National Defense Education Act (1958), 89
National Standards for School
    Counselors, 248
Native Americans, 202
Naturalistic observation, 289–90
Navajo people, 202
NBCC. *See* National Board of Certified
    Counselors
Need assessment, 53–57, 72
  changing populations, 54–56
  current state of need, 53
  data results, 58
  desired state of need, 53, 54, 55, 58
  formal needs assessment, 55–56
  gap between desired and current state of
      need, 53–54, 57
  goals and objectives from, 57–59
  individual and community needs, 54
  informal assessment, 57
  need satisfaction, 53–54, 55
  need scores, 56–57
  outcome goals, 58
Need satisfaction, 53–54, 55
Need scores, 56–57
Needs and interests of consumers and
    providers in systems, 47–48, 49,
    259–60
Needs versus wants, 251, 252
"Need to know" basis, 160, 320
Negative reinforcement, 124
Negligence by parents, 5
Nonlinear relationship, 13
Nonprofessional staff, 90–91
Nonverbal behavior, 143–44
Norms
  of the group, 250
  systemic, 79, 81, 116–17, 227, 248

O

Objective criteria, 261–64
Objectives
  in consultation process, 125–29
  and goals, 126–27
  of systems, 58–59
Objectivity, loss of, 229–37

Observation, 133, 223
Observational information, 24
One-on-one counseling, 7–8
One-to-one direct-service model, 195
Open questioning, 152, 153
Open systems, 50, 69, 70, 76, 78, 79, 80,
    82, 248
Operant behaviors in A-B-C model, 123
Opinion leaders, 99–100
Option generation, 260–61
Organizational consultation, 24
Organizational structure, 76–78
  in system dynamics, 76–77
  See also Administrations
Organizing schema, 122–25, 131
Organ systems, 49
Outcome goals and need assessment, 58
Outcome goals and objectives in
    consultation process, 125–29, 331,
    334–35
Output in systems, 49, 50, 78
Overview, 298
Ownership of consultant and consultee,
    15–16, 25, 172, 179, 185, 189, 226

P

Paper communications, 160
Parables, 242
Paradigm of consultation, 9–10
Parallel systems, 75–76
Paraphrasing content, 145–47, 259
Paraprofessionals, 90
Parent conferences, 3
Parent education, 54
Parents, 90
  as consumers in school systems,
      48, 52, 57
  negligence by, 5
  as providers in school systems, 52
  working with, 8
Parsons's model of consultation, 21–28
  content or process expertise, 24–25,
      30–32
  crisis or developmental nature, 21–22,
      29–30
  modes of consultation, 25–27
  problem and goal definition, 22
  theory and assumptions, 22–24
  See also Consulting model of service
      delivery
Passive aggressive behaviors, 182, 277
Patterns or themes, 158
Peer counselors, 90
Peer interaction, 311
Peer mediation programs, 107
Peer modeling, 131

Peer reinforcement, 227
People in the system, 282
Personal counseling, 3, 14, 15, 218–19, 235, 237
Personal disclosure, 213
Personal involvement with student/client, 229–30
PERT charting. *See* Program Evaluation Review Technique (PERT) charting
Physical environment, 202, 211–12
  of the system, 283
Physical space, 143
Physical systems, 49
Physiological-biochemical responses, 124
Planned change principles, 93–108
  alignment with opinion leaders, 99–100
  compatibility with culture of system, 94–97
  increasing value and power as consultant, 100–105
  move in a crisis, 105–8
  shaping/change in small steps, 97–99
Planning for consultations, 115, 116–18
Planning models, 268–69
Policies and procedures, 72
Population needs in systems, 53–57
Populations
  changing populations, 54–56
  in systems, 49, 50, 54
Positional bargaining, 258
Position or solution to the problem, 248, 257
Positive reinforcement, 124, 211, 226
Posture, 143
Poverty, 4
Power, 323
  blending and balancing, 103–4, 176, 189
  expert and referent, 101–4, 119, 176
  social, 102
  use and misuse of, 176
Practice, 330
  in skill development, 227
Preentry stage in consultation process, 116–18, 331, 333
Prerequisite skills, 200
Prescriptions for intervention, 26, 73, 181
Prescriptive mode of consultation, 26, 118, 130, 178
Presence of something versus absence of something, 172
Preventive model of service, 7, 16, 20, 22, 25, 35
  in consultation, 125, 170, 197, 198, 213, 220

and system change, 87
  See also Developmental model of service
Preventive programming, 37
Principled negotiation, 263–65
Prioritization of goals and strategies, 212–14
Privatization of urban schools, 72
Privileged communication, 119
Proactive role, 11, 16, 57, 133
Probing in questioning, 150
Problem
  construction and reconstruction of, 210
  and goal definition in consultation, 22
  identification of, 198–209, 223–25
  separate people from, 248–59
Problem finding/problem solving, 174–75
Problem-solving abilities, 22
Processes in systems, 49, 50, 57, 60–63
Process expertise in consultation, 24–25, 30–32
Procrastination, 182
Productivity, 24
Product of the system, 283
Professional boundaries, 322–23
Professional development, 228
Professional dialogue, 311
Professional ethics, 119, 140
Professional functioning of the consultee, 218
Professional literature, 311
Professional objectivity of consultees, 228–37
Professional orientation and skills in consultation, 10, 16–17
Program Evaluation Review Technique (PERT) charting, 268–71
Providers in systems, 52–53
Provisional mode of consultation, 25–26, 130, 170, 178
Proximity, 143
Psychological costs, 91
Psychological reactance, 175, 188
Psychosocial problems, 5, 16
Psychotherapy, 218, 235, 237
Public schools, 50
Punishing consequences, 124
Punitive management techniques, 202
Push away, the, 180

Q

Qualitative outcomes, 58, 127
Quantitative outcomes, 58, 172
Questioning, 149–53
  guidelines for, 150–52
  styles of, 142–53
Quick sell/quick buy, 183–85

R

Racism, 4
Rapport, 103, 139
Rational emotive imagery training, 212
Reactance, psychological, 175, 188
Reactive role, 11, 16, 26, 81, 82
Reality and language, 210
Reality-based perception, 224
Referent power, 103, 176
Referring procedure, 117, 160, 256, 312
Reflection of feelings, 147–49
Reframing the resistance, 186–87
Refreezing the system, 300
Relapses, 214
Religious institutions, 50
Remedial-intervention focus, 16, 35, 125, 197, 213
Repetitive mistakes and inefficiencies, 182
Research, marketing, 72
Resistance in consultation, 165–92, 225
　ameliorating the source of resistance, 188
　anxiety about problem finding/problem solving, 174–75
　and consultant insensitivity, 167–69
　and consultant style, 175–76
　consultation as an aversive process, 176–77
　consultee requesting personal counseling, 182–83
　consultee's issues and concerns, 169–75
　and the consulting relationship, 176–79
　control concerns of consultees, 172–73
　defined, 166–67
　expectations of consultees, 169–72
　freedom of consultee, 175
　incongruent expectations, 178–79
　invitation stage, 185–86
　passive aggression, 182
　personal characteristics of consultant, 175–76
　the push away, 180
　quick sell/quick buy, 183–85
　as a reasonable response, 167
　recognizing resistance, 179–85, 189
　reducing the risk of resistance, 188–89
　reframing the resistance, 186–87
　sources of resistance, 166–79
　system-focused consultation, 278
　vulnerable feelings of consultees, 173–74
　working with resistance, 185–88
　"yes, but," 181–82
Resources in job performance criteria, 80, 82

Respondent behaviors in A-B-C model, 123
Responsibility of consultant and consultee, 11–12, 15–16, 25
Restraining force, 265
Return of the investment, 91
Rewards, endogenous and exogenous, 177
Rightsizing, 285
Rigid thinking, 231, 232
Ripple effect, 210
Rituals in a system, 99, 286
Role confusion/role conflict, 295
Role definitions, 90
Role play in learning activities, 228
Rumors, 91

S

SAMHSA. *See* Substance Abuse and Mental Health Services Administration
Schein, Edgar, 286
School-based consultation, 211
School boards, 48
School counselor roles in service delivery, 7–8
School guidance programs, 63
　accountability of, 57
　comprehensive, 57
　process elements for, 61, 62
　as systems, 51
School reform and expansion, 8
　conservatism in, 52
Schools as systems, 47–67
　consumers in, 51–52
　goals and objectives from, 57–59
　history of schools, 50
　process elements for school guidance programs, 61, 62
　processes in, 60–63
　providers in, 52–53
　See also Needs assessment; System dynamics; Systems
Secondary gain, 175
Self-actualization, 21
Self-exploration, 237
Self-knowledge, 224
Self-monitoring techniques, 218, 298
Self-preservation, 90, 167
Self-referral, 116, 117, 118
Self-report, 214
Self-report surveys, 252–53
Self-talk, 123
Sensation in BASIC ID model, 206
Separate people from the problem, 248–59

Service delivery, 3–19
    alternative methods of, 7
    client-focused consultation, 195–217
    direct-service model of counseling, 7–8
    need complexity and quantity, 4–7
    school counselor role, 7–8
    student concerns past and present, 5–7
    See also Consultation; Consulting model
        of service delivery
Sexism, 4
Sexual abuse, 4
Shaping/change in small steps, 97–99,
    128–29, 210
Simple identification with students, 230–31
Skill development for consultees, 226–28
Skilled helpers, 352
Skills
    development of, 212, 297–98
    prerequisite, 200
Social/cultural environment, 202–3, 211–12
Social dynamics and processes, 24
Social factors, 47
Social learning theory, 23–24
Social power, 102
Social–psychological theories, 24
Social status, 102
Social systems, 49–50
Society in crisis, 4
Sociopolitical forces, 89, 285
Solution-focused consultation, 115, 121,
    209–14
Solution implementation, 268–71
Sources of resistance, 166–79, 188
Space utilization, 202
Special educational needs, 4
Specialization of function, 77
Special needs children, 8, 90
"Spread of effect" concept, 23
Stages of consultation process, 331–35, 352
Stakeholders, 214
    in school systems, 48, 52
Standardization, 72
Standards of performance, 58
Standards of practice, 311
    See also Ethics
State of need, 53, 54, 55, 58
Status quo, 71, 77, 78, 79, 81, 87, 93, 94,
    97, 166
Steady state, 72
Strategy development and implementation
    in consultation process, 129–32,
    331, 334
Strengths, 210
Stress management, 22

Structural-functional theory, 78–79
Student concerns past and present, 5–7
Student conflicts, 107
Students
    advocates for, 87
    as consumers in school systems, 48, 52
    See also Client-focused consultation;
        Clients
Student service from a consultation
    perspective, 196–97
Subobjectives, 128–29
Substance Abuse and Mental Health
    Services Administration (SAMHSA), 4
Subsystems, 48, 51, 76–77, 247–48, 256
    See also Systems
Successes, 210, 213–14
Suicide, 4
Summarizations in consulting
    communications, 157–59, 259
Summative evaluation, 326
Sunken costs, 91
Supervision, 311, 312
Support staff as consumers in school
    systems, 48, 52
Surveys, 133, 289
Synergistic interdependence, 69
System dynamics, 68–84
    change in systems, 78–79
    closed systems, 70–71, 76, 81
    counselor consultation, 79–82
    entropy, 71–72, 77
    formal and informal systems, 72–76
    open systems, 69, 70, 76, 78, 79, 80, 82
    organizational structure, 76–77
    parallel or integrated systems, 75–76
    specialization and structure, 77
    See also Groups as clients
System-focused consultation, 35, 36,
    275–308
    artifacts of the system, 286–87, 288
    basic assumptions of the system, 287, 288
    culture and character of the system,
        285–89
    diagnostic tools and techniques, 298–90
    elements of the system, 282–83
    forces impacting the system, 284–85
    naturalistic observation, 289–90
    system analysis and diagnosis, 177–90
    system as the problem, 276–77
    values of the system, 287, 288
    See also Intervention and prevention in
        system-focused consultation
Systemic level of entry, 11
Systemic planning, 249

System modality, 11
Systems
  advocates for, 87–89
  boundaries in, 51
  conflict in unfulfilled needs and interests, 251–55
  consumers in systems, 51–52
  culture of, 94–97
  defined, 49–50
  disequilibrium in, 105–8
  goals of, 57–58
  norms in, 79, 81, 116–17, 227, 248
  objectives of, 58–59
  open systems, 50, 69, 70, 76, 78, 79, 80, 82, 248
  population needs in systems, 53–57
  preservation of, 167
  process elements in school guidance program, 62, 63
  processes in systems, 49, 50, 57, 60–63
  providers in systems, 52–53
  rituals in, 99, 286
  See also Consultant as agent for change; Groups as clients; Need assessment; Schools as systems; Subsystems; System dynamics
Systems analysts, 24
Systems theory, 78–79

T

Tacting response leads in consulting communications, 154, 155–57
Talking around the issue, 241–42
Targeted population, 55
Task analysis, 199–202, 211–12
Taxpayers, 51, 52, 57
Teachers, 75
  as consultees, 196–97, 199
  as consumers in school systems, 48, 52, 57
  support for, 3, 8
  and system change, 88
  training for, 226–27
Team approach, 16, 278
Technical adviser, 24
Tentative conclusions, 238–39
Termination in consultation process, 134–35, 331, 335
Testimonials, 102, 104
Testing, 133

Theme interference, 231–34
Themes or patterns, 158
Theories and consultation, 11, 22–24
Three-legged stool (goals of groups), 249–51
Time Event Charting (TEC) method, 268
Time schedule, 38
Time in solution implementation, 268
Total quality management, 285
Traditional power, 102
Tradition in systems, 92–93
Trainers, 24
Training, 312
Training for consultees. *See* Skill development for consultees
Transference, 234–35
Treatment efficacy, 324–25
Triadic relationship, 11–14, 23, 33, 87, 204, 256, 309, 310, 323

U

Unethical behaviors, 88–89, 188
Unfreezing the system, 299–300
Ury, William, 256, 257

V

Values
  of consultant, 312–14
  of consumers and providers in systems, 47–48
  of the system, 287, 288
Vicarious learning, 131
Video presentations in learning activities, 228
Violence, 4, 105–6
Violence prevention, 8
Vocational counseling, 3

W

Wants versus needs, 251, 252
Win–win solutions, 248, 257–65
Workers, isolation and disenfranchisement of, 277
Workshops, 227
Written communication, 160

Y

"Yes, but," 181–82

Z

Zen philosophy, 185
Zero tolerance policies, 106